All Things Altered

All Things Altered

Women in the Wake of Civil War and Reconstruction

Marilyn Mayer Culpepper

To Jamie and Gil our very dear, very special long time friends — our extended family — with much love and great admiration

Marilyn Mayer Culpepper

McFarland & Company, Inc., Publishers

Jefferson, North Carolina, and London

Library of Congress Cataloguing-in-Publication Data

Culpepper, Marilyn Mayer.
    All things altered : women in the wake of Civil War and
Reconstruction / Marilyn Mayer Culpepper.
      p.   cm.
    Includes bibliographical references and index.

    ISBN 0-7864-1339-5 (softcover : 50# alkaline paper)

    1. Women—Southern States—History—19th century.
2. Reconstruction. I. Title.
HQ1438.S63C65   2002
305.4'0975'09034—dc21   2002008146

British Library cataloguing data are available

On the cover: portrait of Mary Chesnut (from Virginia Clay, *A Belle
of the Fifties*); background art ©2002 ClickArt.

Manufactured in the United States of America

*McFarland & Company, Inc., Publishers
  Box 611, Jefferson, North Carolina 28640
  www.mcfarlandpub.com*

For Tom and my parents

Acknowledgments

The most exciting part of writing this book was the research. For over ten years, librarians and archivists guided and prodded my studies. At the Alabama Department of Archives and History, Norwood A. Kerr in particular and also Ken Tilley and the entire staff were of invaluable assistance in helping me locate manuscripts. Dianne Welch proved most resourceful at the Anson County Library. At the Biloxi Public Library, Murella Powell, Mary Louise Adkinson, Buddy Welch and Ethelyn Gonsoulin were particularly helpful.

I very much appreciated the attention of the staff of the Archives and Manuscript Department at the Chicago Historical Society. During my frequent visits to the Chicago Public Library, Andrea Atelli and Constance Gordon became great good friends and provided me with a wealth of information.

I would like to thank Jacqueline Reid, Janie C. Morris and Stacey Tompkins at the Rare Book, Manuscript, and Special Collections Library at Duke University. Kathleen Cabell, Phyllis Brock Silber, and Sebastian Volcker at the Goochland Historical Society were most most generous with their time and efforts in my behalf. Mark Cave and Pamela Aoceneaux at the Historic New Orleans Collection were tremendously knowledgeable and resourceful on my numerous visists there. Levin Culpepper, genealogist and archivist at the Lauderdale County Department of Archives and History in Meridian, Mississippi, has kindly shared his time and expertise.

I would also like to convey my appreciation to Rebecca Fitzgerald at the Historical Society of Frederick County Maryland; to Betty Cagle at the Lee County Library, Tupelo, Mississippi; to Lee Barnett at the State Archives of Michigan; to Minor Weisiger, especially, and also to Chris Kolbe, Sarah Meacham, Marcella M. Curry, Robert Y. Clay, Bill Luebke, and Alexandra S. Gressitt at the Library of Virginia in Richmond; to Anne Vargo at the Louisiana State University Press; to Carol James and the staff at the Meridian-Lauderdale County Public Library;

to Fred L. Honhart, Dorothy T. Frye, and Debbie S. Hettinger at the Archives and Historical Collection at Michigan State University; to Michael Unsworth, Jane Arnold and Louis Villafranca at the Michigan State University Library; to Grady Howell, Michael Hennen and the staff at the Mississippi Department of Archives and History; to Rendal Jones at the Mobile Public Library; to John and Ruth Ann Coski at the Museum of the Confederacy; to Joseph Ditta, Nick Okrent and Melissa Haley at the New York Historical Society; to Martha C. Carter and Jane Marra at the Spotsylvania Virginia Museum; to Julia Rather at the Tennessee Library and Archives; to Laura Clark Brown at the University of North Carolina at Chapel Hill; and to Vicky Wells at the University of North Carolina Press.

I am greatly indebted to Henry Fulmer and the staff of the South Caroliniana Library at the University of South Carolina. At the University of Southern Mississippi I found Yvonne M. Arnold, Mary Hamilton, Bobs Tusa, Bonnie Cooper Mussiett, and Peggy Price devoted to their work of helping researchers. For many years now Frances Pollard and Janet Schwartz at the Virginia Historical Society in Richmond have given considerable time and energy to helping me with sources for this manuscript. In addition, E. Lee Shepard was very kind in securing permissions from the Viriginia Historical Society. Special friends Carolyn Hoagland, Christy Nichols, Dorrie Souder, Martha Niland, and the late Signe Bates kept eagle eyes out for books and articles that might otherwise have escaped my attention. They also served as sounding boards and provided enthusiasm and encouragement.

My eternal gratitude goes to our family friend and my computer guru, Larry Giacoletto, who answered my incessant 911 calls about computer glitches with incredible expertise and promptness. Without Larry's help, I would probably still be struggling with a typewriter.

I am greatly indebted to another family friend, Paul Souder, who did most of the important photographic work reproduced from old *Harper's Weekly* magazines. Peter Berg and Jerry Paulins of the Special Collections Library at Michigan State University performed an invaluable service in facilitating the use of those magazines.

Yet another family friend, Dr. Richard Bates, contributed (sans office calls or billing) invaluable medical advice concerning nineteenth century medical practices

By far the most important contributor, of course, has been my real editor, my wise, patient, supportive husband, Tom, for whom volumes of thank-yous could never even begin to express my appreciation. I could not make it through life without him.

Contents

Introduction

"Reconstruction is possibly the most misunderstood era in the American past, despite the fact that its scholarly interpretation has undergone enormous changes in the last generation."[1]

While Northerners often gloss over the chaotic days of Reconstruction in the South following the Civil War, Southerners tend to regard the period as fraught with grave, vengeful postwar indignities forced upon the South in order to further prostrate an already defeated, devastated populace. Hodding Carter put it well in surmising in *The Angry Seas*, "It has been almost as unfortunate for our nation that the North has remembered so little of Reconstruction as that the South has remembered so much."

The period of Reconstruction has undergone countless analyses, revisions and revisions, perhaps because the ramifications of the Civil War were so many and so diverse. There are no universals; there are no all-encompassing generalizations that can be drawn. The social, economic, and political changes that pervaded the period differed radically for Southern planters, yeomen, whites, blacks, veterans, women, children—and, of course, for Northerners as well.

This book in no way attempts to solve or fully explain the tumultuous problems of the Reconstruction era, but instead seeks to capture the actions and attitudes of some Southerners—in particular, Southern women—during that turbulent period as revealed in their letters and diaries. Here the term "Southerners" is used generally to denote white Confederate sympathizers. Although many of these Southerners could be classed as "elite"—for they were the ones with the time and educational background to keep diaries—people from many walks of life are included in these pages.

Actually, of course, the "Solid South" was of anything but one mind. In the midst of fire-eating rebels there were loyalists who were convinced

1

the South was making a huge mistake in seceding; in the midst of poverty and sacrifice there were profiteers and hoarders who were making money at the expense of their friends, neighbors, and country. As the war wound down there were "never-give-up" and "let-us-have-peace" factions. Jefferson Davis was vehemently criticized by his detractors, yet to others he was Christ personified. And even the most zealous of any of these partisans could change positions from time to time.

The South itself was an agrarian South, to be sure. (In the 1860 census, New Orleans was the only city later to be included in the Confederacy that was listed in the top twenty most populous American cities; it was number six.) Nevertheless the Southland featured a great variety of crops and climates, and even the farmers were of diverse backgrounds. In addition to farmers, there were hosts of bankers, merchants, ministers, and academicians to be considered.

How to reunite a country after four years of violence and bloodshed that had convulsed the nation? No one seemed to have the answer. Even President Lincoln, in his speech celebrating the surrender at Appomattox, realistically forecast the momentous problems facing America in the days to come: "By these recent successes, the reinauguration of national authority, reconstruction, which has had a large share of thought from the first, is pressed much more closely upon our attention." Perhaps no truer words were ever spoken than his admission that the task was "fraught with great difficulties." The president pointed out that even Northerners were divided in their opinions of how to go about unifying the country: "We must simply begin with and mold from the discordant and disorganized elements; nor is it a small additional embarrassment that we loyal people differ among ourselves as to the mode, manner and measure of reconstruction."

Whatever one's perspective, it is hard to fully comprehend the gravity of the Southern situation at the war's end. Southern homes and farms were in serious disrepair or even in ashes. Southerners found themselves financially ruined: the worthless currency could not even buy a loaf of bread; bonds or stocks were not worth the paper they were written on; bank accounts stood empty. Most livestock—horses, cows, and chickens—had been impressed or stolen and entire crops of corn, wheat, and cotton had been seized. A formerly steady workforce was now liberated and temporarily or permanently dispersed. Many of the Southerners' dearest personal possessions—pictures, paintings, jewelry, pianos, and clothing—had been destroyed, and even such basic necessities as blankets, linens, and bedding—including the beds themselves—had been put to the torch. Southerners looked over fields ravaged by soldiers and battles and shook their heads in despair over the loss of plows, harnesses, and hoes.

Their government, courts, and entire economy were i
had mercilessly shattered their dreams. Some 258,00C
had died, and probably half again that number came
wounded, thousands more mentally scarred for life. 1
forever changed.

Women had little to do with formulating politic
usually had no great input in engineering the financial st   , ~ut they
were part and parcel of the political and financial situation of the times.
Their family bank accounts were depleted, their money was worthless,
their husbands lacked laborers. Women could not vote, but their former
slaves could vote; there were riots and thefts and murders that they did
not participate in, but they suffered the consequences.

My original intent was to focus exclusively on women, but this
proved difficult since most of their problems were intricately intertwined
with the financial, political, labor, and racial concerns of their menfolk.
Therefore, in order to provide a more in-depth understanding of the
upheaval confronting women in the postwar South, some general orientation seemed necessary. The purpose of Part I is to give an overall picture of conditions during Reconstruction and many Southerners' reactions
to them. Hearing the many voices tell their stories may help to deepen
the reader's understanding of the specific experiences detailed in Part II.

Women, of course, were still more or less confined to their "sphere
of domesticity," and not many devoted their diaries to the activities of
the Ku Klux Klan or the neighborhood turncoats. As a consequence, from
time to time Part I includes quotations from and references to men, and
newspaper editorials written by men, that seem to reflect the tenor of the
times. (Men, being more prolific writers and more outspoken than
women, were freer to explicitly and unequivocally express their opinions.)

Clearly this work is not designed to explore in minute detail all of
the profound and confusing aspects of life plaguing Southerners at the
end of the war and during Reconstruction. That task is left to the thousands of other writers who devote themselves exclusively to analyses of
Reconstruction. This book looks primarily at the problems most Southern women faced after the war—women who devoted themselves to nur-
turing the spirits of their despondent, war-weary husbands, or who, as
widows attempted the often debilitating task of managing a farm in addition to supporting a sizable family of young children. These women's
writings document the turmoil of the postwar years and provide a window for viewing something of the lives, roles, and experiences of Southern women. Even this brief examination should help flesh out the picture
of their efforts to cope with the defeat of the Confederacy; of the gloomy
prospects ahead for their families and themselves; of their losses resulting

Introduction

...om the war and from Yankee and "bummer" pillaging; of the labor problems that led to the success or failure of their farms or plantations; of the upheaval accompanying emancipation and Negro suffrage. Southerners' reactions to the troops of occupation, the oath of allegiance, the vast influx of Northerners, and the Radical Republicans' attempts to restructure the South and its people offer insights into the life and times of the women of the Southland.

The excerpts in this book have been purposely chosen from the diaries and letters of less well-known women as well as from women from different walks of life. Some material from African Americans has been used; however, because antebellum laws forbade teaching blacks to read and write, relatively few diaries and letters were written by former slaves. (Some excellent sources of the experiences of former slaves in the postwar years are to be found in the WPA Writers' Project Interviews in the Library of Congress and in books utilizing those sources.)

In my research I found no indication that any white women had marched with the Ku Klux Klan; however, at least one woman revealed in her diary that the women helped stitch the robes for the Klan members. Several women writers clearly approved of the Klan's activities, and several indicated that the Klan offered their only protection from violence. It was in Elizabeth Avery Meriwether's own Memphis home that her husband helped found a Ku Klux Klan chapter. According to her family, Elizabeth attended at least one of the planning sessions, and at that time she proposed giving "respectable" white Southern women the right to vote.[2]

Rather than attempting to draw conclusions for the reader, I have made extensive use of quotations from the writings of the period in my attempt to present a realistic picture of the era. I implore the reader to be aware, however, that vast numbers of the quotations used do not reflect my attitudes but are simply a recording of the words of others. I wish to make clear that the racism expressed by many of these writers does not in any way reflect my sentiments. I am seriously troubled by including the racist remarks of these diarists and letter writers; however, historians remind me that I must be faithful to history. If these writings reflect racial prejudice, that was the way it was—and unfortunately in some cases still is—throughout America and the world.

I am well aware that the letters and diary entries could be presented in their entirety; however, that would entail a great amount of extraneous material, such as "Cloudy all day today," "Tom and the two boys stayed for supper this evening," "Went into town for the mail this morning." For this reason I have chosen to quote only relevant passages. I have, however, endeavored throughout to keep to the original spelling and punctuation of the diarists and letter writers, although in the interest of clarity I have made minor changes to paragraphing and punctuation.

౭౧

Along with death and taxes the sureties of life certainly include diversity. And variety was indeed the order of the day during Reconstruction. Rules and conditions varied from person to person, from area to area, and sometimes from moment to moment. In many areas the oath of allegiance was strictly observed; in other areas it was regarded more casually, observed in some cases and not in others. The freedmen in some locations were docile, obedient, and loyal to their ex-masters; at other times and in other areas they were vengeful and unmanageable. Black codes, apprenticeship laws, and KKK activities differed widely.

Some communities burned Negro schoolhouses and ran off teachers of colored children. In other communities benevolent townspeople helped build and staff Negro schools. Some ex-masters attempted to re-enslave the newly emancipated by offering unrealistic contracts and later reneging on the terms of the contracts. Others gave them land and provided for the ill and the elderly.

Historians themselves, as noted, often hold widely divergent views on Reconstruction. There are those who deem it a "tragic era"; other more modern revisionists consider it a period of progress and enlightenment, a view generally held by most scholars today. Some believe the operations of the Ku Klux Klan provided for the eventual death of Reconstruction. Others felt the publicity in Northern newspapers about the infamous activities of the Klan served to convince Northerners of the need for the continued presence of troops of occupation in order to prevent further violence. Some felt the intimidation of blacks was largely responsible for Democratic victories at the polls in certain areas. Other revisionists believe that the white conservative Republicans' switch to the Democratic party on the basis of race was primarily responsible for eventually bringing down the Republicans.

Reconstruction was unquestionably a period of inconsistencies, and no doubt those contradictions add to the difficulties of interpreting the era. Southerners hated the Yankees *but* loved their capital and their financial expertise. In general Southerners despised the troops of occupation, *but* they acknowledged the need for them for their own protection and for that of their property amidst the ravages of bummers, ruffians, and thieves. Although counting the free black population netted Southern states considerably more seats and clout in Congress, the late rebels were reluctant to give the Negroes the vote. They declared the freedmen too uneducated to vote, *but* they torched Negro schools and threatened the teachers. Indeed, Southerners generally conceded that their former slaves were unlettered and desperately needed schooling—*except* when an education might deprive employers of laborers and make their servants "uppity" and independent. Southerners cherished their homeland *but* left it for Mexico and South America when the going got tough—and returned months later discouraged and disillusioned with their new ventures and convinced that the Southland was not so bad after all. The North lost some 360,222 men in refusing to allow Southerners to leave the Union, *but* fearing a return to power of the old planter caste, Northerners set up formidable hurdles in reallocating them voting rights and permitting them to be seated in Congress.

The capricious diversity and the significant inconsistencies pervading the era make it difficult to employ any statements encompassing all areas, all times, and all people; therefore this book makes repeated use of qualifiers such as "some" and "many," "countless," and "scores."

A chronological organization of the material seemed ineffective, and thus the topical development evolved. However, for anyone possibly needing a reminder of the sequence of events after the defeat, a brief chronological record of events is included at the end of the book.

℘

Following the overall picture of the aftermath of war and some of the challenges of Reconstruction in Part I, a look at the lives of a few specific women in Part II offers more of a personal study of the women of the postwar world, many of whose problems have been identified in a more general way in Part I. With the exception of the Anna Clayton Logan letters, which were published in the Goochland Historical Society publications, to my knowledge most of the excerpts in Part II have not been published before now.

Few women's writings provide so engaging a picture of the domestic scene in the postwar South as the diary of Susan Sillers Darden. The compassionate, family-loving Susan dutifully records a daily account of the dramatic changes brought about during Reconstruction. Susan's pages are replete with the postwar struggles with finances, taxes, presidential pardons, and household help. Even daily living becomes a challenge under reduced circumstances and amidst the crime and violence of the area. The activities of the Radical Republicans, the Loyal Leagues, and the Democratic "clubs" added other important dimensions to life in Fayette, Mississippi, at the war's end.

In the excerpts from the diary of Virginia Carolina Smith Aiken, of Greenwood County, South Carolina, the reader is introduced to a woman who had been accustomed to the best life had to offer before the war, and who now is suddenly faced in the postwar years with penny-pinching and doing without. Coping with the South's endemic financial problems, overwork as a result of throngs of company, a growing family, dozens of extra hands to feed at threshing and ginning time, and a husband increasingly focused on his own career thus distancing himself from family life, Virginia found herself broken down and unappreciated. Virginia's role in helping to provide moral support for a dispirited albeit ambitious returned veteran of the war was a role played by tens of thousands of women throughout the South.

Inability to collect a debt three times that of the $10,000 her father owed brought Anna Clayton Logan, her eleven brothers and sisters, and her parents face-to-face with starvation. Their twelve hundred acre plantation some forty miles from Richmond was sold at a tremendous loss to satisfy the debt; her mother took in boarders, and Anna and her sister rejoiced in securing teaching positions in order to support the family. Such were the vicissitudes of postwar life in Dixie.

Finances—salaries for ministers and building expenses in particular—have posed weighty problems for churches throughout the centuries. Following the defeat, with their money gone and their debts and responsibilities burgeoning, Southerners often dismissed contributions to their churches as non-essential. Margaret Josephine Miles Gillis, wife of an itinerant Methodist Episcopal minister in the Alabama Conference, made a valiant struggle to make ends meet on the minuscule salary accorded her husband. Their financial situation was further complicated by her husband's paternalistic opposition to her teaching. It mattered little that Jo insisted that she "would rather teach than anything else in the world." Both Jo Gillis and Virginia Aiken had been reared in homes of ease and affluence before the war, and their straitened circumstances following Appomattox in contrast to their youthful years of plenty rendered their situation even more traumatic. Jo's deprivations and martyrdom on behalf of her husband (his new clothes, his comfort and his well-being given top priorities) soon led her to an early grave.

To be sure, financial losses were minor compared with the loss of one's husband in battle. In "Plaintive Cries of Pain" the reader meets a lonely widow, Sally Randle Perry, whose husband died in the Battle of Sharpsburg. Now living alone in Dallas County, Alabama, with her two small children, Sally is unable to cope with her grief and her morbid thoughts of the future. Without her husband Sally is consumed with intense anxiety about raising their children. Is she too permissive or too demanding? Too impatient? Too protective? Inexperienced and dependent on the advice of others, she watches her plantation, Ingleside, slowly slip away from her. Unfortunately, Sally's continued inability to come to grips with the new order of things was not an isolated case among Southern widows following the war.

After reading these excerpts the reader may choose to empathize with Southerners following the war or simply judge them victims of their own folly and unworthy of sympathy. Whatever the verdict, these were real women living in a world suddenly turned topsy-turvy.

Part I

MANY VOICES

ℬ 1 ⳩

The Long War Ends

"We had desired peace—an end to the bloodshed and to the impending starvation of women and children. Peace we had longed and prayed for; but not this peace."[1]

Robert E. Lee's surrender to Ulysses S. Grant at Appomattox on April 9, 1865, for all practical purposes, marked the end of the Civil War. Sporadic fighting continued, however, and untold numbers of Southern diehards, unwilling to concede defeat, hoped and waited for a renewed Confederate battlefront in the Trans-Mississippi. Individuals and pockets of resistance throughout the South were bent upon seeing the war fought down to the last man standing.

With the disruption of the rail lines and the dearth of newspapers during the latter part of the war, reliable information in many areas of the South was difficult—and in many cases impossible—to come by. Sherman's "neckties" (train rails given a special twist to prevent their being used again without being sent to a rolling mill) and the demise of Southern newspapers, the result of a scarcity of paper, ink, and editors—or of Union takeover, rendered reliable war news a rarity. Rumor abounded. Even before a rumor could be assimilated, new information had superseded the original, soon to be followed by another contradiction, attended in short order by yet another repudiation. For millions of loyal Southerners any talk of giving up was blasphemous.

Despite being less than forty miles distant from Richmond, Elvira Seddon explained on May 4, 1865 (almost a month after Appomattox) that they were "thoroughly in the dark. We have no idea where Gen Lee and his army are. We don't know what loss he has sustained; we are in utter[?] ignorance of what is transpiring in Richmond. And what is worst of all, we do not see any prospect of a better state of things. For the rest of the war we must be content to live in a state of darkness as regards our friends. Better things are coming, let us wish!"[2]

Two more days brought little relief for Elvira from the awesome burden of suspense. "Where is our army? Who has been killed? Who wounded? What is to be the end of this misery?" Firmly convinced that God was on the side of the Confederacy, Elvira buoyed up her momentarily flagging spirits with "Surely, surely a just God will save us from 'our enemies and the hand of all that hate us.' Let us trust in Him and patiently await His good pleasure, remembering the comforting assurance 'He will never leave nor forsake those who put their trust in Him.'"[3]

Margaret Stanly Beckwith, refugeeing with her family in Lincolnton, North Carolina, was unaware of the surrender at the time she impatiently complained to her journal: "This suspense will drive me mad. Ten thousand rumors reach us each day after day, but not a bit of reliable news...."[4] As one Southern woman confessed: "If we are poor in everything else we are at least rich in rumors. Rumors with which no one can be totally dissatisfied, for they are manufactured to suit every shade and variety of politics...."[5]

During the last days of the war wild rumors circulated that Lee had mined Richmond before he evacuated the city and that the subsequent explosion had killed 20,000 people.[6] Confederates were eager to believe illusory reports that the French had sided with the South and "had taken New Orleans and sunk 3 gunboats in the Mississippi River."[7]

Southern zealots clutched at any possible ray of hope. Sarah Wadley was exuberant over word that it was Fitzhugh Lee's army that had surrendered and not that of General Robert E. Lee. When that report proved false, Sarah clung to the rumor that the general had merely surrendered himself and his rear guard and that the rest of Lee's army had joined Johnston and engaged in a great battle which had ended in a decisive victory for the Confederacy.[8] The most enthusiastically accepted rumors of all, of course, were that Grant had surrendered to Lee.[9]

"To Us All Was Dark"

At first, early reports and even final confirmation of the news of Appomattox met with widespread skepticism. Four years of unceasing struggling, suffering, and sacrificing surely could not end with defeat! Harriet Palmer immediately denounced the news that Richmond had been given up: "All Yankee lies. I don't believe one word of it."[10] News of the fall of Richmond staggered Elvira Seddon and her family. "Our hearts were filled with sadness. Our capital was gone, our ... invincible army defeated, many dear ones doubtless lying on the gory battlefield. Separation from beloved friends at hand, life in the Yankee lines our fate.... To us all was dark. The very exuberance of nature seemed mockery. And then the thought would present itself painfully, 'How long shall we gaze upon this peaceful scene? All will be changed. The fields uncultivated will cease to present their covering of verdance. Evidence of prosperity will vanish, and we will feel thankful if our once large farms yield us a scanty support.'"[11]

With the evacuation of Richmond, Kate Mason Rowland was still firm in her conviction that General Lee "will yet give them [the Yankees] a lesson. The Yankees think the war is nearly over when it is only beginning! The end may be far off and the way a bloody one but Independence is the goal—as certain as the ultimate justice of God...."[12] When the Yankees made the rounds of the homes in Clarksville, Tennessee, asking them to light up their houses in honor of the fall of Richmond, Nannie Haskins was furious: "Fortunately for us they did not come here, I'd rather have seen the house stoned or burned to the ground than luminated for Yanks."[13]

Kate Sperry was yet another of millions of Southerners who despaired over the talk circulating in early April. "Cried all day nearly and never felt so miserable—the reports are worse and worse—I cannot listen to them—no papers and no mail." By April 14th verification of the meeting at Appomattox reached Kate Sperry. "General Lee has surrendered his *whole* army to Grant. O my God, can it be? I never felt so perfectly wretched in my life—there is no hope for us this side of the Mississippi River."[14]

A numbness coupled with disbelief shrouded the South. Harriet Lang recalled that although reports of Lee's surrender drifted in "We could not, or *would* not, believe such a terrible disaster had really happened."[15] When informed of the surrender, Elvira Seddon and her family deemed it "'A Yankee lie!' we say and beg not to be disturbed. In vain! I am haunted by the awful thought."[16]

Charlotte Ravenel registered shock in her diary. "We hear the most exaggerated accounts of things here. To-day's reports are ... Lee's army, 32,000, has surrendered to Grant, and all the men paroled not to fight again during the war." General Lee's appearance in Richmond finally convinced Fannie Dickinson of the reality of the surrender. "Nearly a week has passed since I wrote last. I felt that I could not express my feelings, language could not portray them. Each day we have hoped on, and encouraged each other to hope that General Lee had perhaps not really surrendered, and our affairs in not quite so bad a condition, but certain confirmation has at last arrived. General Lee himself entered Richmond yesterday with his staff. This week has been if anything, sadder than last."[17]

"We Cannot, Will Not Give Up"

"Surrender! Never Surrender!" Kate Sperry wailed, her petition echoing and re-echoing Southerners' inability or unwillingness to accept a defeat that signaled a cruel demise to all their hopes and dreams, that rendered vain four years of unstinting sacrifice and deprivation. Kate Sperry applauded the tenacity of General Johnston who had reportedly threatened some months earlier that "*before he'll give up he'll fight 'til he has to hire a piece of ground to fight on!*"[18] Submission similarly was unthinkable for Elvira Seddon. "I feel the courage of despair and am prepared for any calamity save one, submission. Never, never could I consent to that! Let us fight it out, 'til not a man or a woman survives to bear the yolk of servitude to tyrants! I feel more bitterly every hour; most bitterly as I write."[19] An irate Georgia girl prayed: "Oh! That they would never yield while a man lives to fight...."[20]

Mary Goodwin of Wytheville, Virginia, anguished: "and what now? Shall we give up—cease to fight for liberty? Many think our cause is hopeless & are ready to submit. But I Never! Fight on I would say & let our motto be 'Liberty or Death.' God is hiding his face from us, but he will yet smile upon us, & bless our cause with success."[21]

Several days later Mary continued her tirade. "I cannot believe that for 4 long years we have battled & poured out the best blood of our land on the altar of Liberty for naught. Oh! no I cannot, *cannot believe* that we are whipped, the thought distracts me. It is too humiliating. Subjugation! Oh! bitter word & galling to my very soul. I cannot utter it without a shudder. What have we done that we should be thus afflicted? What have we done to forfeit our claim to Liberty? Oh! Victory why hast thou fled from our banners [?]... Oh! no—thou will return again for we *cannot, will not give up*. Oh! My God open some way of escape for us...."[22]

For Kate, Elvira, Mary and others like them defeat was inconceivable. "We *must* hold out manfully, until an *honorable* peace shall crown our effort," Margaret Beckwith declared. "And we *will* hold out. God helping us, we *will* not betray our trust. The South shall yet be free! It cannot be that they have died in vain"[23] Ellen House refused for one moment to "think that we are whipped. I believe as firmly we will be free as I do there is a God in Heaven." She was sure "we have depended too much on Gen. Lee too little on God."[24]

With the confirmation of the surrender, Lizzie Hardin described the scene in Eatonton, Georgia, their home during their banishment from Kentucky: "Almost everyone in the room burst into tears. Not a word was spoken except when someone sobbed out, 'We are not whipped yet! We will fight in the Trans-Mississippi,' or, 'I hope we will fight till there is not a man left!'"[25]

Upon hearing of Lee's surrender, one woman stuck her knitting needles in a half finished sock and let them rust. "Who could bear to knit, when our army was scattered, our honored and beloved Lee had surrendered, after the grandest and bravest struggle ever recorded in History?"[26]

Although deserters were leaving the ranks of the Rebel army in alarming numbers, loyal Confederates continued to view the situation through rose colored glasses. Sarah Fay's morale surely must have skyrocketed with a letter from her soldier husband written almost a month after the news of Appomattox reaffirming his conviction that "The Confederacy will gain its independence." About a week later her hopes were dashed when he confessed "Everybody but me is whipped."[27]

"Our country gone!" Sarah Wadley wept. "I feel as if all were gone. I had never felt the possibility of this blow, all that makes life glorious. What virtue can be left to one that has no country. Even resignation seems like treason to our principles. It is like darkness, it is so terrible."[28] A devastated Elvira Seddon sobbed: "'We are a conquered people. Henceforth, we must live subservient to Yankee domination. We have no country to be proud of; no flag to point to; the hated stars and stripes are floating insolently over us. Such are my thoughts. No wonder then that I feel like lying down to die. What is life to us? Country gone; property gone; our people crushed under the iron heel of the conqueror. Our very Negroes exalted over our heads. I repeat, what have we to live for? To be 'hewers of wood and drawers of water?' I see nothing in store for us."[29] Another woman grieved: "*A Lost Cause* indeed. Loss of life! Of love! Of property! Oh! maimed hearts and forms and homes, no pen can estimate the extent of your loss!"[30]

Following the news of Appomattox, Margaret Junkin Preston was "struck dumb with astonishment! Why all these four years of suffering—of separations—of horror—of blood—of havoc—of awful bereavement! Why these ruined homes—these broken family circles—these scenes of terror that must scathe the brain of those who witnessed them till their dying day! Why is our dear Willy in his uncoffined grave? Why poor Frank to go through life with one arm? Is it wholly and forever in vain? *God only knows!*"[31]

Having lost two brothers during the war, Pauline DeCaradeuc (Heyward) was devastated by the news of Lee's surrender. "All our brave Generals, unequaled soldiers, my own gallant Brothers, was it for this is that you died? Subjugation! Never! God will raise us yet." In her adamant refusal to accept defeat Pauline insisted: "I *won't* believe our cause lost, so far we are only outnumbered, *in every* fair fight we have been victorious for four years, and it was not, it could not have been for this—never—God who is justice, will accept the sacrifice of the lives of the Chivalry of the South, and give their land its own proud place among nations."[32]

"All Seems Dull and Cold"

As doubts began clouding the heretofore bright optimism of ardent Southern patriots, Harriet Palmer confessed to her diary: "We may be exterminated, but I pray never subjected. I hope I and all mine may be laid in the grass before such a calamity befalls us."[33] By May Sarah Wadley had abandoned all hope. "Oh it is all gone. I am compelled to see it. We are subjugated. I am too sorrowful to weep. All seems dull and cold except when a sudden rush of angry grief comes over me to think of all we were, of what we have done and suffered and now all that we have achieved is gradually slipping away." Sarah's lamentation continued: "Have I indeed imagined the last four years and have they indeed really existed. Oh God. I have never thought the bitterness of this hour would come. I can no longer see one ray of hope. I can no longer see a promise of resistance." Although Sara had expected that a Confederate victory might entail poverty, "suffering perhaps and sorrow but never, never … this. It seems too hard to bear. I will try to be resigned."[34]

Following "the hideous nightmare" of Lee's surrender, Hannah Rawlings agonized: "I felt as if I could lay my head in the dust and *die!* For three days after we learned the fate of our devoted army, I don't think there were a dozen sentences spoken in the family where I was. A stranger would have thought there was a corpse in the house."

Hannah attempted to explain to her sister in Pennsylvania: "You cannot understand how we feel about this thing. You have not watched the struggle as we have, and seen the sufferings of those you love and the insolence of the enemy. We had ministered to the wants of our soldiers, nursed them in sickness and cheered them with kind words until we felt a tenderness for the poorest one in the ranks. They were *ours*. We were proud of them and loved them as the champions of a just cause, and the heroes of many a dauntless deed. God bless them! I hope they may yet grow strong enough to defy those who consider themselves our masters, and to 'rise again and fight for their ain countrie.'"[35]

From Greenville, South Carolina, Jennie King wrote to her cousin: "Oh! How very sad to think that we have no *country*, no *honor*, no *liberty*—words once so very dear to us, now only to be thought of with sadness and humiliation. To think that any people should be subjected to the indignities and insults that are heaped upon us is truly humiliating—surely we have reached the climax of our 'degradation'...."[36]

Other Southerners were too stunned and demoralized to register bitterness. Frances Butler (Leigh) was heartsick upon her arrival in Georgia following the war to look after the family's plantations. "I can hardly give a true idea of how crushed and sad the people are. You hear no bitterness towards the North; they are too sad to be bitter; their grief is overwhelming. Nothing can make any difference to them now; the women live in the past, and the men only in the daily present, trying, in a listless sort of way, to repair their ruined fortunes. They are like so many foreigners, whose only interest in the country is their own individual business."[37]

For some disheartened Rebels, however, there was a momentary rejoicing over the liberal terms offered by General Grant at Appomattox. Sara Handy explained that "First, of course was the "crushing sense of defeat, the helpless and hopeless looking forward to confiscation and possible exile; and having no expectation of amnesty, next to that came astonishment at the liberal terms which Grant had accorded. The Confederates, men as well as officers, owned their horses; and only a cavalry man whose steed has for years been his comrade and best friend, knows what that sentence, 'Let them keep their horses,' meant to men who had fought to the bitter end, and had looked for no clemency from their conquerors."[38]

"A Return to the Union Never!"

Although in time countless recalcitrant Southerners were compelled to accept their fate, they somehow were unable to envision a permanent return to the Union. Early in the war, in May 1862, the Federal takeover of New Orleans had cut away at Clara Solomon's belief that the South could never be subdued; however, it failed to shake her conviction that the country could never by any stretch of the imagination be reunited. Defeat—well possibly, but a return to the Union never! Failure to gain a Confederate victory, she was sure, would be merely a temporary stopgap before another civil war erupted. Registering her loathing for the Yankee troops that were occupying her city she fantasized: "Oh! that we could strike them out as one man. But our time will come, & soon enough they will see the folly of their attempts to restore the Union on the basis of the constitution. A. [her sister] & I are determined *not* to go back, notwithstanding the course taken by all beside. But what a waste of words! *Can we ever be subdued?* Allowing that, can we ever be united in the sacred ties of brotherhood with those for whom we entertain the most rancorous hatred. For a time it *may* endure. But the proud spirit cannot always be claimed, it will break the fetters at any peril & then again there will be a devastation of another civil war."[39]

Any talk of reuniting with the North, Margaret Beckwith maintained, was absurd and passive Rebel acceptance of "restoration" was contemptible. "It makes my blood boil to hear men and women, who call themselves Southerners, talk of 'going back into the Union.' To see them willing to grasp the hands of those who have killed our brothers & friends. Those who would take away our honor, our all."[40] Amanda Worthington's sentiments were even more vitriolic: "Rather than go back into a union with such people I would have *every man, woman and child* in the Confederacy killed."[41]

One zealous Southern woman insisted that Southerners would be willing to sacrifice "Anything—everything will we sacrifice rather than come again under the same government with the hated Yankee! Such are the sentiments of everyone I have seen."[42] For Sarah Wadley and millions like her a future of Southerners standing like criminals waiting for pardon was utterly abhorrent.

While a factious and bitter populace pointed accusing fingers for the defeat at the pre-war, fire-eating secessionists, at Jefferson Davis, at the Confederate government, at the profiteers, at the financial conduct of the war or at myriads of other scapegoats, Sarah Wadley reluctantly admitted that "This is not the time for crimination and recrimination. We have fought much and suffered much. If more could have been done it is now past." In her desperation Sarah threatened: "I cannot bear to stay here. I will never call myself a citizen of the United States."[43]

Talk of "reconstruction" called forth even more violent reactions than even the odious prospect of "subjugation." The Radical Republicans' threatened "Reconstruction" of the South, its politics, its social structure, and its traditions electrified native Southerners. Sarah Wadley bemoaned: "The Yankees talk of mercy, of reconstruction and general amnesty. How hateful are the words. Yes hateful! Their cruelty is more welcome to me than their kindness. I would rather hear the word subjugation than reconstruction; but it will *never* be! It cannot be. We are subjugated I see it now, but oh surely we will not give the lie to all our past protestations. We will not tacitly repudiate the acts of our glorious soldiers, we were right. We were fighting for freedom, for independence. We do not want reconstruction. We do not admit that we were rebels. We do not deny our freedom. Oh say we are conquered if indeed it must be, but never, never let us deny our cause by sanctioning the hypocritical farce of reconstruction."[44]

"A Great Calamity": Lincoln's Death Mourned

The news of Lincoln's assassination spawned yet another wild proliferation of rumors. Reports that years later seem humorous in the light of history were extremely real and frightening at the time. There were reports "that Johnson was the instigator of the plot to kill Lincoln and Seward and that a mob hung Johnson and that Mrs. Lincoln stabbed him with a carving knife and all sorts of rumors ... it's said that one of Mosby's men shot him and exclaimed in the dark (the gas having been turned off) and confusion: 'Virginia is avenged!'"[45] Stories making the rounds had it that the assassination had been the work of "Marylanders robbed of their property by the Yankee government."[46] Widespread fear prevailed among apprehensive Southerners who were convinced that "Andy Johnson will hang all 'rebels' down to captains."[47]

The news circulating in Pendleton, South Carolina, according to Floride Clemson's diary, indicated that "Seward was killed in bed. Now they say Andy Johnson is killed, & two of his cabinet, & that Grant will be dictator, then that Lee is to be president, & Grant vice president; then there is to be a general vote for president."[48] Verification of President Lincoln's assassination met with mixed reviews in the South. Most Southerners, like Sarah Wadley, knew not what to expect. Would the South be accused of plotting Lincoln's death? Would Jefferson Davis and other top CSA officials be the scapegoats for Booth's reprehensible act? Would the entire South be the victim of Yankee vengeance? Would the murder effect more oppressive peace terms? The news, Sarah reported, was bewildering. "What will follow? Heaven only knows ... it must have a powerful effect."[49]

Lincoln was the devil incarnate to most Southerners. Countless rebels were convinced they had been delivered "from our worst enemy," the man who along with the Republican party was responsible for the war and the emancipation proclamation.[50] Ellen House was scarcely heart-broken that Lincoln had been assassinated and rejoiced that "his murderer has escaped." With the rumor that Seward's son had been killed that same night, Ellen deemed it "a pity that the father escaped [being killed too]."[51]

And yet there were a number of rational Southerners who truly mourned the president's death, believing they had lost a potentially reasonable compassionate "binder of wounds." Having read smatterings of Lincoln's Second Inaugural reprinted in the rapidly evaporating editions of their newspapers, some Southerners believed, at least in retrospect, that Lincoln's plans for "restoration" promised far greater merit than the prospect of what threatened to be a convulsive "reconstruction" of former Rebels, their property and their society. Less than six weeks earlier in his Second Inaugural Lincoln had promised to strive on "with malice toward none, with charity for all" and a proposed agenda "to care for him who shall have borne the battle and for his widow and his orphan, to do all which may achieve and cherish a just and lasting peace among ourselves and with all nations."

Years later Sara Handy recognized her father's wisdom in pointing out that Lincoln's death "'is the worst misfortune that was felt to befall us.... Lincoln was the one man in all the North who could well afford to be magnanimous, and—I say it, not forgetting Grant's leniency at Appomattox—was the one man wholly inclined to be so.'" According to Sara's father, Booth had merely succeeded in "cutting the South's throat."[52] Looking back, Mrs. Roger Pryor in her memoir *My Day*, concurred in her husband's conviction that had Lincoln not been assassinated, "The South would never have suffered the shame and sorrow of the carpet-bag regime." Many disheartened rebels feared the South would become the victim of monstrous retaliation at the hands of Johnson. Anne Thom believed: "President Lincoln's death is regarded as a great calamity, because he expressed such conciliatory sentiments, & would have exerted himself to restore peace & order to our distracted country, without confiscation & disfranchisement."[53]

With time to reflect, Cornelia Spencer viewed the assassination of Lincoln with a certain degree of sadness mingled with compassion. After four years of perceiving Lincoln as the antichrist it was difficult for many Southerners to express any deep regret over his death. However, the horror and shock of the assassination rocked the nation. Actually most Southerners knew little about Lincoln other than from the scathing remarks that peppered the vehemently biased Southern press and fired the vitriolic speeches of the demagogues. In the South, Mrs. Spencer explained, "He was always presented to us in caricature. The Southern press never mentioned him but with some added *sobriquet* of contempt and hatred. His simplicity of character and kindliness of heart we knew nothing of;

nor would many now at the South, much as they may deplore his death, concede to him the possession of any such virtues.... But a sense of remorse fills my mind now as I write of him, realizing how much that was really good and guileless, and well-intentioned and generous, may have come to an untimely end in the atrocious tragedy at Ford's Theatre."[54]

"The Vengeance of the Lord": Lincoln's Death Celebrated

In sharp contrast, great numbers of Southerners rejoiced in Lincoln's demise. "Today's news is very cheering," a South Carolina woman wrote. "It is that Lincoln and Seward have both been assassinated, and that there is to be an Armistice."[55]

Tee Edmonds gloated in her journal: "In the midst of our troubles and sorrow the North, too, has been thrown into excitement and trouble. This week Old Abe [Abraham Lincoln] and Seward felt the suffering which they have inflicted on our Southern people. Whilst Abe, hated rail splitter, was in the theater, as much interested as any one probably in the play, one of the actors, to carry out the tragedy and relieve the Southern people of that great bore, fired shooting him through the head. The person, whose name is Booth, immortalized by so daring an act, stepped forward on the platform, waved his sword and cried, 'Sic Semper Tyrannis.' Then he dashed through the crowd and rushed to a horse, which he had hitched conveniently and was off. God bless him for his brave act."[56]

Kate Stone was ecstatic over the news of the assassination. "All honor to J. Wilkes Booth, who has rid the world of a tyrant and made himself famous for generations." Rumors of Seward's death prompted her to exclaim, "I cannot be sorry for their fate. They deserve it. They have reaped their just reward." Two weeks later Kate told her journal: "Many think Andy Johnson worse than Lincoln, but that is simply impossible." Reports circulating in June that Sherman had killed Andrew Johnson, "the detested," led to Kate's conclusion "he deserves killing."[57]

A South Carolina woman described attending church and hearing of Lincoln's assassination. "The general impression made upon the people by the unexpected stroke for our country is that of a happy event. Even the minister so far forgot his position as to make an allusion of a political character in the pulpit, and spoke as if a benefit had been conferred by the murder."[58]

Madge Preston and her husband, William, as Confederate sympathizers living near Baltimore in divided Maryland, observed the city "in great excitement" over the news of Lincoln's assassination and "were careful of their remarks."[59] Pauline DeCaradeuc (Heyward) expressed little grief over the death of Lincoln and responded to the rumor that Seward was mortally wounded with the wish "God grant it."[60] Not a few looked upon the assassination as "Providential."[61]

Clearly Edmund Ruffin harbored no affection for Lincoln and no doubt reflected the opinions of thousands of Southern women and men in writing: "I for one … approve of & rejoice at the slaying of these instigators, permitters, & encouragers of the assassins & robbers, & houseburners, & destroyers of the property of millions of southern victims." Ruffin particularly despised clergymen who devoted their Easter Sunday sermons to making Lincoln a martyr. These sermons, according to Ruffin, constituted "the man-worship, of a low-bred & vulgar & illiterate buffoon, & the near approach to blasphemy, of these holy flatterers." Better, the caustic Ruffin wrote, that Lincoln, rather than being immortalized by being assassinated, would have gone down in history "as a vulgar buffoon" and died "of disease or old age."[62]

One woman having lost two sons in the war and frantic over the fate of a third apparently missing in action, responded to the news with "'Lincoln has been killed! thank God!'" The next day, however, she apparently had second thoughts. "'I have prayed it all out in my heart,'" she said, "'that is, I'm not glad. But somehow, I *can't* be sorry. I believe it was the vengeance of the Lord.'"[63]

Northerners, naturally, took a dim view of Southerners in their midst or in occupied areas who evidenced any show of elation over the assassination. Upon hearing tales of the wholesale destruction of homes and the arrests made of Confederates who were reveling in various areas of Tennessee over Lincoln's assassination, Virginia French was convinced that the soldiers "exerted themselves to draw citizens into some expression of joy over the tragedy—so that they would have a pretext for ill using them." And, indeed, Virginia had reason for concern as her rebellious cousin Mollie was arrested, carried to Tullahoma, Tennessee, and charged with "'rejoicing over the death of Lincoln.'"[64]

Reluctantly, Rachel Craighead and her family draped their Nashville doorway in black crepe in compliance with Union orders, and as the funeral commemoration for Lincoln solemnly wound its way through the streets Rachel sourly commented, "I thought the procession never would get done passing."[65]

A Missouri woman recounted a gruesome story of how her friend, Mrs. Stuart, who had lost a husband and a fifteen-year-old son in the war, had expressed her undying hatred of Lincoln and her absolute delight over his assassination: "'Thank God, the wretch has gotten his just deserts.'" Despite her sentiments she was warned that in accordance with Union orders she must hang black crepe in front of her home as a mourning symbol. Mrs. Stuart's retort was succinct and resolute: "'I'd rather die first.'"

Shortly thereafter, a company of blue clad soldiers observing that the house evidenced no sign of mourning, threatened Mrs. S. "'Every d—rebel must this day kiss the dust for this dastardly act.'" Their orders only served to further enrage Mrs. Stuart, who responded angrily: "'What, I show a sign of mourning for Abraham Lincoln—I, who but for him would not be husbandless and childless today!'" Her impertinence promptly touched off a pell-mell rush through her home by the soldiers to find something black to hang over her doorway.

With yelps of victory the soldiers returned with Mrs. Stuart's long crepe veil—the mourning veil she had worn in grieving for her husband and son. Snatching the veil from their hands she sighed, "'Give it to me, I will hang it up where you wish. Only leave the room, leave the premises; go across the street; you can see me from there....'"

Moments later Mrs. Stuart appeared on her verandah. She was dressed in black and as the soldiers peered across the street they watched Mrs. Stuart as she stood on a chair to thread the material through the openwork of the balcony above her head. Suddenly in a shocking turn of events she kicked the chair out from under her, and to the horror of the onlookers hung suspended from the noose she had intertwined in the veil. True to her word she died before she would mourn for Lincoln, the villain that had left her an inconsolably bereaved childless widow.[66]

Women, of course, constituted a substantial portion of church membership in the South, and over the years they had been duly cautioned by their ministers as to the evils of theater attendance. Numerous members of the clergy, although deeply grieved over the assassination of President Lincoln, also took the opportunity to reproach the president for having been so "wicked" as to attend the theater in the first place. Northern clerics also railed against theater attendance. A newspaper editorial mourned: "True, there is one item in this history over which we wish a vail [sic] of secrecy could have been drawn. Our lamented Chief Magistrate was shot in a theatre. It is inexpressibly to be regretted that he was at a theatre ... if he had not saved his life by being elsewhere he would have saved the Christian public the double shock of not only knowing that their President was dead, but that he fell where they would have wept to have seen their sons alive."[67]

The editorial continued by pointing out that as the model for thousands of young people "he should not have gone to the theatre.... Our Chief Magistrate had no possible business in a theatre. He was the 'minister of God,' and what a place is a theatre for God's ministers!" The clergy reminded readers that while notorious criminals "Paled at the thought," it was a theatrical performer who "was found equal to the infernal task ... the crime of Booth, by which he outranks the most famous regicide of history, is but the fruits of his theatrical life."

Following Lincoln's assassination, some clergymen even drew criticism from their parishioners who were irate over their ministers' praying for President Lincoln's family & his successor. Lucy Fletcher, for example, reported in her diary of being incensed by the prayer. "This is certainly a premature & time serving policy of which I am thankful that none of our Southern *born* ministers have been guilty."

Lizzie Hardin, a Southern zealot, hoped that "he was better prepared for death than we think he was. But for the sake of my country, I cannot but feel glad that he is dead."[68]

"Worse Than Lincoln": President Andrew Johnson

Little optimism prevailed among vast numbers of Southerners over Andrew Johnson and his new role as the president of the United States. In many areas the great distrust of Johnson resulted in a rush to take the amnesty oath before the new president would abolish Lincoln's lenient terms and enact much harsher requirements.[69] Kate Sperry considered Johnson "worse than Lincoln, so that won't do us any good—if somebody would settle Old Andy, why then we would stand a better chance of seeing the Yankees fighting amongst themselves for the *crown*."[70] The rumor of "a probable march of Sherman and Grant upon their own capitol they being unwilling to submit to the tyrannical course of Andy Johnson" spawned great apprehension among some and considerable hope among others.[71]

Following the news of Lincoln's assassination, the increasingly depressed Edmund Ruffin no doubt spoke for untold numbers of women when he bemoaned in his diary: "Now will succeed to the throne, & the enormous power of the Yankee President, the low & vulgar & shameless drunken demagogue, Andrew Johnson of Ten.... He was put on the Yankee ticket for Vice-President merely as being a southern man, by birth and residence, & one of the very few popular southern men who sided with Yankeedom. When he was to be inaugurated, in Washington, the occasion did not prevent his being so drunk as to render his speech 'incoherent' & nonsensical...." Ruffin concluded with the prediction that "his conduct will be as disgraceful as would be expected from his antecedents." Almost gleefully Ruffin rejoiced: "The deserved fate of his predecessor will keep him in continual alarm for his own life."[72]

At the time of the raising of the stars and stripes on Ft. Sumter, Virginia French suggested that "If only Andy Johnson and Parson Brownlow could only go along—one to do up the drinking and the other the cussin of the expedition they would be all arranged." Lucy Fletcher thought the succession of Johnson to the presidency should be proof positive that the South could not possibly be implicated in Lincoln's assassination. "Certainly no judicious friend of the South could hope for an improvement of our situation under Andy Johnson, and much as we despise the miserable sufferers, every generous heart revolts at secret assassination." Johnson, indeed, faced formidable odds what with a ready-made hate constituency. A Richmond woman wrote to her friend Ellen Mordecai: "And now the horrible assassination of President Lincoln, and the Inauguration of that low, miserable wretch, Andy Johnson, who if report says true is the worst enemy the South ever had. What will become of us? I feel almost frantic at times. The excitement produced by this tragical event, is appalling."[73]

Even the thought of her father's possible political association with Johnson was extremely displeasing to Eliza Andrews. Rumors that her father, a Unionist, might be made provisional governor of Georgia embarrassed Eliza, who was convinced that to hold an office under Johnson "would be a disgrace, and my dear father is too honorable a man to have his name mixed up with the miserable gang that are swooping down upon us, like buzzards on a battlefield."[74]

For months after the war, Gertrude Thomas was reluctant to refer to Johnson as "president," admitting that she would call Andrew Johnson "President and own him—him as such when he releases *our* illustrious ex President."[75] Fear for the safety of both Davis and Lee—and, of course, their own futures as well—were frightening aspects of Southerners' reversal of fortunes.

"The War Is Over and I'm Glad of It"

Certainly not all Southerners were loath to see the contest abandoned. During the latter months of the war Rebel soldiers on the battlefield were deserting by the thousands (as many as eight percent in one month), and lonely and destitute women on the homefront longed for the return of their loved ones. While some historians credited Southern women with having zealously supported the war and prolonged its duration for months or even years, other historians suggest that the unwillingness of Southern women to continue their sacrifices helped bring an end to the war.[76]

Desertions in the Confederate ranks had reached epidemic proportions toward the end of the war, many desertions in response to heartbreaking letters from families concerning their destitute conditions on the homefront. Countless rebels soldiers watched their own food, clothing and health eroding and concluded there was little hope of victory. By January 1865, the wife of Confederate General Roger A. Pryor explained, "the common soldier perceived that the cause was lost. He could read its doom in the famine around him, in the faces of his officers, in tidings from abroad. His wife and children were suffering. His duty was now to them; so he stole away in darkness, and, in infinite danger and difficulty, found his way back to his own fireside. He deserted, but not to the enemy."[77]

Some ten days before Appomattox, Gertrude Thomas, despite the fact that her husband had hired a substitute and remained at home safe from the horrors of the battlefield, confided to her diary her longing for the cessation of hostilities. "I may perhaps be glad hereafter that I have lived through this war but now the height of my ambition is to be *quiet*, to have no distracting cares—the time to read—leisure to think and write—and study." Several weeks later, Gertrude's wish came true. (Little did she realize, however, that her greatest problems in life lay ahead of her: financial woes including the bankruptcy of her husband's business, loss of her personal property sold for debt, loss of social prestige, insufficient money to educate her children properly.) "The war is over and I am glad of it. What terms of agreement may be decided upon I cannot say but if *anything* is left us—if we can count with certainty upon enough to raise and educate our children I shall be grateful. It is humiliating, very indeed to be a conquered people...." Reconciliation, she cautioned, would depend on the nation's being "very discreet for the South will prove a smouldering volcano requiring but little to again burst forth. Treated as members of one family—a band of brothers, *in time* we may have a common interest—but pressed too hard upon, our property taken from us—a desperate people having nothing to lose, the South may again revolt...." However, Gertrude promised that with kind treatment she would "endeavour to cultivate friendly feelings."[78]

For millions of Southerners the war involved serious religious ramifications. Southerners' conviction that slavery was sanctioned by God eventuated in ministers and churches themselves owning slaves or even gangs of slaves which the latter often rented out for construction work. Therefore, most Southern churches fervently supported the Confederacy and its attempt to maintain slavery as being the will of God. In turn victories on the battlefield were seen as manifestations of God's approval of the Southern cause; defeats were viewed as God's punishment for personal sins or for public indifference to God's laws. Special prayer meetings held during the war in churches and in private homes and official days of fasting and prayer served to help reinforce Southern sentiment in support of the Confederate cause. For the most part churches denounced deserters, opposed any attempts at compromise, and strenuously objected to any plans of reconstruction.

"It Was God's Will"

The collapse of the Confederacy, in the view of many Southerners, and the oppression of reconstruction were God's vengeance on a wicked people.[79] Countless Southerners who did not subscribe to the punishment rationale resignedly attributed the South's sufferings to God's will, God's long range design for his people.

For some Southerners their religious or moral convictions led them to accept the defeat with quiet resignation. For some who deplored slavery it was God's punishment on Southerners for holding men and women in slavery. For some the war's object "was to break the yoke that the oppressed might go free."[80] For some it was God's chastisement for a wicked society. Margaret Preston asked, "How long, Lord, how long, shall we thy guilty people who deserve all this fierce wrath continue to suffer it!"[81]

Thousands who saw the defeat as God's will shared Virginia French's sentiments: "But it is all over—we have gone down—there is no help for it. It was God's will, or it would not have been."[82] A benumbed Georgiana Walker mourned: "My heart sickens, & I feel that this weight of woe, is almost too much for us to bear! There is but *one* comfort left to us. God reigns, & looks upon this fearful hour. If this be *His* will, we must submit."[83]

Much as she and her fellow countrymen despised the reappearance of the Union flag over the land, Cornelia Spencer insisted that she had never seen any decent man "who evinced any intention of other than an honest acceptance of the situation, and a determination to do their whole duty and make the best of the inevitable." Most people, she maintained, "said they were satisfied that all had been done that could be done, and they seemed to be sustained by the sense of duty done and well done, and the event left to God, and with His award they had no intention of quarreling." An incredible number of Southerners considered death for the cause as a noble sacrifice; it was the responsibility of women to sacrifice their sons and husbands to the service of their country. Thousands assuaged their grief with the conviction that their loved ones had passed on to a far, far better world. Captain John Stewart Walker, of Richmond, Virginia, wrote to his wife praising her for her patriotism. "Your heroic consecration of your husband to the services of our Country, even at the cost of widowhood to yourself, orphanage to our little ones, and poverty to all, demanded even my admiration of your sacrifice, though I thought I had been able before to appreciate the blessing of so noble a wife as I have."[84]

On the other hand the defeat for still others was enough to shake their faith in God. "Sometimes," Grace Elmore wrote, "I feel so wicked, so rebellious against God. If I could but see some light in this horrible darkness, if I could but cease to grope in this wilderness of care, guided only by my own reason, and rest truly and honestly on the belief, 'He doeth all things well.' But as day by day our cares increase; as under the rule of our oppressors, evil after evil unfolds itself; and we see nothing in the future but suffering and humiliation, the heart, the mind will rise and question, yea question the goodness, the mercy of its Maker. We know that with Him a thousand years are as one day, and in his hands are the issues of life, but oh 'tis hard, 'tis bitter to eat the bread of subjugation, to witness through life the humiliation of those around you; to spend a lifetime in the midst of a downtrodden but free hearted people; to see nothing in the future that will compensate for past, present or future suffering. Turn where you will, the waters of trouble surround you; and for our country we see nought but breakers ahead."[85]

With news of the surrender, Kate Foster felt the loss of her two brothers in the service of the Confederacy had been a worthless sacrifice. It was particularly difficult for her to accept their deaths as God's will. "It is not Christian to have such a heart and yet I cannot teach my rebellious heart to be still and know it is God.... When my disappointment at our ill success is less fresh I may learn to say I am content that it is so and know God would not do it except for our own good."[86]

The surrender led Elvira Seddon to question what seemed to her God's abandonment of their cause. The future looked ominous. But surely the South would rise again! "How we shall be taunted with our failure! Oh! My spirit rebels. It is too hard, too hard! I find myself questioning the position of God. Why has he turned His Face from us? Why does he suffer the wicked to prosper? Oh, that He would give me a spirit submissive to His Will! Feeling as I do now, life will be a sore burden. The only thing which at all reconciles me to it is the hope that at some future day we will again rise and again struggle with our hated foe. Resistance, even if it be unsuccessful, will be like balm to my wounded spirit."[87]

As did many nineteen-year-old Southern women, Elvira wished that she were a man enabled to carry on the fight. "Oh! That I were a man! I should take the Carthaginian's oath, and so help me God, I should be a very Hannibal in spirit. How can our men sit down quietly and take insult and degradation as their portion? Ambitions will have no aim. Why distinguish yourself when you have no country to honour? Youth, with all the buoyancy of hope, can catch no ray of comfort for the future. Old age, embittered by sad memories, will sink cheerless to the grave. Were ever a people so cursed? From 'Dan to Beersheba' there will be mourning. Only Negroes and deserters will find existance [sic] tolerable;—they long for—God will visit them with retribution." Elvira denounced the widespread desertion in the Confederate ranks. "How humiliating it is to think that this army was destroyed by desertions. That is the 'Most unkindest' cut of all."[88]

Although traumatized by the defeat, wiser, more mature Southerners were eager for an end to the fighting and a resumption of normal family life. Sarah Espy welcomed peace wholeheartedly even though "it is under subjugation."[89] As she surveyed returning soldiers footsore and disheartened by defeat, Minerva McClatchey wrote: "They seem glad to have the opportunity to do so, but say they were willing to continue the struggle, if there had been the least chance of success. Some of them seem very sad at the thought of abandoning the cause they loved so well and have suffered so much for." Sadly she added: "Some of them behave very badly, stealing horses etc.—one of them stole [her son] Penn's horse a day or two ago in open daylight. He was out near the house grazing and while we were eating dinner he was stolen. We can but illy spare him—good stock."[90]

Countless recalcitrant Southerners continued to hold out hopes for a resumption of the fighting with renewed vigor in the Trans-Mississippi; realists, however, recognized the futility of further warfare. Sara Handy reported overhearing one veteran voice the resolve of vast numbers of his comrades as they made their way home following the war: "'The Southern Confederacy has gone up the spout, and I'm goin' home to plant corn.'"[91]

With time some degree of reality sank in, and Southerners began to acknowledge their military inequalities in numbers and resources. In turn this belated realization gave rise to an ever increasing pride and recognition in the valor displayed and in the sacrifices so willingly made by their unsung heroes on behalf of their country. (This admiration and appreciation later gave impetus to the founding of the ubiquitous Memorial Societies and the Memorial Day observances.) For Elvira Seddon the superior strength and resources of the Federal forces was made manifest on April 13, 1865, as a detachment of Yankees encamped in the Seddons' yard in Goochland County, Virginia. At that moment Elvira Seddon was instantly consumed by an even more profound admiration for the Confederate troops as she observed "As I looked at their fine horses, excellent equipment, and splendid arms and contrasted them with the miserable steeds, and accouterments of our poor men, I wondered that we had been able to withstand the invader at all. Surely, they have had every advantage! A powerful Navy, men at command, and the whole world their arsenal. Contrast in condition and admire our perseverance under difficulties! Cut-off from the aide and sympathy of all nations, overwhelmed by superior numbers, our very resources turned against us! What fearful odds we had to encounter!"[92]

"So Many Bright Faces Were Missing": Homecomings

Whatever their reservations about the surrender, parents throughout the nation joyously welcomed home sons, wives their husbands, sisters their brothers, fiancées their lovers. "Their clothes are being gotten up afresh—their rooms ready—no need to warm up the hearts of those who love them—they are overflowing now," a Tennessee woman wrote.[93] And yet despite the elation, lurking in the dark of night there remained the haunting void of the empty chair, the dear sweet face visible now only in a faded photograph or in the mind's eye of memory. "There was a sadness mixed with pleasure. So many bright faces were missing," another Tennessee woman wrote.[94] "The gallant fellows who have gone down in the struggle—sealing our sacrifices with their blood! May they rest in peace," Virginia French prayed, "and God comfort anew those who mourn for them! Amen and amen!"[95]

For many Southerners there was precious little to celebrate at the war's end. In the South scarcely a family circle remained unbroken. More than 260,000 Confederates had died, a death rate that claimed one out of every four Southern males of eligible draft age (seventeen to forty-five) and a similar number had been wounded.[96] (James McPherson pointed out in his *Battle Cry of Freedom*: "The casualties at Antietam numbered four times the total suffered by American soldiers at the Normandy beaches on June 6, 1944.") Southerners were almost three times as likely to die as were Northern soldiers. By the end of the war "three-fourths of white Southern men of military age had served in the army and at least half of those soldiers had been wounded, captured, or killed, or had died of disease."[97] Some estimates indicate that in certain areas one third of the veterans had lost an arm or a leg.[98]

During the four year struggle one man had given five sons to the Confederacy who had either died on the battlefield or from disease. His two daughters had lost their husbands to the war and his wife had died of grief. And yet, this family simply mirrored the bereavements of thousands of other families throughout the South.[99]

Grief for lost loved ones and a lost cause reverberated throughout the Southland. "In these present days grief has lost all individuality, it is the common property of my people," Grace Elmore mourned. Her own sorrow she saw reflected in the eyes of everyone around her. "Where can one, turning from the darkness in their own life, find cheer in the brightness of another? One cannot escape from the presence of grief, it is the bond that unites us to our friends. I see it in their faces, I hear it in their voices, I know 'tis in their lives. I go from the ashes in my own breast to moan in the ashes of theirs. There is no way of getting away from myself, I see myself repeated in all that I meet. We all dwell in the dreary atmosphere of a sunless day, we all feel the ceaseless dripping of care upon our hearts, we all live in constant dread of the future, and we all look back with a longing, loving gaze upon our buried past."[100]

For Sarah Espy the view from her window provided a constant reminder of the horrors of war. There, close to the house, lay buried her dear son, the victim of diarrhea and pneumonia resulting from his service with the Confederate army.[101] In hearing of the death of a relative, Elvira Seddon commented "His blooming bride is soon transformed to mourning widow. Another sad instance of the ravages of war! She has one comfort. He does not survive to chafe under the weight of tyranny; more fortunate thus than many of his brave comrades."[102]

"Our cemetery filled up fast," one woman recalled. "It seemed like the telegrams of disaster came more frequently on Sundays. Driving up to church we would see groups crying. One day the telegram would be, Mr. Joe Coiner was killed. His wife, children and mother were mourning. Another day it would be, Mr. Hamilton; and his wife and son weeping. Then it would be sons and brothers. War took a heavy toll. We did not know what the day would bring forth."[103]

"Ned Has Come!"

Having lost one brother (Julian) on June 1, 1862, at the Battle of Seven Pines, Margaret Beckwith's prayers were answered with the safe return of a second soldier-brother following the war. "Ned has come!

God be thanked. Hardly recognizable, but what is left of him is here!" Secretly, Margaret registered her thankfulness that at least her brother Julian did not have to live to see the crushing defeat of their dreams.[104]

Ned, of course, was awarded a hero's welcome; the family's joy was unbounded. His return, however, must have opened the floodgates of memories of poor Julian. Tears of happiness surely mingled with tears of grief as the family remembered Julian's mad dash home just days before his death to bid his family good-bye, Julian himself nagged by his dreadful premonition that he would never see his family again. Knowing that Julian was involved in the fighting at Seven Pines, the Beckwiths agonized over terrifying reports from soldiers marching past their front gate declaring that "Julian Beckwith was mortally wounded." Comforting assurances that Julian was "alive and well," were reversed moments later with news that his wounds had been fatal, a report quickly overturned once again with word that he was safe. Finally came official word: "Shot in the forehead, instantly killed—buried on the battlefield." "The war went on," Margaret wept, "but we had been slain." A year later the death of Margaret's uncle had brought yet another blow to the Beckwith household.[105]

Virginia Norfleet's two older brothers had immediately volunteered for service following the declaration of war; however, a younger brother, although a year too young, insisted that he must join his brothers. Reluctantly, believing he should wait a year to enlist, the family gathered round as he proudly donned the handsome gray uniform they had so loving tailored for him. Tearfully and with great misgivings they waved him off to his appointment with destiny. Within weeks the family was devastated to learn that the enthusiastic young volunteer had died of exhaustion from long double-quick time marches and had been buried in an unmarked grave. "My father and mother never saw him again, but the image of that fine form in his new suit of gray with the bright buttons remained with them till the close of life."[106]

Although Virginia's two older brothers survived the four year blood bath, one brother had been taken prisoner and was not released until several months after the surrender. The latter brother's return was indelibly etched in memory. At first the poor, ragged, emaciated form wearily making his way up the road was unrecognizable, but suddenly as the dusty, bedraggled figure drew nearer "we saw that it was our own dear brother that we had not seen for four long years." "We all wept for joy," Virginia wrote, "but think of the sorrow and heartache of my father and mother for the other beautiful son who had gone out with this one, and they could never see him again in this life and never knew where the body rested in the mother earth."[107]

A few week's before Appomattox, Parthenia Hague's brother had succeeded in escaping his Yankee captors and had begun making his way back home afoot, traveling at night and subsisting for weeks on little more than roots, grasses and berries en route. At long last the family's dog, "Drive," announced his homecoming with a furious barking that alerted his parents to the miraculous return of the son "who had been mourned as dead was alive and home again." Sisters and parents devoured their long lost soldier with hugs and kisses, mingled with tears of gladness and shouts of joy. "My brother told me afterward," Parthenia confided, "that he could not move for some time, he was so tightly pinioned when finally taken to his mother's heart."[108] Another of Parthenia's brothers who had been paroled from his imprisonment at Point Lookout in Maryland "footed it" for most of the one hundred and eighty-eighty mile journey from Savannah to Columbus, Georgia. The wild excitement of the return on furlough of Cornelia Jones Pond's husband early in April of 1865 was blighted only by the nagging reminder of his imminent return to his comrades at the battlefront. Any hint of uneasiness over a renewed separation, however, quickly took flight with the news of Lee's surrender on April 9th.[109]

The tragic loss of a husband, a son, or a beloved brother left families and friends devastated by a grief never to be assuaged. When Rachel Craighead and her family paid a "welcome-home" visit to a friend recently returned from the army, Rachel told her diary: "My heart almost bursted to think that my dear noble soldier Brother had been dead 118 weeks, and would never come home. I am sorry but I felt a little rebellious—I can't see why he couldn't be spared but I know I ought not to talk so but try to say thy will oh Lord be done." A few days later she again expressed her resentment: "How envious I am of all whose loved ones are alive to come home." For over twelve years Rachel faithfully and often tearfully recorded a weekly jeremiad of anguish over her brother's death from wounds in the Battle of Perryville. On April 8, 1865, she wept: "It is 115 weeks since Bud gave his life as a sacrifice for his country—Oh! My God if this war had never commenced." As the year 1865 closed down Rachel mourned: "Our hearts are still longing for his return and to know he never will is agony."[110] The weeks passed with seemingly little diminution of her grief—380, 498, 551 weeks. One hundred and thirty-four weeks after his death Rachel was still wearing crepe collars and a veil.

Philip Palmer's return home at the war's ending was a scene of great rejoicing. His sister Harriet exclaimed in her diary, "So Monday exactly 10 weeks since we saw him at the depot, he got back home. It seems like 10 months! So much has happened in the ten weeks and so different from what we expected." Upon hearing that surrender was imminent Philip and members of his company had deserted and headed homeward "rather than be paroled not to take up arms against them." His sister applauded their decision: "And I must admit they were right," she added.[111] Philip's prediction that the Southern states would be returning to the Union, however, merely intensified Harriet's hopelessness and despair. "Never! Never! It can't be so. Why so much bloodshed? Why so many valuable lives lost? Oh, God, grant it may not be so!"[112] Of course, not all of their neighbors accorded deserters an enthusiastic welcome upon their return home, especially those with sons and brothers still risking life and limb on the battlefield. People expected, one North Carolinian confided, that a true Confederate would "go plum through to the surrender."[113]

Months and even years of uncertainty over the fate of a beloved son plagued a mother's hours by day and murdered her sleep at night. Long after the war, distracted parents, frantically worried (and rightfully so) that a missing son or sons might be lying in some unmarked grave near a battlefield, posted plaintive appeals in Southern newspapers pleading for information about their loved ones. The anguished entreaty of Mrs. Mary Arthur, of Canton, Mississippi, in the *New Orleans Daily Picayune* with its tearful description of the hair color, height, weight and physical build of her missing sons surely must have tugged at the heartstrings of even the most insensitive reader. Mrs. Arthur implored her readers for help promising that "any information respecting either of these young men will be joyfully received by a disconsolate mother."[114]

"Glad to Share with Our Soldiers"

At the cessation of hostilities even making it home was a problem. The lucky few who had horses slowly wound their way home on their decrepit, emaciated mounts, while most of the rest of the troops, the railroad tracks having been almost completely obliterated, struggled home afoot, some hobbling distances of hundreds of miles in weary, painful, footsore steps. Mary Whilden, for example, breathed a deep sigh of relief as she welcomed home her husband who had trudged thirty miles to reach her.[115] For some men the long walk home involved even greater privations than the war itself. One returning soldier remembered that for "three days and nights our total supply consisted of one ear of corn to the man, and we divided that with our horses."[116]

Having struggled for months with their own impoverished food supply, Southerners were hard pressed to feed the seemingly endless stream of veterans en route to their far-distant homes, who appeared at their doorsteps begging handouts for themselves or corn for their horses. In

April of 1865 as the procession of exhausted gray-clad men made their way through the Cumberland County area of Virginia, Sara Handy and her family quickly opted to divide their paltry store of provisions with the war-ravaged, ravenous throngs of soldiers. Although they had already complied with Lee's request to put themselves on half rations in an effort to help feed the troops at Petersburg, the Handys generously shared the remainder of their meager supplies "though we knew that we ourselves must go hungry in consequence."[117]

As the hordes of returning veterans poured through Washington, Georgia, Eliza Frances Andrews confessed that she had "never lived in such excitement and confusion in my life." Eliza's father opened their home to "everybody as long as there is a square foot of vacant space under his roof." However, the family was saddened to learn that some of their friends did not call fearing themselves "too ragged and dirty to show themselves. Poor fellows! If they only knew how honorable rags and dirt are now, in our eyes, when endured in the service of their country, they would not be ashamed of them. The son of the richest man in New Orleans trudged through the other day, with no coat to his back, no shoes on his feet." Eliza fervently wished they could do more for their fellow sufferers but confessed "we are all reduced to poverty, and the most we can do is for those of us who have homes to open our doors to the rest."[118]

Returning soldiers, Grace Elmore recalled, "parties of them, mostly strangers would stop for the night." Considerate, knowing the deprivation suffered by most Southerners, many of the soldiers were hesitant to take bread for themselves or corn for their horses. Only when Grace's mother insisted that they partake of the family's breakfast would they consent to enter the house. Knapsacks were replenished and the larder bared "for we were too glad to share with our soldiers."[119] Securing food was difficult enough; however, arriving home in presentable clothing presented an equally onerous problem. Devoid of pants, more than one soldier improvised "blanket pants" made by poking holes through a blanket with a sharp stick and tying them up with ravelings.[120]

Rachel Craighead's diary testified to the unending stream of somber, weary soldiers struggling home afoot after the war, grateful for a crust of bread, a bed of hay, a warm smile. In May of 1865 Rachel recounted in her diary, "There were 20 rebel soldiers stayed with us last night—gave them supper and breakfast—the porch is filled with them now." Five days later she wrote, "We had a sick soldier—besides 15 or so others." Nightly, Rachel's family cared for from ten to twenty exhausted, hungry soldiers. What a rewarding experience, Rachel sensed, to send them on their way rested, their hunger at least temporarily appeased! Unfortunately, tragedy marred the family's pleasure in sharing, when now and then illness and the debilitated condition of one of their transient guests suddenly took their toll in death. Rachel reported sadly: "There was a poor soldier died at Mrs. Yeatman's yesterday."[121]

Not all Southern women responded with the magnanimity of Sara, Grace and Rachel. Women with absent husbands needed to think twice about taking in strangers. During the ebb and flow of soldiers milling through the area during the last months of the war Emily Liles Harris allowed one cavalry soldier to spend the night with her family. "I allowed him to stay but shall do so no more." Rumors about her lodger and the advice of family and friends who thought she "done very wrong to let him stay" caused her to turn down all future appeals. Her decision was not an easy one, however, as she thought about similar rejections that her own soldier husband might encounter.[122]

Kate Stone and her family were relieved and delighted upon the return of her brother Jimmy, although he was "no longer a soldier but a poor discouraged boy." Kate despaired: "We are so glad to have Jimmy safe at home, but oh, what a different homecoming from what we anticipated when he enlisted. No feasting. No rejoicing. Only sadness and tears." Two weeks later brother Johnny returned to the family fold. Johnny's refusal to take the oath of allegiance delayed his return home. Promised free transportation home if he would take the oath, brother Johnny refused the offer and only by selling his horses was he able to scrape together the wherewithal to return to Vicksburg. On a happier note, Kate reported, the boys, not so surprisingly, were wild to meet girls and kept her frantically busy "making bouquets for them to present to anybody, just so it was a girl." Mothers and sisters voiced a special concern that the seasoned returnees might possibly have become inured to the rowdy, rough life at the battlefront and need a refresher course in manners. However, at least one woman observed: "Four years have given these bronzed soldiers many hardships to endure and doubtless many of them will need a course of training to revive their knowledge of the polite arts, though they seem to enter ladies society with a zest, which can only be accounted for by their long abstinence from it."[123]

Here and there as a bedraggled, mud-spattered figure straggled up the lane, a momentarily confused canine sniffed and barked at his returning master, until suddenly recognition set in and the leaping and circling that ensued all but toppled the long absent friend. It was a painful homecoming for one stalwart veteran as he sat down and wept upon returning to his home in Greenville, Mississippi, where he found the town in ruins and his beloved wife, worn and emaciated from the war, chopping weeds in a nearby field.[124]

At least one Southerner found he was unable to enter his own home after the war without first obtaining a permit from the Union officials. His home had been taken over as Federal officers' headquarters and his wife was relegated to a single room. This, however, did not automatically admit her husband without a permit.[125]

The return of Sara Handy's brother-in-law occasioned not only great elation for the family, but also brought forth a most welcome treasure-trove of mules, provisions, and silver which Sherman had allowed Johnston to share with his men following the armistice. The bounty, Sarah exclaimed, "meant salvation, if not from starvation from pinching want."[126]

Memories of the return of a war-weary boatload of exchanged prisoners of war were sure to remain with hundreds of Richmond residents as long as life itself. Early on the day of their arrival word had spread throughout the city of the return of the long-suffering, battle-scarred survivors. As Emily Mason, a devoted southern hospital matron, wound her way through the streets of Richmond in her makeshift "ambulance" on her way to gather up the soldiers and transport them to the hospital, door after door opened with women bringing out their own family dinners to be delivered to the returning soldiers, the ladies softly murmuring, "We can eat dry bread to-day."

At the riverside, there was hushed anticipation as the steamer hove in sight and cautiously edged in toward the dock. The suspense was relieved with a deafening cheer from the crowd and music from the band rent the air. It was an enthusiastic although feeble response as the "load of dirty, ragged men, half dead with illness and starvation" returned the cheers of the excited families and well-wishers gathered on the dock. The band struck up "Dixie" and slowly and painfully the heroes began tottering down the gangplank to be ravenously devoured by the kisses and embraces of their loved ones. Soiled bandages swathed aching heads, empty sleeves dangled from gray-clad shoulders—here and there a crutch, a cane, a trouser leg folded back. Emotions ran high.

Suddenly, out of the crowd a child's voice rang out. "Oh, look mama, look, there's papa!"

Eyes brimmed over. "There was not a dry eye of those which had been dry before—& there were few of those."[127]

℘

Certainly not all of the returning remnants of the Confederate army were orderly and well mannered. Soldiers frustrated by the surrender and annoyed with the hoarders and the stay-at-homes sometimes took out their resentment in crime and violence. Savage bands of guerrillas looking for easy access to food and treasure or simply bent on high adventure roamed the countryside. Riots ensued as disgruntled soldiers stormed Confederate warehouses and commissary depositories. In May a Georgia woman told of a Texas regiment, among the over fifteen thousand soldiers who passed through Washington, Georgia, en route home after the surrender, that grew dissatisfied with their rations and created a riot by breaking into the commissary department, assaulting the quartermaster's stores, and appropriating whatever mules and horses they wanted. Disorderly civilians, servants, and children joined in the pillaging and "paper, pens, buttons, tape, cloth—everything in the building was seized and thrown on the ground." Unwilling to fire on their own men, the provost-guard did little to stop the looting; however, "nobody seemed to care much," one woman admitted, "as we all know the Yankees will get it in the end, any way, if our men don't."[128]

Reporting from their refugee home in Tyler, Texas, on May 27, 1865, Kate Stone wrote: "Anarchy and confusion reign over all. Jayhawking is the order of the day. The soldiers are disbanding throughout the Department and seizing Government property wherever they can find it. The Government offices here have been sacked."[129] Despite the turmoil and general appropriation of supplies, Kate was pleased that the pillaging by Confederate soldiers would prevent the goods from falling into the hands of the Yankees. Actually the Stones were beneficiaries of the distribution of stores from the ordnance department. Friends secured ammunition and writing paper for the Stones, the later being a particularly welcomed acquisition.

"They were in bad spirits, poor fellows!" Elvira Seddon observed as a contingent of Confederate soldiers rode up to their home apparently on their way home from Appomattox. "And well they might be! After a hard struggle of four years, what was their reward? A formal surrender of arms, of rights, of all that man hold dearest!"[130]

"Women Can Bear It"

Very possibly women found buoying up the spirits of the returnees one of their most difficult tasks. Calling on eloquence and climaxing with a caustic touch in her final words, Cornelia Spencer described the heartfelt welcome accorded the weary heroes. "So we endeavored to play out the play with dignity and self-possession, watching the long train of foragers coming in every day by every high-road and byway leading from the country, laden with the substance of our friends and neighbors for many miles ... wondering where it would all end, and that we should have lived to see such a day; reviewing the height from which we had fallen, and struggling, I say, to wear a look of proud composure, when all our assumed stoicism and resignation was put to flight by the appearance, on a certain day, of a squad of unarmed men in gray, dusty and haggard, walking slowly along the road. A moment's look, a hasty inquiry, and 'Lee's men!' burst from our lips, and tears from our eyes. There they were, the heroes of the army of Virginia, walking home, each with *his pass* in his pocket, and nothing else. To run after them, to call them in, to feel honored at shaking those rough hands, to spread the table for them, to cry over them, and say again and again, 'God bless you all; we are just as proud of you and thank you just as much as if it had turned out differently'; this was a work which stirred our inmost souls, and has left a tender memory which will outlast life. Day after day we saw them, sometimes in twos and threes, sometimes in little companies making the best of their way toward their distant homes, penniless and dependent on wayside charity for their food, plodding along, while the blue jackets pranced gayly past on the best blood of Southern stables."[131]

Parthenia Hague echoed Mrs. Spencer's sentiments, insisting that the ragged gray returnees "were just as dear to the hearts of their kindred at their ruined homes, as if they had come marching in triumph, with olive-wreaths encircling their brows."[132]

Upon his release from being imprisoned at Fort Delaware, a dispirited Matthew Jack Davis set out for the fifteen hundred mile trek home without a cent in his pockets. En route home his welcome at his various stopovers astonished him, yet at the same time served to document the response of millions of grateful, caring Southern women. Following supper at New Castle, Delaware, a gathering of women enveloped Jack's little party. "Instead of stiff formal bows as I had expected, each rushed around us to shake hands with us, each striving to reach us first. Old ladies cried, young ladies, beautiful young ladies wept over us."[133]

Eliza Walker told of her husband's approaching a covered bridge at Eufaula, Alabama, on his long walk home and of being ordered to halt by a surly Federal guard. "Who are you?" the guard demanded in a gruff voice. With fire in his eyes the soldier spat out, "I am a paroled soldier from General Lee's Army!" For the briefest second there was a pause and then in apparent admiration for a soldier having waged a courageous fight, the guard responded solemnly: "You're a gintleman, sir. Pass on."[134]

In utter desperation Grace Elmore reflected on the country's enormous losses, expressing her own hopelessness and the concern women everywhere felt for their dispirited husbands and brothers. "Oh, sometimes I wish for death, 'tis living death to live so. We women, suffer not for ourselves alone, but for our men, so weary and worn. For the casting down of their high hopes and noble ambitions. Women can bear it, 'tis their province to endure, and they at least are spared the feeling of personal humiliation, which every man must experience; but the chief bitterness to them is to witness the chafing of those high strung men, most dear to them, under the conqueror's rule."[135]

"Could you have seen some of our soldiers as I saw them after the surrender," Hannah Rawlings wrote her sister, "it would have wrung your very soul. They seemed almost heartbroken. Those who had marched without faltering up to the cannon's mouth and faced death in its most horrid forms, were now completely unmanned. Tears flowed from 'eyes all unused to weep,' and strong men were so overcome by emotion that their trembling lips could scarcely utter a word."[136]

Among the careworn veterans, of course, were tens of thousands of soldiers who returned home so gravely ill and emaciated as to be barely recognizable from the hardships of their ordeal. When Marion Briscoe's father neared home from his service with the Confederacy, Yankee stragglers accosted him and ordered him to dismount. They then took off, Marion wrote, with "his beautiful horse, the only thing he had left, and he came slowly up to the back of the house. My mother seeing him mistook him for a tramp."[137] Elizabeth Allston registered astonishment at the "pitiful sight" of her brother upon his return home—"so ill and changed, we were not surprised that he had had typhoid fever."[138]

Unfortunately, thousands of those who were somehow lucky enough to return home had only days or months to languish in the bosom of their families before the ravages of war took their toll and beckoned them to join their fallen comrades. (An estimated 140,000 Confederates returned home with wounds, many of which would require nursing care and hospitalization for a lifetime; other returnees came home with conditions that rapidly proved terminal.) Women's courageous work in the field of nursing during the war continued on a more personal level in their own homes after the war. Husbands, fathers, and sons who returned from the war physically and mentally scarred for life necessitated infinite care from loving family members who devoted much of their lives to changing bandages, cooling fevered brows, or reassuring and reorienting the victims of traumatic nightmares and terror-stricken flashbacks. Soon thousands of these same women were forced to assume an additional role as the family's breadwinner.

A South Carolina woman rejoiced over the safe return of her brother Alick. As the family smothered the gaunt, young soldier with embraces they were shocked to discover the "strong, robust man" they had sent off to the war had returned "wrecked in health and spirits. Four years of camp life had been too great a trial for his constitution, and he returned to us, barely twenty-one years of age, with scarcely strength to walk." Two months later in May a second brother returned home from the battlefields in the same emaciated, debilitated condition. The family's lack of nourishing food sent the family begging for help from more well-stocked neighbors and friends, who generously contributed food from their own tables to help nurse the brothers back to at least a semi-healthy condition. For a brief time the family delighted in once again being a united family; however, "before a year had passed they were both laid to rest under the church-yard sod."[139]

The scourge of disease and fevers that swept the South following the war exacerbated the ex-Confederates' woes. Prime victims were returning veterans despondent and enervated from their battlefront experiences. Mrs. Gordon Rice recalled the sudden death of her uncle and young cousin. The losses left an older cousin ("scarcely more than a lad" and already greatly enfeebled from service with the Confederate troops) with the responsibility for the welfare of his mother and the need to put several plantations which were in various stages of decay back in working order.[140]

Elizabeth "Betty" Meriwether had good reason to be apprehensive about her Memphis home. General Sherman in a fit of pique in 1862 during the Federal occupation of Memphis had confiscated Betty's personal property and banished her from the city in retaliation for her partisan Confederate loyalties. After the war as Betty and her children returned from their two year exile, Betty found her home occupied, but in fair condition compared to the ravaged condition of most of the homes around her. It was a pleasant surprise for her to find that the family occupying her home were kindly disposed and well aware that the true owner eventually would be returning and claiming ownership.

In the yard out front, however, it was a different story. There a contingent of newly freed men, armed with saws and lumber, were embarked on plans to cut down the trees and erect a house on the front lawn. It was "abandoned land," they claimed, and free for settlement. Although her sympathies lay with the freedmen (she and her husband, believing slavery wrong, had long since freed their slaves and sent them to Africa) Betty was indignant over their appropriating private property for their own uses. After repeated confrontations and a session with a lawyer, the men packed up their lumber and gleefully rode off, smugly informing Betty that they had found better "abandoned land" closer to town.

Rumors were grim about the fate that awaited the defeated South. As the would-be "squatters" moved on, Betty's fears were somewhat assuaged. Betty's husband had not yet returned from the war, however, and it was with considerable uneasiness that she looked toward the river where at Fort Pickering "were encamped more than two thousand Negro soldiers and three thousand white Yankee soldiers. All these, I knew, hated me and mine; I was alone with three little children; my husband was I knew not where—perhaps a captive on his way to some Northern dungeon."[141]

Women, as well, had suffered pain and deprivation during the war, some even having sacrificed their looks and their health to the "Cause." The war had prematurely aged many a woman. Anne Thom admitted that her husband thought she looked "*very old.*" And well she might! "He little knows the load of care which has rested upon me for the last four years, & which, God knows, I have tried to bear bravely and cheerfully, but which I fear has left an impress on my heart and face which can never be effaced."[142]

As with all wars one wonders: "Were the war's greatest sufferers those on the battlefield or the women left on the homefront?" Picturing a grief-stricken woman (and there were thousands) benumbed by a telegraph wire which read "Shot through the heart—buried where he fell," one compassionate soul inquired: "She stands here in the sunlight; he lies asleep by the Potomac. It is well with one of them, but which one? Alas! The pity of it. I often wonder which suffered the most—the boys at the front or the women who remained at home. The boys who went into battle ... I wonder if these men suffered more than the women who remained at home and fought life's battle silently."[143]

Gloomy Prospects Ahead

℠ Joyous as their homecoming had been, the outlook for the future was anything but promising for millions of returning veterans and their families. The courage and enthusiasm that spirited the fighting men and refugees throughout the war melted as they surveyed the chaos and devastation that greeted them.

Emily Liles Harris was jubilant over her husband's safe return from the war. The responsibilities of managing their farm near Spartanburg, South Carolina, their ten slaves and their seven children had weighed heavily with her during his absence. Faithfully Emily had kept a journal for David while he was away. Now as David surveyed the destruction following an early hailstorm in May 1865 he summarized in his diary (*Piedmont Farmer*) the situation confronting thousands of returning veterans and their families. "I think that this is the time that tries mens souls, pockets and his bowels at the same time. The Lord only knows what is to be the fate of our unlucky country. I much fear that the worst is yet to come. Raids, mobs, & thefts is the order of the day. It seems that our unfortunate country is drifting to ruin as fast as the Tide of Destruction can carry it. Our currency has entirely failed. No one will take a 'Confederate dollar' for anything. (An hundred dollars would not buy a good drink.) We have no other money, consequently the prices have suddenly fallen flat. All trading is done by bartering. For everything that is sold, provision is demanded, & no one have provision to give. All is at a standstill & wondering what will be done next. All anxious to see, yet all fearing to know."

"The Original Memorial Day." Drawing by Frank Spangler, probably created for the *Montgomery Advertiser*, April 27, 1934. (Alabama Department of Archives and History.)

Jennie Stephenson painted a melancholy picture of the times. "Staggering under a weight of disappointment, the weary, heartsick men and women, yes, and children too, drew their breath for the long silent agony of readjusting themselves to the new state of being. Poverty was on every hand. All was new about them, and yet the same old land marks stood to remind them of the irrevocable past, and to keep alive the old habit of thinking and doing. But there was always the negro under our feet, but not to obey us, and we knowing nothing but to direct him."

As she watched her father, her unsung hero, in his declining years, Jennie Stephenson's heart ached. The war and reconstruction had rendered him a mere shadow, both financially and emotionally, of his former self. As you "see him now going steadily to work, with the heavy care of a large, dependent family, with expensive tastes and ideas of life, as a matter of course, drop for him a tear of sympathy, as he took up the new life in the old groove. Would that my pen could do him justice, words fail me but … he is my hero and my heart's adoration is the best tribute I can bring."

As time passed Jennie grew further distressed over the lack of wherewithal that prevented her brothers from going to college. Her older brother turned to farm work, her younger brother found work as a clerk in a drug store. "Life for them was to be a hand to hand fight, with no help from a full coffer or mental training of a college course."[1]

"We all feel that we are in a great prison," a Richmond woman wrote, "and live from day to day & from hour to hour in constant dread & expectation of, we hardly know what."

Another desperate woman registered her frustration regarding labor, violence, and the future in an 1866 letter to a friend. "I am so sorry to hear of your failure this year in planting…. Nothing has been made here; the seasons and the interventions [?] of both Black and White Yankees with our Negroes have caused an entire failure. God only knows how our people will be fed. Robbery and the incendiary torch are my nightly anticipations. My land is lying idle. All that I have left is the house we live in down [?] Church St., and a small house in the upper part of the city. We have to hire out a portion of our house to help us to live. I lost twenty thousand dollars, and twenty odd Negroes. All of my sister's property was in Confederate bonds and Negroes, and all of Mother's too, except one piece of city property and five thousand dollars. So you see we cannot help the others. All could be endured if I could but have the hope our country will be free, and my children get an education. God has dealt mercifully with us, and I try to submit to His will."[2]

Although the tangible losses at the time were horrendous, Grace Elmore mourned the sacrifice of many of the South's most brilliant, most promising leaders on the battlefield and the ensuing diminution of vitality and potential of the enfeebled returnees. Subjugated and humiliated in defeat, they were now simply devoting their abilities and talents to eking out a living—a situation that boded ill for the South. "To see these noble hearts," she continued, "being drained of the milk of human kindness, to know that both mind and heart are being cramped by the hand of the oppressor. I grieve for all, but especially for those whose minds and inclination fitted them for public life. Who would have found happiness to themselves and profit to their country, in the exercise of their talents and energies, for the public good. I grieve to think of the effect this blight will have on many…. How many a high strung spirit will be broken, how many men, who would have been a glory to their Country, in the councils of our South, [now] are doomed to waste in idleness their highest powers, and expend all their strength in gaining bread."[3]

"Their Owners Are Ruined": *Financial Losses*

Returning veterans were greeted with banks that had failed or closed; bridges, factories, public buildings burned or in ruins; railroads and the postal system almost nil; newspapers a scarce commodity; back taxes that foretold bankruptcy; estate litigation that could last thirty years and still leave families insolvent. Patriotic Southerners had poured all the money they could scrape together into the Confederacy and by the war's end they were penniless.

Before the war, for example, Nannie Scott's father had owned seven plantations, but by the end of the war every acre he had owned was lost to his creditors. Members of the Ball family, who had owned more than a dozen homes in Charleston in addition to some twenty plantations on the Cooper River outside the city, experienced disastrous financial decline following the war. Several lost control of their lives and turned to alcoholism. When only 29 workers (before the war he had managed 620) signed his first labor contract, William Ball faced hard times as he attempted to make a living as a sharecrop landlord. Soon he found it necessary to move out of his Charleston mansion and rent it in order to pay for the taxes and insurance. Little by little pieces of the Ball properties were sold to "stay afloat." A descendant later pointed out "There was no land, no inheritance, no slave money."[4]

Elizabeth Allston Pringle told of the loss of her father's seven plantations, two farms in Anson County, North Carolina, a house in Charleston, eleven thousand acres of timber, plus other holdings as a result of the war. With the exception of one plantation awarded to her mother by right of dower, Elizabeth lamented: "Of all this principality not one of the heirs got anything!"[5] An owner of six plantations in the

Sea Islands fled when Port Royal was overtaken. In short order her house was torched, her estate confiscated and sold for back taxes, and she was left impoverished, the object of charity. Poverty, however, was the least of her tragedies. Her two sons had died serving with the Confederate troops, a daughter earned eight dollars a month doing menial work, and her granddaughter had to be given up for adoption.[6]

In 1866 Alabama's Governor Patton cited $500 million in property losses in that state and some twenty thousand widows and sixty thousand orphans resulting from the war.[7] The freeing of 300,000 slaves amounted to one-fifth of the state's population.[8] Alabama claimed destruction of some $300 million; Louisiana cane planters lost $100 million.[9]

At the close of the war Louisiana was plagued with the South's ubiquitous problems of lack of capital, lack of laborers, lack of credit, heavy prewar mortgages, theft and vandalism, and worn out equipment. The aforementioned troubles coupled with the deterioration of the levees, the breakdown of the drainage systems, the regulations of the Freedmen's Bureau, and a Federal excise tax of three cents per pound on sugar led to the almost complete annihilation of the sugar industry in Louisiana. Credit, of course, could be had at interest rates of 10–15 percent; however, depreciated land values made it that much more difficult to come up with adequate security for a loan and a good many formerly affluent sugar planters were soon financially ruined. As a result of the war, losses to the sugar interests including land and slaves were estimated to be as much as $193 million.[10] The 1865 Louisiana sugar crop was reduced to one tenth of the 1861 production.[11]

Hundreds of planters attempting to raise sugar cane in Louisiana after the war found it exceedingly rough going. In December of 1872 one woman wrote: "We have failed to make expenses on this place.... I tell you it is disheartening work to see around me daily the absolute signs of decay which the planting interests exhibit—Everyone is terribly blue. The condition of affairs in Louisiana is positively terrible." Three months later she worried: "If we fail to make a good crop this year we are lost."[12]

Not only did sugar planters suffer, a report from East Louisiana in December of 1865 indicated that about 2,500 bales of cotton, 800 hogsheads of sugar, 3,000 barrels of molasses were produced in contrast to the 40,000 bales of cotton, 30,000 hogsheads of sugar and 90,000 barrels of molasses produced in the area in former years. Newspaper articles cautioned that "no one need enter the planting lists with any hope of making a fortune." Furthermore at least one writer predicted only half of "last year's planters will re-embark in the business, and the remainder go in because it is keep in or starve."[13]

Frances Butler (Leigh) was shocked over conditions in the Sea Islands: "This part of the country has suffered more heavily than any other from the war. Hundreds of acres of rice land, which yielded millions before the war, are fast returning to the original swamp from which they were reclaimed with infinite pains and expense, simply because their owners are ruined, their houses burnt to the ground, and their Negroes made worthless as labourers. It is very sad to see such wide-spread ruin, and to hear of girls well-educated, and brought up with every luxury, turned adrift as dressmakers, school-teachers, and even shop girls in order to keep themselves and their families from starvation." In describing the plight of one young lady who was engaged in making underclothes to sell as a means of support for her family, Frances wrote admiringly "It is wonderful to me to see how bravely and cheerfully they do work, knowing as I do how they lived before the war."[14]

From Mississippi grim statistics revealed that although Mississippi entered the war as the fifth wealthiest state in the country (thanks in part to its enormous cotton production), the state as a result of the ravages of war emerged four years later at the bottom of the list. As noted out of the South's white population of five million some 250,000 did not return after the war.[15]

"Some with Empty Sleeves":
Physical Losses

Compounding the financial losses, and far more devastating, of course, were the thousands of veterans who arrived home minus a hand, a foot, a leg or an arm. In the first year after the war Mississippi appropriated one-fifth of its revenue to provide artificial limbs for needy veterans. Other states made similar provisions, many continuing their allotments for ten and fifteen years after the war.[16] In many cases the wounded veteran who was physically or mentally incapacitated was often more of an economic hardship to his family than those who had been killed in action.

On the streets, in the churches, at public gatherings ubiquitous scenes of mangled bodies, disfigured faces, canes, crutches, dangling shirtsleeves and empty trouser legs folded back tore at the hearts of friends and bystanders. The heartrending congregation at an Episcopalian schoolhouse church in Cuthbert, Georgia, where many of the attendees were patients from nearby hospitals, brought Eliza Frances Andrews to tears. "They came, some limping on crutches, some with scarred and mangled faces, some with empty sleeves, nearly all with poor, emaciated bodies, telling their mute tale of sickness and suffering, weariness and heartache. I saw one poor lame fellow leading a blind one, who held on to his crutch. Another had a blind comrade hanging upon one arm while an empty sleeve dangled where the other ought to be. I have seen men since I came here with both eyes shot out, men with both arms off, and one poor fellow with both arms and a leg gone. What can our country ever do to repay such sacrifice?" she asked.[17]

"Most Thoroughly Plundered": Loss of Property

Those fortunate enough to return home intact in body and mind were indeed lucky if they found their homes spared the torch, their fields uninjured by battles or marching soldiers, and possibly a scanty supply of food to tide them over until a new crop could be planted and harvested. The predominately agrarian South suffered incalculable losses. Sheman's march to the sea, for example, had involved damages of $100 million; the destruction of over 200 miles of railroad; the theft of 1,500 good mules; the confiscation of up to 60,000 horses and untold numbers of cattle, poultry, hogs, sheep; the demolition of an infinite number of field crops, farm buildings and implements, houses, factories, mills and warehouses.[18]

Philip Sheridan had kept his promise to General Grant that following his march through the Shenandoah that "The Valley, from Winchester up to Staunton, ninety-two miles, will have little in it for man or

"Ruins on Main Street, Richmond." (*Harper's Weekly*, April 22, 1865.)

beast." In addition to the destruction of 1,200 barns and 71 flour mills, Sheridan's army in the three month period from August 10 to November 16, 1864, had seized or destroyed "435,802 bushels of wheat, 3,772 horses, 10,918 cattle, 12,000 sheep, 15,000 hogs, 77,176 bushels of corn, 12,000 pounds of bacon, 20,397 tons of hay...."[19] Sheridan explained in his memoirs, "Death is popularly considered the maximum of punishment in war, but it is not; reduction to poverty brings prayers for peace more surely and more quickly than does the destruction of human life...."[20] By scourging the countryside Sheridan vowed he would make the people "sick of the war."[21]

Ann Jones personalized the Shenandoah Valley statistics by describing the devastation of their home and farmland. "They shot the fowls, shot the Pigs, & carried them away in Bags, killed altogether *every hog* Strother had for his next year's support & and many shoats, nine or ten Shoats which we succeeded in putting out of the way were all that was left. They found out where the corn had been secreted took almost *every bit*, carried off green corn, took quantities of Hay...." Inside the house chaos prevailed as jewelry, pistols were taken, boxes of glass, china and books were broken open, and every knife for the table was stolen. Even so, Ann was grateful that the pillaging had not been worse for "Many persons have suffered more than we have, poor things!!"[22]

Cornelia Spencer was horrified over the devastation of Sherman's army in the vicinity of and for twenty miles around Goldsboro, North Carolina: "the country was most thoroughly plundered and stripped of food, forage, and private property of every description.... Not a farmhouse in the country but was visited and wantonly robbed. Many were burned, and very many, together with out-houses, were pulled down and hauled into camp for use. Generally not a live animal, not a morsel of food of any description was left, and in many instances not a bed or sheet or change of clothing for man, woman, or child...."[23]

On one plantation outside of Raleigh, North Carolina, Sherman's troops divested the Negroes of most of their clothing and food and broke open the house where "weather-boarding, flooring, and ceiling [were] carried off, every window-sash and glass broken out, and every article of furniture for house or kitchen either carried off or wantonly destroyed. Barns, cotton-house, and sheds were all torn down; blacksmith's carpenter's and farming implements carried off or broken up; three carts and two large wagons, with their gear, destroyed; the fences burned; and a large number of mules and horses pastured on the wheat-fields; all of my mules and horses there (seventeen in number) carried off; fifty head of cattle, forty sheep, fifty hogs, and a large flock of geese and poultry either taken off or wantonly shot down; a quantity of medicine, some excellent wines, brandy, whisky, and two hundred gallons of vinegar were taken. Wagon trains went down day after day, till 150 barrels of corn, 15,000 pounds of fodder, 12,000 pounds of hay, and all my wheat, peas, cotton, etc. were carried off, leaving the whole place entirely bare...."[24]

From June 1864 through to the end of the war Minerva McClatchey had watched helplessly as successive waves of Union troops ravaged the family plantation near Marietta, Georgia. Much of the town of Marietta had gone up in flames as Union troops marched through in November of 1864. Shortly thereafter, however, there was a jubilant reunion with her husband upon his return from middle Georgia where he had sequestered his slaves in the hopes of escaping Sherman's army. Rebuilding, Minerva discovered, was akin to starting over. Everywhere fences were down; farmland was "ploughed up" from breastworks, and forts, and encampments; farm animals, horses, cows, chickens, sheep had been stolen or perversely destroyed. Minerva despaired: "Where a subsistence for man and beast is to come from until we can make a crop, is the question. Rails are to be made to enclose every inch of ground to be cultivated (except some few scattered ones). The mule is not doing much good. Provisions of all kinds are very scarce."[25]

One woman told of the devastation wrought upon her refugee quarters in Barnwell, South Carolina. Although the house was not burned she reported there was "corn in heaps upon the floor where it lay mingled with the contents of the trunks and drawers in the wildest confusion. Every blanket, quilt and sheet had been stripped from the beds and carried off, ornaments of various kinds had either disappeared or been broken, and from a handsome India shawl several strips had been cut for scarfs. In the parlor the top had been thrown from the piano, some keys broken and wires cut, the music and books lay strewn about the room and yard, and a valuable violin of Mr. Taylor's had been taken, while most of the pictures had sabre thrusts here and there in the canvas; perhaps a feeling of superstition alone had saved the mirrors from destruction, for they were almost the only unbroken articles in the room."[26]

When Margaret Ward returned from her refugee life in Atlanta and Augusta to her Rome, Georgia, home just two weeks before the surrender, she found the house standing but the fences down, much of the furniture gone, and everything in a state of confusion. Guerrilla bands, composed of deserters from both armies, had savagely pillaged homes and fields in their wild search for food and loot. "They would rush into a town, dressed in blue clothes, and rob somebody, on the ground that he had been unnecessarily loyal to the Confederacy, and the next day they would come dressed in gray clothes and would rob or murder some other people because they had affiliated with the North."[27]

In the absence of the owners, many of the homes had been appropriated by what Mrs. Ward called "white trash." Mrs. Ward discovered valuable items from her home and those of her friends next door in the possession of a Mrs. Hawkins whom Mrs. Ward termed "as common as could be." Mrs. Hawkins was convinced that Rome residents who had abandoned their homes fearing an enemy takeover of the town had forfeited all their property and "that she and others like her had a right to it all."[28]

Nettie Henry and her family suffered right along with their white owners as Sherman's men devoured Meridian, Mississippi. Nettie's recollection of the demolition in her own words was recorded years later by interviewers with the WPA Federal Writers' Project. "When word come dat dey was coming, hit sound like a moanin' wind in deh quarter: ever'body was sayin', 'Deh Yankees are comin! De Yankees are comin!' Us chullum was scared but hit was like Sunday, too—nobody doin' nothin—and we march around deh room—dey wouldn' let us out on deh road—an sorter sing-like 'Deh Yankees are comin!' Well, deh come. An deh burn up seventy houses an all deh sto's an tear up deh railroad tracks and tote off every'thing deh coundn' eat. I don't understand nothin' bout how come dey act like dat. We ain't done nothin' to 'em." As in other areas some houses were saved by their owners providing accommodations for several of the officers. "Deh left deh house and didn't bother deh fam'ly cause dey called dey-sefs company, but deh good lord know Mr. Greer didn invite 'em. But deh Cap'ns bein' there kep riff-raff so-jers frum tearing up ever'thing."[29]

Actually whole towns and villages had been erased by battles and burnings. Kate Sperry told of an area near Memphis that had been so devastated by the war that one "would not have known there ever had been a town there…." From Bluffton, South Carolina, Louisa Seabrooke reported that in her area "out of eighty comfortable dwellings, only twelve shattered houses remain."[30]

Upon his return home one Southerner found "…not a stick, board of fence is left, even our well is filled up, and the nails culled from the ashes. Nothing but chimneys remain."[31] Franklin, Virginia, according to Virginia Norfleet, had been a growing town in antebellum years but had been reduced to sixteen people by 1865.[32]

"Times Is Hard and Worse a Coming"

The prospects facing the tired, dispirited soldiers who drifted in on the way to their homes were indeed gloomy. Throughout the Southland women saw the same scene reenacted as that pictured by Harriet Lang:

"A ragged, weary body of men, returning after years of hard fighting and privations of every kind, to their ruined homes and farms, to begin anew the struggle for a living. Nothing to look forward to, no stock, no money! Labor at a premium, the slaves feeling their freedom so that they refused to work! The entire south in utter poverty."

One Southern soldier, a former major general in the Confederate army, returned home at twenty-nine years of age, one leg gone and with "a wife and three children to support, seventy emancipated slaves, a debt of $15,000, and in his pocket $1.75"[33] (It was indeed fortunate that young veteran at least had a *home* to return to.) Another Southern patriot arrived home only to find his $50,000 in Confederate currency worthless, his fifteen or twenty slaves freed, and his 700 acres of land "of so little value that he could not mortgage it for enough money to purchase a box of tobacco."[34] Harry Hammond, who in antebellum years had been accustomed to a life of ease and luxury, returned home after the war owning "a pipe. Some tobacco, and literally nothing else." Even merchants who had been longtime associates denied him credit.[35]

Even professional people knew not where to turn. Generals and privates alike were hard put to know where to look for remunerative work. Mary Custis Lee in a letter to Emily Mason in September of 1865 wrote that "General Lee has decided to accept the position offered him at Lexington. I do not think he is very fond of teaching but is willing to do anything that will give him an honorable support."[36]

Mrs. Roger Pryor shared her husband's frustration at the conclusion of the war. "There was no hope there [Richmond] for lucrative occupation. He had no profession. He had forgotten all the little law he had learned at the university. He had been an editor, diplomat, politician [Congressman] and soldier [General], and distinguished himself in all four. These were now closed to him forever! There seemed to be no room for a rebel in all the world."[37]

For most Southerners the future looked dismal indeed. An Alabama couple were both to the point and realistic when they wrote from their home in Rogersville in February of 1869: "Times is hard and worse a coming. We have about half anough to eat and about twice as many chills as we want."[38]

Upon occasion a bright light appeared on the horizon when a sudden windfall almost overnight miraculously turned poverty into sufficiency. Upon his return from the war Hilary Herbert, of Greenville, Alabama, found his father and Hilary's entire family dependent on him. His father was $5,000 in debt, his sister's land was unsaleable, and the only real money in the family was forty-five cents in silver. With dim prospects Hilary opened a law practice and through skillful maneuvering was miraculously able to secure the return of his client's cotton. Ecstatic over realizing a munificent $300 fee for his services, paid in $20 gold pieces, Hilary triumphantly passed out the gold coins to his jubilant family. "There is no more prospect of starvation for us. Here is twenty dollars apiece for you; don't let me have it if I call for it hereafter but save it until the last exigency shall come. I will keep this two hundred and twenty dollars and look after the family."[39]

"Absolutely Penniless"

Shortages of food, clothing, housing, and other necessities of life had become critical during the latter months of the war. By the war's end thousands of Southerners were desperate for provisions. Huge taxes on farmers during the war; the impressment by the Confederate government of horses, mules, and produce; the theft and pillaging by Yankees—as well as Confederates; cropland laid waste by battles and encampments of soldiers, droughts and insect infestations left thousands of Southerners destitute of money, provisions, raiment, and equipment.

A Georgia woman explained that prior to the war their property had been worth $200,000. By 1867 "an attempt to cultivate it [the land] with hired labor has only created debts, which, increasing at interest, we can perhaps never pay." She continued, "Since last fall we have been living without any ostensible means whatever.... We have several times not had a cent in the house, nor a week's provisions."[40] In Charleston, three maiden ladies who before the war owned their own home and subsisted on a capital of $40,000, were left penniless by 1867. During the war their money, as well as the proceeds from the sale of their house when the city was shelled had been invested in Confederate securities which by then were worthless. The sisters, one an invalid and the other two ravaged by cancer, confessed they were down to their last twenty cents and in dire straits.[41] A man who before the war was paying taxes on $180,000 worth of property lost everything; by March of 1866 his family was scattered, and he was discovered wandering the streets as a beggar.[42]

Alexander Thom was heartsick not only over his own losses, but also those of his brother. "Wat" had attempted to oversee his brother Pem's money while his brother was in Europe on Confederate business; however, the complete upheaval of the Confederate economy resulted in huge losses for both brothers. In a letter to Pem he wrote: "It is a clean sweep. I had tried my best to save your property but to no avail,—its loss affects me quite as much as my own affairs." Wat attempted to explain: "There is such a social convulsion that property of all kinds seems mostly

Top left: Eliza Frances Andrews. (From Eliza Andrews, *The War-Time Journal of a Georgia Girl.*) *Clockwise from top right:* Varina (Mrs. Jefferson) Davis, Mary Chesnut, Mrs. Roger Pryor. (Photographs from Virginia Clay, *A Belle of the Fifties.*)

worthless. At all events the future must decide. I had about $15,000. Confed. Money in Richmond at the time of the evacuation. The bank & all burnt. This is of little moment as it is of no value. Half, or there-abouts, belonged to you."[43]

Many women widowed by the war were left as the sole support for four, five, six, or more children. Some were known to have walked twenty miles for musty meal to feed their children "and leave the impress of their feet in blood on the stones of the wayside ere they reached home again."[44] One's heart aches for a distraught widow seeking help in locating the burial spot of her husband and explaining her destitution following the war. "I have heard by the kiness of Mrs. Gregorie that you was the lady that was with my dear husband in his last moment and oh my dear friend how can I be grateful oh how can I thank you anuff for you kiness to one so dear to me.... One request I ask of you to rite to me and let me no what burying ground my dear husband was entered everything I had was destroyed by the enemy but a small poshion of my stock wich if it had not bin left I do not know what my sufference wold of bin with five little cilden and one a baby in my arms which my loving husband never seen...."[45]

Particularly deserving of sympathy were the wives or mothers of small farmers who with the loss of their husbands or sons "were left helpless, with no idea of business. One by one their Negroes went for debt, piece by piece their land, till nothing was left."[46] After the death of her husband one woman found her resources added up to the grand total of twenty-five cents.

In January of 1864 food became so scarce that Mrs. Mary Edmondson of Phillips County, Arkansas, was reduced to catching and eating snow birds, doves, red birds, flickers and larks. "How sad," she wrote, "to feed upon instead of feeding and protecting innocent bright creatures."[47] Even the heretofore affluent Grace Elmore found it "queer to be without money." Her brother needed fifty cents to pay for a gun to protect the family and Grace had "not a cent, neither has sister Ellen. She writes she has spent her last twenty-five cents."[48]

"Thousands of delicate women," Cornelia Spencer explained, "bred up in affluence, are now bravely working with their hands for their daily bread; many in old age, and alone in the world, are bereft of all their early possessions. Thousands of families are absolutely penniless, who have never before known a want ungratified.... Nobody is ashamed of himself, or ashamed of his position, or of his necessities. What the South wants is not charity—but generosity."[49]

In a letter to her elder sister Clarissa in Pennsylvania and written August 9, 1865, from Orange County, Virginia, Hannah Rawlings reflected on the South's desperate need for clothing at the end of the war. By then Hannah was left threadbare, having patched, mended, turned inside out and re-re-altered clothing until there was precious little left. "In fact there never was a time-serving politician who underwent as many metamorphoses as a garment in the hands of a Southern girl during the years 1863 and '4," she wrote. "We had come to regard a patch or a neatly darned rent, rather as a *badge* of distinction than a reproach. It was 'a la Confederate,' therefore as it should be. We would not think of spending money upon a dress when our soldiers were naked and hungry in the field."[50] In asking for a loan for money to purchase new clothing ("am in need of *everything* both underclothing and dresses") she explained that Confederate money had become "waste paper" or a possible substitute for wallpaper—an observation scarcely news to any Southerner.

As Hannah continued, the letter became a recital of the reversal of fortunes of her family and friends. "There is not a family within the circle of your acquaintance in Spotsylvania that has not been reduced almost to indigence. Four years ago the Holladays of Prospect Hill were quite wealthy, and now they lack the commonest comforts of life.... Henry H who had become one of the most *flourishing* men of this *very flourishing* vicinity, has lost nearly everything. His large mill was burnt by the enemy last summer and he has not now the means to rebuild it." A year earlier a brother-in-law had watched Sheridan's troops make off with all of his horses and mules, and most of his crops and food supplies, "leaving his family consisting of upwards of a hundred persons (white and black) without a morsel to eat." Monetary losses and the departure of about one hundred slaves left him with "nothing now but his land, a portion of which he will probably be obliged to sell."[51]

Other friends, Hannah reported, "are no better off. They must all begin the world anew." A widowed sister had "neither cow nor garden, and was without money," and most days, Hannah continued, she has "been utterly at a loss to know where dinner was to come from." Hannah, herself, was no stranger to hunger and want as she told her sister: "I have eaten bread made from meal that was so sour and musty, I was obliged to hold my breath while I swallowed it."[52]

"They Must Cry for Their Bread"

Appeals for help—as a last resort even from Northerners—revealed the pitiable situation of poor and formerly wealthy farmers alike. Southerners from all walks of life found themselves reduced to writing letters pleading for aid from the various relief societies organized in the North to help provide their former enemies with the basic necessities for survival. "You have no idea of the frightful prospect ahead of us unless something is done," one writer warned. Another petitioner reported that "Many of our best families who before the war never had to deny themselves a single luxury now have to live as best they can. They have now large and valuable plantations but no means to cultivate them."[53]

A letter to the Southern Famine Relief Commission, War Department, on January 10, 1867, from some of the leading citizens in the Lancaster District in South Carolina appealed for aid for some "two hundred families in this District ... widows and orphans or helpless persons, who have no provisions anything like adequate to their wants for the present year. These people have no means at all with which to buy, & the case is plain and beyond dispute, that unless they are relieved by contributions from those who are more favored they must cry for bread & their cry be unanswered—they have no way of getting it, & it is absolutely out of the power of their fellow citizens here to give them aid."

A request for aid from Montgomery, Alabama, written on January 31, 1867, revealed that there were some 40,000 people in the locality who would need to be fed through public or private charity until they could raise a crop. One minister told of being without flour for almost a year. Few of his parishioners could spare extra money to contribute to the church and therefore he was considering giving up his ministry in order to support his sick wife and children. He explained that he had one gallon of meal and fifty pounds of salted pork and little hope for any more. Having served as a chaplain at a military prison at his own expense, he admitted that he would greatly appreciate help from Northerners whose sons he had ministered unto during the war. A physician from Virginia complained that he had few patients able to pay for his services and begged for a loan to help the blacks. Countless letters detailed extensive property losses, the work of lawless bands of camp followers.[54]

Although many felt it degrading to accept aid from Northerners, pride often took a back seat to acute need. One determined woman tried to make a living by opening a seminary in Wilmington for young ladies. However, she soon discovered that everyone was so poor that she would have to give up the school unless funds and books could be obtained from sympathetic Northerners. A former senator in the Virginia legislature explained that he was greatly in need of help. In December of 1863 his family had escaped with only the clothes on their backs when seven shells passed through their house during the bombardment of Fredericksburg.[55]

The generosity of strangers was often replicated by Southerners themselves. It was indeed a great time of sharing. Despite the widespread poverty prevailing throughout the South, Southerners were incredibly generous in sharing what little they had with those even less fortunate. One woman explained: "No one was so poor as not to be able to give from her little stock." During her mother's illness, the writer recalled that gifts of a small flask of brandy, a small sack of flour, and a cup of sugar offered as a caring, neighborly gesture by a friend were considered too dear to be consumed by the family and "were repacked and sent immediately ... to some other sufferer more in need of them, and who being in the country could not secure them on any terms." Such treasures "made at a sacrifice for the sick were sent from one friend to another until they reached the original source. Such self-forgetfulness as exhibited by the Southern women has rarely been seen," the woman concluded.

Sick soldiers also had to be fed and once again Southerns shared their mite, she continued. "Each lady pledged herself for so much, and that was redeemed even if her friends had to go on short commons. Little children were willing to be denied when the sick soldier was the recipient of their bounty."[56]

"As Wretched a Soul as Lives in This World"

Once the trees and fence rails in an area had been despoiled by an encampment of Yankee [or Confederate] soldiers[57] and one's store of blankets had been sent to the men on the battlefront, the certainty of bitterly cold days and nights loomed ominously ahead. It was a great stroke of luck not to have had one's cows seized or butchered by enemy troops—or impressed by the Confederate government. However, it was not enough merely to have a cow; animals too needed food to survive. The destruction of vast areas of farmland, the departure of tens of thousands of farmers and overseers to the Confederate army, coupled with the government's requirement that ten percent of the year's crops to be turned over to the government left many farmers—and city dwellers—destitute for forage to feed their domestic animals.

As the war wound down the Joseph Barton family found themselves with five children under the age of seven, "the youngest an infant entirely dependent on cows milk." Joseph Barton's letter to General Sheridan revealed the family's desperate plight. "I have two cows but not one thing to feed them on and take the liberty of applying to you for feed for them. I have no means of sending for feed but my House is not five miles from Winchester this side of the Calvary Pickits, & if General you can send feed to me it will relieve from suffering five children & one of them apparent

"The Last Relic." After the war, women often sold family heirlooms to survive. (*Harper's Weekly*, December 12, 1868.)

starvation, as it is too young to take any thing but milk & this I cannot longer have without feed."[58] Unfortunately the feed was never sent and the baby died.

Even when aid was forthcoming, however, the disruption of the railroad systems (two thirds had been rendered inoperable) added to the problems of transporting any available supplies to needy farm families. Without money or farm wagons it was impossible for many farmers to haul the provisions that had been donated to their homes—or, of course, to send any of their own produce to market.

Financial worries, naturally, tended to encompass the entire family. Even children were caught up in the anxieties of their elders. Overhearing her father agonize over his financial problems was a frightening experience for Marion Briscoe, who as a child was terrified that the family would be carted off to the almshouse. "My father would walk up and down the room at night declaring in loud tones that we were going to the poorhouse. I would hide behind a chair and cringe with fear, believing that the next morning I would awake to find a wagon waiting at the gate to take us there. My mother tried to encourage him and refused to listen to such talk, but in her heart she felt afraid to pull aside the curtains and peep into the future. This environment affected me beyond anything that the grownups could understand, or surely they would have tried to put a little brightness into my baby years."[59]

Even blacks who had long before been accorded their freedom found life difficult after the war. A Natchez "woman of color" chronicled in her diary the decline of her family's fortunes during the postwar years.

Catharine Johnson was the daughter of literate and prosperous parents, her father a successful Natchez businessman. Both parents had been freed in the 1820s and interestingly enough had owned slaves themselves. Just as with white slaveholders, the desertion of their bondsmen and women had resulted in severe financial losses. Catharine's efforts to find remunerative work by teaching school went for naught. In about 1872 she wrote, "I am as wretched a soul as lives in this world. The times are so hard and seem to be growing worse every day. I believe that to all our other ills and troubles is to be added that of poverty. For every year we grow poorer and poorer. We can't get our rents and for two terms I have toiled in the Public School and received nothing but a lot of worthless warrants for my pain." (Catharine was apparently paid in warrants, issued by the school board, and worth very little.)[60]

For many Southerners the destitution that loomed ahead somehow made their deprivations during the war seem trifling in comparison. Virginia French of McMinnville and Tullahoma, Tennessee, worried: "We hear nothing from Henry French or anybody who owes us money, and we need it very much indeed. God knows when or how we are to get any, and where the preparations for next winter are to come from, which we will need so much—which we greatly need now. I did not feel our poverty so much during the war, somehow...."[61]

"What Else Is to Become of the Negroes"

Contrary to popular thinking, not all slave owners were cruel, demanding masters. Thousands of slaves were given religious instruction, medical attention when needed, and a limited amount of personal freedom. Only about 1,800 of the South's 384,000 slave owners had one hundred or more slaves. Most owners had fewer than ten. Often there was a close personal relationship, particularly between domestic slaves and the members of the family.

The economic problems that brought such dire consequences for the farmer/planter's immediate family also encompassed the extended family of ex-slaves, freedmen men and women who chose to remain with their former owners rather than to strike out on their own. Most planters were hard put to scrape together the money to pay field hands. At the war's end, as noted earlier, thousands of former slave owners now found themselves in an impoverished condition and unable to feed and clothe their former servants. Destitute for food for themselves and their families they were at a loss to provide for others. What to do with these hungry dependents posed a serious dilemma for conscientious, caring former owners. It was hoped some solution could be found to temporarily support their ex-slaves as a stopgap before hiring or contracting with them to help with the planting, cultivating, and harvesting of a new crop. One planter, for example, told of having ample land and ninety hands but no way to support them—or to feed his farm animals. He was most sympathetic with the freedmen who had no alternatives other than vagrancy and theft.

In the fall of 1865 Mary Jones received a letter from her brother written in desperation. Late planting and drought had reduced his crop to almost nil and he was at his wit's end to know how to support his workers. "Alas, our future is dark—and grows darker! ... it is impossible for me to keep all of our people, even if they should stay. And to turn them off—although they seem so indifferent to me—will be painful."[62] Maggie Lindsley shared her father's distress in his inability to pay wages to his people. "But he will help them all to start in life for themselves," she added proudly.[63]

For countless plantation owners the problems of supporting aged and infirm blacks unable to work and small children too young to go out in the fields or do housework grew formidable. Living a hand-to-mouth existence themselves, planters found it impossible to feed the growing numbers of elderly disabled freedmen. With no family to help support them in the quarters the only recourse seemed to be to have them sent to the poorhouse. Frances Butler (Leigh) was pleased that her father had "agreed to support the children for three years, and the old people till they die, that is, feed and clothe them. Fortunately, as we have some property at the North we are able to do this, but most of the planters are utterly ruined and have no money to buy food for their own families, so on their plantations I do not know what else is to become of the Negroes who cannot work except to die."[64]

Thus ran the litany of destitution of thousands upon thousands of indigent Southerners. As Margaret Junkin Preston wrote during the postbellum days: "I suppose poverty was never so honorable before in the history of the world, as in the ex–Confederacy of 1865. For six months after the surrender, anything that had cost money was looked upon with suspicion. Where had that money come from? Was it clean money? For the true ex–Confederate had not a dollar to bless himself with."[65] One writer confessed that he would scarcely know what to do were he to be given a little aid. If he used the money to buy food, he would be destitute for clothing, and if he bought clothing he would suffer for want of food.

"How Shall the South Begin Her New Life?"

For Northerners there was the Grand Parade in Washington in May 1865, and within a matter of weeks more than 600,000 men were discharged from their units and sent home via government transportation on the railroads.

Most Southerners, however, as noted earlier, were forced to walk home, sans food, sans money, and for most men sans horses or mules. Begging food on the way, lucking out now and then when a kindly stranger offered a night's lodging in a barn or tool shed, the disheartened men trudged across the Southland, alone or in small groups of two or three. Some had lost an arm or a leg, others had undergone such traumatic experiences that it would be months or years—or never—before they could successfully resume their prewar careers or even attempt the support of their families. Some were so broken in spirit that they would never be able to revert to a normal life again.

Jennie Stephenson explained in her memoir that she was heartbroken to see the changes in her father following his return from Appomattox Court House to his devastated and ruined home. "It was not strange that some, like my father always went about hereafter in a subdued, stunned softness, that made the hearts of those about him bleed to see. No murmuring only the quiet taking up of the things so new to him, and all with a spirit so chastened as to make him say for the first time in his life, he felt thankful for the necessities of life."

Her father's demoralization was scarcely surprising, Jennie explained. "Ah, no wonder my Father was a changed man, for this the home of his birth and manhood, had been a pride and a delight. Now all was desolation. Even nature's landmarks were removed." Some 250 acres of timber had been cut down. "Quarters, barns, overseer's house, out houses, and fencing were all gone…. Not a dwelling to be seen in all that region of country, not a house, save the four square walls of our old home." Such was the devastation of their farm that Jennie, standing in the midst of the remains on an afternoon's sortie out of Petersburg with friends, had to inquire where they were.

"My mother's spirit," Jennie continued, "was more elastic. She was not so crushed. She soon rallied, and bought us pretty things, and did wonderfully in readjusting herself to the changes. But she was not the head. The responsibility of providing did not rest upon her. Woman, at this time in the South, was the sheltered, protected one, leaning on the stronger arm of man for support. My Mother's occupation had not been swept away from her. Her household duties, though much simpler, were left in somewhat the same shape, but to my Father, a whirlwind could not better have carried away his means of supporting and equipping this large, household for life."

A Virginia woman wrote dejectedly: "Wat returned home on the 21st disappointed & spiritless, & I fear it will be a long time before his naturally elastic temperament, or family endearments will restore his cheerfulness. Indeed, the gloomy anticipations which now fill every heart, effectually banish everything like happiness."[66]

The story of Frances Fearn and her family (although a family much better off than most) and their return from Europe following the war serves to paint a picture of the apprehension and confusion confronting Southerners as they attempted to start over. Hoping to have better control of their properties in the North, the James Fearns left their plantation home near New Orleans and waited out the war in Paris. At the war's end as they headed back to the Crescent City, Frances confessed to her diary (*The Diary of a Refugee*) her apprehension concerning the quality of life awaiting them. "The conditions in our part of the country are still very unsettled, the events of the last months indicate clearly that the reconstruction is going to be a long, tedious, and trying time for the Southern States." The loss of two sons in the war cast a pall over their return. "Then we are uncertain as to whether we shall be able to save enough from the wreck of our fortune to enable us to live even in a very modest way." Worried over the loss of their sons and the war's toll on her husband's health she wrote: "The spirit is willing but the poor heart has suffered so much anxiety and sorrow during those terrible four years that I fear it has reached its limit."[67]

In Louisiana a bewildering new life awaited them. The cataclysmic upheaval of the postwar world had completely overturned their heretofore secure, sedate world. "Here we are back again in the dear old Crescent City. It takes all our courage and fortitude to face these new and strange conditions of life. The inevitable consequences of war are all about us, everyone is adrift, social and business conditions are disorganized, the permanence of home seems a mockery." Doctors quickly advised against her husband's attempting to rejuvenate the plantation, and therefore it must "be put up for sale," Frances mourned.[68]

As Frances had predicted, plans for and the enactment of reconstruction proved both devastating and frustrating. Everywhere there seemed to be an "endless discussion of the heart-breaking measures that are being enforced as the means to restore conditions that can never be accepted by our people.... There is a difference of opinion even among our own people as to what methods should be pursued." One of Frances' greatest regrets was that they had not had time to train and better prepare their former slaves for emancipation, "that this tremendous power that has so unexpectedly been placed in their hands might have been used to some good purpose." Younger men, she mused, "perhaps those who come from afar, without handicap of the older systems, may stand a better chance to revive sugar-making and work out new and fresh ideas along different lines."[69]

Following the North's victory a defeated, despondent people who had lost a quarter of a million men and two billions of dollars in slave property attempted to pull themselves together and to start over. Begin again! Southerners shuddered. Where could one summon the courage to start all over again, now when mere survival sapped all one's strength?[70]

"How shall the South begin her new life?" Cornelia Spencer asked. "How, disfranchised and denied her civil rights, shall she start the wheels of enterprise and business that shall bring work and bread to her plundered, penniless people? How shall her widows and orphans be fed, her schools and colleges be supported, her churches be maintained, unless her rights and liberties be regained—unless every effort be made to give her wounds repose, and restore health and energy to her paralyzed and shattered frame?"[71]

For most Southerners lack of money, barren fields, severe labor problems and even nature itself posed seemingly insurmountable deterrents to a new beginning. Refugees fortunate enough to have a home to return to found their fields overgrown with weeds, their homes distressed and neglected, furniture, pictures, and carpets mutilated, destroyed or scattered across the countryside. Memories of happier days and absent loved ones hovered as gray ghosts amid the emptiness. Home had forever changed. Although Kate Stone and her family returned from their refugee life in Texas to a home in Louisiana far less ravaged than most, the loss of two brothers in the war clouded Kate's much anticipated homecoming to Brokenburn. "But if the loved ones who passed through its doors could be with us again, we might be happy yet. But never, never, never more echoes back to our hearts like a funeral knell at every thought of the happy past. We must bear our losses as best we can. Nothing is left but to endure."[72] Again, Kate repeated: "Everything seems sadly out of time. But no thoughts like these. We must be brave, and to give way to the 'blues' now is cowardly."[73]

"The Confederate Money Does Not Pass at All"

Southerners' attempts to begin life anew were essentially complicated by the South's desperate financial situation. Scarcities, inflation, the blockade, hoarding, speculators, the repeated issuance of Confederate bills all combined to depreciate Confederate currency until finally by the last months of the conflict it had become almost worthless. (As the war closed down the South had suffered an inflation of more than 9,000 per cent.)[74] One writer told of a cavalry officer who shortly before the end of the war found himself in dire need of a pair of boots. Locating a pair in a small village country store, sale priced at two hundred dollars, the officer tendered a five hundred dollar Confederate bill to the storekeeper, who, in turn, regretted that he had no small bills for change. "'Never mind,' said the cavalier, 'I'll take the boots anyhow. Keep the change; I never let a little matter of three hundred dollars stand in the way of a trade.'"[75]

The demise of the Confederacy, of course, signaled the complete collapse of the already shaky Confederate financial structure. Banks had been forced to close or suspend operations. Loyal Southerners having supported the war effort by pouring their money into bonds, now found themselves penniless, their bank accounts wiped out, their bonds turned into scrap paper.

In their generous, conscientious responses to their government's seemingly incessant appeals for money and supplies during the war loyal Confederates had been bled dry. As the Confederates' situation worsened, the appeals became ever more frequent and ever more urgent. Even as late as April second, the day before the Federal takeover of Richmond, the Rebel government was making frantic requests for aid for the army. Elvira Seddon and her father took the afternoon to journey to the Goochland County Court House (Virginia) to hear an impassioned plea[76] begging local residents to contribute generously to relieve the acute shortages plaguing the Confederate troops. "He proceeded thence to prove that Gen. Lee's Army *would be forced* to leave Rd. [Richmond] were not his troops supplied with the necessaries of life. These necessaries he declared must be supplied by the people and that right early or this all would fall in the hands of Yankee thieves. Would the people make these contributions? Could Virginia resist an appeal made by their beloved Gen. in chief in favor of that gallant army which has stood so long, a bulwark of defense? No! Surely No! Would not each family promise to support 1 soldier at least for 6 months or a year? The plan was feasible. Why should it not be practiced? All were anxious to do their utmost. A committee was formed and resolutions agreed to. A good deal was contributed on the spot. I hope the good cause will prosper," Elvira added.[77]

Debtors, of course, sought to pay back their loans at prewar prices and in depreciated currency. Creditors refused such schemes, but often waited in vain for their money. Sarah Espy was angered when people who owed her money attempted such tactics. Ever alert Sarah rejoiced over recognizing devalued currency in time to refuse it.[78]

Clearly Confederate money was not even worth the paper it was printed on. At least one Southerner who had buried his Confederate bills in his yard for security, decided it was not worth the bother to dig them up even for souvenirs after the war. Another man bragged about purchasing $1,080 of Confederate money for "four bits." Others used the bills to light their cigars. Trunkfuls of Confederate money served as paper bills for children to "play store with."

Hard cash was almost impossible to come by even for formerly prominent, well-to-do families. No one was willing to accept Confederate bills after the war for services or for goods. Sarah Wadley and her family, after attending church in Monroe, Louisiana, were faced with the embarrassment of being unable to come up with the minuscule boatman's fee required to ferry them to their nearby home across the river. "The Confederate money does not pass at all in Monroe now and the ferryman refuses to take anything but specie or greenbacks! I suppose we shall have to stop going to Monroe as we have neither of these."[79] (One may recall a similar situation experienced by Mary Chesnut in her return after the war to their home near Camden, South Carolina.) The Hardins, heading home following their two and a half year exile in Georgia, attempted to sell some of their jewelry in order to gather up enough money to continue on their way to Kentucky. Apparently there was little interest in the valuables for no one could pay for luxuries in anything but Confederate bills which were, of course, worthless.[80]

Soon after the "peace" there was a frantic search of sofas, pillows, overstuffed chairs for the retrieval of a cache of hidden money or jewelry which, of course, would mean bread for the ensuing months. Most Southerners anticipating an enemy attack during the war years had secreted their gold and silver in old stumps, in birds' nests, in the ground, under bushes, behind pictures, under mattresses, in pillowcases, or in other ingenious hiding places. Most, unfortunately, found their treasures had been discovered and confiscated. Owners had a vast array of choices to blame for the thefts: Yankees, bummers, returning Confederate veterans, neighbors, or servants.

Rumors in mid–March of 1865 of Yankee troops scheduled to descend on their Goochland County, Virginia, property had sent Elvira Seddon and her family into a flurry of packing up valuables to be stored with neighbors and silver and crystal to be cleverly secreted away. "They are upon us now we are sure. What a fate awaits us! In going through the rooms collecting various small articles I inwardly bid adieu to these scenes. I think of all the happy days I have passed in my dear home, and I feel sad, very sad when I picture it reduced to a pile of ashes."[81] For days every sound of gunfire or clatter of horses' hooves set off panic attacks.

The Seddons were among the lucky ones, however, for a short time later their goods were recovered from neighbors and their silver unearthed from its hiding place. By April 3 the Seddons' home had survived but Richmond had fallen to the enemy.

Sarah Follansbee was relieved to find their treasure-trove, hidden above the windows, intact. Others, she reported, "when after the surrender they went for it [their valuables]—found it gone. Mrs. Metcalf had *planted* $1,000.00 in two deeply dug holes in her cellar, where she had deposited it after covering the window and every crevice that light could gleam through, and doing it at midnight, when every darkie was supposed in bed and asleep. She found the first deposit—gone—but rejoiced in the other $500."[82]

Those who miraculously retrieved their cleverly squirreled away resources found precious little to buy, the few articles that were available commanding astronomically high prices. Sarah Follansbee pointed out that "the markets were not supplied with but with the very plainest of provisions."[83] In a frantic attempt to spend her few remaining Confederate dollars before they became absolutely valueless, Sarah Follansbee quoted prices such as twenty-five dollars for a broom, five dollars for a pail of greens, ten dollars for a pound of beef, and fifty dollars for a small pig. Even those prices, Sarah thought, were "quite reasonable" in view of the tremendous escalation of prices during the war.

Indeed, prospects for starting over were anything but encouraging for millions of Southerners whose pockets were empty and whose farms and homes lay in ruins. In the towns (or what was left of them) schools, colleges, courts, businesses, medical practices had been disrupted or abandoned during the war years. Now, returning teachers, lawyers, physicians, ministers found themselves at a loss for students, clients, patients, or parishioners who had money to pay for their services. Harriet Kershaw Lang's father returned from the war without a dollar, and Harriet remembered his desperate attempts to raise money to resume his law practice by selling many of the family's heirlooms.[84]

In lieu of cold hard cash, goods and services were exchanged by barter: a skirt or blouse traded for a turkey or turkeys; so many physician's calls for so much corn or so many shirts; boarding house accommodations paid for in sacks of potatoes. Trading clothes for food was common after the war. When asked how his sisters were getting along, one young man replied, "Their complexions look badly," he explained, "but that is not surprising, when you consider how long they have been eating old frocks."[85]

Even the eminent Mary Chestnut discovered that it was quite impossible to purchase food with Confederate money, and each day she found herself bartering dresses from her wardrobe for eatables. "So we are devouring our clothes," she told her diary.[86]

Farmers, both black and white, brought their produce to market where they traded chickens and eggs for hats or veils or vests. On May 13, 1865, Edwin Fay, stationed with the Quartermaster's Department of the Confederate Army at Opelousas, Louisiana, wrote his wife Sarah: "Confederate money will buy nothing here, not even a glass of rum. I cannot pay my board except with tithe provisions and now people wont pay their Tithes preferring to pay in Confederate Money which is worth only one cent on the dollar."[87]

"My father was taking up his law again," Marion Briscoe recalled, "but his clients were hard up also, and often he brought home commodities in payment for his services."[88] The Philadelphia Committee backing Margaret Thorpe's school for newly freed blacks in Virginia had requested a tuition charge of five cents a week; however, the teachers readily settled for "corn meal, eggs, potatoes, pork, old worn out hens or any other edible" as payment. One rabbit, for example, could pay for a whole month's schooling.[89] Even some private schools and colleges accepted students whose tuition was paid for in provisions.

"We Made About Twenty Bales": The Farmers' Plight

By the war's end farmers were desperate for money to buy seed for a new crop, to mend fence rails and worn-out equipment, to find some temporary replacement for farm implements that had been stolen or "pressed." Huge tracts of land had been completely denuded as Union (or Confederate) soldiers, either in large foraging parties officially detailed by army headquarters or in small independent groups acting on their own volition, succeeded in ravaging the countryside. Large areas that had once been good cropland had been trampled and scorched and would be unproductive for years to come. As noted in Chapter One, the indiscriminate destruction of homes, including family heirlooms, pianos, pictures, paintings, clothing, and china, left only "Sherman's sentinels," the brick chimneys standing amid the blackened rubble of family homes and farm buildings. Stragglers from both armies supplemented the Union foragers in scavenging homes and farmyards, appropriating whatever they needed—or wanted—at the moment, leaving owners destitute and disheartened. The Confederate government itself had further added to

the problems with their "tax-in-kind" requirements and the impressment of crops, horses, mules, wagons, and farm implements for use by
the armies. Thousands simply gave up farming forever. Elizabeth
Reynolds, for example, reported that upon finding their home useless without barns, cattle or servants, the family abandoned their farm
near Fredericksburg, Virginia, at the end of the war and moved into
town.[90]

The return to cotton production was no easy matter after the war.
Fortunately, Kate Stone's mother found it a rather simple matter to get
advances in New Orleans thanks to the high price of cotton and Northern capitalists who were eager to invest in the southern staple. However,
labor difficulties (Negroes demanding wages of $20 to $25 dollars a month
plus rations, the departure of former hands, the difficulty in obtaining
new laborers, and discipline troubles in the fields) constituted an important part of the problem of resurrecting their plantation. The Stones and
thousands like them watched helplessly as cholera decimated the ranks
of the Negroes and glanders infected the mules. In addition there was
flooding—*and* the army worms. "Then the water came up and we were
nearly overflowed. The cotton planted was very late, and when it was
looking as luxuriant and promising as possible and we saw ease of mind
before us, the worms came. In a few days the fields were blackened like
fire had swept over them. We made about twenty bales and spent $25,000
doing it."[91]

A disappointed Kate reported that there was absolutely no money
for personal luxuries, that all the money went to the Negroes. Mrs. Stone
was adamant about giving the workers their fair share, believing it "not
honest to spend the money on anything but making the crop. All in this
section have suffered in the same way, and for awhile they seemed stunned
by their misfortunes."[92] Ill fortune continued to plague the Stones when
the floods of 1867 rose to the doorstep of Brokenburn, drove the Stones
from their home, and forced them to seek shelter with friends in the area
until August. The next year with the threat of extensive flooding Kate's
brother rented drier quarters for the family at Rose Hill. Extra money
continued a scarce item for the Stones. Straitened circumstances made it
impossible to send Kate's sister away to school for two years and Kate's
brother Jimmy, refusing to continue his financial dependence on his older
brother, abandoned what appeared to be a promising medical career. It
was indeed a cause for celebration in the fall of 1868 when Kate's brother
sent money for new winter clothes. "We have lived on very little of late
years, little bought that was not absolutely necessary." Needless to say
Kate and her sister were "jubilant at the prospect of new dresses and bon-
nets."[93]

"A Rich Man's War and a Poor Man's Fight"

Poor people, as in all wars, suffer the brunt of the war. Sarah Espy, although better off than many, echoed the complaint of thousands of Southerners who insisted that the war was "a rich man's war and a poor man's fight." As neighbors sold off their possessions and moved to safer territory to avoid the Yankees, Sarah expressed a touch of envy. "They are well off, and are going to wealthy friends whereas I, and many others, have no friends and our children even barely boys, are taken from us and put into the service. There is a great wrong somewhere, and if our Confederacy should fall, it will be no wonder to me for the brunt is thrown upon the working classes while the rich live at home in ease and pleasure." Sarah resignedly commented on the plight of a cousin who was "in great distress" over being left at home with small children and a lame son. "But so it is. Such as she, must bear it. There is no remedy."[94]

"Virginians Drawing Their Rations from the Federal Commissary." (*Harper's Weekly*, February 11, 1865.)

"The Open Door of Bankruptcy"

Without resources Southerners found the paying of taxes nigh on to impossible. Bills for back taxes became a primary concern and owners now bereft of funds watched as their property was confiscated or sold for trifling sums at auction. Newspapers were replete with ads for acreage for sale by owners unable to come up with the money for unpaid taxes. Other owners, having somehow raised the tax money, were now faced with the dismal prospects of farming without their former enslaved black workforce. Lacking money to hire workers and floundering under the share crop system, thousands of planters saw no alternative other than to put their property up for sale.

Not only back taxes but current taxes took a heavy toll on Southerners. In Mississippi, for example, the state levy for 1871 was four times what it was in 1869. For 1873 it was eight and one half times as great, and for 1874 it was fourteen times as great.[95]

The devaluation of land and heavy prewar mortgages, along with the South's litany of postwar problems, rendered it hopeless for countless farmers to ante up the money for taxes. According to William Harris in 1870, two million acres were held by public authorities for nonpayment of taxes and by 1875 some six million acres, or one-fifth of the land area of Mississippi, had defaulted to the state government. As Eric Foner pointed out, however, much of this land remained in the hands of the owners, as they somehow borrowed enough money to pay off their debts or as friends and neighbors devised schemes to thwart the auctions.[96]

As the taxes on Southerners increased in the postwar years despite the fact that ten of the Confederate states had been denied readmission to Congress, many saw similarities to the Revolutionary War argument that "taxation without representation is tyranny." South Carolina's Provisional Governor Perry queried, "Are not ten States deprived of representation, while their citizens are taxed without their consent? Is that a republican form of government?"[97]

Southerners were further incensed over being taxed to support not only their own veterans and their dependents but also those of the Northern section as well. A sizable portion of the South's heavy state taxes went to the maintenance of their disabled veterans and the support of the war's tens of thousands of widows and orphans. In the North such aid was provided by the Federal government, money which came in part from the Federal taxes levied upon Southerners. In other words, Southerners were taxed to support their own ill and indigent countrymen through their state taxes and in part for Northern veterans through their Federal taxes.

Borrowing money to pay taxes, to settle debts, to establish businesses, to replace worn out farm equipment, or as advances on future harvests frequently led to an escalation of even greater financial indebtedness. The collapse of the Confederacy sent Ella Gertrude Clanton Thomas's world into a tailspin. Accustomed in her youth to wealth and luxury as the daughter of one of Georgia's richest men, Gertrude was subjected to tremendous humiliation and anguish following the war as she watched even her own personal property, inherited from her father, lost to creditors or sold for taxes.

For the previous four years the Thomases, as patriotic Southerners, had invested heavily in Confederate bonds. In July of 1863, Gertrude Thomas had mentioned in her journal her husband's sale of cotton and his investment of $15,000 in Confederate eight per cent bonds. All, of course, were lost at the end of the war. Borrowing soon became a way of life for Gertrude's husband, Jefferson Thomas. Whatever ability he lacked as a planter and businessman, he certainly made up for in his talent for borrowing money. Jefferson Thomas owed money to his own brother and sister, to Gertrude's family, to cotton merchants, banks, businesses, and dozens of individuals.[98]

Gertrude Thomas watched helplessly as her bountiful inheritance was sold to meet her husband's mounting debts. "For two years I have watched a death struggle, have heard every sigh, every groan, have seen the anguished brow, the convulsed lip—have seen *the mask off*...." For Gertrude Thomas her husband's agonies reverberated in every fiber of her being. "My life, my glory, my honour have been so intimately blended with that of my husband and now to see him broken in fortune, health and spirits."[99]

Gertrude's financial woes, a result of the war and her husband's "bad management," were devastating, forcing her to take a lackluster teaching position and to make supreme efforts to economize in an attempt to help relieve the family's financial difficulties. Among her greatest concerns were worries over the lack of money to educate her children and, as a consequence of their impoverishment, seeing their sons engaged in menial field work. "Sometimes I do not know if I do right in acting as I do. For several years I have practiced close economy and of what avail is it. Last winter Turner was out of school and among all my troubles none worried me more than to see him engaged in work which any Negro could have done as well."[100]

With news of a husband's borrowing large amounts of money, a woman's ever-present postwar anxieties soared to new heights. Marion Briscoe's mother was beside herself upon learning that her husband had borrowed $50,000 to buy a "Health Resort." Marion's father had grown up at his father's resort in Hot Springs in Virginia, and his experiences there had colored his plans for his family's future. One day, Marion recalled, he "came in and told my mother that he had borrowed fifty thousand dollars and bought the Buffalo Springs. I shall never forget my mother's horror. She told him that we were ruined and that he would never be able to pay it back. She argued that no one would ever be so wild as to think of making any money from an obscure little resort like that. However, it was not easy to turn my father from his purpose, and soon he was settled to work out his problem." (Fortunately the venture proved to be a great success!)[101]

Attempts to pay off pre- and postwar loans often created instant paupers. When Jennie Stephenson's father was forced to sell his townhouse in Petersburg, she recalled, he borrowed money from a friend and asked him to buy the house for him. At the auction the house was "knocked off" to her father's friend, but the debt constituted a stranglehold on her father for the rest of his life. Payments on her father's two $10,000 life insurance policies had stopped because of the war, and the nine hundred dollars paid off by the one company evaporated in the purchase of supplies to rebuild the farmhouse and to purchase half interest in a cow in order to keep his family in milk. "The pinch of poverty during the war was hard," Jennie confessed, "but that was an episode that most of us hoped would end in glory. But straightened circumstance were now abiding, they had come to stay and that too just where all had been so different. Where now were all the hopes of college bred sons and daughters, of finished education? Where the start in life for those youths and maidens, just budding into men and women. Only those who passed through that furnace of domestic and social change, can tell the sufferings my parents bore." For vast numbers of Southerners war—and the Reconstruction—were indeed hell.

Borrowing or buying on credit, of course, could prove hazardous for debtor and creditor alike. Operating a store, for example, turned into a disastrous venture for hosts of enterprising Southerners. Extending too much credit could close down an owner's business in short order. With little hard cash at their disposal, customers buying on credit frequently found themselves so entangled in their own financial troubles that declaring bankruptcy was the only solution. A Mississippi woman operating a store in Woodville learned the hard way about the bankrupt law when many of her customers delinquent in paying their bills took the easy way out by declaring themselves insolvent. Betty Beaumont took a dim view of her chances of collecting on the mumbled promises about "paying later." To Betty far too many people were eager to "get rid of all individual liability, and as worldly pilgrims to enter the open door of bankruptcy, and drop just outside the heavy load of indebtedness...."[102]

Not a few devious Southerners saved themselves from financial ruin by transferring at least some of their money to bank accounts in England or France during the war. Others, to secure their property from confiscation, deeded over their land to wives or relatives. Some insolvent Southerners, having thus turned over their property, could later declare bankruptcy and begin life anew debt-free. Some resorted to the lien system whereby planters could pledge a certain amount of their crops in return for a loan. Fortunately even when land was forfeited there was usually a specified period whereby the land could be redeemed, and hundreds of planters somehow found the resources to eventually recover their property.

Economy, as Gertrude Thomas admitted, was the byword in most Southern households. Families who had heretofore felt little need for practicing economy were suddenly forced to tighten their purse strings and their belts. Harriet Palmer's father cautioned, "I need not say we can not be too economical in this matter. We are worse off this year (1870) than any since the 'Union came in.' I speak from certain knowledge."[103]

While her husband sought remunerative work as a lawyer in Texas, Cordelia Jackson valiantly wrestled with family finances at home after the war. Already in straitened circumstances Cordelia must have been particularly dismayed with the news that her husband's minuscule earnings might be paid in greenbacks. "And in that case," her husband wrote, "we will have tight screwing to live." Earlier that year (1866) he had warned her: "If I don't succeed pretty well this trip I don't see how I am to get through for another month. But I say nothing about economy as I know you will incur no unnecessary expenses."[104]

Apparently William Ker's sister looked to her brother for at least partial support—or perhaps as a good source to touch for a loan. Her brother's January 1869 letter, however, expressed his humiliation at owing money and his displeasure over his sister's extravagances. "If you knew how harrassed I am about our prospects, and how galling it is to me to think that I am *always* to have debts dragging me down, you would feel sorry for me, and I think you would not spend money simply because you have it—for I cannot imagine what occasion you have for spending much. I feel like giving up entirely, for the more I struggle and just when I think I have cause to feel a little relief, something occurs to bring everything before me. I had rather have a man shoot at me than ask me for money that I owe him and cant pay him, and I never go on the streets, that I don't feel like dodging men, lest they should dun me. If I live a thousand years, I don't think I should ever get over this feeling."[105]

"Cotton Stealing Is the Order of the Day"

Intricately tied to Southerners' financial difficulties were their astronomical cotton losses. Both wealthy planters and small cotton farmers suffered from the Confederate government's wartime warnings to growers to refrain from planting cotton and instead devote their fields to food crops to feed the army. Several states passed laws restricting the production of cotton. The limits were two bales per hand in Arkansas, one acre per hand in South Carolina, and three in Georgia. In some areas planters were heavily taxed for planting large cotton crops, and in most states overplanting was severely frowned upon. This policy lead to the decrease in cotton production from 4,500,000 bales in 1861 to 30,000 in 1864. (In later years many historians cited the restrictions on growing cotton and an early discouragement in 1861 of exports to England as having helped bring about the South's weakened economic condition.) By 1865 cotton that had been selling for thirteen cents a pound in 1861 was selling outside the South for $1.90 a pound.[106]

After the defeat, reverting to cotton production entailed a reorganization of farm work. Newly freed blacks often ignored or refused to participate in the vital but back-breaking rigors of "chopping the cotton" (hoeing the weeds away from the cotton plants). This, of course, became one of the factors that contributed to the drastic reduction in the number of bales per acre.

Lack of "horse-power" (the result of Confederate confiscation and Yankee theft of horses and mules) further complicated life for the plantation owner as well as the small farmer. A South Carolina farmer explained that he had "lost every mule and horse by Sherman's Army except the one I retreated on. The three I purchased after the army passed are quite indifferent, being good eaters, but extremely old and lazy."[107] One writer complained that by the end of the war horses and mules were in such short supply that many were stolen "while their owners were riding them." Anna Logan wrote that a friend of hers "was being borne to the grave when the hearse was stopped on the way to the cemetery and the horses taken [impressed]."[108] Other serious crop losses resulted from the Confederate government's collection of the "tax-in-kind" levy of ten percent of all farm produce and meat for the army.

During the war years untold numbers of cotton bales had been captured by the Federals or had been burned by their owners to prevent their falling into the hands of the enemy and, as one Virginia woman declared, to "show the world how truly we are *in earnest*."[109] Kate Morrissette told of one unlucky bride's wedding gift of 200 bales of cotton (worth about $50,000) that "went up in smoke" in connection with the takeover of Montgomery, Alabama, in April of 1865.[110] Authorities estimate that the destruction of cotton by the Northern armies and by the Southerners themselves amounted to a loss of 2,500,000 bales.[111]

Amanda Worthington, of Washington County, Mississippi, explained in her diary that early in the war (in 1862) her family had burned some two hundred bales of cotton not wanting "those rascally Yankees to get any of it." Years later in a more expansive report the family stated that in 1863 some 20,000 thousand bales of Confederate cotton hidden near their home had been confiscated by Federal troops including several thousand bales of the Worthington cotton. The capture was so enormous that it took a detail of Yankees (with the help of one hundred wagons and six hundred mules appropriated from farmers in the area) a month to haul away the cotton. In the wake of the raid almost two hundred of the Worthington's servants made their departure.[112] In February of 1865, the Federals demanded the keys to Margaret McClough's gin-house and she and her husband watched helplessly as thirty-five bales went up in smoke.[113] Additional cotton losses were incurred by owners who abandoned their cotton as the Federals approached or who hid their bales in the woods where the elements took their toll.

Of course, countless bales of the South's cotton disappeared thanks to the greed of its own people. Some of the South's less conscientious cotton producers, reluctant to limit production or unwilling to sacrifice their cotton for the sake of the Confederacy, concealed their cotton and surreptitiously made deals with both the North and the South for its sale. Case in point: Following the death of her husband in 1863, Adelicia Acklen of Nashville, Tennessee, hurried to their Louisiana plantation and through ingenious maneuvering succeeded in having their cotton sent to Liverpool, her $2 million profit in greenbacks making her one of the richest women in America.[114]

Cotton was often seized with little or no regard to property rights. Vindictive Federals often viewed all cotton in the former Rebel states as "spoils of war" that rightfully belonged to the victors.[115] In December of 1864, during the Union take over of Savannah, Sherman's Christmas greetings to President Lincoln read: "I beg to present you as a Christmas Gift the City of Savannah with 150 heavy guns and plenty of ammunition and also about 25,000 bales of cotton."[116] Within the time span of a few months the total seizure of cotton in Savannah had amounted to 38,500 bales [117]

Yankees were joined by bummers, blacks, or even disgruntled neighbors who proceeded to strip families of their cotton. "Cotton stealing is the order of the day" an article in the *New Orleans Times* of June 6, 1865, proclaimed. Were it C.S.A. cotton or private stock, Yankees, Negroes, fellow Southerners—all were eager to lay hands on the precious commodity. Laborers en route to market driving wagons filled with bales of cotton were often hijacked and both wagon and cotton stolen. Hungry, unpaid returning veterans saw the cotton as "their due." One writer, no doubt divested of cotton himself, complained bitterly: "People say they have fought hard for four years without pay, and now they propose to pay themselves." And, unfortunately there was little the owner or the now defunct Confederate Government could do about it. "C.S.A cotton," the writer continued, "seems to be an especial object of cupidity. It

is difficult to prevent it. The Confederate Authority is not recognized—
yet Federal authority [has not] been established, and thus the country is
suffering all the grief of the interregnum, or, more properly, of anarchy."[118]

"I'm Sure I Sent Some
Honest Cotton Agents"

With the collapse of the Confederacy tens of thousands of bales of
cotton, owned by the Confederacy or held as security for loans, were
seized by Union agents (and by impostors pretending to be Union agents
or flaunting a fake order from some vague authority). Estimates indicate
that some three million bales of cotton of the five million on hand in 1865
were seized by cotton agents.[119] (It should be remembered that in 1872
some claimants were reimbursed at least in part for their losses.) Angry
Southerners, of course, were quick to accuse government agents of seizing cotton "without any evidence that it ever belonged to the Confederate Government." A newspaper editorial complained: "If anyone has
failed, or is reported as having failed to pay the tax on cotton, they at
once seize it and refuse to adjudicate the claim alleging that they have
no authority to hear and determine the proof of ownership...."[120]

Privately owned cotton on docks or in warehouses awaiting shipment to England or being stored by planters speculating on a rise in cotton prices was often summarily appropriated in the name of the U.S.
government. Alice Palmer, for example, protested the seizure of her
grandfather's cotton. In September of 1865 the Federal authorities refused
to allow her grandfather to move his wagonloads of cotton to market.
Union officials maintained that "everyone furnished cotton to the Confederate government at the beginning of the war" and therefore it could
now be taken as captured property. That philosophy prompted Alice to
caution: "Everybody that has cotton I think had better get it off as quickly
as possible."[121]

Some agents indiscriminately seized every bale of cotton (both public and Confederate) they found. Not a few unscrupulous agents succeeded in secretly appropriating countless bales for themselves as a means
of augmenting their own personal bank accounts. Agents and laborers,
both black and white, insidiously grabbed handfuls of cotton, stashed
their plunder and in time rebaled it for their own gain. Some unprincipled schemers concocted a nefarious plot to demand a ransom from owners for the return of their cotton. Other agents, appropriately termed

"rogues and fortune hunters," greedily insisted on heavy bribes from the owners not to confiscate certain stores of private cotton.[122] A New Orleans newspaper repeated an article from a Marion County, Texas, newspaper that claimed that "two-thirds of the seizures which have been made in this section of the State have proceeded upon fictitious and fabricated claims by which the Government has not been benefited, but which has resulted in filling the pockets of the Treasury Agents and those who follow them around to profit upon the ruin and misfortunes of our people."[123]

John William De Forest, Freedmen's Bureau agent in South Carolina, expressed little admiration for many of the revenue agents sent by the Federal government to the South. He deemed them "small help to the government" and added "one wonders that the South did not rebel anew when one considers the miserable vermin who were sent down there as government officials."[124] Their corruptness and immorality De Forest considered beneath contempt. Secretary Hugh McCulloch was aghast at the illicit activities of his agents: "I am sure I sent *some* honest cotton agents South; but it sometimes seems very doubtful whether any of them remained honest very long."[125]

In addition to cotton losses in the fields, from Federal treasury agents and from local thieves, there were, of course, huge losses at sea incurred in the shipments of cotton to England. In 1867 Celena Carnes of Bishopville, South Carolina, wrote of her husband's disastrous losses as a result of a shipwreck and the decline in the price of cotton. "Everybody talks of hard times particularly the merchants who have lost a great deal by the fall in the cotton market. Mr. C continues hopeful however, notwithstanding he has been particularly unfortunate in that line, having made a heavy shipment of cotton to Liverpool, and lost every bit by the wreck of the vessel—he seems to care only about the dreadful state of politics existing here, the Negro authorities over us, and the illustrious notorious Dan Sickles. What are you going to do in VA? Our freedmen are doing well compared with many other places in this *Territory*. We have been so successful with ours and hope they'll continue to do well."[126]

To minimize the importance of the tremendous loss of cotton to Southerners as a result of the Confederate government's wartime restrictions on growing cotton, their own destruction of ten of thousands of bales to prevent its capture by Union forces, the seizure of cotton by Federal government officials after the war, the labor difficulties engendered by emancipation, and the postwar vagaries of nature would seriously distort a realistic picture of the South's financial situation following the defeat.

℘ 3 ℭ

A World
Rife with
Changes

℘ For both former owners and slaves Emancipation brought with it dramatic changes. For a time general confusion prevailed. Clara Barton in her work in tracking down missing men of the Union Army told of being besieged by freedmen as she began her investigation in Andersonville, Georgia. Some blacks had been told by their employers that Lincoln had indeed been murdered and now they would no longer be free. As many as a hundred newly freedmen and women appeared at Miss Barton's tent each day (some having walked twenty miles following their day's work), to learn whether they were truly free people or still slaves.[1]

Throughout the South, Freedmen's Bureau officials were hounded by questions from former slaves desirous of understanding their status. Many expressed a lack of confidence in their former owners, believing that if they remained on the plantations their situation would be unchanged. Naturally, the freedmen were exceedingly skeptical about signing contracts with their ex-masters when they were unable to read the stipulations. Most were under the impression that "the soil had changed proprietors" and that they were now owners.

"De Tried and Tried to Keep Us as Slaves"

With news of the surrender and the freeing of their slaves, most planters followed a plan similar to that of Sara Handy's father, who called his slaves together and explained to them that they were free. "'I have no money,'" he told them, "'and I cannot promise you wages; but while you are free to go, you are also welcome to remain, and earn a living for yourselves and your children by your labor, until you can do better for yourselves, or I can do better for you.'" Many quickly packed up their meager belongings and left at once. Others, usually house servants, opted to remain with their former masters.[2]

Emancipation signaled untold problems for plantation owners. Not a few former masters, impoverished by the war and with no tangible income in sight, became alarmed by the prospect of attempting to feed and clothe these scores of newly freed people for the ensuing months or years. Some former masters believed their only option for the good of their "servants" and themselves was to send them on their way. Sometimes freedmen who wished to remain were told they must leave. One ex-bondsman reported: "He said he couldn't take care of us, that times had changed and he had no money left."[3] A Louisiana ex-slave remembered being sent to an orphans' asylum with a brother and sister. The brother soon died, the sister was quickly adopted, and after a long stay he at last was taken by an Opelousas man.[4]

While former slaves hoped for new life and independence, their former masters regarded their emancipation with regret and in some cases denial. A former slave recalled that his owner refused to tell them they were free. "De tried and tried to keep us as slaves."[5] And, indeed, countless masters did keep their servants in ignorance of their freedom for months or even years. It was August of 1865 before David Harris and many of his Piedmont South Carolina area neighbors informed their slaves of their freedom and then only because they were ordered to do so by Yankee officials.[6]

In other instances owners were so incensed with the freeing of their slaves that they took to violence. Numerous former slaves bore physical evidence of the displeasure of their former owners over their newly acquired freedom. In sheer anger or in a supreme effort to detain their former "servants" some former slave owners resorted to gross physical abuse. Ex-slaves sought out the "Freedmen's Man" complaining of having been mistreated and brutalized by their former owners, some "with the marks of brutality still painfully visible." One woman arrived at the Bureau displaying the cuts and bruises resulting from beatings from her former master. Two old men brought in the "hickory sticks with which they had been beaten."[7] Seventy-five years later Henrietta Butler still bore mute testimony of her "mean as hell" mistress's almost biting off Henrietta's finger in anger over her being set free.[8]

Although Freedmen's Bureau officials sought to investigate and adjudicate cases of actual mistreatment, for the most part they were adamant in instructing most of the freedmen (those not misused or physically abused) to return to their former owners on farms where workers were in great demand "as long as their rights were respected and wages paid."[9]

"Free and Can Do as You Please"

Slaves reacted to news of their freedom with emotions running the gamut from jubilation to fear. One ex-slave recalled that the first word of his freedom came when a Union soldier arrived at his plantation and announced to the crowd: "You's free and can do as you please—now, and forever and forever." One former slave vented his elation by picking up a stick and beating on his master's grave in repayment for all those whippings incurred during his enslavement. Mrs. Irby Morgan recalled the reception by her servants of the news of their emancipation: "drums beating, banners waving, Negroes running, shouting, yelling, looking like lunatics just escaped from the asylum. Among the number, my cook ran by me, with her white apron tied to the end of a broomstick, shouting and cheering at the highest pitch of her voice, jumped the fence, and was gone." At least one faithful servant, however, registered disgust at their behavior. "Joe walked out into the yard with the children, and said: 'I am so mad with them fool niggers. If they are free, they are free, but not to make fools of themselves.' He said: 'Now, if you please, look at the poor white trash them niggers is running after.... I tell you now they won't get dis nigger. And I thank God I know who my friends are.'"[10]

A black Mississippian, Sam Broach, who had been sent to war to wait on his young master, remembered hearing little about freedom until end of the war. Sam admitted to an interviewer with the WPA Writers' Project: "I didn hear nothin bout slaves bein free, didn hear no talk bout freedom a-tall twell we got home from der War. Der white folks talked bout it some, an dey try, off an on, ter tell us, but we didn pay hit much mind. Den der Surrender come on us. Den dey wuz talkin, but hit was all bout sompen far off, seems like, We didn understand nothin bout it twell long time afterwards when we get ter studyin' how come dis thing happened and dat thing happened, hit was because der Surrender done come on us."[11]

Sam Broach explained the situation. "We stayed right on, lived right on dare at der Broach place. An after while, dis one would die or move off or somebody git mar'ied or sumpem an change up, and we'd start'm ter farmin fur somebody else. Dats how I come ter be living here on dis place, jes working like we been er-doin, come der War." Sam continued: "I rec'lect sumpen bout hearin tell niggers wuz votin', but I didn pay no tention ter hit. I never did vote, no'm." Even as late as 1937 Sam was still professing affection for his former owners. "I loved 'em. I loves 'em now. When I wuz at der War wid em, I wuz near bout white wid em. If I hear bout anything happenin ter em, I cry quick. But I loved my ole mistis better'n anybody."[12]

"Our old servants stayed with us until the end of the war, some longer," a Mississippi woman recalled. "But we had so little money for wages, or even food, and only knew how to sew and mix cakes, ourselves. The North thought emancipation would solve the Negro problem, and all would go well, not seeing that the real problem was the presence of the Negro in the United States. I suppose people would never do anything if they could look far enough ahead!"[13]

With the passage of time not a few ex-slaves, hounded by the problems concomitant with freedom, actually longed for a return to the "good old times." One admitted that as he had not had to work very hard as a slave he had been happy in his master's care. To the contrary, however, thousands of others testified to their incessant mistreatment and abuse as slaves.[14]

"True as Steel"

Accounts differ considerably about the behavior of slaves with the news of their freedom. Sara Handy wrote that their freed people "behaved admirably; gave us no trouble, but remained and did their work as though there had been no change in our mutual relations."[15] Cornelia Spencer took to task Northern letter-writers for painting a picture of wild and irresponsible behavior on the part of Negroes following their liberation. "They behaved well during the war; if they had not, it could not have lasted eighteen months." With their emancipation, she pointed out, their "fidelity and steadiness" continued with little trace of exultation over their former masters.[16] Cautioning a friend she wrote: "Don't you believe your 'eye-witnesses & ear witnesses' of our cruelty to our poor Negroes. Exceptional cases there are no doubt, as in everything but believe me 990 in every 1000 of our people are kindly disposed towards them, & if they will behave themselves will befriend them."[17]

A South Carolina woman commended their behavior: "I do not believe there is any other people upon the face of the earth who would have behaved so well under the circumstances of so suddenly acquiring, not only freedom, but citizenship, as our Negroes did. For months we were almost at their mercy, and it was the exception when one of them took advantage of it."[18] A Georgia woman asked: "True the coloured people are not now as they were during the war but we trusted ourselves to them then. Why not now?"[19]

Another woman, who no doubt spoke for scores of her countrymen, reported that "The negroes, without exception, had been true as steel; they never wavered in their fidelity, and, although pretty well assured by their visiting friends (who nevertheless stole all they could from them) that they no longer owed service or obedience, they refused neither, but in every capacity evinced docility, concern and affection." Many homes, the writer continued, had been saved from burning during the war when the raiders' torches were wrested from them by the "servants."[20] A Freedman's Bureau official in North Carolina commended the newly freed blacks for their diligence and industry. "Contrary to the fears and predictions of many, the great mass of colored people have remained quietly at work upon the plantations of their former masters during the entire summer."[21]

Margaret Preston was surprised by the reaction of several of their servants when her husband dismissed four of them thinking it best to make some changes. "Anakee has lived with him 25 years; he was grieved to give her up, and she wanted to stay. Old Uncle Young manifested no pleasure at the idea of freedom. It is astonishing how little it seems to affect them; they seem depressed rather than elated."[22]

Margaret Ward extolled the loyalty of the slaves during the war "They certainly behaved well—wonderfully well. I think the people of the South owe the negroes of that time a debt of gratitude for their good behavior, because there were many, many homes that were entirely at their mercy. There was an adjoining plantation where there were no men except one crippled old man that couldn't go into the army, so we were dependent for protection and for the running of the farms upon these negroes, and on the whole they did wonderfully well."[23]

George Eggleston also found much to praise in the reactions of their former slaves. The newly emancipated people at his home were informed of their freedom and told they were free to leave or remain. If they wished to continue working they were assured of being given provisions and clothing and wages at the end of the year. Every Negro assented to the offer and "they lost not an hour from their work, and the life upon the plantation underwent no change whatever until its master was forced by a pressure of debt to sell his land."[24]

Shortly after the war's end Lucy Irion (Neilson), of Columbus, Mississippi, remarked that despite their Negroes being affected with the Yankee fever, they "have behaved remarkably well; none of them show any disposition to set up for themselves yet awhile. Some people have lost all of theirs, and a good many of our citizens have been arrested for whipping their servants."[25] Later in December of 1871 Lucy reported that their Negroes had emerged with dignity and money in their pockets. "Nancy and Woos will have $235.00 coming to them. They have saved every cent of their wages. That is doing well for them."[26] In fact the family considered selling their old home to one of their former servants, retaining the land and certain farming utensils, and thus being entitled to one third of the crop.[27]

As Southerners commenced rebuilding their dismantled railroad system, blacks quickly found remunerative employment in construction work. A railroad superintendent lauded the industry of his Negro employees, calling them the very best of workers. They were "always willing, zealous, and faithful," he maintained, "and will work very hard and in the most disagreeable labor for any one who treats them well."[28] Considerable numbers of planters and businessmen considered blacks much more reliable than white laborers.[29]

"A Heavy Leavin' of Slaves"

Not all Southerners applauded the behavior of their former "hands" after the war. A decidedly different scene from those described above took place on other farms or plantations where blacks took off with the wind, convinced that they were not truly free until they had left their plantations and taken on a new name other than their masters' surname. Just days before Appomattox as rumors of their impending freedom spread throughout the slave quarters on the farms and plantations around Richmond, blacks migrated en masse to the cities or simply abandoned all work entirely, awaiting the land and mules they were sure would be supplied by their Yankee saviors. Elvira Seddon, the eldest daughter of James Seddon, Secretary of War, CSA, wrote from her home in Goochland County, Virginia, of the visit from a neighbor announcing that "his servants had stopped all work." Alarmed at the situation, the neighbor called his people together and told them "they might work or not, just as they pleased, but that in one thing he was determined and that was that they should not remain on the place unless willing to support themselves." Elvira continued her account with: "I heard this morning that all his able-bodied men left last night. Dr. Walker's have behaved in a similar manner. Our's will soon go do likewise, no doubt."[30]

Two days later on April 6, 1865, Elvira reported that three of their men had left. Yet another neighbor complained that twelve had taken off from their place "taking with them every horse left on the place." By this time Elvira was envisioning a fate far worse than the departure of their slaves. "I feel perfectly indifferent to their movements. So many misfortunes are crowding upon us now that the loss of negroes is comparatively unimportant. If choosing to remain to perform the most menial offices of the establishment, we shall feel thankful; if not, I suppose we can find white labor. At all events we have our own hands, and we must turn them to account."[31]

Three days later Elvira observed that "Several negroes had taken their departure from this place and others from each of the neighboring farms. We were not surprised. There is no accounting for their conduct." Later she added: "Poor deluded creatures! Little do they know the fate which awaits them."[32] A Kentucky woman confessed "It is hard to judge them. I believe slavery is best for them, but I can't expect them to think so. And I reckon after all if I were a Negro I would be running off too."[33]

In associating the plantations with their debilitating years of slavery and fearing entrapment and re-enslavement by their former owners, many blacks swarmed to the towns convinced that "freedom was free-er" there. Later the appearance of the vigilante groups and the Ku Klux Klan prompted still other blacks to become suspicious of their former owners and also sent them scurrying to the cities. As a result, according to Eric Foner, "Between 1865 and 1870 the black population of the South's ten largest cities doubled, while the number of white residents rose by only ten percent."[34]

A Norfolk, Virginia, woman described the exodus from the plantations. "Slaves were runned from the plantation 'dout nothin' but us han's, no house to shelter us, and no food. We jes' had to make hit de best dat we could. Dis, you see, caused mo' crime 'specially stealin' 'mong us slaves. Dis caused a heavy leavin' of slaves after freedom from de country to flocking to dem large cities and towns lookin' fer wurk in order to get a livin'. Many hired dem selves to po' white farmers fer little or no wages to wurk on de farm as a wash woman and whatever she could do."[35]

Despite their inability to find work and their crowded, squalid living conditions, countless blacks sought a new, different life in towns which offered churches, possibly schools, and often Freedmen's Bureau offices. Eliza Frances Andrews deplored the casual attitude of the Yankees in tearing down the temporary shanties erected by the newly freed Negroes. Seeking protection from the elements the freedmen, thanks to their indifferent treatment by the Yankees, were forced to live out in the open air with only tree branches, a blanket, or a lean-to of boards stashed against a wall for shelter. As might be expected their miserable poverty and the deplorable huts and shanties knocked together for housing served to contribute to the soaring crime rates. "I hate to go into the street, because in doing so I have to pass that scene of wretchedness and vice,"

Eliza wrote. "They live by stealing—and worse. Everybody in the neighborhood suffers from their depredations." As a true Southerner Eliza, of course, believed the Negroes had received far better treatment under the protective aegis of their former owners. "I wonder the Yankees do not shudder to behold their work."[36]

Rather than congregating in the towns and cities where opportunities for work were considerably diminished, freedmen were repeatedly urged by the military, the Freedmen's Bureau, and their former owners to return to the plantations where work was plentiful. Roaming off to crowded areas usually resulted in disappointment for the blacks, and in congested areas, vagrants were picked up by the police and jailed despite the fact that they had committed no offense.

Soon this floating population and the proliferation of shantytowns peopled by transients or by newly freed men and women, some working odd jobs, others simply exulting in their freedom and refusing to return to the confines and minuscule remuneration of plantation work, gave rise to vagrancy laws and apprenticeship laws. Under the vagrancy laws blacks—and whites—found to be with no lawful employment or business could be imprisoned or fined. The apprenticeship laws involved attempts to bolster a flagging labor supply, as well as to provide homes for dependent Negro children. The laws, passed by white legislatures, stipulated that orphan children of freedmen must be apprenticed out to "some competent and suitable person" until in the case of males they reached the age of twenty-one or in the case of females until eighteen. In April of 1866 Narcissa Black, for example, told of going to court to have a sixteen year old former slave bound to her for five years. One man bragged that he had hired two freed men and eight bound apprentices who were required to serve from two to eighteen years, and added "so in some degree I am a slave holder yet."[37] As a result of the apprenticeship laws hundreds of black orphans were sent North. Many Negroes, Whitelaw Reid observed, experienced a more difficult time after emancipation than before as they were constantly "trusted less, and watched more."[38]

"Most of Those Who Left Have Returned"

As would be expected, blacks exulted in their newly acquired freedom. All too often, however, there was great confusion between freedom from slavery and freedom from work of any kind. One black considered "no man free who had to work for a living."[39]

"The field negroes are in a dreadful state," a South Carolina woman complained. "They will not work, but either roam the country, or sit in their houses. At first they all said they were going, but have changed their minds now. Pa has a plan to propose to them by which they are to pay Grand Pa so much for the hire of the land and houses; but they will not come up to hear it. I do not see how we are to live in this country without any rule or regulation. We are afraid now to walk outside of the gate." A few sentences later she added, "The negroes are in the most lawless and demoralized state imaginable. If this is what the Yankee intended they have made their work complete. We have to keep everything under lock and key, and can call nothing our own now."[40] Theft was not always based on need, an ex-slave chuckled. It was as much for the fun of fooling Ole Massa as anything else. "We stole so many chickens that if a chicken would see a darkey he'd run right straight to the house."[41]

In the fall of 1865, upon their return from their refugee home in Tyler, Texas, to Lamar County, Texas, where Kate's mother had quartered an overseer and one hundred thirty slaves, the Stones "found nearly all the Negroes in a state of insubordination, insolent and refusing to work. Mamma had a good deal of trouble with them for a few days. Now they have quieted down and most of those who left have returned, and they are doing as well as 'freedmen' ever will, I suppose. We were really afraid to stay on the place for the first two days." Kate continued, "Our future is appalling—no money, no credit, heavily in debt, and an overflowed place. No wonder Mamma is so discouraged."[42]

Elizabeth Allston Pringle told of the tense moments when her mother was greeted with threatening crowds of their former bondsmen as she attempted to regain the keys to her barns which in her absence the Federal officers had taken from the overseer and given to the Negroes. Fortunately a serious confrontation and possible violence was avoided. Elizabeth's mother kept her cool, spoke familiarly with members of the hostile throng, and eventually the tension lifted and the keys were returned to her.[43]

Naturally the whole concept of freedom was confusing to formerly enslaved blacks. Not surprisingly they sought to emulate their role models and what they saw as their former owners' life of travel, partying, and leisure. Inexperienced in handling money, having had their work and almost every aspect of their lives dictated to them since birth, the dazed, bewildered freed men, devoid of land, tools, skills, money or credit, were at a loss to know how to handle their emancipation.

Actually how could any realist possibly expect anything less than chaos at the end of the war? Four million former slaves suddenly found themselves free to work, to not work, to challenge employers, to go to school, to travel, to live where and as they wished and with whom they wished, to own property, to frolic, to purchase guns and liquor, to attend a church of their own choice. The erratic behavior of millions of blacks could scarcely be condemned. Told that their owners' land would be divided and awarded to them, threatened by rumors that if they returned to their masters they would be shot; told that they were entitled to the crops they essentially had produced, reminded of the sins of their owners in holding them in bondage, blacks felt righteous in wanton acts of theft and seizure of property. No wonder blacks by the thousands dropped their hoes in the fields and fled to the cities in order to escape cruel owners and to seek a better life in a new environment. Even many of those who remained on the plantations were reluctant to return to the arduous work of raising cotton.

Understandably, as a Mississippi woman pointed out, the newly freed men and women anticipated at least a modicum of recognition and adamantly refused to submit to their former rules of labor, or to passively follow their employers' directions. "They gave the employers to understand that it was their turn now; the whites had had their day, and they were ready to fight for their rights; they possessed their freedom and would have equality."[44] Most longed for a little land of their own on which to raise food for themselves and their families.

A fortunate few ex-slaves were given land to farm on their own by their former owners. At the time of the surrender, Frank Durr, a former slave of E. A. Durr, of Marion, Mississippi, recalled that he had accumulated about two hundred dollars, his savings from his work and yearly gifts from his owner. When his former owner informed him that he was free and urged him to get a home of his own, Frank turned over his two hundred dollar nest egg in return for part of Mr. Durr's plantation and two months later settled in on his own land. Taught to read and write by his former master, he was thus able to manage his affairs with remarkable success.[45]

Amanda Stone rewarded one of the Negroes who had faithfully cared for their Louisiana home during the Stones' refugee sojourn in Texas with a plot of land rent free.[46] A North Carolina planter divided up his 5,000 acre estate and gave each of his former slaves who remained with him a specific plot to work on his own. In addition to his regular wages each worker was given time to work his own fields.[47]

Over the years a few grateful former slave owners made provisions in their wills for land to be given over to their servants. In her will a Louisiana woman deeded several hundred acres of her land to her former servants "to give them a start in life."[48] At his death William Lee's former master gave him forty acres, four hundred dollars, and the overseer's house. A Virginia woman's former owner saw to it in his will that his Negroes were given much of his land including the mill, the blacksmith shop and other buildings. "He give some to all o' dem. My mother 'herited dis lan' from him. It's 100 acres. Some niggers got 150, 200, er 250 acres each."[49] Some blacks reported that although they were given land "some of de po' white trash took it away from de slaves."[50]

"Our Negroes Will Never Be as They Were Before"

Emancipation and the problem of what to do about millions of formerly enslaved freed blacks (about one third of the South's population) proved equally baffling to both Southern and Northern whites—as well as to the newly freed men and women themselves. Harriet Palmer surveyed the situation with alarm. "The institution of slavery is ruined. If we ever get through this terrible war, our negroes will never be as they were before." And "What is to become of us?" she queried. "Truly the Yankees could not have adopted a more effective way of ruining us than they have done by filling the negroes with all sorts of nonsense of freedom and going to live in the islands."[51]

Freedom, of course, was an entirely new concept for newly freed slaves. Years later Nettie Henry, of Meridian, Mississippi, recalled in an interview for the WPA Writers' Project: "After deh Surrender, niggers got mighty biggity. Most of 'em was glad jes to feel free. Dey didn't have no better sense. Dey forgot wouldn't nobody to take care of 'em. Things wasn't healthy, an my mother an me kep close to our white folks.... I don't know how come things got so unnatchel after deh Surrender. Niggers got to doing all kinds of things what deh Lord didn intend 'em for, like being policemen an all like dat. Hit was *scan'lous*. Course, hit was deh Yankees done hit. Dey promise to give ever' one of 'em forty acres an a mule, an a lot of 'em didn have no better sense than to believe hit, and go ahead an do whut deh Yankees tell 'em."[52]

Fortunately, at least a few residents of Meridian were willing to rent land to blacks, and Nettie Henry recalled that her family "lived nice, on land rented from white owners." As was true of whites, Nettie's black family had a difficult time without horses or plows, these having been carried off by Yankees. "But we dug up deh grown wid a grubbin hoe an raise pun'kins an plenty of chickens an ever'thing.... An my white people was good white people, wasn't brutish.... I don't know nothin bout no meanness."[53] Simon Hare epitomized the turmoil experienced by many of the Lauderdale County, Mississippi, freed people and confessed to a WPA interviewer: "Come de Surrender, de colored folks had a bad time.

Didn' know how ter make a trade no more'n nothin'. Didn' have nothin', not even a hat." There were mixed feelings about emancipation and the integrity of their former owners, Simon recalled. "Some was glad ter be free, some was sorry because dey was wuss off, work a year an' git nothin.'" Once Simon's master told them they were free, "he didn' do nothin' mo fer us. Colored folks didn' have sense enough ter know how ter get on, wasn' use ter doin' fer deyse'fs. Had a bad time."[54]

"A Mutual Distrust Exists Between Them"

Some Southerners and most Northerners accepted—or in the case of the latter advocated—the eradication of slavery. Yet millions of racists, as well as seemingly unbiased citizens (and even abolitionists in both sections of the country) were radically opposed to making voters, jurors, government officials, fellow workers, or social equals of the freedmen. Millions of Northerners shared the racial biases of their former foes.

A lengthy analysis of racial prejudices here would be futile; they are still to be overcome. And the Federal government's successes in establishing the freedman's equality with the white man in society—to legislate equality through amendments and civil rights acts—also involves countless tomes. By the war's end—and, of course, well before—prejudice existed on the part of both blacks and whites. Southern whites looked upon their former slaves with contempt and apprehension while newly freed blacks eyed whites with fear and suspicion.

Assistant Commissioner of Freedmen's Bureau Rufus Saxton summed up the situation saying: "I think that the former slaveholders know really less about the freedmen than any other class of people." Slavery involved concealment of emotions and attitudes by the Negro slave and resulted in a general proclivity for deceit on numerous occasions. "The freedman has no faith in his former master, nor has his former owner any faith in the capacity of the freedman. A mutual distrust exists between them."[55] Cornelia Hancock also commented on the antagonisms of both parties. "You can lay this down as a law, the Rebels are as mean as they can possibly be and the Freedmen are ignorant as they possibly can be except their instincts (which are always good) and with the two conflicting elements you may know there can be no flattering state of affairs."[56]

"Our country is in a deplorable condition," Anna Maria Green wrote. "Many fear a war of races, and indeed it seems impossible for the white men to submit to negro rule.... It is certainly a distressing state of affairs when negroes hold conventions in our state and indeed have every right of suffrage and civil power. Men look ominously at one another and wonder what the times will bring forth. And poverty and ruin stalk through the land. Military despotism our only authority."[57]

Mutual distrust naturally bred the suspicions and rumors which gave rise to the racial unrest which pervaded the era. Over the years inestimable numbers of freed blacks were assaulted or murdered for attempting to leave plantations, for disputing contracts, for entering white churches, or for not stepping off sidewalks to allow white pedestrians to pass. In Memphis and New Orleans in 1866 widespread racial riots erupted in violence and death. (The Memphis riot is considered to be the first modern race riot in the United States.) In the Memphis riot, although only one white man was injured (other sources indicate two white men died), forty-six Negroes were killed and more than eighty were wounded. In the New Orleans riots four white men died and ten were injured; quite a contrast to the thirty-four Negroes killed and more than two hundred injured. (The numbers killed and wounded in the New Orleans riot vary slightly according to different sources.[58] Despite poorly kept records, clearly more blacks were victims of racial unrest than whites, for, of course, efforts to meet violence with violence on the part of blacks found them seriously outnumbered in men and arms.)[59]

Black-white confrontations in towns and throughout countryside, although less cataclysmic than full blown riots, were common occurrences, and most women's diaries made note of at least one or more outbreaks of racial violence. Within weeks after Appomattox, Gertrude Thomas recorded details of a riot in Augusta, Georgia, initiated by Confederate soldiers embittered by defeat and fearful of the Yankee troops of occupation that were about to descend upon the city. As the soldiers were breaking into stores and making off with their plunder, blacks seized the opportunity to threaten to burn down houses, and before the violence could be put down it had cost the lives of two men.[60]

Louisa McCord Smythe was shocked by the violence in the Charleston area. Envisioning the omnipresent threat of confrontations, she protested: "The riots in the streets were frequent and the alarms more so. Some terrible things happened. Young men of our acquaintance were beaten to death in the streets by negroes. At the slightest alarm, apparently without a word, the streets would be filled by 'our men' each with his gun in his hand and we never knew when the whole city would be bathed in blood." Despite the appalling behavior of some blacks, Louisa Smythe had high praise for several Negroes whom she credited with saving her and her husband from serious injury upon several occasions. She sympathized with blacks that she adjudged "to be in a pitiful position between two fires. They knew that their interest and their affections lay with the white people, and yet they were so afraid of the turbulent element among their own people that they were obliged often to pretend to what they didn't feel."[61]

Typical of the era's racial unrest was the 1871 riot in Meridian, Mississippi, during which thirty blacks lost their lives. Nettie Henry described the rioting to a WPA Writers' Project interviewer. "Well, things kep on getting badder and badder.... An things got so bad, deh *Kloo*-Kluxes started ridin at night and '*sposin*' of bad niggers." Violence erupted when, following the burning of a store, several blacks "doin' devilment" were arrested and accused (falsely, according to Nettie) of starting the fire. A confrontation arose with each race accusing the other of lighting the fire. In the courtroom two days later tempers flared and a riot broke out when the judge was accidentally shot and killed, allegedly by one of the black men on trial. "Then ever'thing buss loose." As darkness came on the blacks returned to their quarters. Later that night Nettie and her owners, peeping around from behind the curtains, saw "all deh show'nough white men come marchin out Seventh Street on deh way to dey quarter...." A small army of whites (perhaps Klanners) were seeking to lynch the Carpetbag mayor. "Hit didn sound like no ever'day marching; hit sound like judgment day.... I spec Seventh Street was lined wid women folks doin jes whut we was doin, cause most of em's husbands an sons an sweethearts was out there in dat march-line." That night and in the ensuing hours five Negroes were lynched; still more were to be killed in the several days of rioting and hunting down of Negroes. Only when it was promised that the mayor would leave town did the trouble subside.[62]

Racial troubles touched off "a great state of excitement," according to Betty Beaumont, with the murder of a white man in his store near Woodville, Mississippi. A search for the killers (supposedly blacks who had been goaded by labor leaders to avenge the wrongs suffered during their enslavement) brought throngs of infuriated white men to the Woodville area, and in very short order the town was deserted by the freedmen who fled to the woods for safety. Farming came to a standstill as their pursuers scoured the area for the fugitive murderers. Frightened mothers and wives thronged Mrs. Beaumont's hotel as they took refuge from what was threatening to explode into a violent confrontation. Finally after several days of rioting and suspense the passions of both blacks and whites simmered down and fortunately life returned to normal once again.[63]

"Slavery Degrades the White Man More Than the Negro"

The legacy of white supremacy was not easily uprooted. Most Southerners were convinced that blacks were childlike, ignorant, uncivilized, and improvident. In New Orleans at an Independence Day celebration in 1866 the mayor, speaking from the grandstand prior to the reading of the Declaration of Independence, made his stand clear (a view held by countless Southerners) that "he differed from one expression of opinion in that document to the effect that all men were created equal. The nigger could not be considered the equal of the white man; and as the writer of the Declaration, Mr. Jefferson, was a slaveholder, it stood to reason that he could not have meant to include the nigger in that assertion."[64]

A Freedmen's Bureau officer succinctly summarized the postwar attitudes of countless former slaveowners toward the newly freedmen in noting that although "they have a kind of affection for him as an old servant…they have direct hostility to him as now being in the condition of a freedman claiming the rights of a freeman."[65]

Southerners were irate, to say the least, at having their former slaves (most of them unskilled and illiterate by virtue of antebellum laws that

"Whipping a Negro Girl in North Carolina by 'Unreconstructed' Johnsonians."
(*Harper's Weekly*, September 14, 1867.)

prohibited the educating of slaves) suddenly being catapulted into situations which completely reversed the former master-slave relationship. To be compelled to accept ex-slaves as legislators, public office holders, and as social equals was anathema to most Southerners. Schooling blacks was viewed as arming them with potentially dangerous power. Schooling blacks and whites together, of course, was unthinkable. Making voters of freedmen (with the passage of the Fifteenth Amendment), while Southern men, as a result of their participation in the war, were deprived the franchise added fuel to an already smoldering situation.

Southerners were horrified by the fraternization of white girls with black soldiers, and a black-white marriage was totally abhorrent. However, more than one Southern woman questioned the morality of the ubiquitous prewar black-white, master-slave sexual relationships. In the eyes of many Southern men their antebellum intimate relationships with their female slaves were an acceptable aspect of Southern manhood. (In most cases children of a white planter and a black slave were sold or willed to offspring by the plantation owner as readily as non-related blacks.) However, the *marriage* of a white male to his black mistress resulted in a public outcry. Probably, as Gertrude Thomas mused, that because of miscegenation "Southern women are I believe all at heart abolitionists ... the institution of slavery degrades the white man more than the Negro...."[66]

Although she very definitely disapproved of "mixed marriages," Gertrude Thomas, as did a few of her contemporaries, morally questioned the generally pervasive *acceptance* of a white Southern male's sexual activities with his black slave as contrasted with the public's *outrage* at the marriage of an owner and his black slave. Stirred by the public wrath in the case of the marriage of a white man and his mulatto slave, Gertrude Thomas wrote of the father of the bridegroom: "I can well understand his horror of that kind of marriage. I can appreciate his feeling perfect antipathy to having negro blood mingle in the veins of his descendants but I cannot understand his feeling of indifference to having that same blood flowing through the veins of a race of descendants held in perpetual slavery—perhaps by other men."[67]

Basic to Southerners' distrust and suspicion of their former slaves, no doubt, was their incessant fear of being overpowered by blacks. Long before the war, Southerners had agonized over the very real potential of a Negro uprising. In most Southern states, particularly in Mississippi and South Carolina where in some areas blacks outnumbered whites seven to one, the threat of an insurrection was a constant companion. Now as power increased for the blacks, fear of a possible rebellion intensified among the whites. In antebellum years blacks were forbidden to own guns and slave quarters were searched regularly for the presence of weapons. Once the bans were lifted, many blacks made a firearm one of their first acquisitions. After the war in many areas arms were freely sold to the freedmen and as members of the militia former slaves were even provided with guns and trained in their use. This, of course, struck fear in the hearts of millions of property owners, especially lone women, where the potential for an uprising was not treated lightly. One frightened female explained in her journal, "The negroes are exhibiting such a degree of excitement over their freedom that I feel very uneasy at our being in a house alone. I have made James, Valley's father [former servants] grind a carving knife down until it has assumed the shape of a dagger. This I will keep about me and use it if necessary ... if I should be called upon to defend myself against the insult of a negro...."[68]

"Only to Find Themselves Where They Started"

With good reason, newly freed blacks grew increasingly suspicious of whites. Not a few slaves continued to be held in bondage long after the war, their owners refusing to inform them that they were free. Interviews with former slaves in the WPA Federal Writers' Project revealed that seventeen percent of those who testified to their masters' actions at the end of the war charged their former owners with deliberately prolonging slavery.[69] One such deception involved a young girl who was kept enslaved for six years after the war.[70] A Georgia planter kept his black workforce in bondage until the fall of 1865.[71] (Probably until after the cotton crop was harvested.) Some heartless owners told their former slaves that although they were free their children would be held in bondage until they were twenty-one. A Mississippi man refused to return her daughter to a former slave then residing in Memphis, saying, "As to recognizing the rights of freedmen to their children, I will say there is not one man or woman in all the south who believes they are free, but we consider them as stolen property—stolen by the bayonets of the damnable United States government."[72] While some former owners offered their ex-slaves a choice of remaining on the plantation or leaving in search of new homes and new opportunities, other owners, as noted earlier, viciously kicked, whipped and even fired at newly freedmen who opted to leave. Some newly freedmen were physically restrained by chains at night to prevent their leaving.

Not a few newly freed men were duped by unscrupulous extortionists who hit on a lucrative plan to sell painted sticks to gullible freedmen who were assured that they could drive the stakes into the ground and this would entitle them to any acreage they wished to claim.[73] A Virginia man told of a "bagger" who came to church one day. "Had a badge an' ev'ything. Said de gov'ment sent him. Come walkin' into church one Sunday an' tole de colored people dat he come to see who needed land. 'Course dey all needed it, even de preacher. Opened up his bag an' showed us all de stakes de gov'ment had give him. Wanted to know where was de secesh land in de county. Well, de next day most ev'body met him out on de lands b'longin' to Marse Jack Turner dat had died in de war. Took out dem pegs an' tole de Negroes to go 'haid pick dere land. Ev'body scrambled to git de bes' pieces, den he tole 'em dey would have to pay one dollar in United States money fo'dey pegs. Some did an' some didn't. Dem dat got de money staked off de land like he said, but it didn't do no good. One day Yankee troops come ridin' out from Richmond lookin' fo' dat 'bagger.' Said he didn't belong to de gov'ment, an' didn't have no right sellin' nollan' or givin' it away. Don't know whether dey caught him or not, but dem colored folks dat had bought stakes sho' was achin' to get dey hands on him."[74]

Some former bondsmen were charged one dollar to have their names registered in Washington, a payment which they were told would enable them to obtain free land. Blacks were cautioned not to mention the charge to anyone as it might endanger their chances of getting their due.[75] Still other opportunists tricked freedmen into paying two dollars each for "land warrants," properties to be awarded them following the Federal government's anticipated confiscation of their former owners' plantations.

Greedy Northern speculators coveting more and more land found the inexperienced Negroes easy prey for their nefarious schemes of plying them with bad whiskey and inducing them to sign over any property they had been given or had bought. Promising to hold the deeds "for safe keeping" or appropriating a deed as payment for some small debt, speculators wrested much of what little property the poor unlettered freedmen might possibly have acquired. An officer told Elizabeth Hyde Botume, "'All the good the Yankee teachers do to the freedmen is neutralized by the harm done to them by the Yankee sharpers.'" "I must confess," Elizabeth declared, "'carpet-baggers' sprang up in this vicinity like caterpillars over the growing cotton-fields. The poor contrabands might well exclaim, 'Save me from friends, and I will take care of the enemy!'"[76] Still other groups, the Ku Klux Klan and other white racist groups, terrorized untold numbers of Negroes who had been granted or were somehow able to purchase land and sought to drive them off of their property in an attempt to return them to their antebellum subservient roles.

Not only were many of the Negroes duped and harassed by white

Southerners, but the later enactment of the various Black Codes, which in some areas prohibited Negroes from owning weapons, selling liquor, preaching without a special license, or traveling without permission from their employers, severely curtailed their rights as free men. Additional restrictions served to exacerbate already fragile black-white relationships.

Freedmen who innocently made major purchases at stores operated by avaricious employers found at the end of the year that they had no money coming, their store bills totaled more than their wages. One student interviewer of former slaves condemned the system saying that despite the fact that slavery had been abolished it was disheartening to see Negroes who would "toil day after day in the fields till the end of the year when they are told by the owners that they are yet in debt—which means that they must toil yet another year, only to find themselves where they started."[77]

"Thrifty Little Farms": The Challenges Facing the Freedmen's Bureau

The Freedmen's Bureau (officially titled the Bureau of Refugees, Freedmen, and Abandoned Lands) instituted by the Federal government in March of 1865, just as the war was closing down, proved a godsend to many formerly enslaved blacks. Designed to help provide food and relief to newly freed blacks (and whites) the Bureau's assignments included protecting and educating the former slaves and readying them for independent, productive lives. In creating the Bureau lawmakers envisioned the process of educating and grooming them for self-sufficiency as necessitating a lengthy period of education for the freedmen and an immense readjustment in attitude on the part of whites. (Overall the activities of the Bureau were viewed by irate white farmers as being biased on behalf of the blacks, while the blacks on the other hand accused the Bureau of favoring whites.) The long range thinking of many Freemen's Bureau officials as well as that of countless other Americans was that the newly freed blacks should be educated and encouraged to develop lives of self-sufficiency rather than remaining permanently dependent on governmental assistance.

As part of their work, Bureau representatives were assigned to oversee the signing of labor contracts in order to prevent the exploitation of blacks by white employers, and also to enforce adherence to the contracts to the benefit of both parties. As might be expected the engineering of the contracts proved to be a tremendous hassle for the Bureau—and for both parties concerned. The stipulations of the contract (signing in the

A representative of the Freedmen's Bureau tries to keep angry crowds apart. (*Harper's Weekly*, July 25, 1868.)

presence of a Bureau official, for example) were particularly annoying to employers when the negotiations necessitated travel to a Bureau office some fifty miles away. Further complications arose when bewildered freedmen, anticipating a future life of leisure with land and money that would be freely distributed by the Federal government, refused to work under any arrangements, and furthermore refused to leave their former owners' property. Wary freedmen resisted signing contracts, convinced that their former masters' lands were soon to be divided up and be made an outright gift to them. (A North Carolina woman's workers need not have waited around for her to parcel out any land. Adamant, to say the least, she confided to journalist Dennett: "One o' my gals, Jane, told me they was to have land given to 'em for themselves. 'Don't think you'll git mine,' I told her, 'for I'll cut your throat first.' Confound her impudence!"[78])

Other freedmen complicated the system by signing by the month rather than for the year. Bureau officials urged Negroes who were reluctant to sign contracts to work out agreeable terms with employers, insisting that it was an absurd notion that signing a contract would return them to slavery. Authorities warned, "Your danger lies exactly in the other direction. If you do not have some occupation, you will be treated as vagrants, and made to labor in the public works."[79]

Planters, too, sought help from the Bureau. Frantic employers headed straight to the doors of the Freedmen's Bureau for help with former slaves who were unwilling to work or who ignored contracts and walked off in the middle of the hoeing or picking season. The following exchange perhaps best epitomizes the plight of untold numbers of planters throughout the South. At his wit's end in trying to cope with his former slaves who would not work and whom he could not feed, one planter begged for help from the Freedmen's Bureau. "Well," the government official responded. "simply run 'em off." "But they won't leave," the planter declared. "Well, then take them to court," the official advised. "Oh, but we have no courts!" the planter soberly reminded him. On another occasion an official's advice met with derision when he advised a disgruntled employer that the only solution to his situation was to sue the delinquent worker. "Sue him!" the employer scoffed, "He ha'nt got nothing to collect on."[80] In time a Montgomery planter had reached the boiling point: "I have a large plantation on the Alabama river. I have seventy-five negroes; they are all free, and, damn 'em I can't drive 'em off my place. They are hanging around, eating up all I have. I threatened to shoot them if they didn't leave; but they won't go. I had eighty-seven shoats; they have eat up eighty of them.... Damn 'em, I believe I *will* shoot 'em when I get back. A few days ago I told a number of the boys I would shoot them if they didn't leave. Said they, 'Where shall we go?' Said I 'I don't care if you go to hell.'"[81]

Once the contracts were signed the Freedmen's Bureau's next most challenging job was seeing that the contracts were upheld, that is, attempting to resolve the incessant complaints of blacks against whites (primarily cases of the blacks' inability to collect back wages from whites) and the repeated accusations of whites against blacks involving the division of crops and failure to abide by their contracts. Employers, as proof of their loyalty to the United States government, were to have taken the Oath of Allegiance before appealing for help from an officer of the Freedmen's Bureau. That stipulation alone (sometimes although not everywhere enforced) served to encourage former Rebels to take the oath.

The Freedmen's Bureau's insistence upon contracts did not always solve the problems of the workers, for some dishonest employers "padded" the charges for food, clothing, and doctor's bills to be deducted from the freedmen's wages. Cornelia Hancock, a New Jersey Quaker who served as a nurse during the war and stayed to become a teacher of freedmen in South Carolina, was thoroughly disheartened as she listened to the endless stories of poor, illiterate blacks being cheated out of their earnings by greedy landowners. "The rascality that has been practiced upon the Freedmen by the northern Speculators, unjust Bureau Officers, etc., beggars all description. Mr. Bowen, the colored people's advocate, tells me of much that is going on upon the islands. The friction of the wickedness in this world I wonder does not take fire and consume it." Cornelia Hancock expressed a wish voiced by millions. "How I wish the Government had apportioned them some confiscated land at the close of the war. Had that been done, by this time [1868] thrifty little farms would have been the result." Instead, she wrote, the planters were mercilessly taking advantage of the blacks and leaving them penniless.[82] Officials were particularly irate over proprietors who secured their part of the crop and then called in the Ku Klux Klan or other racist groups to frighten the freedmen into leaving the area with only one tenth of their rightful share.

Unscrupulous farmers found themselves considerably advantaged over their helpless employees in their control of wages or crop divisions, their operation of "company stores," or their esoteric bookkeeping. Marcus Hopkins and thousands like him were incensed by the outrages and swindling being committed by whites against the blacks. As a civilian officer in the Freedmen's Bureau in Virginia in 1868 he found himself besieged with complaints of freedmen unable to collect pay for their work, their employers seeking to line their own pockets by refusing to pay their laborers the wages promised.[83]

Unfortunately, mathematics was a problem for the newly freed blacks, many of whom considered one-sixth of the crop a better deal than one-third of the crop, and employers often took advantage of this miscalculation.[84] Other freedmen under contract for "half the crop" were convinced that if six days' work a week would raise a full crop then certainly three days' work was all that was needed to raise half a crop.[85] In the case of Mrs. Gordon Pryor Rice, of Charlotte County, Virginia, it was her husband who came out on the little end of the deal. When her husband's renter failed to allot Mr. Rice his fourth of the crop, Mr. Rice inquired, "'Where's my fourth, Joe?' 'You ain' got no forth, suh,' was the reply; 'Der warn' but three waggin loads.'"[86]

Some scheming landowners cheated their workers by setting up what amounted to "company stores" and sold goods—and whiskey—to their workers. All too often freedmen ran up debts that negated their shares in the crop to the end of the year and therefore they were eager to move off to another plantation and cease "working for a dead horse."[87]

"The Land Was Theirs, They Had Toiled on It All Their Lives"

On his tour of the South as a reporter for *The Nation* John Richard Dennett was invited by General Ely, chief officer of the Freedmen's

Bureau in northern South Carolina, to accompany him on one of his visits to towns in his district. The excursion was an eye opener for Dennett who could observe firsthand the confusion and complaints from whites and blacks, laborers and employers over land and contracts. The turmoil of the times was reflected in the rampant racism, violence, and disorganization that characterized the district. One of their first stops was with a woman in a log cabin where the self-sufficient woman and her husband lived in almost complete isolation. The "problem solvers" found it rough going to appease the couple. They had lost all of their black workers and the woman was ostensibly "mighty glad of it." She wished "the niggers had been at the bottom o' the sea."[88]

One poor mulatto told General Ely of having been strung up three times by a Federal officer and members of the home guard on rumors that he was in possession of a gun belonging to the government. Despite the man's consistent denials that he had a weapon, the men continued their demonic pursuits. The man feared for his life as a result of his having brought his complaint to Bureau Chief Ely; however, he admitted as he began to cry, "I hasn't got anything in the world but myself, for I hasn't got any family, nor any parents, nor any land, nor any money, and I know I is not to be any worse off in the grave than I is now." The case was referred to the proper authorities, and at the same time investigations were also ordered into two other reports of hangings in the area.[89]

Throughout the trip Ely was showered with questions from employers and employees concerning "rights and duties," and his previously announced talk to the freedmen at Edgefield village was enthusiastically attended by some two thousand blacks. As a Freedmen's Bureau mediator, Ely explained to his audience that they would not be given land by the Federal government, but instead they must work and earn the money to buy land. The Negro and the planter needed each other, he pointed out, and through honesty and hard work the Negro could considerably improve his situation. However, workers should be cautious, Ely reminded them, in signing a contract, and once the worker has signed he must conscientiously abide by the terms agreed upon.[90]

In many areas the Freedmen's Bureau dicta were law, and failure to comply with the Bureau's regulations could quickly land an employer or householder in jail. One Columbia, South Carolina, woman protested that the choice for many citizens lay between "protecting the lives of yourself and family and going to the nearest county jail." She further observed: "Scarce a day passes that we do not hear of some white person in trouble."[91]

Yet another important function of the Bureau was to furnish transportation for Negroes to help them in returning to their home plantations, to assist them in finding profitable employment, or to enable them to reunite with family members who had been sold and moved to distant areas. The latter had become an all consuming effort on the part of the newly freed men and women. Following the war, vast numbers of former slaves immediately set about combing the Southland searching for wives and children from whom they had been separated as a result of a sale, a gift, or a bequest by their former owners. Husbands spent weeks and even months walking hundreds of miles to locate their loved ones. One man was known to have walked six hundred miles looking for his wife and children. Nettie Henry explained that her father, owned by a different family from her mother's, had been forced to move with his owner to Texas during the war. Following emancipation, he at once set out to rejoin his wife and children in Meridian, Mississippi, walking "most all deh way frum Texas." Negro newspapers carried ads offering rewards for help in locating family members.[92]

Blacks (and whites) seemed to be constantly on the move. The *Nation*, in December, 1865, pointed out that "more than one thousand Negroes monthly were in transit through Columbia, S. C." By 1866 in an attempt to curtail travel for pleasure rather than for a more permanent reuniting of families or gainful employment, the Bureau began placing considerably greater restrictions on travel.

Scores of additional headaches for the Bureau presented themselves. Problems involving the eviction of blacks from their former owners' property confounded the owners, the Bureau, and the blacks. Southerners who had abandoned their homes and fled in the face of an enemy attack often discovered upon their return that the freedmen had taken possession of their buildings and fields and were exceedingly reluctant to give up ownership. Some Negroes with the hope of permanent possession had "moved their things to massa's parlor, for to keep it while he's gone."[93] Further complications arose for Confederate soldiers returning from the war who were given explicit orders preventing them from evicting freedmen who were raising a crop on their property. Furthermore former slaves who had planted a crop were entitled to "full compensation for their labor."[94]

Hosts of observers, including Elizabeth Hyde Botume, Mary Ames, and Margaret Thorpe, described the almost insurmountable difficulties of returning the abandoned lands in South Carolina, Georgia, and Florida to their white owners after the war. The Bureau's attempts to "reconcile conflicting interests" served basically to exacerbate the antagonism between their ex-slaves and the returning white owners. Sherman's Special Field Order No. 15 setting aside land "for the benefit of refugees and freedmen that had been congregated by the operations of war, or had been left to take care of themselves by former owners" had led the ex-slaves to believe that the land was permanently entrusted to them. Much of the Sea Island land had been divided up and allotted to Negroes; therefore the return of the former owners to reclaim their property created an ever increasing distrust on the part of the freedmen.[95]

The change from slaves, to squatters, to freed men and women, and now to evictees involved cataclysmic changes for the former slaves. Mary Ames, working for the Freedmen's Bureau in 1865, reported in her diary that it took a visit from General Saxton and General Howard to disperse the freedmen who had taken over the homes of their former owners on Edisto Island. General Howard spoke to the people, telling them that "the owners of the land, their old masters, had been pardoned, and their plantations were to be given back to them; that they wanted to come back and cultivate the land, and would hire the blacks to work for them."[96] The announcement met with great outbursts of "No, never!" and "Can't do it!" In some areas the former owners were met by parties of forty or more Negroes armed with guns and threatening to kill owners who returned to repossess their property.[97]

On the Warren plantation on the York River, Margaret Thorpe, one of the scores of "Yankee teachers" who journeyed south to teach blacks after the war, paid a special visit to the freedmen still living on the Warren Farm. Having been ordered to move away within the month, the blacks were immensely distressed as to where they could go. "We told them Mr. Warren did not want them to live any longer on this land, and that they will find places provided at Yorktown where they can stay until they decided where they wish to live, but they declared they would not move, the land was theirs, they had toiled on it all their lives, without wages. The Union soldiers had told them they might remain there as long as they lived."[98]

The freedmen found their eviction difficult to comprehend. Surely, they argued, they were entitled to the land, their just due after a lifetime of service. Margaret Thorpe admitted that she too had difficulty in persuading them—or herself—of the justice of the order. "Where is the compensation for years of toil, for they have nothing to show save hardened hands and scarred backs?" Margaret asked. "Where the compensation for the children that were torn from their parents arms, and sold to the fiendish slave-driver? Where the compensation for the men and women whom God had joined, torn apart and beaten because they wept? Where the compensation for the mothers who saw their daughters sold to a fate infinitely worse than death? And Oh! is there a woman on earth who thinks aught can compensate those young girls?"[99]

And yet as much as the Yankee teachers empathized with the dispossessed blacks they found themselves torn by sympathy for the returning owners now despoiled of all their property and possessions. Although some managed to regain their property "others went into small dwellings and hired houses. Their property had been confiscated, and their possessions scattered. They had neither houses nor furniture nor servants. Many ladies most delicately reared were obliged to take up menial service. With all our hearts we pitied them and deplored their misfortunes."[100]

Following the war when the Daniel Hunts deemed it safe to return to their home in Ripley, Mississippi, they found their two "servants," in whose care the home had been left, adamant in their refusal to give up the house. Earlier the Hunts, fearing a Yankee takeover, had left their plantation for safer territory. Hoping to save their home from being torched by the Federals they had placed Uncle Tom and Aunt Tildy in charge of cooking and caring for the Union officers who would overrun the property. The Hunts' return and claim to their home infuriated Uncle Tom, who insisted that "This is my house; I saved it, and I don't give it up!" In gratitude that the house had indeed been saved, and to avoid trouble with the former servants and with the Federal officials, the Hunts "built the Negro a very nice house and barn and gave him 10 acres of land."[101]

In addition to the staggering problems with freedmen over property rights the Freedmen's Bureau and the Federal government also found themselves embroiled in ownership battles with irate Confederates who returned to find their homes and lands occupied by white Northerners. In their absence, while refugeeing in safer parts of the country or during their service with the military, owners discovered their land had been confiscated and sold or leased by the Federal Treasury Department as "abandoned property." In order to recover their property owners were forced to appeal to the courts and/or pay an inflated amount of back taxes. Many of those unable to come up with necessary funds watched helplessly as their property was sold at auction for ridiculously paltry sums.[102]

"A Perfect Nuisance"

Workers for the Freedmen's Bureau wore many hats as "judges," "problem solvers," "advisors," "listening ears." Yet despite their valiant efforts to ameliorate differences and correct injustices their personal relationships with native Southerners were for the most part disastrous. Southerners, as might well be expected, were less than enthusiastic about the Freedmen's Bureau. Blacks, people were convinced, were being awarded preferential treatment while whites were being relegated to the status of second class citizens. An article in the *New Orleans Daily Picayune* of March 4, 1866, castigated the Bureau and its operations: "for all practical purposes, to harmonize the races, promote restoration of order and the revival of industry and prosperity, its operations and influence are worse than vain and useless: they are in the highest degree irritating, anarchical and oppressive. Nothing would go further to promote the general peace, good order and prosperity of the South than the abandonment of the whole scheme."

Mary Custis Lee, wife of General Lee, was certainly not alone in denouncing the presence of the Freedmen's Bureau. In a letter written in May of 1866 from Lexington, Virginia, she declared: "We are all here dreadfully plundered by the lazy idle negroes who lounge about the streets doing nothing but looking what they may plunder during the night. We have been raided on twice already but fortunately they did not get a great deal either time—But all thru' the country the people are robbed nearly as much as they were during the war—& they can illy afford to lose any thing now. When we are got rid of the freedmen's Bureau & can take the law in our hands we may perhaps do better—If they would only take their pets North it would be a happy riddance."[103]

In 1866 President Johnson's veto of the Freedmen's Bureau Bill calling for the extension of the life of the Bureau was applauded by most Southerners. The New Orleans *Daily Picayune* noted that "throughout this State the contacts between the planters and freedmen for the present year have been made without any regard to the regulations prescribed by the bureau. The freedmen claim the right of making their own contracts, and we do not see how, under the doctrines admitted by all and contended for with so much ardor by the Radicals, this can be denied them. They object to being treated as children or insane persons, incapable of making bargains and regulating their habits, their food, their clothing, the hours they are able to work, and the holidays which they desire. They prefer, too, to settle their disputes with their employers, without the intervention of outsiders and officials, who are too apt to exact fees and compensation for their services. In other words, they are for the application of the principles of free trade to their transactions."[104]

That the Freedmen's Bureau Bill was passed despite the president's veto infuriated most Southerners. Countless ex–Confederates insisted that the Bureau was made up of "meddlesome, envious, suspicious, sectional set of men" existing "not to protect the rights of our citizens, nor to prevent wrongs to the freedmen, but, through false and suborned testimony, to convict honest citizens who are attending to their own affairs, of disloyalty to the Government."[105]

The editorial insisted: "There is not an intelligent, honest citizen in the Southern States, we care not to what party he belongs, who does not regard these military tyrannies at the South—these Freedmen's Bureaux, as they are called—as a perfect nuisance, having nothing whatever to recommend them, either in the aspect of a protection to the black race or the white. This is the unanimous opinion, repeated over and over again by our planters and farmers, and by intelligent visitors all over the South." The writer was convinced that the Bureaux rendered the freedmen uncontrollable, disputatious and unwilling to work.[106]

In his diatribe the writer went on to depict the Freedmen's Bureau as an injurious influence. "The Bureau although organized for protection and benefit to the freedman, has been an injury to him, and has had a demoralizing effect upon both races. The Bureau does much to sow the seeds of suspicion and ill feeling between the freedmen and whites, without affording protection or benefit to the former. The agents are generally men who are totally unacquainted with the character and habits of either the negro or his former master, and consequently do evil to both races when they intend good."[107]

The Bureau was also given a bad press by an officer traveling in the South who, in a report to President Johnson, pictured the deplorable conditions of the itinerant Negroes shacked up along the roadsides under canopies of tree branches—or just stars—awaiting the division of their owners' lands. "Nearly everywhere I learned that the agents of the Freedmen's Bureau had been more energetic to disturb the peace of society than to promote the welfare of the poor wandering colored people."[108]

Disparagers of the Freedmen's Bureau took pride in pointing to the collapse of the Freedmen's Bank that left large numbers of Negroes impoverished and embittered. Although the Bank and the Bureau were separate entities, the involvement of Bureau officials in the creation and perpetuation of the Bank, the endorsement of the Bank by the Bureau, and the zealous support and encouragement given the bank as a safe place for the deposit of freedmen's savings, served to so intertwine the two institutions as to make the Bank almost an auxiliary to the Bureau. Freedmen were repeatedly urged to put their money in "The Freedmen's Savings and Trust Company," which operated thirty-four banks in the South as well as banks in New York, Pennsylvania, and the District of Columbia. Unfortunately, as a result of inexperience on the part of its managers, the general business depression of the time, and the dishonest activities of the District of Columbia "ring," the Bank floundered and finally collapsed in 1874, taking with it the savings of countless distraught freedmen.[109]

Other critics of the Freedmen's Bureau accused it of overstepping the authority of the Federal government in meddling in employer-employee relationships and fostering false hopes among the Negroes about being allotted land and farm animals. Great numbers of people believed the administrators to be incompetent and working to foster the aims of the Republican party. Frequent newspaper editorials chided the Freedmen's Bureau for failing to encourage the ex-slaves to become more self-reliant and to realize that they must "depend on their own merits, and trust to their own efforts for successful rivalry with the rest of the community." An editorial in the New Orleans *Daily Picayune* read: "For these and other good reasons, we regard the existence of the Bureau a positive evil, especially to the freedmen."[110]

Officials of the Freedmen's Bureau almost to a man testified to their exclusion from the society of ex–Confederates. Rarely if ever were they invited into the homes of former secessionists and almost never to the social functions of people in their area. One Northerner told of a Charleston woman who rejoiced in the North-South enmity saying, "she hoped that bitterness would continue; she wished to see it continue to her dying day, and never wanted it obliterated or modified."[111]

An observant Northerner who had become increasingly annoyed with the abuse heaped on Negroes and the Freedmen's Bureau in the press and the open threats to Northerners engaged in cotton production on South Carolina plantations, finally confronted a disgruntled rice planter who was struggling to regain his fortune. "How do you expect to succeed" he asked, "if you continue to abuse the negro, which is your laborer, the northern man, who is your capitalist, and the bureau which is your mediator to arrange your relations with your laborers?"[112]

☙

Despite its detractors the Bureau (before its suspension in 1872) with the help of Northern charitable organizations, such as the American Missionary Association, was responsible for providing both whites and blacks with some 21 million food rations, for finding good homes for countless numbers of war orphans, for establishing greatly needed schools, hospitals and colleges for the newly freed blacks, and for encouraging free elementary education for all Southerners. During its existence the Bureau was credited with spending more than $5 million in helping to establish some 3,000 schools in the South.[113] It was at that time that Fisk, Atlanta, Howard, Morehouse, and Talladega colleges for Negroes were organized.

Unfortunately the efficiency of the Bureau suffered as a result of the overwhelming numbers of people needing aid. Also many Northern (and, of course Southern) whites believed that blacks should be given only temporary help. Their future, it was thought, depended on their own initiative and effort, and that after a reasonable amount of assistance they should become permanently independent of governmental hand-outs.

Overall, the Freedmen's Bureau, questioned by Northerners and universally detested by Southerners, is judged to have been America's first Federal welfare agency. Even during its short life, the experiences of the Bureau provided valuable lessons for what in later years would explode into a multitude of government welfare agencies.

𝔰 4 𝔠

Help
Wanted

𝔰𝔠 As the newly freed men deserted the plantations, flocking in droves to the cities, they left their former owners in dire need of workers to plant, cultivate, and harvest the crops. Want ad columns pleaded for farm workers. The May 12, 1865, issue of the *New Orleans Times*, for example, carried a help wanted ad for fifty white laborers to work on a plantation five miles from New Orleans with the alluring promise of "cash every Saturday night."

Labor shortages became even more critical with the refusal of black women to continue working in the fields. In deploring the sad state of the cotton crop in Mississippi in 1866, an article in the *New Orleans Times* cited the problems of the lack of laborers, particularly female workers. The writer looked back to the years prior to their emancipation when women "were among the most effective and reliable workers." "Few of them are now seen in the fields at all," he pointed out, and in a derogatory tone continued: "They are indulged by their husbands, affect the manner of white ladies, stay at home looking after the children, or, if they go abroad dress as finely as possible. Formerly known only as Dinah or Chloe, they now announce themselves as Mrs. Carter or Mrs. Middleton," until the heat of summer bore on and then "many of them are leaving the farms, wandering about from place to place, hunting job work, and half the idlers are continually stealing and committing trespasses about in the country."[1]

Understandably, freedwomen were extremely anxious to set up housekeeping for themselves and refused to return to field work. Interminable days of backbreaking work under a murderous sun followed by frenzied evenings devoted to preparing meals and tending to the needs of their young children had left them prematurely aged and debilitated.

111

Objecting to the freed women's habitual recourse to feigned or real health problems in order to escape heavy duty work, planters resorted to various strategies to keep women at work in the fields. Issuing different colored tickets to indicate the actual days worked as well as cutting down on rations proved to be effective measures.[2] In time, however, financial necessity sent many women back to work in the fields.

"Thankful to Pay Their Way Back": *Immigration Societies*

When prospects for procuring reliable workers at home appeared dismal, commissioners of immigration were set up in various southern states and money was provided for agents to travel in the North and to Europe to confer with newspaper editors, write articles, and give talks testifying to the tremendous opportunities available in their particular areas.

Land companies based in both New Orleans and New York took out newspaper ads promising to "Sell, Lease, or Rent Cotton Sugar and Farming Lands; also to furnish White Labor (German, Swiss, Irish or English) and Machinery of all kinds and descriptions, such as Cotton Gins, Cotton Mills" and "all kinds of Agricultural Implements too numerous to enumerate. Also, Garden Seed, Fruit and Ornamental Trees of every description."[3] Other entrepreneurs announced themselves agents who were "authorized to sign contracts for the immigration of laborers from India or China."[4]

Sizable newspaper ads were designed to attract large numbers of workers from Asia, Europe, and Canada. In South Carolina immigration societies were organized to try to procure farm workers from Germany and the Scandinavian countries to come to work on the plantations.[5] Unfortunately the new recruits often proved less than satisfactory. One plantation owner hired one hundred German immigrants, and within a matter of weeks thirty-five had deserted.[6] Dr. Esther Hill Hawks reported the disastrous experiment with white labor by an employer who hired fourteen Irishmen for his plantation only to have them leave within a fortnight. "Not one of them could be hired on any terms to remain and work here."[7] When Frances Butler Leigh and her husband imported eight English laborers to work on their plantations, the results proved ruinous. Although one worker remained, at the end of the second year the Leighs "were most thankful to pay their way back to England and get rid of them."[8]

Four years after the war Southerners still entertained the idea of importing Chinese laborers to work in the cotton fields. An appeal in the *New Orleans Times* of September 17, 1869, promised that "...if we can only procure 100,000 Chinamen to help us with the next crop, we shall, with the favor of Heaven, demonstrate that there is life in the old land yet." There was even wishful thinking that many of the Chinese laborers brought from Asia to work on the railroads in California would choose to migrate to the South to replace the black workers. As for enticing Chinese laborers southward Frances Butler (Leigh) explained: "There seemed to be a general move in this direction all through the Southern States, and I have no doubt was only prevented by the want of means of the planters, which, as far as I personally am concerned, I am glad was the case. Just then, however, we were all very keen about it, and it sounded very easy, the Pacific Railway having opened a way for them to reach us."[9]

For numerous reasons efforts to attract large numbers of Asians or Europeans as workers on Southern farms fell far short of expectations. For some possible recruits there was a disinterest in competing with Negroes; for others a dissatisfaction with the climate or with the living conditions, or a fear of the inhospitality of the area's unreconstructed rebels, or a concern over the changing economic conditions.[10]

Southern Hospitality or "Bitterness and Dissent"?

Actually, Southerners were of two minds about enticing Northerners to move South. Desperate for workers, they needed laborers who would work with or even replace their emancipated Negroes. Northern money and industrial expertise they welcomed with open arms but Northerners as competition in farming or business were abhorred.

Enterprising Northerners who journeyed south to take up temporary or permanent residence among the ex–Confederates were given a far different welcome from the enthusiastic acceptance promised by many of the South's editorial writers. Most Southerners shunned, threatened, maltreated and even sent packing Yankees they saw as competition to their "territory." Seeking to restore the South's traditional reputation for hospitality, Southern newspapers carried lengthy articles repudiating the charges of ill-will and animosity. A writer for the *New Orleans Daily Picayune*, for example, vigorously denied General Sheridan's widely circulated assessment that "a spirit of bitterness and dissent exists here" to such an extent that troops are necessary "to give security to Northern capital and Union people." Fearing that Sheridan's statements could do irreparable harm to the Southland by discouraging further acquisition of Northern capital and by extending the reign of occupation of the Southland by Union troops, the editor insisted that not enmity but true Southern hospitality prevailed. Surely Sheridan must have found "the people of Louisiana inviting and extending the hand of welcome to capital from every country, and to all people to settle here and help us build up our State, our great city and our homes. We should be madmen if we did not do it," the editorial continued. "Why, General if there be any people in the world who are genial, who are famed throughout the wide world for good nature, hospitality, liberality of sentiment and sociability with such as come properly introduced and recommended to them, sometimes with generous confidence bordering on indiscretion, it is the people of Louisiana."

Another editorial two days later concluded, "We are recognized as peacefully disposed and honorable people, who will keep all their pledges to the letter, as well from the obligations of good faith, as from the conviction that a harmonious renewal of free and cordial intercourse with the men of capital and enterprise at the North, is our surest and speediest remedy for the disorders that affect the State. Whoever says otherwise, is the dupe of a pitiable ignorance or the slave of a wicked, uneradicable prejudice."[11] A great many unhappy Northerners, however, thought and even retorted, "Prove it!"

Laborers, Employers and Contracts

Experienced planters as well as new planters soon discovered that securing steady, reliable workers often became nigh on to an impossibility. Planters who clung to their determination to make a success of cotton production struggled through various trial and error stages of renting the land to the newly freed men or when possible paying wages. Most, however, eventually settled on "sharecropping," the owners providing the seed, the farming equipment, sometimes the rations and clothing for their workers who in turn were given a percentage of the crop.

Although it would seem logical that the paying of wages would have been the most practical solution to the arrangements between employer and freedmen, it must be remembered that hard cash was extremely scarce in the South following the war. Southerners' money was worthless; a bushel basket full of bills would not buy a quart of milk. With the total collapse of the economy, money to pay wages, to purchase farm animals or equipment, or to replace broken-down farm tools was almost non-existent.

Furthermore, handling money was an absolutely new experience for the recently freed men and women, and all too often, thanks to swindlers, they were quickly parted with any wages they had received. What little money they did retain was often frittered away on ornamentation and trivialities. Often times, as noted earlier, workers ended up owing a "company store," operated by a plantation owner, more than could be covered by his year's wages. Greedy employers sometimes deducted fines and charges for food and clothing which left their workers with precious little to show for their year's work.

Ella Wilson told of her employer's contemptible behavior in refusing to pay her family anything, either in wages or in crops. "'We didn't get no half. We didn't git nothin'…. We hadn't done nothin' to him. He just wanted all the crop for hisself and he run us off. That's all.'"[12] Actually, paying wages often turned into a losing proposition for employers as well as employees. When Mary Catherine Killebrew, of Clarksville, Tennessee, took over the management of the family's farms with the help of her two sons, she deemed the expenditures incurred in wage labor an expensive experiment. "I did not get back a third of the money I paid out for hand hire," she complained.[13]

Renting land to freedmen also proved discouraging to farmers when at the end of the year they found they were unable to collect the pre-agreed upon rent. Furthermore, in numerous areas laws forbade the renting of land to freedmen. Thus in time sharecropping, backed up by labor contracts, evolved as the most efficient employment system for both planters and freed people. Often whole families of workers were involved in the contractual agreements.

Whatever the terms of employment, wages or sharecropping, the need for contracts was absolutely vital. Without the all important contract, laborers and employers alike could incur devastating losses. Workers could walk off at the height of the harvesting season, or employers could withhold wages or shares at the end of the year. As the Stones prepared to return to their home in Louisiana, Kate mused: "It seems an ill-advised move to take the Negroes back unless they could be bound by some contract to remain on the place, and that is impossible." Actually she doubted that any of them would remain with them once they reached Brokenburn.[14]

Naturally the employer-employee problems were myriad: workers wanted more money, employers wanted more work from their laborers. Some ruthless planters even forced the signing of contracts at gunpoint or attempted to force their laborers to sign lifetime contracts.[15]

Not infrequently former bondsmen refused to sign a contract feeling it demeaning or that somehow it would be used to return them to slavery. Furthermore many freedmen refused to work at all until the promise of forty acres and a mule was fulfilled. Their former masters had supported them all of their lives, surely they would continue to do so, work or no work on their part.

Frances Butler's experiences on their plantations typified the postwar labor problems of thousands of Southerners. Hoping to salvage what they could from their properties after the war, Frances Butler[16] and her father, Pierce Butler, set out in 1866 for their rice and cotton plantations on Butler's and St. Simon's Islands. By then many of their former slaves had returned to the plantations and staunchly refused to work for anyone but the Butlers. Although the Butlers were given a heartwarming welcome by several hundred of "their people," there quickly ensued problems (rundown buildings, worn-out equipment, inclement weather, army worms and capricious laborers) that at times seemed insurmountable. Following her father's death in 1867 Frances took over as manager of their plantations and at that point she ran head on into seemingly endless troubles.

Settling up at the end of the year often ended in serious arguments between wage laborers or sharecroppers and their employers. Disgruntled workers insisted they were entitled to more money than they received and angrily contested the bookkeeping. Frances Butler's (Leigh) meticulous logbook accounts of days missed failed to convince her workers that they were not being cheated. Suspicious of a female manager, chary laborers refused to accept her authority. Frances's face must have reddened upon receiving the ultimate put-down when one worker testily retorted, "You see, missus, a woman ain't much 'count."[17]

After years of having had no choice but to obey orders, the freedmen found the novelty of contesting authority an interesting, challenging change. Now in disputing their wages and contracts they sought to assert their independence and newly acquired status. For some blacks it became a game, for others it was a deadly serious business. Frances Butler (Leigh) was driven to distraction arguing over contracts with workers—one wanting a certain provision in his contract, another wanting something else. Attempting to make fair, uniform contracts with several hundred laborers put Frances to the test. Some refused to work on Saturdays, some agreed to work in the mill but not in the field, some would work at one job but not at another, some refused to sign a contract until it came down to a last ditch "sign or leave" mandate. Not surprisingly the wrangling often brought on "a violent attack of hysterics afterward from fatigue and excitement."[18]

Of course, contract signing days were not the only irksome days. Frequently rumors started in the fields about wages, or hours of work, or assigned tasks. It was then incumbent upon Frances to bring out the contracts which she read slowly, stressing the words, "'The undersigned freed men and women agree to obey all orders and to do the work required of them in a satisfactory manner, and in event of any violation of this contract, they are to be dismissed from the place and to forfeit all wages due to them.'"[19] The reading usually quelled the discontent—at least for a few days.

In time Frances instituted the quasi-satisfactory arrangement of paying twelve dollars a month with full rations. (In other areas workers were making twice that amount, but probably with no rations.[20]) At the end of the month each worker received six dollars, the other half of his pay being withheld until the end of the year. (This system no doubt served to bind workers to the plantation and prevent their slipping off to another job or to a life of leisure. To wander off, of course, meant forfeiting their full due at the end of the year.) By 1876, however, Frances had settled on a plan of paying straight wages once each week.

In 1866 in a contract apparently filed with the Freedmen's Bureau, Rebecca Smith agreed to pay her workers sixty dollars for a year's service. In addition each laborer would receive two suits of clothes and one acre planted in cotton. In order to minimize the numbers of lost days, the workers were required to pay Rebecca fifty cents for each day they were absent from work and were also responsible for their own medical expenses.[21]

The Confederacy's demise also brought immense changes in Sarah Espy's life in Cherokee County, Alabama. However, by signing a contract with two "hands," Sarah secured help with her farm, the men to receive one sixth of the entire crop. On July 3, 1865, Sarah recorded in her diary: "I contracted with Jane & Dick to serve the remainder of the year such being the federal law. I give them their victuals & clothing, the proceeds of their patches, & they are to perform their duties as heretofore. The freedom of the negroes will not be ratified until Congress meets which will be in October." (For some Southerners the unconditional freedom of their former slaves was in a state of limbo, for the Thirteenth Amendment was not declared in effect until December 1865.) Often, one notes, an important feature of the contract was the provision that the laborers be given a parcel of land to farm for themselves, thus Mrs. Espy's reference to "patches."

The irresponsibility of white as well as black workers caused harried planters monumental headaches as well as thousands of dollars in lost income. As they struggled to make a go of their plantation, Sally Elmore Taylor and her husband discovered contracts with laborers were easily negotiated but not so easily enforced. At crucial harvest time or cotton picking time the entire crop might be lost when "at dawn, the whole residential picking force would stampede to some other plantation for a kind of frolic, or because the cotton being more freely opened, was easier and more rapidly picked, and was paid for by weight wherever it was picked."[22]

Broken contracts and men working on shares and then leaving without warning provided constant worries for Gertrude Thomas and her husband. The differences between ordering slaves about and tiptoeing about with hired help proved frustrating to Gertrude and to her husband as well. As the new year dawned in 1871 Gertrude hoped that her husband would have fewer troubles as the months passed, but that was not to be. Help seemed to disappear and reappear with haphazard regularity. "...Young has moved today and Edmund and Mary expect to go tomorrow and Sam was missing this morning and Uncle Robin whom he thought he had engaged for this year has not come back. These are hands he had last year (just passed) and he has made little or no effort to secure them for another. Young was the best man he had on the place and I am sorry he has gone. Edmund will be no loss. He is indolent and impertinent at times. Diania (Young's wife) is cooking and milking for me...."

"When one servant leaves a place," Gertrude continued, "they use their influence to prevail upon as many of the others to go as they can. Mr. Thomas had hired a white man Mr. Simmons and he told Turner that Edmund compelled Sam who is only 14 years old to leave this morning. He left before his month was out. Mr. Simmons is at present the only man or boy on the place in our service and he has a chill every other day since he has been here...."[23]

By the latter part of May the situation for the Thomases showed little improvement. "I see little difference in white or coloured labour," Gertrude complained, noting that "the loss of three hands who have contracted with him is quite disheartening to Mr. Thomas...." Despite the theft of pigs, chickens and other farm animals by two of their "hands," the Thomases chose not to dismiss them only fearing "to engage others equally dishonest and perhaps not so good fieldhands...."[24] From Richmond in the summer of 1865 Betty Ross wrote to her brother Pem: "I fear the new labour system will work very badly. I wish every negro could be taken away & their places supplied by whites. The present state of things is hard to bear."[25]

Employment in helping to rebuild the nearly defunct railroad tracks throughout the South offered attractive and remunerative work to the freedmen. With prospects of jobs with the railroads, newly emancipated men took off from the fields with the speed of lightning. Marie Rice depicted a time in Charlotte County, Virginia, when during the busiest season all of their black workers deserted to take higher paying jobs as pick and shovel men working for the railroad.[26]

Grace Elmore enumerated her problems with contracts with the newly freed help. "We have truly said good-bye to being ladies of leisure, my time is fully occupied, often not having time to sleep. Rise at 5 o'clock, dress, come down to see after breakfast, then, a multitude of small cares; among them reading to Jack his contract, which he ought to know by heart. For every day he makes some demand and when I decline, said 'But Miss Grace, ain't it in de contract,' whereupon I take him, gravely to the library and read the document signed by the parties in the presence of the Yankee Colonel Haughton; and which he told Jack was binding. I sometimes get very impatient.... So Jack has the contract read and explained every day before his work is over. For, if he does not make a demand, he is sure to refuse one of mine."[27]

Of course, contracts did not necessarily assure diligent, conscientious workers. Complaints about their workers' indolence and improvidence were almost universal among farmers. When Sally Taylor chided a black servant for only making $70 at the end of the year when with a little more effort he could have drawn considerably more, he responded: "If I can live all the year and keep warm and all of we eat and I git $70.00, I aint ask no more from the Heavenly Father—I ain't want to work for no more." Sally also suggested that he could do the work of an overseer; however, he clearly had no interest in that job. "...Missis I aint goin oversee no *free* niggers."[28]

The Elmore family registered shock at the scanty production record of their workers. When the crops were gathered, Grace reported: "it was one bale of cotton of 500 pounds and a little one of 150 pounds. As for corn, that was taken from the fields before it was ripe, so that at the close of the year there was not provision enough to run the place. Our crops used to be 60 or 75 bales, several hundred bushels of wheat for market, and corn enough to feed a great deal of stock and 200 negroes.... A Yankee soldier came over to see that justice was done in the division, but even he could not help expressing disapprobation when the negroes claimed the big bale instead of the little one, whilst Albert and I could not help laughing at the humor of the whole farce, which was just as apparent to the negroes as it was to us."[29]

"We Must Part with Our Beloved Home": Giving Up and Moving On

Even with considerable advice and a modicum of financial aid from family members, Mary Jones[30] discovered managing a plantation in the postwar years an overwhelming task. Mary suddenly found herself "reduced from affluence to penury" after the war, and consequently without the means to assist their former "servants" with their problems of adjustment following their emancipation. Time and time again Mary's letters alluded to the "deplorable state" of affairs on her plantation. The blacks, she complained, "will not contract or enter into any engagement for another year, and will not work now except as it pleases them. I know not from day to day if I will have one left about me on the place. Several of them refuse positively to do any work."[31]

Altercations over contracts and the irresponsibility of workers resulted in increasingly unpleasant encounters. Mary was indignant when her laborers (apparently persuaded by some outside source that Mary was attempting to deceive them), suddenly refused "to strike another lick with the hoe" in dissatisfaction with their contract. Since the contract had been suggested and approved by a Federal officer, she immediately ordered the ringleaders to meet with her and an official at the nearest Freedman's Bureau. There, after some floundering on the part of the agent, she was assured that actually there was no standard form for labor contracts and that her document was entirely legal. In answer to her frantic appeal for order to be restored upon her plantation, the agent threatened to put the ringleaders in irons if they did not return to their work. The confrontation seemed to settle the contract dispute at least temporarily; however, Mary made clear to them her resentment over their distrust of her concern for their well-being.

"I have told the people that in doubting my word they offered me the greatest insult I ever received in my life," she wrote. "I had considered them friends and treated them as such ... but that now they were only laborers under contract, and only the law would rule between us, and I would require every one of them to come up to the mark in their duty on the plantation. The effect has been decided, and I am not sorry for the position we hold mutually. They have relieved me of the constant desire and effort to do something to promote their comfort."[32]

Labor disputes coupled with overseers' expenses, market fluctuations, rain, drought, caterpillars, and a host of other troubles finally induced Mary Jones to give up even trying to meet expenses, to say nothing of making a profit, on the Montevideo plantation in Liberty County, Georgia. Mary complained to her daughter: "I sometimes feel I must sink under the various perplexities of this situation.... I have come to the determination that if a purchaser can be found, we must part with our beloved, our long-cherished home. I do not see how I can keep it up, dependent as I am upon a manager for the oversight and upon the false and faithless freedmen as laborers. If there was hope of improvement in the future, I could endure any temporary trials; but I am convinced the condition of things will grow worse and worse."[33]

Underscoring Mary's gloomy outlook was her report of a large meeting of blacks at which "Assurances [were] given that the coming year forty acres of land would be given to each, and our lands confiscated and given to them, to whom they justly belonged. All here were present. A fearful state of things! Where will it end?" Distraught over her continued problems with free labor, Mary finally gave up and in 1867 reluctantly moved to New Orleans to live with her married daughter. Finding it "no longer safe or prudent" to remain in her beloved home, Mary resigned herself to the reality that "All things are altered."[34]

Problems in securing workers and in effecting workable contracts caused countless other farmers to give up, put their land up for sale and move elsewhere. After months of back-breaking work attempting to make a success of their plantation, Louisa McCord Smythe and her husband discovered "there was no money in it—at least plenty went in it and none came out." Sadly, as she and her husband left to join his family in Charleston, Louisa conceded: "And so the dream of making a home at Lang Syne was over and my poor mother and Hannah were once more wanderers."[35]

One plantation owner, typical no doubt of thousands of others, revealed his difficulties getting along with the freedman in his fields and admitted that he was "making money backwards very fast."[36] Laura Buttolph voiced the hopelessness of her situation in a letter written on August 10, 1867. "No redress in case of difficulty with the freedmen here.... Military paralyzing all efforts to make them work. Country ruined: South has no future! Things worse and worse. No help as far as I can see. People generally dissatisfied with their homes; too poor to go away. Seasons unfavorable; too poor to live at home! We have no potatoes, corn, or anything else. We rented out our places, and the crops having all failed, we will realize nothing."[37]

Nature along with labor problems combined to defeat many a Southern—*and* Northern farmer as well. Discouraged after three successive crop failures when caterpillars devoured the cotton crop on the St. Simon's plantation, Frances Butler (Leigh) wrote: "This gave the deathblow to the Sea Island cotton, at least as far as I was concerned, for I had not capital enough to plant again after losing three crops, and the place has never been planted since, but is rented out to the negroes for a mere nominal rent, and they keep the weeds down and that is about all."[38]

In 1871 Frances married the Reverend James Wentworth Leigh, an English clergyman, and together they attempted to put the rice plantation on a more profitable basis. Frances's husband, James, pictured the disastrous conditions noting that "formerly, in six of the Southern States, 186,000,000 bushels of rice were sent to market, in 1870 only 72,000,000 were raised. The original planters having been completely ruined by the war, the planting in many cases carried on by negroes on their own account in small patches. As the Agricultural Commissioner, in his report, has lately stated, 'The rice-planters were driven from the Carolina and Georgia shores during the war, labour was in a disorganised and chaotic state, production had almost ceased, and at its close, dams, flood-gates, canals, mills, and houses were either dilapidated or destroyed, and the power to compel the labourers to go into the rice-swamps utterly broken. The labourers had scattered, gone into other businesses, and those obtainable would only work for themselves on a share contract.'"

"'Many of the proprietors,'" the commissioner continued, "'were dead, and more absentees, and inexperienced men from the North or elsewhere assumed their places. The rice-fields had grown up in weeds or tangled shrubbery, the labour of separation was discouraging, and the work of cultivation greatly increased, giving unexpected gravity to the accidents and contingencies of the season.'"

James Leigh corroborated the official's report. "The picture is by no means overdrawn, and even now, in our own neighbourhood, there is scarcely a planter whose plantation is not mortgaged, and whose crop is not the property of his factor who has advanced him money to plant with. They plant on sufferance, and live from hand to mouth as best they can."[39] For a few years the Leighs devoted themselves to resurrecting their rice fields on Butler's Island, but in time they rejected the hassles of plantation life in favor of the altruism of church life, and elected to live permanently in England, leaving their plantations in the hands of an agent.

"I Do Hate House Keeping"

Securing dependable domestic help proved almost as vexing as hiring field hands. Struggling to find capable, experienced help, Sarah Williams uttered women's age old lament, "I do hate house keeping." In spite of their distaste for housework, vast numbers of Southern women found the unaccustomed tasks of washing, ironing, dusting, and cooking suddenly thrust upon them following the war. Amanda Worthington told her diary "...we have most of the housework to do all the time, and one thing certain, it does not make me like the Yankees any better...."[40] Gertrude Thomas thought perhaps it would have been wise for her to keep a "record of the trials to which Southern housekeepers are exposed." When she complained to her husband he simply responded with "'So much for the blessings of freedom!'"[41] A Virginian uttered a universal complaint: "We can get no servant we can rule or control."[42]

A Georgia woman fretted: "Negroes are a great trial and nuisance, yet it seems impossible to get along without them in this country. We expected to pay $5. a month for Beckie. To-day her master told S. he must have $8. I had been so tired with her all day, that my first thought when S. told me was that I would give her up before I would pay such an exorbitant price for a girl twelve years old. We have been talking it over however, and have concluded it is best to keep her as we do not know where to get another."[43]

Without question, competent, faithful cooks, housemaids, waiters, washers and ironers were in great demand throughout the South. Mobile, Alabama, residents clamored for white house servants to work for a salary of fifteen dollars per month; New Orleans women promised eighteen to twenty dollars a month; other areas offered varying wages. Ann Hardeman was pleased that so many of their old slaves returned to work for the family as hired servants; however, she soon discovered that what she considered exorbitant wages being paid to their servants and the indifferent attitude of their servants toward work made shifting to wage laborers an expensive undertaking.[44]

From Hancock County, Georgia, Sallie Bird apologized in a letter to her daughter for her preoccupation with "that all pervading topic," the difficulties in obtaining domestic help. "Just imagine how we are situated, not a negro on the place, but Nina.... I am perfectly quiet and hope to get servants, but can't tell. Things do not look promising as yet.... A great many persons have no servants as yet...." The negroes "won't make contracts; hoping for more and more."[45] One lucky woman could see the handwriting on the wall and admitted that she "would like to know how to make every article of my clothing for one of these days I may have it all to do with my own hands; now I am fortunate enough to have some one to do it for me."[46] In September of 1865 Tryphena Fox wrote her mother: "There are plenty of free negroes to be hired but there are so many objections to most of them & they all put on so many airs, that it is difficult to find a good one."[47] For Pauline DeCaradeuc (Heyward) their myriad troubles with servants were an "annoyance, but in the scale of life these are minor weights."[48]

Even very young children were caught up in the "servant problems" of their elders. Betty Herndon Maury, as early as August 1862, smiled at overhearing her small daughter's conversation while "playing ladies" with her friend.

"Sallie: 'Good morning, ma'am. How are you today?'

Nannie Belle: 'I don't feel very well this morning. *All my niggers have run away and left me.'*[49]

"I Am Glad They Are Gone"

Surprisingly vast numbers of diarists breathed a sigh of relief as their former slaves took flight. With news of the emancipation, Nannie Scott's mother exclaimed, "'Now I am free.'"[50] Mary Harrison was happy to see two of her family's "servants" leave: "They are both good for nothing, both being diseased. The only fear is they will soon be back."[51]

Gertrude Thomas confided to her diary that she experienced a certain relief in the responsibility she had felt for the family's slaves. "...I am not the person to permit pecuniary loss to afflict me as long as I have health and energy. As to the emancipation of the Negroes, while there is of course a natural dislike to the loss of so much property in my inmost soul I cannot regret it—I always felt that there was a great responsibility—It is in some degree a great relief to have this feeling removed. For the Negroes I know that I have the kindest possible feeling—For the Yankees who deprive us of them I have no use whatever. I only hope I shall see very little of them."[52]

Although the flight of Samuel Agnew's servants entailed considerable extra work for his wife, Sam was resigned to the family's fate. Sadly he lamented that he "never expected that my wife would have to come to the wash tub, but so it is." Two days earlier Samuel had noted, "Our negroes are all gone now. The negro yard is silent and dark. George and Franky were off this evening for their new livings. I am glad they are gone, I did not fancy their lolling about here not doing one hands turn."[53]

When one of her departed ex-slaves sent the Yankees back to her home to free his wife and children, their former owner, a Virginia woman, angrily exclaimed [I] "sincerely hope I may never see a member of that family again."[54] (Her sentiments no doubt went double for her ex-slaves and tens of thousands like them. Unfortunately, however, many discouraged blacks humbly returned hat in hand to their former owners once they discovered field and domestic work offered about the only opportunities for unskilled black workers.)

The departure of their "servants" was a loss welcomed—at least ostensibly—by Margaret Beckwith. "For some time Jane had been behaving her worst. We were looking around to see how we could get rid of her. When, much to our relief, after sending in supper, by one of the children ... she went to house-keeping in a dwelling twice the size of this house, not a hundred yards off. On finding that she and her family had cleared out, we very quietly took possession."[55]

Despite her elation in Jane's departure, Margaret guiltily recalled that she owed Jane a great debt of gratitude. Two months earlier Jane had been their salvation when she and the other servants shared the food they obtained from Yankees, who were camped nearby, with the Beckwiths. "But for her, we should have starved for everything we depended on was destroyed. She kept us supplied. Strange, as long as she felt we were in danger, she remained faithful. As soon as the Yankees moved off, she became worthless. They must have filled her with notions."[56]

Another former slave owner also retained a sense of gratitude to former slaves. "He and Horace watch over us in every way, and mind our discomfort and privations greatly. I shall never forget either, Horace so courteous, never forgetting by word or deed his position; faithful (in all the excitement of a new freedom, and an intense satisfaction in that freedom to his race), to the affection born of past kindness and care."[57] Yet another South Carolina woman had high praise for the Negroes' loyalty during the spring of 1865. "To the eternal honor of the negroes be it spoken, that many of them aided and sustained their former owners in these trying times, with a devotion as surprising as it was noble."[58]

In a touching reversal of roles, Jennie Stephenson in her reminiscences of her father told of the affection for his old master of one of her father's former slaves, then a tenant at their farm. During one of the darkest periods of their postwar financial difficulties, "His foreman, Jim Johnson, came to him, bringing money he had laid by, and begging his Master to accept it. He said that he had been working for himself for more than a year, and did not need it, as he could easily make more."

In September of 1865 Catherine Hammond wrote to her brother praising the loyalty of many other former slaves, but also wishing to get rid of "many of the useless ones. 300 mouths to feed is no small charge."[59]

"*I Must Now Be My Own Servant*"

In December of 1865 Sarah Espy of Cherokee County, Alabama, recounted problems with Jane, household help with whom she seemed to have had a contract. "She has been giving me trouble for some time. Wished to do as she pleases, regardless of her contract." By the end of the month Jane had moved off with her "plunder." "I could not help feeling sorry to see her go; she has in many ways been faithful & I shall miss her much. Besides, I have no idea that *freedom* (so called) will be any advantage to her. I must set up now, a new way of life. After having had servants for 50 years I must now be my own servant or subject myself to having a stranger in the family which I do not by any means like."[60]

While some Southerners happily bade their servants good-bye, many soon found themselves inextricably caught up in the exhausting, time-consuming routine involving hot stoves, hot ovens, hot soap suds, hot flatirons, dirty floors, and unmade beds. Four months after Appomattox, Eliza Frances Andrews reported the reduction in their establishment from twenty-five servants to five, two of the latter indisposed. As their servants Dick and Emily departed with their children to strike out on their own, both families shed tears. For the most part she and her sister found little objection to doing the housework "for we do it so much better than the negroes." However, by the end of the day they often found themselves in a state of complete exhaustion. A bevy of unexpected overnight and dinner guests brought on a case of utter fatigue: "I never was so tired in my life; every bone in my body felt as if it were ready to drop out, and my eyes were so heavy that I could hardly keep them open. I don't find doing housework quite so much of a joke as I imagined it was going to be, especially when we have company to entertain at the same time, and want to make them enjoy themselves."[61]

Kate Foster found that doing the washing by herself for six weeks was definitely not all fun and games and complained "came near ruining myself for life as I was too delicately raised for such hard work."[62] And, indeed, confronting those mountains of sheets and household linens was a daunting task. Wash days, involving hauling out the "wash pots," building a roaring fire beneath them, jugging at the tubs' amorphous contents writhing in boiling water, wrestling the soggy bundles onto temperamental clotheslines, all the while gambling on the tenuous promise of enough sunshine to air dry the sodden array, somehow never turned out to be the week's most eagerly anticipated day. As her servants began disappearing Mary Chesnut was left with only a few retainers and sighed, "If I do a little work it is quite enough to show me how dreadful it would be … *if I should have to do it all*."[63]

"We find the cooking," Margaret Beckwith admitted, "easy enough, as there is very little to do; but the washing is the rub, though we contrive to do very well & find the clothes improve in appearance." Nevertheless she still maintained, as for their departure: "Joy go with them, I would not have one of them back, as a precious gift."[64] In what appeared to be a quid pro quo arrangement, Jennie Stephenson's family struck up a shrewd deal with a former servant. "Our own servants were never in our employ after the surrender, save one, who rented a house of my Father's in Blandford and paid the rent in the family laundrying."

Offered little alternative, many Southern women took the loss of their servants in stride. "Our servants have all left us," Sarah Wadley wrote, "and we have now only one hired woman and one little girl; we have all the house work to do but we are now so accustomed to this that it does not trouble us much."[65] From Winchester, Virginia, during the chaotic turnovers of the town, Fanny Barton explained: "As for the servants going off *we are charmed now* that they are gone. Their places are for all filled by much more capable ones & we work ourselves very little more than we ever did. I make the most beautiful bread you ever saw & I assure you I am proud of the accomplishment...."[66]

Fortunately, when Sarah Espy did the washing for the first time in her life she found it turned out not to be "the dreadful job I always took it to be."[67] (The acquisition of a "washing machine," as one would expect, proved an immense saving in time and energy both for women who did their own laundry as well as for those who were fortunate enough to be able to hire a "washer woman." A South Carolina woman extolled the virtues of the new machine. "It washes the clothes beautifully.... The colored clothes cannot be washed by it, but whilst the white clothes are boiling the colored clothes can be washed.... I think the wringer is a capital thing, the clothes dry in a short time after they are hung out."[68])

"A Sharp Antagonism Between the Two Races"

The pleasure felt by former owners at seeing the last of their former servants was nothing compared to the ecstasy experienced by many blacks in parting with their former masters. The farewells were often less than amiable on the part of both the employer and the employee. Resentment frequently continued long after the separation. A woman told of being greatly embarrassed upon encountering one of the family's old "servants" on the street months after their parting. The former slave loudly "cursed her for everything, wished the whole Darden family was in the hottest spot."[69]

All too often a sense of bitterness accompanied the departure of their servants. A South Carolina woman reflected on the situation: "Three weeks since the servants left.... We have gone through so much, that this breaking of old ties has excited but little feeling, both parties are very indifferent, and the most that is felt is a polite and gentle interest in the affairs of each other. In most instances there is I believe a bitter feeling, and a sharp antagonism between the two races. I almost think they are natural enemies and that only their relative positions bound them together in affection, as well as by law."

The same writer was quick to point out a similar indifference and even enmity on the part of Northerners for the black race. "For we see this antagonism just as strong in the Yankees as in the Southerner, and with no reason whatever, they seem in private life to consider the negro worthless, and to treat him as such. Already they do not hesitate to express utter contempt for the race, and while they insist upon our treating them as equals, they show their scorn and indifference, in every way, to this same race."[70]

"...And This Is Their Return"

Although thousands of Southerners were delighted to see an end to the responsibilities that slavery entailed, others were angered by the freedmen's growing independence—actions and mannerisms they termed "uppity." Most diarists were offended by what they considered a lack of gratitude on the part of their former slaves.

Mary Mallard, writing from New Orleans, thoroughly resented what she considered impertinence and perversity in her servants. Clearly Mary considered the departure of a black servant she had nursed through a case of yellow fever as typical of former slaves' ingratitude. "I have seen for some weeks that she was becoming disaffected and surly, so that it did not surprise me when she gave notice she would leave. Since then she has not found the fine offers she spoke of, and I think she is quite miserable; but I shall make no effort to retain her, although I feel very sorry for her, and shall continue to do what I can for her."[71]

As her help disappeared, one by one or in groups, Mary Jones mused: "My life long (I mean since I had a home) I have been laboring and caring for them, and since the war have labored with all my might to supply their wants, and expended everything I had upon their support, directly or indirectly; and this is their return."[72] By mid–April hosts of Richmond servants had taken off for what they hoped would be greener pastures. Their departure, Fannie Dickinson wrote, touched a nerve. "Today our servants have all left. Father offered them higher wages but they preferred to set up for themselves. This is indeed the unkindest cut of all. I cannot write about it."[73]

"You Must Reply Respectfully"

Many former slave owners, no matter how resigned to emancipation they had become, refused to abandon their assumed racial superiority and insisted that they and the members of their families be addressed as "Mr." and "Mrs." and "Master" and "Miss." Gertrude Thomas was a stickler for a certain respect she believed due her and her family from the newly freed blacks. When Henry, one of the servants, failed to say "Yes, sir," to Turner (Gertrude's young son), Gertrude called him to task. Henry, drawing himself up to the full stature of his newly acquired position in life, retorted that although he would respond with a "Yes, sir," to Gertrude's husband, he would not so reply to a boy of eighteen. He further reminded her that he could leave if he so wished.[74]

Gertrude, annoyed by his "impertinence," halted further talk and remonstrated: "'I repeat to you that while you are in our employment you must reply respectfully to Turner or leave. You can do as you please, but I should tell you the same if you were the only servant to be hired in the state.' I told him this and came in. I do not know whether he will go or stay. I should prefer his remaining for hands are scarce but respect is a quality I demand from servants even more than obedience. I can over look neglected work but cannot tolerate disrespect." Gertrude knew better than to attempt to force servants to call Turner, "Master" Turner or their daughter "Miss" Mary Belle, appellations she was sure the freedmen would consider demeaning to their new status.[75]

Sally Taylor also demanded a similar deference from her black servants for her position as a white employer. On one occasion Sally summarily dismissed a kitchen servant for calling her "Sally" Taylor instead of "Mrs." Taylor. Accepting their former slaves as equals was extremely difficult for many Southerners and utterly impossible for others. In explaining the above mentioned firing Sally Taylor confessed that as she was unable to accept United States dictum: "I did not regard her as my equal."[76]

Even transplanted Yankees insisted on deferential treatment from their servants. Blanche Butler Ames (a Northerner, although at the time—January of 1874—she was living in Jackson with her husband, the Governor of Mississippi) reprimanded her cook for not addressing her properly. "What did you call me—you are to say Madame when you want anything of me." In a letter to her mother she added haughtily "the colored people here are not nearly as well trained as they are in Washington."[77]

Frances Butler (Leigh) was offended by the lack of respect shown her by her black workers—a situation that she attributed to "Negro adventurers from the North." Furthermore, Frances insisted that black workers remove their hats when speaking with her.[78] In a warning to insolent workers Frances made clear her distinction between employer and employee. "'You are free to leave the place, but not to stay here and behave as you please, for I am free, too, and moreover own the place, and so have a right to give my orders on it, and have them obeyed.'"[79]

"An Irrepressible Conflict"

Women's complaints about the loss of and incompetence of domestic help comprised one of the foremost topics of conversation among employers. Queried about the conditions of household affairs subsequent to the war, Margaret Ward insisted that the situation had steadily worsened over the years. "The servants are growing more and more incorrigible all the time. They have no idea of the binding force of a contract or of any moral obligation. They leave us at any time they choose; they go from house to house, and we can place no dependence upon them at all. This is the way they are doing; and if you dare to correct them or to suggest that their mode of working is not the best, or not the one you approve, they will leave you, or else be insolent about it."

"It is a very hard life that we housekeepers here lead," Margaret continued: "It is actually dangerous to invite company three days ahead, because you cannot depend upon your servants staying with you so long or doing what you want them to do if they do stay." Years later, Margaret Ward explained it was almost impossible to get white household help. Many poor white women simply refused to go out as domestic servants believing that service is synonymous with slavery. "They make no distinction between free domestic service and compulsory servitude—regular old-time slavery." As for actually employing white servants Mrs. Ward was aghast at the idea, accusing white household help of being slovenly and utterly indifferent to an employer's directions or suggestions. The poor whites, Mrs. Ward, insisted were "very inferior as servants." They were looked down upon by even the colored help, who assuming an air of superiority, disdained to eat their cooking.[80]

Charges, of course, were rife concerning their servants' indifference to their work and their inexperience. An article on the front page of the *New Orleans Daily Picayune* of May 3, 1866, charged that many servants "know little of the duties they should perform, and care less about fulfilling them; and, with some creditable exceptions regard themselves as entitled to be waited upon, rather than under obligation to wait upon those who employ them. Whether this is due altogether to the passage of the civil rights bill, or to natural depravity may be doubted but so it is, families who pay out their money freely for service fail to get it. Servants who desire to perform their duty and to receive pay for it, would do well to direct their steps to this city from the North and West, and from across the ocean."

Although white female employers generally believed in their inherent superiority over black employees, the situation upon occasion was reversed. The *New Orleans Times* on May 14, 1869, reported that some "freed ladies" considered it "beneath their station" to work even in the house for people they deemed "white trash."

With news of their emancipation, as noted earlier, many freedwomen vehemently rejected field work in particular and sometimes all work in general. Remembering their years of abject servitude, freed women often turned up their noses at work as maids or household "help," considering such work beneath them. Early on, the *Daily True Delta* of New Orleans urged blacks not to let indolence or arrogance deter them from accepting positions as household servants, otherwise, the paper warned, whites will take over. "We have told the freed blacks, time and again, that unless they should go cheerfully to work and labor, and deport themselves as servants, capital would soon bring a class of laborers and 'helps' here, between whom and them there would be an 'irrepressible conflict.'"[81]

Citizens accustomed to luxury who still could afford household help, the article cautioned, would hire whites if blacks were not available. Once the government stops the "rations business," freed men and women "must work and support themselves and those dependent upon them," the writer pointed out, "for there is no one else to do it." (Since millions of blacks could neither read nor write, one supposes that white readers of the *Daily True Delta* reiterated that dire prediction to any indolent freedmen within hearing range.) In response to the rumor being circulated that one hundred Irish girls were to be imported as domestics, the paper made it a point to caution the newly freed men and women that they "will soon find themselves wandering vagrants, while Biddy and Bridget will reign supreme in the kitchen and backyard of the better classes of the South."[82]

∞

Whites as well as blacks found readjustment difficult after the war. "It was hard to settle down to work after four years of unsettled life in an excited and anxious condition, " Virginia Norfleet recalled. In time, however, she reported that both employers and workers "went to work with a vim that brought good results...."[83]

℘ 5 ℃

*The Rocky Road
to Reconciliation*

℘) Christ's commandment to "love your enemies" fell on deaf ears—even among the most pious Southerners. A world turned upside-down by defeat, death, destruction, and devastation; an economy in chaos; former slaves suddenly accorded equality—any or all of the above scarcely augured a cordial reunion with the source of those woes. Painful memories of the heartless pillaging and mayhem strategies of the Federals' "all-out war" campaign left Southerners bitter and demoralized. Yankee demolition that was designed to lower morale on the Southern homefront, curtail food supplies throughout the Southland, and thus hasten an end to the war achieved precisely those results.

Mrs. Gordon Pryor Rice and her fellow parishioners in Charlotte County, Virginia, were enraged when the English clergyman conducting services at their church counseled the congregation: "Now bear in mind 'Love your enemies' *means* something. It means for you, 'Love the Yankees.'" Mrs. Rice was furious: "How outrageous! What a perversion of scripture to drag it into politics in that way! A preacher has no business with such subjects; he should confine himself to preaching the Gospel!" Lucy Fletcher, wife of a Richmond minister, despised the swarms of Yankees that took over Richmond in April of 1865. "It is a galling sight to see the streets filled with Yankees, black & white. (We feel just as much respect for one, as for the other.) Our Capitol square lined with blue coats, remembering that these are the people who for 4 years have been slaying our brethern, and desolating our land, burning and ravaging our homes, insulting & robbing our defenceless women and grey haired men. Has not their cry ascended to Heaven! Wilt Thou not come for our deliverance O Lord?"[1]

No doubt Father Abram Ryan represented thousands of Southerners

133

"Reconstruction." (*Harper's Weekly,* August 5, 1868.)

in protesting the huge influx of Northerners and what he termed "their satanic hatred of Southern people." In September of 1866 he complained that the Knoxville area "is completely deluged with Yankees. Yankee ministers—Yankee schoolmasters & schoolmarms—Yankee merchants—Yankee doctors and lawyers and Yankees of every calling imaginable. They are pouring in—pouring in—every day and heaven knows when they will stop. I suppose however it is the same all over the South. Every car from Virginia is crammed with them. They're as bad as the plagues of locusts in olden time. You see that my feelings towards these people have undergone no change. I can't bear them—'tis no use trying."[2] Most Southerners seemed to agree that it would be easier to love one's enemies if they kept their distance.

The blatant animosity felt by both Southern men and Southern women toward the triumphant Northerners was adroitly expressed by Jim Selby: "Forgive they never can & they would be unworthy men and women if they could or would. To the end of time, the name of 'Yankee' will be considered as the most degrading epithet that can be applied to mortal man."[3] Seething with bitterness, Hannah Rawlings, writing from Virginia, predicted: "The feeling here against the North is intense, 'tho smothered. It will never pass away. Mothers will teach their young children to abhor the slayers of their fathers and brothers, they will teach it to them from their earliest infancy. Had I sons, this is the religion that I would inculcate from the time they could lisp: '*Fear God, love the South, and live to avenge her!*' That is short and easily remembered."[4]

One observer caustically described Southerners' antipathy for Northerners declaring: "they [Southerners] are haughty and overbearing and insolent, and they do not propose, if they can help it, to allow any one to associate with them politically, socially, or commercially, unless he has been a rebel or has given the rebellion his support, or comes up to their standard. They never speak of a federal in any other way than as a 'Yankee.'"[5] In a conversation with a Freedmen's Bureau official, one ex–Confederate soldier expressed a loathing of Yankees that no doubt succinctly reflected the consensus of tens of thousands of Southerners. "I hate you; I do not love you; I always shall hate you."[6]

Surprisingly, or perhaps not so surprisingly, the process of reconstructing Southern men turned out to be an easier task than that of reconstructing Southern women. For returning soldiers, despite being war-weary and discouraged, there was a certain element of euphoria in somehow having survived the slaughter which had indiscriminately snuffed out the lives of hundreds of their messmates and comrades. Somehow men having experienced firsthand the kill-or-be-killed inevitability of war were considerably more forgiving than were the women of the South. They had experienced enough of battles and bloodshed to last an eternity. For women their sacrifices of fathers, sons, husbands, brothers, and fiancés to death and disease, their commitment to the cause, their contributions in providing food and nursing care, their sufferings and privations during the seemingly endless struggle made anything less than total victory seem empty and unacceptable.

Hatred of the Yankees was almost universal among Southern women. Several months after Appomattox, a Mississippi woman wrote: "The deep fire of hatred burns as fiercely in my bosom now as it ever did and I feel that I can never forgive them the injuries they have done to me & my country." For that woman any interest in "the affairs of the United States Government will never have power to interest me, unless they get into war with some foreign power, then indeed will I watch with eager eyes & pray God that the United States may be humbled and brought low even as we have been."[7]

Augusta Jane Evans (Wilson), a popular novelist of her day and one of the foremost propagandists of the Confederacy, vented her hatred for the North in a letter dated February 3, 1866. "...the strongest wish of my heart is, that I may live to witness—to *enjoy* the dire retribution,—The awful Nemesis, which if God reigns in heaven, must descend upon that *Synagogue* of Satan—New England. The wrongs inflicted upon us, I expect neither to forgive nor forget, until a terrible punishment overtake...."[8] Although grief stricken over the loss of two of her sons to the Confederate cause, one woman wrote her husband, "There is but one consolation in their having been taken from us ... that after four years of hardships, privations, and sufferings in their Country's cause, to return to their home under such harrowing circumstances (as *now exists* and *ever will*).... I say Death is preferable."[9]

For the distraught Kate Foster it would be impossible ever to blot out the infinite list of wrongs the North had perpetrated against the South. Kate was convinced that the sacrifice of her two brothers in the war had been for nothing. Blaming the Yankees for "the everlasting wounds on my heart," Kate found her hatred for "our oppressors" escalating by the day.

Her inability to forgive the Yankees sent Mary Goodwin on a guilt trip. Considering herself as "the vilest of sinners," she felt she "had sinned, seriously sinned, & I determined with God's help to overcome it, though for a moment I was tempted to renounce Christianity." Mary continued: "For four years, but more especially during the last 3 months, I have experienced, and lately I fear have cherished, a feeling of the most intense hatred for the Yankees...." (Surely millions of Southerners shared Mary's sentiments sans the guilt!)[10]

Typical Southern attitudes were recorded by George Eggleston when he overheard the conversation of two women, the younger of whom stated, "'I'm sure I do not hate our enemies. I earnestly hope their souls may go to heaven, but I would like to blow all their mortal bodies away, as fast as they come upon our soil.'"

"'Why you shock me dear,' replied the other; 'I don't see why you want the Yankees to go to heaven! I hope to get there myself some day, and I'm sure I shouldn't want to go if I thought I should find any of them there.'"[11]

Actually, a special place in Heaven should be awarded women, according to Margaret Ward, as compensation for their war and postwar trials. A Southern woman who arrives at the Celestial City "ought to go very high up," she declared. "I think she ought to get up where she could look down on all the Yankees, for she will be one of those that are spoken of as coming up through great tribulation."[12]

Almost twenty years after the war when asked whether she blamed Northerners for the problems Southerners were facing, Margaret Ward rejoiced in expressing her pent up hostility: "Yes I blame you for a great deal of it. I think if you had staid at home and let us go out of the Union we would have avoided all this trouble. I don't see what you wanted to keep us in for. When we wanted to go out you wouldn't let us, and then when we got back you kept all the time dinging and dinging at us as if to make us go out again. You 'reconstructed' us as though we had never known anything at all, and as though we were indebted to the Northern people for the very first ideas of civilization."[13]

"Hatred of Anything That Has a Yankee Uniform"

As tangible expressions of their distaste for Northerners, Southern women refused to call on Northern ladies who had invaded their sacred territory. As Federal troops of occupation appeared in Tyler, Texas, Kate Stone held only disdain for Capt. St. Clair who "has completed his disgrace by being the only man in town who will entertain a Yankee and the first to take office under the new rulers. The general feeling of contempt for him is too deep for words."[14]

Women often drew up their skirts in passing Northerners for fear of contamination. As George Benham explained, "They would drop their veils, and turn their faces away; and if by some chance, we got a glimpse of their features, the expression was anything but complimentary to us."[15] One woman was overheard to threaten her unruly child with the worst fate she could possibly conjure up: "If you don't behave, young lady, I'm going to leave you and let the Yankees catch you!"[16]

Offered a spate of new books to read, Kate Stone was disgusted as "most of them are by Yankee authors and are unreadable trash." Even the sound of war songs sickened Kate Stone; their notes seemed to touch new wounds. "It is best not to waken bitter memories by familiar heartfelt songs."[17]

Although the contingent of Yankee soldiers who encamped on the family's Goochland County property near Richmond proved themselves considerate and courteous, Elvira Seddon was not about to be deceived. "At their hands we have to expect degradation and insult. They are affecting conciliatory manners now, but in their hearts they hate us, and now that we are in their power, they will make us feel the weight of their displeasure. I want them to be harsh. I want our people to feel what [a] dreadful thing it is to lose our rights. They will be forced thereby to rise again, and I trust to fight successfully."[18]

Shortly after the soldiers left, the Seddons discovered the disappearance of their turkeys and the family's sulky. Elvira shuddered, feeling that the Yankees had "polluted" their property. As the officer in charge departed, Elvira commented: "making a polite bow, he mounted a splendid horse and rode off, apparently much to his own satisfaction, certainly greatly to ours. When these rascals are on the place I feel that it is polluted. It is galling to see them walk about insolently, looking so conscious of their power and of our impotence. How long, Oh Lord? How long? Can we bear it for a lifetime?"[19]

Despite her Massachusetts heritage, Tryphena Holder Fox had

developed decidedly pro–Southern sympathies during her experiences as a tutor for a Mississippi family and her subsequent marriage to physician David Fox of Louisiana. Tryphena wrote her mother in the North, "The one great fault of my life now is my *ingrafted* hatred of anything that has a Yankee Uniform, but I am going to try to overcome that & render good for evil—If I could only see you and tell you how I came to have so strong a prejudice, you would not wonder. We have all like thousands of others here in the South suffered terribly—have been cold & hungry & almost naked & homeless, for *the victor* & it is hard to forgive."[20]

The imprisonment of Jefferson Davis also drew fire from loyal Southerners. With the news of the surrender Southerners were fearful that all rebel leaders, Davis, Clay, and hosts of others would be immediately hanged or executed. (Actually it was a Northern leader who was killed— and at the hands of a Southerner.) Despite what seemed to some vindictive Northerners as rather lenient treatment of Jefferson Davis, Southerners became incensed over his pursuit and capture and what they considered his cruel treatment during his imprisonment. Even ex–Confederates at odds with Davis over his conduct of the war protested his being shackled in irons in his feeble condition and his being needlessly monitored by a guard every fifteen minutes of the day and night. In time as Davis's health continued to deteriorate, the Northern press took up his cause and thanks to the effort of Mrs. Davis, Horace Greeley and other notables not only was Varina allowed to visit him, but the Davises were given a four room apartment at Fort Monroe. In addition Davis was given full parole of the fort and allowed untold numbers of visitors. Nevertheless, Southerners saw Davis as their martyr and his treatment they felt represented further humiliation to an already embittered people.

Zealous Southerners such as Pauline DeCaradeuc (Heyward) revered Davis as "the purest patriot, the greatest statesman, and wisest administrator that ever lived." Pauline wished for her own death were it "to save him from sorrow, and the humiliation which are to be heaped upon his great soul." Suspicions that Davis was a conspirator in Lincoln's murder enraged Pauline. Yankees, despite their "vileness consistent with their entire conduct," she maintained, would be unable "to cast one shade on the spotless purity of that brilliant star."[21] Florence Anderson concurred with Pauline's assessment of Davis. "It is hard that he should be called to suffer either life-long captivity—or be ignominiously executed—for he has done his part nobly. In all charges of corruption among the Confederate officials, few southern men can be found who implicate Mr. Davis, though many are bitter in their denunciations of the Congress— and the Department officers. Truly he did walk between Immortality and the scaffold."[22]

One woman's unsolicited comment to a fellow railroad traveler epitomized the veneration accorded the Confederate president during his imprisonment and trial. "I will tell you what I think of Jeff. Davis. I think he was a greater and better man than Jesus Christ."[23]

"They Know They Are Marked Men": *Southern Unionists*

Although not "Yankees" in the most contemptuous sense of the word, loyal Union people in the South, even after the war, found themselves perpetually, and at times increasingly, subjected to the deep-seated animosity of their ex-confederate neighbors. (Southerners were certainly not unanimous in their support of the Confederacy. Loyalties divided even families as was true of one North Carolina family of five brothers who actually succeeded in dividing their loyalties equally—two brothers served with the Union army; two with the Confederate army; and one hid from both armies.[24])

Unionists had taken more than their share of abuse from Confederates during the war, and even after the war, their property and often their very lives were secured only by the Federal troops of occupation. Hosts of Unionists and Northern immigrants feared that once the Union troops were withdrawn the open hostility and violence of former secessionists would force them to leave the Southland. In an 1866 diary entry, Esther Hill Hawks, doctor, teacher and traveler in the South, succinctly assessed the plight of loyalists. "At present the poor men who have remained true to the Union are the most unfortunate, they are despised by the rebs and their lives only safe so long as the military are in power; They are not sought for offices, and strict surveillance is kept over them. They know they are *marked men*, and only tolerated for a season. The bitter reflection must often come to them that it would have been better for them to have been *traitors* than loyal to their country if this is the return she makes for what they have suffered."[25]

The records of the Freedmen's Bureau and the journals of travelers in the Southland were replete with reports of Unionists being hanged, robbed, their homes burned, their crops destroyed. One official told of a young woman walking sixty miles to safety in the snow and sleet with her infant, "her house having been burned over her head."[26] Unionists, particularly veterans of the U. S. Army, were not only victims of their neighbors' hostility but also were singled out as deserving targets for Ku Klux Klan violence. Unfortunately, even the Federal government, for whom they had made such tremendous personal and financial sacrifices, accorded them little help or appreciation.

Cornelia Hancock was particularly sympathetic to the two Union women with whom she lived. "They have been Union through the whole war; have fed the Union prisoners; harbored Jeff's deserters and done many hazardous things for the Union cause. They are literally stripped of everything; robbed by the Rebels. They feel very bitterly towards President Johnson as they think so much has been returned to the rebels and they who suffered so much left in such abject want. I know they deserve it and had I the power of the President I would set such people on their feet mighty quickly." Later she wrote, "Poverty stares nearly all the inhabitants in the face and if President Johnson could only feel it in his heart to help the loyal people, both black and white, instead of the aristocrats who, day by day, are receiving back their lands, assuming their insolent demeanor and straining every nerve that they can may again rule the land. There seems to be no encouragement for the Union people of the South. The number is small but they are tired and I would be glad to see them more prosperous."[27]

The contempt Southerners felt for the Unionists in their midst was only scarcely less than their abhorrence for Yankees in general. Earlier Confederates had burned Catherine Minor in effigy for her pro-union sympathies. Owner of plantations in Louisiana and Mississippi, Catherine admitted she had made herself "very unpopular by not agreeing with the rest of my associates who were infatuated." Rebel women called Catherine "little Yankee" and one lady told her she "ought to be put in a corral with them." The troops of both armies had laid waste her fields and impressed or confiscated her stock, farm buildings, and farm implements. At the war's end Catherine testified "we had nothing in the world: we lived within our resources. We wove our own clothes for the Negroes, our people; we were very much reduced and then we were so anxious for some greenbacks, we sold our clothes to get some." By 1869 Catherine's husband had died and as the provider for three young children, she found herself in desperate circumstances, her plantations devoid of almost everything from fence rails to seed cotton. At the war's end, it often seemed that Northerners were oblivious to the sacrifices Southern Unionists had made and the services they had rendered on behalf of the North. Sometimes it took eight years for the Southern Claims Commission to process their claims, and often any reimbursements were awarded at only a fraction of Unionists' wartime losses. Catherine Minor was finally awarded $13,072, slightly more than one fifth of her claim for $64,155, which had already been scaled down from actual losses. Expenses for the transportation of witnesses to Washington and lawyers' fees left Catherine with slight compensation for her trouble. Shortly before his death in 1869, Catherine's husband turned to alcohol and "refused to go North for medical attention, saying 'that his treatment from his old friends and associates had been such that he didn't care whether he lived or died.'"[28]

"Insulting, Overbearing, Threatening": Occupation Troops

In many areas, the humiliation of defeat was further exacerbated by the presence of Negro troops of occupation. Southerners' financial losses in the emancipation of their slaves was devastating enough; now their being subjected to demeaning orders and restrictions levied by black Yankee soldiers constituted a severe blow to their social status and self-image. Gertrude Thomas's aversion to black domination was commonplace. "So long as negro soldiers guard and Negro men make laws for us just so long will the feeling of resentment linger in our minds."[29]

Federal authorities were inundated with complaints that the black soldiers were not subjected to sufficiently strict rein on their activities. "They are insulting, overbearing, threatening. They intrude upon the premises of the citizens, without leave, to visit the 'colored ladies,' as they call the servants, and if ordered off, they make belligerent demonstrations which alarm and disturb the peace of the family. Appeals to the military authorities are not followed by the prompt and certain punishment which is so necessary to keep Sambo in his place."[30]

New Orleans residents called attention to the unsoldierly-like conduct of some of the colored troops of occupation and chided liquor merchants who contributed to their delinquency. "It was not an uncommon sight to see them drunk on the streets insulting everybody they chance to meet. We are aware that it is almost impossible to keep soldiers from getting drunk, as long as we have in our midst a set of low-down thieving white men who will sell them whisky."[31]

Two months after Appomattox, Pauline DeCaradeuc (Heyward) on a visit with friends and relatives to Aiken, South Carolina, encountered her first black troops at the depot and registered her displeasure at their presence. "They were the first black troops I ever saw, I felt every imaginable emotion upon seeing them, they, who two or three months ago were our respectful slaves, were there as impertinent as possible, pushing & jostling us about ... it was all like a pandemonium of black demons, so intense was the noise & confusion."[32]

White soldiers of occupation were scarcely more tolerated than their black brothers in uniform. They were spat upon, jeered at, or snubbed by most Southerners. Now and then a Southerner would admit that the Northern troops of occupation behaved in a manner far better than had been expected. Most Southerners, however, deplored their existence, particularly former Confederates who became victims of the postwar assaults by malicious, vindictive Northern soldiers (or guerrillas) hell-bent on their own hedonistic pursuits. When Pauline DeCaradeuc's father attempted to prevent two Yankee soldiers from ravishing his home in search of liquor, "one of the men struck him over the head with his musket, which being so wholly unexpected, knocked him down, then they fell on him and kicked him and knocked him with their guns until he was insensible...."[33] Fortunately Pauline's father's injuries were not serious; however such acts of violence, and there were many, merely added to Southerners' antipathy for the loathsome troops of occupation.

A Mobile girl wrote of the Federal occupation of the city that had taken place three days earlier. The blue-clad soldiers, she reported, were "the vilest looking set of creatures I ever saw. I always thought that our men were dirty enough, but oh! I think it would take someone who is better in describing filthiness to describe them. Even their officers are not fit to go into a lady's house."[34]

In Richmond, the Federal troops of occupation were treated with the same contempt that greeted them in most areas of Rebeldom. A Presbyterian minister's wife remarked caustically: "I do not *know* of a single instance in which they have been treated with anything more than the most distant politeness. I have *heard* of one or two wealthy & fashionable families where the young ladies have so far lost their self-respect as to allow these gilded officers to wait on them, but no one of my *acquaintance*."[35]

A South Carolina woman complained, "The city is garrisoned, a Yankee wretch at every corner. We hold our parasols between us and Yankee faces, but we can't escape a sight of their hateful blue legs and feet." The same woman chafed, "How devoid of all generosity all magnanimity are the Yankees, how indecent their jeers over our fallen lot. How low their jokes, over the capture and imprisonment of our fallen Statesman and Patriot, our well beloved President Davis; how fiendish in their anticipation of his death. How disgusting this people, in all their attributes."[36]

"I don't think I should be half so Southern if it were not for these stupid troops," Virginia French reflected. "I begin sometimes to feel quite charitable towards the North but the moment I catch sight of these blue things I am full of resistance and rebellion. How I do hate them! And how I want to let 'em know it to the full!"[37]

Although the fighting was over on the battlefield, Virginia's observations echoed the feelings of much of the Southland. "There is a great deal of rebellion yet to be crushed, or allayed, or gotten rid of in some way and of course, as usual, the Federal authorities are pursuing whatever policy will tend to intensify the hatred of the South towards them." Particularly irksome to Virginia were the Federal orders that men were to cease wearing their gray uniforms and women were to refrain from making any gray goods to be used in wearing apparel. "Yet the Yankee blue flaunts before our eyes as hatefully as ever," Virginia lamented.[38]

Strict martial law, with General Sickles in authority, prevailed in Charleston, South Carolina, Louisa McCord Smythe recalled. "His military orders would be issued and published in the newspapers. By them we had to live. As they all tended to degrade the white and uplift the black population there was constant friction between these two elements which resulted frequently in street rows and murders."[39]

To Grace Elmore the Yankees had irretrievably abridged every vestige of freedom in the South, and the 1865 Fourth of July celebration seemed somewhat ironic. In a city (Columbia, South Carolina) ravaged just months earlier by Sherman's troops and now garrisoned by the enemy, and where basic rights were suspended and personal property had been burned and confiscated, the concept of freedom appeared farcical. "Even as I write I hear the shouts of our enemies mingled with those of our slaves, as together they celebrate the 4th in feasting, and eulogizing Freedom and 'The Union.' Oh, Liberty, how many crimes are committed in thy name. Here are the Military celebrating the 'Declaration of Independence,' in a city over which they stand guard, which they burned and pillaged, and whose people fought and won the same right they celebrate. Whose people now sit in the ashes of their former greatness, hearing in bitterness of spirit the sounds of their rejoicing. Is it not a hideous mockery?"[40]

More than ten years after the war and following a Fourth of July celebration in Charleston, Alice Palmer announced: "I am a greater Rebel than ever. Oh, how it makes my blood boil to see those Yankees all mixed up with our men."[41]

North-South enmity was a two way street, of course. Northerners vehemently objected to the presence of Confederate flags in their line of vision. Alice continued her letter noting that on the opening day of the Centennial in Philadelphia, a family, formerly of Charleston, flew the state flag of South Carolina, only to have it torn down and trampled underfoot. Pubic sentiment, according to Alice and the newspapers, indicated that "South Carolina had brought all the trouble on the country and that no symbol of hers ought ever to be allowed on any public occasion without receiving like treatment." Caustically she added, "Much love they have for us."[42]

"In Terror of Our Lives"

In truth, much as Southerners loathed the presence of Yankee soldiers, areas occupied by either white or black Union troops provided Southerners with much needed protection from marauding gangs of thieves, ruffians, and desperadoes, who roamed the countryside seeking money, vengeance, adventure—or all of the above. In some areas citizens actually petitioned against the removal of Federal troops, having found them a blessing in serving to curtail the activities of the Ku Klux Klan and in helping prevent black-white conflicts.[43]

The turmoil of the times was recorded by a discouraged George Eggleston during the early days following the war. "It is difficult to comprehend, and impossible to describe, the state of uncertainty in which we lived in this time," he wrote. "There was no State, county, or municipal government in existence among us. We had no courts, no justices of the peace, no sheriffs, no officers of any kind invested with a shadow of authority, and there were not men enough in the community, at first, to resist the marauders, comparatively few of the surrendered soldiers having found their way home as yet."[44] In the ensuing months the presence of military rule seemed to Sara Handy "a little thing, after having been without any government at all, and in terror of our lives."[45]

Fanny Berry, of Petersburg, Virginia, explained that "When de Yankees come dey sot de niggers free an' de niggers went on wukin' jus' like dey did befo' only now whut dey make is dere'n an' dey don't have tuh take et an' put et away in de master's barn, An' de whites couldn't say nothin' 'cause dey was po'as de niggers an' besides de Yankees were dere to watch 'em."

"But after while de Yankees went on back up North, an' den de 'po'hickories' got tuh acting up. Dey would put on de ole uniforms de Yankees done lef' behin' an' go ridin' all over de lan' at night in bands jus' ah shootin' up all de niggers dey saw. Dey would shoot 'em daid an' ride on. An' some one finally sent word up No'th to de Yankees an' de Yankees come aridin' back an' dem ole whites was jus' as nice an' pleasant fo' a while as could be. Long as de Yankees was aroun'. But soon's de Yankees leave dey start in again. An' don't you know, Yankees had tuh come back tuh Appamattox three times fo' de whites leave us po' niggers alone?"[46]

"This Oath, or See Yourselves Plundered": Pardons and the Oath of Allegiance

In May of 1865 President Johnson issued his Amnesty Proclamation, whereby former rebels could obtain pardons by taking the Oath of Allegiance to the Federal government. Although his proclamation made amnesty available for most Southerners, there were certain exceptions. Confederates worth as much or more than $20,000 in taxable property (and several other excepted classes) were excluded from amnesty, but were eligible for a special pardon from President Johnson provided their petitions were deemed valid.

Pardons, of course, were of vital importance to every storekeeper, minister, lawyer, businessman. It was mandatory to secure a pardon in order to operate a business, conduct church services, provide legal counsel, buy or sell property, and in some cases take the marriage vows. Within days after the surrender Mary Fontaine wrote from Richmond, Virginia, of the rash of marriages taking place. "We had a number of sudden marriages last Sunday. An order being issued Saturday, that after Monday all persons marrying must take the oath before procuring licenses, there was considerable confusion created among certain Confederate officers, who were looking forward to marriage in the Spring."[47]

Needless to say, being forced to profess allegiance to the Federal government was particularly humiliating to Southerners; securing a pardon, however, involved taking the Oath of Allegiance. A special "Ironclad Test Oath" was a prerequisite for civil servants, military and naval officers, attorneys, judges.[48] Unfortunately, few Southerners could honestly subscribe to the Ironclad Oath testifying that they had never voluntarily given "aid, countenance, counsel or encouragement to persons engaged in armed hostilities" against the United States, and untold numbers of men were removed from office or prevented from assuming public offices based on their inability to take the Ironclad Oath. Subscribing to the "loyalty oath," however, wherein the individual pledged to "support and defend the Constitution of the United States, against all enemies, foreign and domestic, that I will bear true faith and allegiance to the same..." was indeed irritating although considerably less restrictive. Prior to Appomattox, of course, most Confederates in Federally occupied areas had already been required to take the oath.[49]

Countless Southerners objected to the amnesty oath believing the Emancipation Proclamation to be unconstitutional. (Swearing to sanction the abolition of slavery was next to impossible for many Southerners.) Others, believing they had done nothing to repent, simply refused to take the oath on principle. Mary Farrar Wilkinson's husband died at the Battle of Second Manassas, and it was understandable that she would be unwilling to take the Oath of Allegiance when the Federals took over New Orleans. Her recalcitrance resulted in her temporary imprisonment in the Rampart Street Prison after which she was sent by General Butler to Vicksburg. Following the siege of Vicksburg she embarked on a continuous effort to keep ahead of the Union troops. After leaving Vicksburg she found temporary sanctuary in Columbia, South Carolina, finally returning home to New Orleans after the war.[50]

As she was being ordered out of Savannah by the Yankees for her "imprudent letters," Rosa Postell was at a loss as to know where to find refuge for herself and her five children. Inquiries about removing to Philadelphia were met with the ultimatum that she would be allowed passage only if she took the oath. Having lost one son in the war and suffering extreme anxiety over the fate of her other two soldier sons Rosa was infuriated that anyone could conceive of her acquiescing to the requirement. "I could not give utterance to my feelings of indignation," Rosa fumed. "I compressed my lips, cast my eyes down, and gave a most significant shake of my head as a reply." A few weeks later, however, Mrs. Postell was compelled "to take THAT OATH!" as a requisite to receiving letters concerning a second son, Chase, who lay dying of wounds during the last days of the conflict. Rosa wrote to her prisoner-of-war husband: "I did it, that I might receive my letters at *this time*, when I was almost crazy to hear something of my dear Son, whom I fondly hoped would live. [He had been reported wounded, and had eventually succumbed to his wounds.] So I now advise you to take *that oath*, that you may be allowed to leave your prison...."[51]

As the paroled soldiers began returing home, even many of the most devoted Rebels advocated their taking the oath. Florence Anderson summarized the change in attitude in a letter to a friend. "I was opposed to such a course when we had a cause, a Government which demanded loyalty, but now I can see no good from a prolongation of the period of captivity which can only be eventually terminated in this way. I advise all paroled prisoners and those still in confinement to give preference to the oath, as I cannot endure the thought of so many who are the rightful owners of the land being alienated, unless there could be a hope of future independence, which there is not."

Catherine Edmondston's diary entry of July 28, 1865, reflected the hypocrisy and the festering resentment of Southerners forced to take the Loyalty Oath. "On Monday, Father and Mr. Edmondston were forced, in order to protect themselves, to take the oath of allegiance. They say to us, 'This Oath or see yourselves plundered by Yankees and negroes alike; This Oath, or turned out of your house and loved home.' Swear anything—both possible and impossible—say light is darkness—heat is cold—Andy Johnson is a gentleman—Seward is truthful—Yankees are honest—what you will! I assent to it all, and hate you while I do it." Catherine continued: "Yes Yankee nation, 'cute' as you are, you cannot fathom the depth of hate, contempt, & rage with which you have filled the breast of every true Southron." Venom poured forth as Catherine told of her brother's request for a pardon "at the hand of his high mightiness Andy Johnson for the crime of being worth more than $20,000." The attitude of tens of thousands of Southerners was denoted by Catherine as she raged: "He [Johnson] has exalted himself by pulling others down. In the seething cauldron, the thickest scum ever rises to the top!" Catherine concluded with: "for all this [forced profession of allegiance] we hate you!"[52]

Emily Mason, a dedicated Civil War nurse, in seeking a pass to journey north after the war, was stopped and questioned as to whether she had taken the oath of allegiance. Testily she took issue with the interrogator. "No," she replied, "and I never will! Suppose your wife should swear fealty to another man because you had lost everything? You would expect her to be more faithful because of your misfortunes." The commandant acknowledged the analogy and granted her the pass.[53]

Louisiana residents who were charged two dollars and fifty cents to take the oath hotly protested the assessment. Apparently those were paltry fees, for pardons were handled by "pardon brokers" who charged from $150 to $200 for their services. (Women, summoning their feminine wiles, often proved to be successful "brokers." One female broker even tangled with the famous detective La Fayette C. Baker, who directed the capture of John Wilkes Booth. Baker devoted several chapters of his *History of the United States Secret Service*, pages 589–646, to the intriguing story of his troubles with Mrs. John R. Cobb.) In many occupied areas taking the Oath of Allegiance was a prerequisite to being allowed access to the Yankee commissary stores—a condition that prompted large numbers of hungry albeit hesitant Southerners to take the pledge.

Despite their irritation, millions of Southerners gritted their teeth and for the sake of their families and their careers took the oath. For the less conscientious, however, it was not difficult to make unspoken, mental reservations in taking the pledge. (Prior to Appomattox countless rebel soldiers solemnly took the oath, were paroled, and quickly took flight to rejoin the Confederate army.[54])

Not a few Southerners following "the recent unpleasantness" were hypocritical and believed that a compulsory oath was not at all binding. Others who took the oath, simply to restore their citizenship, treated it "in a frivolous and sneering manner." Such levity naturally provoked the authorities and finally at least one provost marshal was instructed to administer the oath "to those only whom he had good reason to believe would honestly observe it."[55]

"I Will Do What My Conscience Approves Of"

For the more scrupulous Southerners, taking the oath presented a nagging moral dilemma. Southerners required to take oath in occupied areas during the war and those forced to submit to it following the war faced the same wrenching personal conflict. "It is deeply repugnant to every feeling of our hearts, but how else can we get the necessaries of life?" Mary Edmondson queried. "We are cut off from our own people and almost every means of making our support. I do not yet think I can take an oath to save us from starvation and utterly disregard it as others have done and yet to renounce all that are dear to me is *utterly impossible*."[56] The situation became even more traumatic when Mary's physician husband was arrested and then temporarily released to attend to his patients—but with strict orders to return and take the oath or go to prison. An anxiety-ridden Mary devoted untold hours to fasting and praying over the sinfulness of her husband's taking a false oath; however, at the last moment her prayers were answered when a friend interceded for him and he was not subjected to taking the oath.

Ella Tazewell was dismayed by orders that Southerners who refused to take the oath of allegiance in New Orleans were prevented from engaging in business or teaching "both from the pulpit or in schools." She added, "Nothing can be done ... no one who has not subscribed to this can ask any favour, be heard in any court, or expect any protection whatever, except from personal violence; and moreover, whoever takes this oath is also forced to indorse the Emancipation Proclamation, and all acts of Congress relative to slavery that have been, or will be passed, the said acts to be confirmed, or rendered void by the action of the Supreme Court."[57]

Ella continued, "With the exception of few, very few, the whole population have taken the oath, the panic is intense. Tho' our household have not done it, and as far as human beings can say, will not, yet I do not blame any who have. Some have reasoned this way: if they do not submit to the terms their property will be taken from them, and thus they will yield assistance to the Gov. they detest; others have done it merely from love of money, and they ought to be despised, but the majority, and they principally women, have done it for protection. It is said through the town that all who refuse,—in other words the 'disloyal', are liable to be turned out of their homes, & possibly negroes put in, or quartered on them, for a previous order says they are to be treated with respect, and are on an equality with the whites. To look around it would seem so."[58]

For Ella subscribing to the oath involved a serious tug of war with her conscience. Even though refusing to take the oath might mean the loss of all their property, Ella was deeply concerned with the sin of perjury. "Pray that grace may be given me to do my duty; it will be hard to give up all here, not as property,—for I do not believe we care more for that than we should,—but there are associations with one's home that cannot be severed without distress. I was born in this house, and here my Father and blessed Mother breathed their last,—every tree and plant has a memory connected with it. But what is all this compared to a false oath?"

"Man is not to live forever," she reasoned. "Earthly possessions, however dear, must be left, and how awful it will be to appear before our Maker with a perjured soul. We are urged on every side, indeed implored, not to turn such a large property into the hands of our enemies, but that reasoning does not satisfy us; Ten, yes I believe half of that number, would cover all who have resisted, hundreds who have property to protect, and thousands who have scarcely food and raiment, and they do not consider they have done wrong, or that the oath is at all binding, and their hearts and feelings have not changed. They would most eagerly renew their allegiance to our Gov. tomorrow. But Doctor, is this right as a *Virginian* and as a *Christian*? But still I feel charitably toward them, as no one who has not witnessed the panic can imagine it. If the town was being bombarded it would meet with greater calmness." It seemed so very wrong to Ella to take the oath when the boys who "are fighting for us" discover that "their fathers, yes, and mothers and sisters have taken the oath." (Fortunately Ella's family had been healthy. "Our physicians have not been allowed to practice for months. We have so much to be thankful for, not a case of sickness has occurred in our family to require a doctor's advice."[59])

During the Union occupation of Nashville, Rachel Craighead railed against taking the Oath of Allegiance. "All I can say is that I can't help myself. I never hated to do anything so bad in my life. I pray to God that all the sin may rest on the heads of our enemies." Despite whatever reservations attended her taking the oath, Rachel was faithful to the terms of the pledge. Rachel explained to her diary: "The Parole says I cannot write or speak against the Govt. It is very difficult for me to bring myself to

take [it] but I'll have to so I cant write anything more against our enemies after tonight so goodbye."[60]

It took time—and persuasion—for loyal Confederates to agree to
subscribe to the oath. The decision to take the oath was particularly traumatic for POWs, such as Joe Selby [apparently the nephew of Jim Selby],
men whose release was conditioned on their willingness to subscribe to
the oath. Although taking the Oath of Allegiance would mean release
within weeks, Joe Selby, a POW at Fort Delaware, found it difficult to
agree to the oath while there were still armies in the field. "*All* of the men,
and a majority of the officers will accept it, believing that the Confederacy is 'gone up.' My name will be called to morrow, and I am totally
undecided what to do. I have swore allegiance to the 'Confederate States,'
and there being yet two armies in the field, my conscience tells me, it will
be perjury to give up until they surrender, or are dispersed, and yet many
highly intelligent officers have decided to do so. I am sorry it was not put
off until Johnstons surrender, and think it premature. I regard an oath as
a very solemn and binding thing, and if I take it, will abide by it, in all
things. Rest assured of one thing, I will do what my conscience approves
of, let the result be what it may."[61] Joe waited until May 13, 1865, to
finally take the amnesty oath.

Confederate Captain George Washington Nelson Jr., a prisoner of
war at Fort Delaware, faced a similar situation. When asked for a third
time, "Wash" and 2,300 of his fellow prisoners agreed to take the Oath of
Allegiance. "God alone knows the struggle I have had," he wrote his fiancée,
Mollie. Not only was his own integrity at stake, but how would Mollie
react? Would she summarily reject him as having compromised his honor?
"Wash" begged Mollie to write him immediately with "a little comfort—
for the cheering word that you will sustain me in the path of duty and conscience." Mollie and others like her quickly responded to their crucial roles
as comforters and nurturers in not only acquiescing in but in enthusiastically applauding their loved ones' decision to accept the oath.[62]

Southerners who consistently refused were often induced to take the
oath when they became victims of local terrorists. Nannie Scott's father's
wheat crop, for example, was completely destroyed as a result of his reluctance to agree to the oath.[63] Only after taking the oath was Elizabeth
Allston's (Pringle) mother able to secure help from the government in
obtaining the return of the keys to her property from the former slaves
to whom they had been given.[64] Even some Northerners in various capac-
ities were compelled to pledge their loyalty. As a teacher from the New
England Freedman's Aid Society, one of Elizabeth Hyde Botume's first
assignments upon her arrival at Hilton Head was to go to the provost-
marshal's office to take the oath.[65]

Naturally, authorities, including provisional governors (Sharkey, Johnson, Perry, for example) urged former Confederates to take the oath, pointing out that slavery was a dead issue, that "African slavery ... is gone, dead forever, never to be revived or hoped for in the future of this State."[66] Governor Johnson, of Georgia, likened the necessity of taking the oath to a tender mother subjecting a child to "a bitter pill which must be taken because ordered by the Doctor."[67]

"If Required *to Pray for Lincoln"*

Yet another source of conflict, one particularly annoying to Southerners, was the insistence by officers of the troops of occupation that the Confederate prayer for President Jefferson Davis be discontinued following the war's end and that prayer for the president of the United States, Abraham Lincoln or later Andrew Johnson, be reinstated in church services. Diary after diary depicted the writer's irritation with this seemingly despicable order. This attempt to regulate their innermost thoughts, their prayers, and to dictate the subject of their appeals was totally abhorrent to most Southerners. (Following secession Southerners had insisted that their ministers' prayers be offered not on behalf of Lincoln but for the president of the Confederacy, Jefferson Davis. Clergymen who inadvertently continued reciting the prayer for the president of the United States abruptly revised the liturgy after watching members of their congregations rise up in protest and leave the church en masse.) Clergymen in occupied areas during the war who omitted the prayer for the president altogether (so as to avoid the mandate to pray for President Lincoln, a plan devised by countless ministers to skirt the issue and to avoid hypocrisy) was totally unacceptable to the authorities. Churches failing to comply were threatened with closure, and in some instances, recalcitrant ministers were banished and their congregations disbanded.

The Reverend Dr. Alex Marshall of St. John's Chapel in Charleston, South Carolina, for example, ran headlong into big trouble in April of 1865 on two counts: by failing to take the Oath of Allegiance and by omitting the prayer for the president of the United States during his church services. When called in by the authorities to account for himself, the Reverend Marshall admitted that prior to the Federal occupation of Charleston, he had, of course, included a prayer for the president—of the Confederacy. Since the Union takeover of Charleston, he wished to give no offense and therefore had omitted the prayer altogether. His frank admission merely served to further incense the officials who immediately informed the Reverend Marshall that no clergyman who omitted the prayer from his service would be allowed to officiate in Charleston.

With this ultimatum, the Reverend Marshall then communicated the orders to his congregation and "dismissed them without holding any service." Believing the prayer to be a "political prayer," the Reverend Marshall discontinued his services at St. John's Chapel, and penned a note to the officials: "I am not yet at liberty to take the Oath of Allegiance to the United States." This was the last straw for the Federal authorities with this obstinate pastor, and the Reverend Marshall was ordered to "be sent beyond the lines of the army, and be forbidden to enter the city of Charleston during its occupation by the United States troops...." (In addition his personal property was to be confiscated.)

Even the congregation was subjected to the officials' wrath. The Federals announced that the Reverend Marshall's punishment was intended as a warning to worshippers at the church who had covered for the reverend and not reported the omission to the Federal authorities. "They are also warned that they will hereafter be marked persons, and any act done, or word uttered, in justification of his disloyalty, will subject them to a like punishment."[68]

Countless writers, including Sarah Follansbee, living in Montgomery, Alabama, for example, corroborated the problems involved by the Federal authorities' draconian orders that the prayer for the president of the United States must be read as part of the traditional church service, otherwise services at those churches failing to comply with the order must be discontinued.[69] Instructions to his clergymen from the Protestant Episcopal Bishop of Alabama, the Right Reverend R. H. Wilmer, in June 1865, ordering them not to pray for the Federal occupying authorities, resulted in his suspension and that of other clergymen from their duties and the closing of their churches.[70]

In early April during the occupation of Richmond, the provost marshal summoned the city's Episcopal and Catholic clergymen to a meeting for a serious discussion of the church liturgy concerning the prayer for the president. Wisely, in order to quell further dissension, it was decided to leave the decision whether to include or omit the prayer during church services up to the discretion of the church officials. Lucy Fletcher, wife of a local Presbyterian minister, theorized: "I suppose our ministers would none of them officiate, if *required* to pray for Lincoln, as has been done in other places." In short order, apparently the Federal officials had had enough of magnanimity, and Lucy reported, "The Episcopal churches were all closed yesterday, in consequence of an order from the Commanding General, that the Prayer for the Pres. U. S. should be read! This I consider the worst form of tyranny. I could not pray for our own Pres, or my own child *under orders.*" During the Union takeover of Wilmington, North Carolina, during the last days of the war, when the rector of the Protestant Episcopal Church refused to pray for Lincoln instead of Jefferson Davis, the church was seized, the pews and pulpit removed and the church made into a hospital. About the same time the Methodist Church was appropriated by the Federals and given over to Negroes.[71]

As the Federals occupied Mobile in April of 1865, one young resident wrote her cousin of her annoyance at the officers' insistence on having the Confederate flag over their church replaced by the United States flag and at the additional stipulation that parishioners pray not for Jeff Davis but for President Lincoln. "They need not think they spite anyone by doing so.... Even if they do wish us to pray for Old Uncle Abe, we can very easily sit up instead of kneeling when we get to that part of the service."[72]

In her reminiscences Louisa McCord Smythe told of her church in Columbia, South Carolina, being closed as a result of the minister's refusal to read the prayer for the president of the United States. The minister, notified that the church would be turned over to a black congregation were it to remain vacant one more Sunday, conducted regular services the following week. With the reading of the prayer for the president the parishioners, who had been kneeling throughout the service, stood up as if on cue, thus registering in the presence of the Federal officers in attendance their supreme contempt for the order. That spontaneous act of defiance persisted as roguish perversity in the weeks and months to come.

As late as May 21, 1865, Mary Goodwin, prior to her knowledge of the capture of Jeff Davis, told her diary, "We still pray for the President of the Confederate States, though we don't know that there is such a personage." One week later Mary wrote: "Today father [a minister] omitted the prayer for the Pres. of the CS for the 1st time as it is believed that he has fallen into the hands of the enemy." She added "What a mysterious Providence it is that has brought us so low. But we can only trust that all will be well at last."[73]

The following Sunday when Mary Goodwin's father attempted to offer the prayer for the president of the United States, Mary reported that he trembled visibly and finally dissolved into tears. It was the day of Holy Communion and Mary admitted that when Communion was administered, "I did not feel that Charity for our enemies that a child of God ought to feel to be justified in coming to Communion. We are commanded to love even our Enemies, & as individuals I do not *hate* them or at least would do them no personal injury. But as a Nation as *Yankees,* I do dislike them intensely. I cannot, *cannot* love the Yankees...."[74]

"To Bring About the Education of Blacks": Schoolteachers from the North

Southerners were annoyed, often angered, and at times given to violence as a result of the influx of Northern teachers who invaded the Southland to teach the blacks to read and write.[75] In 1866 the American Freedmen's Union Commission and the American Missionary Association along with other church groups supported hundreds of teachers.[76] Basic to Southerners' aversion, of course, was their heritage of racial supremacy and the persistent threat of the potential power of an educated black race. In addition untold numbers of Southerners were indignant at the educating of black children before thousands of white children were provided teachers and books. So great was the opposition against the teachers and the schools that at times black schools were maintained only through the presence of the Yankee troops.[77]

The brother of O. O. Howard, commissioner of the Freedmen's Bureau, testified that he had never seen in South Carolina "any who felt interest enough in it [education of blacks] to advocate it, or to take any measures, either in their legislature or elsewhere, to bring about the education

PRIMARY SCHOOL FOR FREEDMEN, IN CHARGE OF Mrs. GREEN, AT VICKSBURG, MISSISSIPPI.—[See Page 394.]

"Primary School for Freedmen in Vicksburg, Mississippi." (Harper's Weekly June 25, 1866.)

of blacks." Most seemed to deem it a folly although there are a few "who are not so much opposed to it."[78] Most felt it would be detrimental to labor: Blacks would not work so well and their absence in the fields would reduce the labor supply.

For some Southerners their displeasure was not so much the fact that their former slaves were being educated, but rather the suspicion that the hated Northerners would fill their young pupils' heads with liberal, Yankee ideas. (Actually, Radical Republicans did, indeed, find many of the teachers an excellent medium for the promulgation of Republican ideology.) Rumors that the Yankee teachers were instructing their "scholars" in patriotic Union songs such as "John Brown," "Rally Round the Flag," and "Three Cheers for the Red White and Blue" proved true, at least in Cornelia Hancock's school in South Carolina. Unable to come up with the precise words to all the songs, Cornelia sent a request northward for copies of the songs to be used with her newly freed charges.

Many conservative Southerners were convinced that southern men rather than northern women should be engaged to teach the newly freed blacks. Prevailing thought concluded that "A Negro educated by a northern teacher would be taught to hate the southern heritage, whereas a Negro educated by a Southerner could be taught to revere the South's way of life."[79]

Letitia Dabney Miller could find little good to say about the New England schoolmarms. "A Southern woman would starve before she would teach Negroes, in the South, though she was quite capable of going as a missionary to Africa. So the Negroes (all ages wanted to learn) were turned over to the rather fanatical Yankee schoolmarms, who broke down all the old barriers, old restraints, and knew not how to erect new ones. Then began the outrages and lynchings, followed by reprisals on both sides, the Negroes always getting the worst of it."

Much of the racial unrest Letitia Miller blamed on the Yankee teachers. "This was after the New England schoolmarms with their inflammatory teaching had broken up the old relations. I don't mean they taught crime. But they inflamed the minds of the Negroes by telling them how unjustly they had been held down. Negro suffrage and Carpetbag government helped."[80] Case in point: Anna Gardner, a teacher sent to the Southland by the New England Freedmen's Aid Society, garnered the wrath of the Albemarle County populace with her zealous crusade to inculcate doctrines of equality and self-worth in her black pupils. In answer to Anna's appeal in 1867 for a donation to her school, the editor of the *Charlottesville Chronicle* responded that the white residents of Charlottesville believed Anna was far outreaching her role as a teacher, duties that should have been confined to teaching the 3 R's. "The idea prevails that you instruct them in politics and sociology; that you come among us not merely as an ordinary school teacher, but as a political missionary; that you communicate to the colored people ideas of social equality with the whites. With your first object we sympathize; the second we regard as mischievous, and as only tending to disturb the good feeling between the two races."

Anna's response was brief and to the point. "Mr. J. C. Southall, I teach *in* school and *out*, so far as my political influence extends, the fundamental principles of 'politics' and 'sociology,' vis:—'Whatever you would that men should do to you, do ye even so unto them.'" Certainly Anna's assessment of the ex-slave holders as "those alien and hostile people ... primitive in appearance and habits" or "those subtle, slippery Virginians," in no way dispelled her reputation as a meddling fanatic.[81]

Numerous detractors criticized the Yankee teachers for being too free in their relationships with the freedmen and interested solely in the financial returns from teaching. Southerners loudly denounced the Yankee women's familiarity with their black pupils. People were stunned when an Augusta, Georgia, teacher was observed to have kissed some of her young black students, and local white residents took offense at her repeated insistence that Negroes were as good as white people.[82]

Even white Southern women who took up the teaching of blacks also came in for their share of the criticism. When Tougaloo College, established for the schooling of black men and women, opened in 1869 near Jackson, Mississippi, the *Vicksburg Herald* ridiculed any "lady" desiring to teach at the school. "A lady who is capable of teaching at all must be in sore need if she has to resort to a colored school to eke out a precarious existence and we hope the time will never come when any true daughter of the South will ever be put to that necessity."[83]

Antipathy for the northern schoolmarms and Negro schools in general, including those sponsored by the Freedmen's Bureau, were at times, and even often, the subject of caustic editorials in southern newspapers. In defense of the teachers and the education of blacks, Freedmen's Bureau officials valiantly sought to repudiate the disparaging charges. One Freedmen's Bureau official accused the newspapers of taking the "occasion to abuse the school mistresses and others in charge of the schools by publishing innuendoes and articles charging the school mistresses with actual crime or complicity in crime, all of which charges are untrue." The official continued by explaining that the newspapers accused the teachers of exacting money from the children and noting that were a child attendee to be accused of any petty offense, the schools and the bureau would be subjected to slurs and aspersions in the press. At least one woman was harshly rebuffed by a white employer for her presumptuousness in calling on the family of one of his servants to urge that the daughter be sent to school.[84]

"Here Comes Hell"

Yankee schoolmarms were laughed at, stared at, scoffed at, threatened, and ridiculed. Cornelia Hancock and the teachers at their Mt. Pleasant, South Carolina, school for freedmen quickly discerned the resentment harbored against them by their Southern neighbors. "Everyone hates us with a bitter hatred here. They would be glad if a consuming fire would come over the land and annihilate both the contrabands and their teachers." On the train en route to Charleston, Cornelia wrote of the ex–Confederates using "the most vituperative language against the Yanks. We were marked on the whole way and the people said every kind of disagreeable thing in our hearing but would not condescend to speak to the 'Yankee nigger teachers' as they call us." Once the military left the area around Charleston and Mt. Pleasant, Cornelia reassured her mother in Salem, New Jersey, she would leave too. "The rebels would be just as likely to tar and feather us now as in former days and would go unpunished for the deed too."[85]

Dr. Esther Hill Hawks, a northern physician who journeyed South to teach blacks, told of Southerners' treatment of northern teachers. "There is nothing to[o] mean to say of the teachers and no inducements could prevail on them to offer us any civilities or take one as a boarder— and every impediment is thrown in the way of the schools and their success." Sarah Jane Foster was living testimony of the disdain that many Southerners accorded "nigger teachers." Local residents of Martinsburg, West Virginia, where Sarah had come as one of a contingent of Northern Freewill Baptist teachers to help educate the freedmen, were outraged by her conduct in walking in public with black men and visiting her black pupils in their homes. Fearing personal ostracism her landlady turned her out, and various other residents refused to board her. When Sarah became the object of threatening letters and the subject of vicious town gossip, her superiors transferred her to Harpers Ferry and ultimately refused to rehire her for another year. Sarah's treatment was certainly not unique in the postwar South. Her successor had taught at Charles Town, had to be escorted to her school by an armed guard, and kept a "good axe an six-shooter at the head of my bed at night." Some months later Sarah was hired by the American Missionary Association to teach in Charleston. As a missionary teacher she was religious, but not fanatically so. Her religion, however, helped make her a true believer in black-white equality.

For her black charges Sarah gave her time, her heart and her life. In June of 1868 at age twenty-eight Sarah died of yellow fever contracted during her teaching duties in South Carolina.[86]

In Cuthbent, Georgia, Sarah Campney's welcome was less than hospitable as a chorus of "Here Comes Hell" greeted her arrival. In Charlottesville, Virginia, Anna Gardner complained that even the university students took it upon themselves to terrorize the schoolmarms.[87]

In a diary entry in November of 1870, Blanche Butler Ames observed the utter contempt held by "Southern ladies" for the Northern school teachers who had come South to conduct schools for the Negro children and their parents. By successfully establishing a school for black children in Holly Springs, Mississippi, a courageous Mrs. Gill quickly incurred the wrath of the townspeople for her efforts on behalf of the recently freed blacks. "Every Northern woman who takes up her residence in Holly Springs," Blanche wrote, "is informed that she must give up all idea of intercourse socially with the 'Southern ladies' if she receives or returns Mrs. Gill's calls."[88]

On the surface, at least, Southern women seemed to register greater disdain for the teachers than Southern men, behavior perhaps attributable to ingrained Southern chivalry on the part of the men. Mary Ames noted that many of the planters who came to Edisto Island hoping to retake possession of their property "were gentlemen ... but when they were in possession and were joined by their families, it was different. The women ignored us."[89] Whitelaw Reid wrote of several North Carolina women who snubbed a young officer who apparently evidenced too great an interest in the Negro schools. Reid wondered: "The men of North Carolina may be 'subjugated,' but who shall subjugate the women?"[90]

Hosts of Southerners, even those in want of boarders, refused to take in lady schoolteachers from the North "who were there for the purpose of teaching colored schools." According to O. O. Howard's brother who was an inspector in the Freedmen's Bureau serving in South Carolina, Georgia, and Florida: "They would never receive on any social equality the lady teachers who go down there, whatever might have been their social position at the north. They never receive them into social equality, and they try to make it uncomfortable for them. In fact, I have had great difficulty to contend with in locating female teachers, particularly in towns. It has been almost impossible to procure boarding-places for them. People who need the pecuniary advantages of keeping of boarders would refuse to receive teachers into their families because they were negro teachers."[91]

Even liberal Southerners refused to board teachers of blacks for fear they themselves would be ostracized or become subjects of verbal or possibly physical abuse. In Canton, Mississippi, residents were steadfastly "determined not to have any freedmen's schools, or any damned Yankees in the place."[92]

Not just teachers but even the children of teachers of ex-slaves were subjected to insults and slurs from their white classmates and friends. Some white children were so disparaged by their neighbors for attending the few experimental biracial schools in existence that their parents reluctantly withdrew them from classes. Elizabeth Hyde Botume told of two bright young girls "from an old Southern family" who in the absence of any other school in the area eagerly attended a school for freedmen's children. Within two months they were removed by their parents as a result of peer pressure from friends and neighbors.[93]

In numerous areas almost anyone attempting to help set up schools for blacks brought forth the ire of the local residents. Here and there a few planters, hoping to retain some of their best workers, maintained schools for the children of their black help. This too was frowned upon. A Northern "speculator" and his brother who had taken over a plantation in Yazoo County, Mississippi, were shocked by the attitude of native Southerners who were indignant over their audacity in organizing a school for their black workers and their families. Even more outrageous apparently was their hiring of a white Northern woman to teach. The townspeople were horrified by the idea of "'A white lady teaching a Niger school!!!'"—certainly a crime against her "sex and her race." Insults flew thick and fast. The teacher was shunned from the start, and as the brothers passed in the street local women would "gather their skirts about them and turn away." Men would barricade their passage to the post office.[94]

"The White People Forced Them to Leave the Country": Violence Against Teachers

In some areas opposition to the teachers and their schools became violent. Frequently Yankee teachers were refused rooms or buildings in which to conduct their classes. Ku Klux Klan members or gangs under various names such as "White Caps," "Pale Faces," or "Knights of the White Camellia" believed the Negroes were "getting too smart" and undertook to vandalize and burn buildings and churches used as classrooms. Schoolmarms were pelted with stones, their windows smashed, and male teachers were even threatened with hanging if they did not leave town. Some female teachers received terrifying letters, drawings, and messages promising dire consequences if they continued to teach, threats which frightened them into abandoning their schools and leaving the area. In Columbus, Georgia, a committee of local women was appointed to call on the teachers and urge them to leave town. Fortunately the military arrived and the visit was aborted.[95] One spirited Northern female teacher prudently responded to the threats of personal violence by obtaining a gun and spending her free time in target practice before the greatly subdued townspeople.[96]

The widely publicized whipping incident of Colonel Huggins in Mississippi focused nationwide attention on the appalling situation involving the education of Negroes in some areas of the South. In 1870 Colonel A. P. Huggins, county superintendent of education in Monroe County, Mississippi, first encountered trouble with the local residents when he applied for membership in the local church and was denied admission for the crime of having served in the Federal Army. Problems quickly escalated when he was discovered helping establish Negro schools and assisting blacks in achieving social equality. Huggins was soon confronted by the Ku Klux Klan and informed of the Klan's policy of first issuing a warning, then administering a whipping. Finally, he was told, if an individual did not obey the Klan's ultimatums, the offender would be killed by the Klan en masse or privately by assassination. Although Huggins put up a brave fight, a severe whipping induced him to leave the area, and in short order the story of his beating made headlines throughout the country adding substantially to the Klan's bad press in the North.[97]

A group of disguised men visited Mrs. Sarah A. Allen, an Illinois teacher, one evening and forced her to quit her Negro school in Monroe County, Mississippi. Unable to secure housing with white townspeople, Mrs. Allen had taken up residence in the home of a black family, where the men called to inform her that she must discontinue her school as the local residents did not want Radicals in their area, especially Northern teachers. Furthermore they vigorously objected to the heavy school taxes being levied upon them. Unfortunately, Mrs. Allen was merely one of a host of Northern teachers to be ordered to leave. Sarah Cole and Polly Day conducted Negro schools in Pontotoc County, Mississippi, but their advocacy of social equality "became so odious that the white people forced them to leave the country."[98]

Mississippi teachers were certainly not alone in being subjected to violence and mistreatment. School buildings were stoned in Glasgow, Kentucky; teachers were insulted with obscene language in Oxford, North Carolina; mobs burned schoolhouses in Maryland and in Oxford, Georgia.[99] Students at the University of Virginia terrorized women teachers in Charlottesville with frequent raids and insulting language. In Ellaville, in Milledgeville, and in Cuthbent, Georgia, female teachers were threatened and harassed. The incidents of white resistance to the education of blacks was almost interminable.[100]

"*Freedom from Ignorance Is Power in Any Country*"

On the other side of the coin and in marked contrast to the skeptical critics were advocates who looked upon Northern teachers as God fearing men and women engaged in a praiseworthy undertaking.[101] Radical Republicans, parents and the pupils themselves joined in singing the praises of the teachers and their work. Here were conscientious, enthusiastic teachers eager to meet a desperate need for education for a heretofore deprived populace.

Surely the schoolmarms themselves must have felt rewarded by their pupils' passionate yearning for an education. Southerners were often surprised and at the same time apprehensive of their former slaves' thirst for knowledge. Antebellum laws prohibiting the teaching of slaves to read and write had engendered an intense desire in freedmen to acquire an education. A Virginian recalled: "Aftuh da wo' everybody went school fer to learn. Ol folks, young folks, everybudy, went night school 'an day school...."[102] One young boy, for example, walked four miles to school three days each week and then shared his pair of shoes with his sister thus enabling her to attend school for the other three days.[103]

A North Carolina resident exclaimed, "No one can realize the earnest manner and eager desire these people exhibit for knowledge, without being an eye-witness of the same." Often parents came with the children to see for themselves the books, the classes and the northern teachers. First, there was laughter from the aged parents and then tears of joy. "Poor creatures!" the writer observed, "What a world has been closed to them and now, how their minds hunger and thirst to enter it!"[104] Countless observers delighted in seeing the children take such an interest in their schooling and marveled at their speed and ability in acquiring new information and new skills.

Reports concerning the school in Edenton, North Carolina, gave excellent marks to their pupils for attendance, progress and unrivaled perseverance. "They carry their beloved books every where with them, improving every opportunity of pursuing them. On their way to and from school, and at recess, we can see them in little groups, walking and studying, the more advanced kindly assisting those not so fortunate." One eager young "scholar," after completing his day's work of chopping wood, studied his lessons for evening school "by the light reflected upon the verandah through the windows of the room where we were taking tea."[105]

There was a special incentive, of course, to learn to read in order to be able to read the Bible (a goal not unappreciated by the church-backed schools.) Nettie Henry told an interviewer for the WPA Writers' Project about her former owners' helping to teach them to read and write after the war. "An den we carried our Blue Back Spellers to Sunday School, an a ole Baptist colored preacher would teach us out of hit, cause he say, deh same words is in dis book what's in deh Bible, an you chullun learn 'em deh way deh is fixed for you to learn 'em in dis here Blue Back Speller, and den you can read 'em in deh Bible, an deh first thing you know, you can read deh Bible."[106]

Cornelia Hancock envisioned great potential for the newly freed blacks. "They are in favor of education for the masses of their color and freedom from ignorance is power in any country. I think now the schools are doing more toward reconstruction than congress. For all congress can do Andy [President Johnson] can undo and what the schools are doing no politician can ever undo."[107]

"We Encourage a Feeling of Self-Respect"

If Southerners were critical of Yankee teachers for teaching what they considered "liberal ideas," they at least should have been grateful for the Northerners' work in providing social services and in inculcating moral and religious values in the youngsters. (It was understood by numerous church organizations that their teachers would help take over the religious education of the Negroes.) It took but a few brief meetings for most Yankee teachers to realize that rendering assistance to the newly freed blacks involved considerably more than just teaching children (and adults) to read and write.

Yankee schoolmarms and workers for the Freedmen's Bureau found their work cut out for them in helping to care for the poor and downtrodden. Many conducted night classes for adults in sewing, knitting, and healthful living. Margaret Thorpe and Martha Haines, sent by the Friends' Association of Philadelphia in 1866 to teach the freedmen in Virginia, were appalled at the abject poverty of many of the blacks (and whites as well) in their Williamsburg area. At a Negro settlement nearby they discovered ten women and children living, or rather starving, in one room. In another room a one legged woman was attempting to care for four children, and in yet another room they found a ninety-year-old man without food or even a bed. One woman, a former slave owner who had fallen prey to the destitution that pervaded the South following the war, swallowed her pride and begged the teachers for clothing for her eight children, some of whom were down to one wearable garment each.[108] It was obvious the newly freed people required more that just book learning.

Margaret and Martha, as was true of most "Yankee teachers," not only taught the three R's, but also sought to instill in their pupils moral lessons as well, urging upon their youngsters the need to be honest, punctual, clean, upright, and responsible. In addition they dispensed medicine, clothing, farm tools, and garden seeds.

The blacks, Margaret explained, wished to earn enough money to pay for the things they needed and were not anxious to be beggars. Whenever possible the teachers sold cloth to them for very nominal amounts to enable them to make clothes for themselves. "In this way we encourage a feeling of self-respect and independence; of course the number of those who buy is much smaller than the number of those to whom we give. It is nothing short of heroic to live and work as some of these people are doing, the land is so terribly poor and the white people have so little money, and at the stores everything is about double the price charged for the same in the North."[109]

In May of 1865, New Englanders Mary Ames and Emily Bliss braved ridicule from their Northern families and boarded a steamer headed for South Carolina where as teachers of blacks they met with a chilly reception. They, too, discovered teaching the basics of reading and writing was only a small part of their responsibilities. Cleanliness, truthfulness, gardening, and religion became important aspects of their work with both young and old pupils. Among their greatest challenges, however, were their constant attempts, along with other Freedmen's Bureau officials, to reconcile the old owners and the "squatter" blacks. As was true of other Yankee teachers their presence continued to grate on wives of the locals who did their best to ignore them.

෨

The success stories of Yankee schoolmarms and the establishing of black schools were myriad. The increasing interest in black education and the need for college educated black teachers soon prompted the founding of black colleges such as Howard University, Fisk, and Morehouse. Interviews with former slaves and free blacks bear eloquent testimony to the inspiration provided by the Yankee teachers and to the later accomplishments of their young charges. One woman went North with her Northern teacher, worked her way through school, and returned to the South to teach in the Albemarle County schools for some fifty years.

A Richmond man related having had his early schooling in the New England teachers' classrooms, then continuing with his education and becoming a teacher, and later a successful lawyer following his graduation from Howard University Law School.[110]

It would be a serious mistake to assume that all Southern blacks were illiterate, brow-beaten field workers. An impressive number of blacks, some who were inspired by Yankee schoolmarms, some who were freed by their owners, some who purchased their own freedom, some who became successful following their emancipation at the end of the war—grew to be prosperous businessmen and accumulated considerable personal wealth and property.[111]

ഌ **6** ය

The Radicals and Reconstruction

ഌ) In the years following the war Lincoln's plans for "Reconciliation" or "Restoration" and Johnson's lenient amnesty program, which many believed foretold the return to power of the antebellum aristocracy, met with violent opposition on the part of the Radical Republicans. In an attempt to make the South more democratic, to make sure that all the bloodshed had not been in vain—and to build power for the Republican Party, the Radicals insisted on a far more drastic "Reconstruction" of the South than that advocated by either Lincoln or Johnson.

Radical Republicans feared that were the antebellum aristocracy to regain power the appalling carnage of the past four years of the war would have been for naught. The emancipation of the slaves would allow for greater Southern representation in Congress, and if the old regime were restored to power, the Radicals reasoned there would be a war fought in Congress that had only recently been concluded on the battlefield. In order to further empower the Republican party and secure its perpetuity, the party leaders saw the logical solution to be obtaining voting rights for blacks and through persuasion or coercion converting them into the Republican ranks. With this in mind, the Republicans set about helping to organize blacks into ubiquitous "Loyal Leagues," complete with secret rituals and patriotic ceremonies. The popularity of the leagues spread like wildfire and even Negro women members of the Loyal Leagues aided and abetted the cause by pledging not to keep company with men who refused to join. (The Democrats in turn enticed Southern whites into "Democratic Clubs" that further escalated the racial discord of the times. See the Darden Chapter, Part II.)

President Johnson, according to the Radical Republicans, was far too indulgent in accepting former rebels into full citizenship and representation in Congress, actions that they considered would serve to negate Republican power. (Many historians refer to the years 1865 through 1867 as the Presidential Reconstruction period and the years from 1868 through 1877 as the Congressional or Radical Reconstruction period, although the two periods blurred depending on individual perspective.)

Radical Republicans saw Johnson's presidency as becoming much too liberal. Southern planters, they were convinced, were reassuming their antebellum position of superiority, and Neg-roes, despite emancipation, were being forced to continue their servile role in the old "master-slave caste system." To the Radicals it appeared that although the war had freed the slaves, little else had changed

"The First Vote." (*Harper's Weekly*, November 16, 1867.)

in the South. The tremendous loss of life had been to no avail. For a variety of reasons Radical Republicans—some true idealists, some seeking a Republican Party dominance, some looking for economic gain and improved business conditions—determined that the South should never again be enabled to leave the Union, and should unconditionally be prevented from acquiring the potential for any future warfare. The nation should be a democracy in every aspect, and the newly freed men must be accepted as equals and accorded equal rights.

Countless editorials in Northern newspapers reflected the Radicals' growing discontent with Johnson. An article in the *Chicago Tribune*, for example, queried: "Is it possible that President Johnson intends to turn the few loyal whites and the blacks over to the mercy of the traitorous pro-slavery aristocracy? If so, he is an unworthy successor of the great and good man who preceded him, and Congress will have to undo the work that should never have been done, and return the South to the military authorities until the population has become sufficiently loyal, by reflection and immigration, or some other agency, to be safely entrusted with the management of the State."[1]

A few days later another article in the *Chicago Tribune* reported: "The present policy of reconstruction in the South meets with little favor in the minds of the loyal masses of the North. People cannot get reconciled to the idea of the admission of eighty whitewashed rebels into the House of Representatives, and twenty senators into the upper branch of the stripe of Toombs, Mason and Wigfall. The result of this procedure, if not prevented by Congress, instead of bringing peace and harmony, will breed new conflicts, and factions, and turmoils."[2]

Reports of the situation in the South and the potential for an amicable return of former rebels to the Union was strictly polarized. Several travelers, including General Grant, toured the South and returned home with reports of a quiet resignation on the part of the former rebels in accepting their defeat. On the other hand unsettling accounts from other travelers and shocking reports in major newspapers throughout the North led congressmen to grow increasingly concerned over the attitudes prevailing toward the Federal government among their recently defeated foes in the Southland. Were Southerners accepting their defeat gracefully, albeit resignedly, or could it be possible that a renewed rebellion was brewing? Were Southerners in the insurrectionary states harboring hostilities that would thwart the authority of the Federal government? Were ex–Confederates at all repentant? How were the newly freedmen being integrated into society? Would the admission of Southern delegates to Congress at that time simply be restoring the leading rebels to power? With representation constitutionally based on population, the emancipation of blacks would increase the South's representation in Congress and with increased power the South could rise from the ashes as a dominant force in Washington.

In December of 1865 a joint committee of both houses of Congress, the Joint Committee on Reconstruction, was appointed to study conditions in the South to determine whether the ex–Confederate states should be entitled to representation in Congress. The testimony was discouraging. Johnson was outmaneuvered as the Radicals used the reports to advantage in their efforts to replace Johnson's leniency with Radical Republican grass roots Reconstruction. One observer told the Committee: "I think that instead of growing more willing to accept the situation, they are showing a more intense feeling of bitterness towards the government." Another insisted: "I think they have no patriotism for the Union. They appear to be now as much devoted to the cause of the rebellion as they were during the war."[3] A North Carolinian observed that "It requires no great keeness of sight to behold, here in eastern North Carolina at least, that the spirit of secession is as rampant as ever in the hearts of a majority of the people."[4] An officer in the Freedmen's Bureau spoke of the hostility of many of the Southern people toward the Federal government. "There is evidently no regret for the rebellion, but rather a defence of it, and only a submission to the circumstances of the case as a conquered people. They everywhere defend the principles on which the rebellion was commenced."[5]

A sub-commissioner of the Freedmen's Bureau reported: "I find the people generally very bitter, so much so that I consider it dangerous for any federal officer to go unescorted through that country [Mississippi]. Particularly between New Orleans and Vicksburg, or between New Orleans and Jackson, it would be dangerous for a man to be seen in blue clothes." Another man in speaking of Alabama pointed out: "In a few counties civil law has scarcely any prevalence or force, and gangs of ruffians, mostly operating at night, hold individuals under a reign of terror.... The City of Mobile also appears to be largely under the dominion of rowdyism, and animated almost throughout by active hostility to the freedmen."[6]

One observer spoke of an influential group in Texas that exhibited "a fine Union element" and appeared well disposed to the authority of the Federal government. "But a large majority of the white people of Texas were still disloyal, and still entertained a hope of re-establishing slavery. It was common for them to tell their former slaves, now free, that the proclamation of emancipation would be set aside. There was also a sort of disdain exhibited towards the northern people, and a disposition to spurn the federal authority." General W. E. Strong corroborated the reports of a pervasive aversion among Texans for Northerners. "The most intense hatred is shown by many of the citizens of the country [Texas] towards northern men, officers and soldiers of our army, and the United States government." Yet another interviewee declared that "Unfortunately, it has been a common sentiment in the south that northern people were their inferiors; and during the war this sentiment was increased—their songs, their speeches, their literature, all tending to belittle the 'Yankees.'"[7]

Hundreds of pages of similar testimony before the committee led Congress to believe that all was not sweetness and light in the South and that a withdrawal of the troops of occupation would constitute a serious error. It was the conclusion of the committee that "the so-called Confederate States are not, at present, entitled to representation in the Congress of the United States."[8]

As the Radicals gained power in the North in numbers strong enough to override Johnson's vetoes, they fought to put their plans for a fundamental reconstruction of the South into operation. Many of the basic Republican aims were embodied in a speech delivered by Thaddeus Stevens, one of the foremost leaders of the Republic Party, at a meeting in Lancaster, Pennsylvania, on September 6, 1865. Stevens and the Radicals insisted that all slaves be freed and armed, that the old planter caste system be destroyed, and that condign punishment be inflicted "on the rebel belligerents, and so weaken their hands that they can never again endanger the Union...." Many Radicals, including Stevens, believed the property belonging to the large land owners should be confiscated and divided among the land-poor whites and newly freed blacks. Convinced that the wealthy Southern planters had instigated the war, the Radicals sought to change the entire fabric of Southern society in order to achieve a democracy instead of what appeared to be an aristocracy. Republicans envisioned the seizure of the land of wealthy proprietors which would then be sold to help pay the national debt brought on by the war and at the same time would serve to create an extensive yeoman class of small land owners. It was the national government's right to give laws to the conquered Southerners and "abolish all their municipal institutions and form new ones," Thaddeus Stevens proclaimed. "The vanquished in an unjust war must pay the expense."[9]

Needless to say, countless Southerners, enraged over the Radicals' plans for Reconstruction, believed they had submitted "not to the United States, to the Union, but to the Radicals, led by 'Generals' Stevens, Sumner, Chandler, etc." Not a few Southerners argued that the activities of the Radical Republicans were "struggling as effectually and more threateningly to subvert and change the Government than the armed Confederates in the field."[10]

Southerners, bitter over the demise of their hopes for a successful, independent Confederate nation, did, indeed, hope for a return to antebellum days—i.e. economically a submissive, obedient, even though emancipated work force, and socially the continuation of the tradition of white supremacy. It was enough to be a defeated nation—now to be subservient to the hated enemy who had come to seize their land and dictate their every action was almost a fate worse than death. (For some, Edmund Ruffin and others who chose suicide, of course, it *was* a fate worse than death.) To be second class citizens and watch their former slaves assume important political offices and enjoy voting privileges that relegated white Southerners to a minority was insufferable.

"This Right of Suffrage"

The social aspects of the new Constitutional Amendments (Thirteenth, Fourteenth and Fifteenth Amendments—mandating black-white equality) were difficult enough for Southerners to accept; however, the political aspects, particularly the allocation of voting rights to the freedmen, were extremely bitter pills for Southerners to swallow. One could scarcely expect Southerners to be thrilled to see the enfranchisement of their former slaves while they themselves were disfranchised. An article in the *Raleigh Daily Sentinel* detailed a dinner "attended by three former governors, a former justice of the state supreme court, one or two former members of Congress, and several other distinguished men. The only person in this august gathering who could vote was the black man waiting on the tables."[11]

Even in the North giving the Negro the vote was a hotly contested issue. Only five Northern states extended voting rights to Negroes. In 1865 in Wisconsin, Minnesota, and Connecticut proposals for Negro suffrage were defeated as were similar proposals in New Jersey and Ohio in 1867 and Michigan and Pennsylvania in 1868.[12] Illinois discouraged free Negroes from entering the state by imposing a fifty dollar fine on each person—a law that was not repealed until February of 1865. Surprisingly Charles Sumner, Horace Greeley, and O. O. Howard acknowledged the need for educational qualifications for voters, and even Thaddeus Stevens and William Lloyd Garrison, along with other of Garrison's fellow abolitionists, entertained serious questions as to Negro suffrage.[13]

For the most part, Southerners felt voting rights for blacks should be conditioned on their owning property, a requirement that would, of course, disqualify most former bondsmen. A *New Orleans Times* editorial read: "Wherever voters greatly outnumber property holders, property will assuredly be unsafe. When voters have property and intelligence, there is some hope that they may 'find their interest in the interest of the community' and be anxious to secure a consistent, honest, economical and straight-forward administration." The writer continued, "Were universal negro suffrage to be added to the white universal suffrage now existing in the South, the security of both life and property would be greatly weakened."[14]

A few farsighted Southerners accepted the enfranchisement of the newly freed blacks as an inevitable fact and urged the people to help the new voters by "enlightening their understanding." For others, including Anna Maria Green of Milledgeville, Georgia, emancipation and Negro suffrage were further manifestations of God's will, "a Divine providence which he will carry through without further suffering to the South.... What are the hidden secrets of God's government men cannot discern."[15]

Most conventional Southerners, however, looked upon Negro suffrage as part of the North's vengeance against the South. To former rebels it seemed hypocritical of Northerners to attempt to force Negro suffrage on Southerners while in many Northern states blacks were denied the franchise. Southerners, of course, were outraged at allowing blacks to vote who were unable to read the ballot or to sign their names. (It was estimated that about 97 percent of Southern blacks were illiterate.) In July of 1867 Susan Darden watched as "The negro men all went to Fayette to register their names so they can vote; it is a disgrace to civilized people to have ignorant persons, like negroes, voting."[16] A Kentucky woman was clear and concise in explaining the political consequences of Negro suffrage: "If the Negro votes, the Black Republicans will retain the power, and if not the Democrats will come in."[17]

Now and then a transplanted Northerner recognized the problems the enfranchisement of Negroes would engender. Margaret Thorpe, a Yankee teacher of blacks, and several of her friends expressed their reservations. "Oh this right of suffrage to a people utterly unprepared! We already see a change in the feeling of some of the men toward us, for we oppose with all our strength of will and tongue their efforts to get into office, and we tell them how utterly unfit they are; this perhaps will make them angry, and they will accuse us of 'trying to keep them down.'"[18]

Surprisingly, even some of the newly enfranchised blacks found it strange that they were allowed to vote and yet their former owners were not. Frank Durr, of Marion, Mississippi, later confessed that "I thought it very strange after I was enfranchised and allowed to vote and my best friends [his former owner and other notables of the town] were disfranchised."[19]

Here and there, of course, were women who sensed a certain injustice in the fact that all men, blacks and whites, were entitled to vote (after the universal pardon), yet all women were denied the franchise. When Ned, a young Negro of Elizabeth Hyde Botume's acquaintance, was pounced upon by the Radicals as a potential voter in 1867, he was greatly confused about the issues at stake. Elizabeth smiled wryly: "Poor Ned! He did not know that with all his ignorance and credulity his name was of far more value than ours, because he was a man, and we only women. He could cast a vote which he could not read, and help to make laws of whose import he knew nothing."[20]

As a solution to the overwhelming number of newly enfranchised blacks voting a Republican ticket, the irrepressible Elizabeth Meriwether shocked her neighbors by proposing "that the men consider enfranchising 'respectable' Southern white women to counterbalance the votes of black and white men targeted by the Klan." Unfortunately, her suggestion met with little support.[21]

"Agitators Are Sallying Through the Country": The Making of Black Republicans

The Radical Republicans' plans to reconstruct the South by making loyal Republicans of freedmen were clearly designed to minimize the power and influence of the former aristocracy—the ex-slave owners. At the same time the plans would also help to ensure the political control of the country for the Republican Party. By fair means or foul the Republicans sought to register any male black who could even vaguely could be considered of voting age. Republican canvassers went after potential black voters with a vengeance and in some areas ninety percent of the eligible freedmen were registered to vote.[22]

Prior to each election the freedmen were persuaded—or coerced—into voting the Republican ticket. Thus thousands of ex-slaves often became political pawns in the hands of carpetbaggers and scalawags who engaged in a relentless campaign to organize blacks throughout the South, warning them that their very freedom depended on a Republican victory, that a defeat at the polls would assuredly mean their return to slavery once again.

Radicals were quick to reap the advantages of organizing blacks into secret societies (clubs) and reminding them of their rights and the wrongs of their former owners. (The Southern branch of the Union League in the North was known as the Loyal League and consisted primarily of Negroes.) The league staged parades, held barbecues and meetings, denounced the Democrats, and warned blacks to support the Republican Party. A Mississippi woman remarked: "Nearly every Saturday the town is crowded to excess by the negroes, who appear of a riotous disposition, and being much encouraged by their leaders, rarely attend to their plantation duties when these agitators are sallying through the country, thus giving their employers much dissatisfaction."[23]

Agitators could induce the freedmen to leave their work at a moment's notice. "They at all hazards go, taking their horses and mules out of the ploughs, and, at their preconcerted signals, every man on the plantation is mounted and gone, those who have nothing to ride following in the rear." Mrs. Beaumont continued: "There is no law to govern labor; the white man has to submit to all the neglect caused by these political meetings to strengthen radical rule. Everything is in a very unsatisfactory condition;—the only labor we have cannot be controlled, and politics, with ignorance, make the crop suffer."[24]

"Soon the lowest types of white people were being sent into the South to arouse the Negroes with incendiary speeches," Marion Briscoe complained. "One orator, who had assembled them behind closed doors, would shout: 'My friends, you will ride in the streetcars with white women if you please. If you go to the theater, you will sit where you please, in the best boxes if you like.' There were men who mingled freely with them promising to divide the white man's acres if they would vote the Republican ticket. Of course, it was no wonder that the white people felt vague uneasiness when they lay down at night."[25]

Marie Rice could recall "none save kindly intercourse between Negroes and whites until days of election approached. It was natural that on national questions the Negroes should vote with the party which freed them; but, as everyone knows, State politics were poisoned by the army of 'carpet-baggers' who invaded the South after the Civil War. These men, often the dregs of society, and always unscrupulous, obtained ascendancy over the mind of the Negro and used him for their own ends. They convinced him that political predominance of his former owners would mean putting him back into slavery; and, in secret meetings, they exacted from him an oath to vote always with the Republican party."[26]

Prior to election day, Mrs. Rice wrote, she had observed a general feeling of good-will between the black workers and their employers; but at election time all was different. "The Negroes went to the polls en masse to vote contrary to the whites, even upon matters wherein the interests of both races were identical." This perversity, Mrs. Rice recognized as "a deep seated antagonism, a blind distrust of us."

The heavy concentration of Negroes in many areas of the deep South guaranteed Republicans their eagerly sought after victories at the polls. Although Southerners were outraged over the extension of the suffrage to blacks and although they often cried out against what they called "Negro rule," it should be remembered that in only three states (South Carolina, Mississippi, and Louisiana) were Negroes "in the government in any considerable numbers." As historians today emphasize, "Negroes did not rule anywhere in the South." Furthermore not all of those Negroes elected to office were what many Southerners deemed a rag-taggle group of illiterate blacks—in fact several had college degrees from prestigious American and European colleges.[27]

Both parties used devious means in attempting to gain votes. Buggies were sent to ensure the vote of the aged and infirm. Registration forms were stolen to prevent black voters from exercising their voting rights. On the day of an election freedpeople were deceptively informed that elections had been canceled thus preventing even their appearance at the polls. In an article in the *New Orleans Times* of November 29, 1865, the Republicans announced the election of H. C. Warmoth as "delegate to Congress by 1900 votes! and whereas the vote would have been much larger if not double, but for the interference of men, late traitors, and others who broke up the ballot-box and arrested commissioners of election in one parish, and impeded and prevented the election in other parishes."

Rash promises resulted in blacks arriving at the polls carrying halters for the mules promised them by unconscionable Republicans. On the other hand unprincipled Democrats sought to discourage Negroes from voting by cautioning them that their registration would be used as a means to tax the blacks and would engage them in military service. Before elections there were "Negro Hunts" in which scores of blacks were hunted down and murdered.

A South Carolina foreman explained that he and his men were coerced into voting the Republican ticket. Each of the Negroes who had voted the Democratic ticket had been punished: the foreman's cow had been killed, another man's colt had been killed, another freedman's rice crop had been destroyed.[28]

Some Conservative Democrats threatened their workers with instant dismissal if they voted the Republican ticket. One Virginian avowed that his "boss man take the names of the slaves and vote for them. Know nothing about a free ballot." Other Democrats discouraged blacks from voting by pelting them with stones and threatening them with gunfire. Rioting erupted at numerous polling stations. Charles Stearns, for example, reported seeing a Negro knocked down and another stabbed for voting the Republican ticket. Further atrocities would surely have occurred, Stearns insisted, had it not been for the presence of soldiers.[29] Liquor, of course, bought hundreds of votes, and bogus ballots brought about landslide victories. "The colored vote can be bought for a trifle," a Mississippi woman wrote. The Negroes, she noted, "believe that these carpet-bag officers are instrumental in keeping them out of slavery; therefore they can be used very profitably."[30]

Riots were commonplace throughout the South during election time, and now and then cannons were fired to frighten blacks away from the polling places. Some Democrats even made personal calls at the freedmen's homes to advise them against voting for Republicans. Bridges were burned to prevent blacks from voting. Large numbers of blacks and whites came to vote armed with clubs and guns. Democrats attempted to counteract Republican appeals to blacks by insisting that the Democrats, not the Republicans, were the true friends of the black man. Speakers sought to win over blacks by ominously proclaiming, "My colored friends, you are ruining the white people of the South, and yourselves as well, by running after the carpet bagger and voting the Republican ticket. If it goes much further, colored men, I am for war and blood, war to the knife, and the knife to the hilt."[31] Freedmen were often threatened that they would not be hired the following year or that they would not be given necessary medical attention if they voted the Democratic ticket. In attempting to prevent a black landslide one polling booth reported that "a mule had eaten up the ballot box."[32] Of course, ballots being counted by candlelight could easily be and frequently were switched or dumped in the fireplace.[33]

As might be expected the newly freedmen were not the only voters experiencing confrontations and deception at the polls; white conservatives also came in for their share of woes. Elections were rife with political maneuvering and downright dishonesty, and often conservative whites found it involved considerably more than simply taking the loyalty oath to enable them to run for office—or to vote. A northern Virginia man, Robert Barton, told of having taken the Oath of Allegiance, having been nominated for the office of county clerk, and having won the election. However, the "anti–Southern element" succeeded in inducing the officials to throw out all ballots of voters they thought might have been dishonest (or insincere) in swearing to the amnesty oath. Despite the fact that Barton still had chalked up a majority of votes, the officials, clearly opposed to his election, disqualified him on the ground that he had once taken an Oath of Allegiance to the Confederate States, an act which he vehemently denied. Nevertheless, his opponent was awarded the office.[34] Although his punishment was not disfranchisement or disqualification for office, a white Kentuckian who "voted the wrong way" told of being sent thirty-six soldiers to feed as chastisement.[35]

Many conservative white Democrats became so discouraged by their inability to "make a difference" in the balloting that they sometimes stayed at home on election day. One woman complained of the lack of white turnout at the polls. "A colored man beat Mr. A. Sheperd at the election by 8 votes. If the white men had turned out as they should have done, I reckon he would have gotten the most votes."[36] Small wonder the conservatives felt their votes counted for nothing: voter registration in the ten unreconstructed southern states in 1867 was reported to be about 635,000 white registrants and 735,000 blacks. Some Democrats did not go to the polls hoping that the vote to hold a constitutional convention would be invalidated by a lack of registered voters casting their ballots.[37]

In the elections, returning veterans, of course, were held in great esteem by the conservatives. Men who did not participate in the war effort and who were deemed "cowards" by fervent younger Southerners continued to be viewed with contempt. In October of 1865 Amanda Worthington was provoked over the results of an election. Her two favorite candidates "were defeated and by men who have never been soldiers too, and I am perfectly disgusted with the people who voted for those 'stay-at-homes.'"[38]

That the newly freedmen would join the Republican ranks whole-heartedly should have come as no surprise. Actually, how could former slaves be blamed for accepting the best offer? The Republicans promised a rosy future of independence and prosperity. To the freedmen the Democrats seemed to advocate a return to the enslavement of the past.

Secretly Gertrude Thomas was among those who defended the Negro and his alliance with the Radicals. From a remarkably enlightened, rational perspective she reasoned: "Just here I must take occasion to say that I do not in my heart wonder that the Negroes vote the radical ticket, and to have persuaded them otherwise would be against my own conscience. Think of it, the right to vote, that right which they have seen their old masters exercise with so much pride, and their young masters look forward to with so much pleasure is within their *very grasp*—They secure a right for themselves, which it is true they may not understand, but they have children whom they expect to educate. Shall they secure this right for them or sell their right away? It is within their grasp. Who can guarantee that they will ever have it extended to them again?"

In a thoughtful analogy Gertrude reasoned that were she, a woman, granted the vote, she would be extremely reluctant about voting to have that right withdrawn. "If the women of the North once secured to me the right to vote whilst it might be 'an honor thrust upon me,' I think I should think twice before I voted to have it taken from me. Of course such sentiments smack too much of radicalism to promulgate outside of my own family & though I do not say much, I think Grant will be elected and I don't think if we can have peace that it will make much difference, as he says 'Let us have peace.'"[39]

As he attempted to put his wife's plantations on a paying basis James Leigh also came to the defense of the newly freed men, explaining, "The poor negro has since the war been placed in an entirely false position, and is therefore not to be blamed for many of the absurdities he has committed, seeing that he has been urged on by Northern 'carpet-baggers' and Southern 'scalawags,' who have used him as a tool to further their own nefarious ends." A Mississippian wrote of the behavior of the freedmen in the area: "Recently freed from a repressing slavery; clothed with a freedmen's most sacred right, the right to vote; and placed above their former owners with power to oppress; their mind instilled with bitter hatred against those they had lately served; and made the blind, unreasoning dupes of wicked and designing men, the wonder to me is that they were not very much more vicious than they proved to be."[40]

"Hundreds of Northern Speculators"

It took little time for Northerners to size up the situation in the Southland and seize the opportunity to move in for personal gain. Two months following Appomattox a writer for the *Mobile News* reported: "One may find the representatives of almost any named city in the West and North within ten minutes walk from the Custom House. The heavy produce and grocery man of Chicago runs against the dry goods jobber of New York, while the bustling, rushing adventurous Memphian comes into collision with the more substantial broker or prospective banker of New Orleans."[41]

Countless farmers, their homes, buildings, money, cotton, work force gone, simply gave up in despair and sold out to the highest bidder. With money in extremely short supply on the part of both buyers and sellers, property traded hands at give-away prices.

The situation was a heyday for speculators. With the high price of cotton and land selling for as little as thirty-five cents an acre, thousands of Northerners were enticed to move south and try their hand at raising cotton. Some Northerners rented property, some bought land, some came as field hands, while some speculators bought into a crop for one-fourth of the profits.

Even while the war was still raging Northerners were quick to cash in on Southern homes and croplands abandoned by their owners in the face of an enemy attack. In June of 1864, Mary Hough received a letter from her soldier husband describing the land around Murfreesboro that months before had been absolute desolation. "Now one short year what a change. The whole surrounding country including the very battlefield of Stone River excepting the graveyards, and forests is one vast cotton field, planted and owned or rented by Northern men, and worked by hired negroes."[42]

During the war, the Federal government had taken over abandoned plantations and leased them to "loyal" persons. Along the Mississippi River it was hoped that plantations operated by loyal citizens would help to facilitate the government's unobstructed navigation of the river and at the same time provide work for newly freed blacks. (Although lessees were bound to employ freedmen as laborers, unfortunately many of the lessees were motivated considerably less by loyalty and patriotism than by gain and greenbacks. All too often concern for the labor force of black workers appeared of secondary importance.)

Frances Lauderdale's collection of letters from her brother Willis Lauderdale, a telegraphic operator in St. Louis, and his brother Sam, detail experiences typical of hordes of Northerners, who following the

capture of Vickburg attempted to make a fortune—or at least a prosperous livelihood—raising cotton on plantations rented from owners living
along the Mississippi. It seems somewhat surprising that more than a year
before Appomattox, while bloody battles were still being waged in the
East, Northerners were moving by the hundreds into certain Union occupied territories where they were convinced they could more effectively
and more profitably raise cotton than native Southerners.

In March of 1864 Willis explained to his sister that in seeking to
better his condition "in a worldly point" he had spent six weeks traveling around scouting possibilities. In Vicksburg, he sized up what he
thought would be precisely the opportunity he was searching for. "Here
I found hundreds of Northern speculators who were engaged in all sorts
of trades. Cotton carrying being the great business. I also found many
going into Cotton raising. This struck me as the best thing I could go
into." With apparently little trouble he and brother Sam were fortunate
in renting a plantation about ten miles out of Vicksburg from a Mrs.
Bolls, a widow lady "who has a Plantation of 250 Acres under cultivation with fine gin house, good Negro Quarters, good fences, fine Residence, and house handsomely furnished. Mrs. Bolls is 39 years of age
with five interesting children. The war has left her as it has all the Planters
without money, Mules or Slaves, consequently she is unable to grow Cotton." Under the terms of the agreement Willis would pay her one fifth
part of the cotton crop to be raised and allow her and her family "egress
and ingress to and from her said residence." Stipulations from the government included hiring freed slaves as workers, keeping a store on the
plantation and selling to the hands. Fear of problems from enemy raiders
were, Willis thought, minimal: "As I am so near Vicksburg and surrounded by our Troops, I dont anticipate any danger from the Rebels.
All the Plantations along the Big Black River from the Rail Road Bridge
for twenty miles down are being worked by Northern Men, giving the
owner a small share of the Crops."[43]

According to Willis, he expected little trouble from the Confederates because "The owners of the places are all widows or nearly all, very
few exception, and they—the most of them—have sons or friends in the
Southern army, and as the farms are leased of owners in such a way that
if the crop is raised, they receive a certain per cent of the net proffits, and
if the crop is destroyed or fails, they receive nothing ... you see at once
it is for their interest that the crop is raised. It is not so on the Mississippi, there the farms are what are called 'Abandoned Plantations' and
are leased from the Govt and it is quite natural that the owners should
not like to see them worked by Yankees. I rather think most of them have
been broken up by the rebels already—running off the mules & taking

the supplies. Two I know of have been rented out twice, lost all their money & property and have gone north quite sick of southern life and planting cotton."[44]

Unfortunately, hopes to be free from molestation by rebel raiders and loyal Confederate neighbors were soon dashed when six of the Lauderdale brothers' horses were stolen and several of the plantation buildings were set on fire. Once the brothers professed to be from Missouri and opposed to much of the Federal government's administration they were accorded more kindly treatment. Throughout all their exchanges with Confederate sympathizers, however, they carefully tiptoed around the subject of politics and their northern heritage.

Sam Lauderdale wrote his father that Northern planters' fears were somewhat allayed by an order from the Federal commander for the District of Vicksburg, Major General Henry Slocum. In Sam's words the order stated that "where one of the planters were raided the property of all citizens within a circuit of ten miles from the farm raided would be taken & sold to make good the planters loss, and where a life was taken, $10,000 would be the remuneration, the money to be paid over to the friends."[45]

For awhile the Lauderdale brothers' life was good; their cotton "as fine cotton as ever was seen," they bragged to their father. Torrential rains and weeds had failed to dampen their spirits. Then suddenly, as so many speculators discovered, the army worm arrived to devour most of their beautiful crop and wipe out the phantom profits. By November of 1865 Willis, as did hundreds of other Northerners, decided trying to raise cotton was a no-win project for inexperienced planters, and instead Willis opted for work in St. Louis selling insurance. Meanwhile Sam had succumbed to a combination of "a western climate," fever and bowel disease.[46]

"We Know of No Place That Presents as Many Advantages"

For as many reasons as there were individuals Northerners journeyed South, some for what appeared to be golden opportunities, some to live out their lives in the warmer climes, some to devote themselves to improving the lives of former slaves. Countless "entrepreneurs," however, quickly became disenchanted and soon returned to their homes in the North. For the most part Northerners appeared to have been attracted by the bargains in southern land and the possibility of making huge fortunes in cotton production.

Following the war northern newspapers pointed to the great bargains in lands throughout the South. Land that had once sold for one hundred and fifty dollars per acre now could be purchased for two dollars and two dollars and fifty cents an acre. Other land that once had been valued at one thousand dollars an acre went begging for five dollars an acre.[47] A South Carolina estate worth $15,000 brought in only three hundred dollars; another worth $24,000 was obtained for eighty dollars.[48] Editors predicted that many of the large plantations would be divided into small units "with the view of their purchase and cultivation by Northern farmers of moderate means."[49]

Real estate agents, such as Henry Clements Collier of Charlotte, Dixon County, Tennessee, had a field day in negotiating contracts between northern buyers and southern sellers.[50] Brokers eagerly championed the Southland as the land of opportunity for Northern men of vigor and intelligence. In Columbia, South Carolina, in 1871, for example, a real estate agent in response to an inquiry from a Pennsylvania man enthusiastically extolled the virtues of the state's capital. "We know of no place that presents as many advantages to a business man and capitalist, as does Columbia, at the present time, and would advise you to run down to see us, and become convinced for yourself."[51] So ran the barrage of appeals for Northerners to come South to buoy up the Southern economy.

Northern speculators looked to immense profits to be garnered from organizing associations for the purpose of raising colonies to purchase land and settle in the South. One such organization, the Manhattan Company, in April of 1869, boasted of a membership of over a thousand persons, and promised that many Southern gentlemen were involved in securing land for the organization's members "in the most fertile parts" of Georgia, Virginia, and East Tennessee for settlement.[52] Newspapers carried ads not only for the sale of thousands of acres of land (21,972 in North Carolina, for example), but also for mills, factories, and mines "which need Northern enterprise to set them going."[53]

For many Northerners the South's fertile soil and mild climates promised instant riches, and for a time a "Southern fever" prevailed. Convinced that Southerners were lazy and ineffectual, Northern entrepreneurs were sure that by employing Yankee methods and technology combined with northern practicality and vitality they could far surpass southern cotton production records. A Boston lecturer, for example, professed a popular Northern notion that Southerners really knew "next to nothing about cotton planting." Once Northern farmers, utilizing good old fashioned Northern efficiency and know-how, took over the plantations, the speaker predicted they could be run much more efficiently and would soon be producing bumper crops.[54]

Yet despite their economy and highly touted "expertise," thousands of inexperienced Northerners, as previously noted, were forced to abandon their grandiose schemes for making a fortune—or even a living—by planting cotton. Numerous speculators were all but ruined when they encountered problems of desertion of laborers, the delay of late planting, a smallpox outbreak, the thefts of laborers, machinery breakdowns, an army worm plague—as well as other less cataclysmic crises.[55] All too quickly Northerners found there were a great many lessons to be learned about southern temperatures, southern laborers, and "old seed" that refused to sprout. Frances Butler (Leigh), for example, pointed out the disastrous consequences resulting from the practices of some of her Northern neighbors.[56]

After successive crop failures and ephemeral profits, vast numbers threw in the towel and humbly trekked back northward or stayed on and embarked on more remunerative avenues of work. Smothering a smug "We told you so," planters jested that the "'sacred soil' resisted immigrants' efforts to restore its fertility by 'deep plowing and Northern methods of tillage.'"[57] Untold numbers of discouraged Northerners simply turned their backs on personally resurrecting "King cotton" and turned their attention instead to securing political offices.

"As If We Were So Many Criminals": The Benham Family's Story

Among the hundreds of accounts of Northerners who flocked to the South seeking instant riches to be gained in cotton production was the story of the George Benhams. In his book *A Year of Wreck: A True Story by a Victim*, Benham recounts the details of his catastrophic first year as a planter in Hebron, Mississippi, in 1866, a fiasco that reflected the problems of numerous Northerners bent on reviving and revolutionizing cotton production in the South.[58]

The opportunity for making $114,000 in four years on the investment of $22,000 was simply too promising a return to pass up for George Benham. Apparently nothing could dissuade her husband from leaving his well established drug store business and heading south; however, Mrs. Benham was considerably less enthusiastic and responded to the move resignedly with a quiver in her voice and a tear in her eye. "'You must be the judge [George]—our home here is delightful, and it will be a little trying to leave our friends and go so far away; but if you think it for the best, let it be so.'"

Once land in Hebron, Mississippi, was secured the picture looked rosy indeed until suddenly dark clouds began to appear when mounting hidden costs began eating away at their savings. A thousand dollars was needed for house-rent, untold numbers of dollars were required for repairs of the house, a thousand dollars for cotton seed, and twelve hundred dollars for an overseer—worries the Benhams quickly dismissed in anticipating the immense margin of profit to be gained at year's end. A "fool's errand" to Lexington, Kentucky, to purchase surplus army equipment merely served to augment the initial expenses.

It was a shock to the Benhams when their welcome by Hebron residents turned out to be considerably less than the fabled southern hospitality. Instead, the potential for violence in the area had a chilling effect on their first days in their new home. At night the sounds of gunfire and human wailings bore testimony to the distressing news that one or two murders routinely took place in the village each week. Even more frightening was word that one of the most recent crimes had been perpetrated by "mischievous boys" on a Northern man recently settled in the area. A village merchant casually admitted that "These things are very common here; boys will be boys. For myself, I regret it very much—don't consider it treating the new-comers just right; but there seems to be no remedy for it."[59]

Congenial neighbors also proved to be a myth as people quickly made known their abhorrence of Yankee adventurers. On a mission to borrow the temporary use of a coffee mill, Mr. Benham and the Benhams' cook, Jane, were viciously rebuffed by the lady [!] of the house next door. "'Go, back, you nigger,' she screamed out, 'tell that d_____ Yankee woman I have two very nice coffee-mills, very nice ones, but not for her to use.'" Adding a warning about the need for the Benhams to be wary of the water they drank from their cistern, she dismissed them with the sinister threat, "Arsenic is good diet for Yankees."

Lacking matches, in desperation and expecting to approach Aunt Chloe rather than the neighbor herself, Jane undertook a second trip next door for a coal of fire to start her own kitchen-fire. Her reception was even more vitriolic than before. Threats and abuse were heaped upon poor Jane and in a rage the woman screeched that the Yankees "were a pack of mud-sills, come down into this country to rob and plunder from them what they had left from, 'the wa'. 'Yes,' she said, 'I will let them have a coal of fire, but it will be in the shape of a torch touched to the house some dark night.'"[60] A short time later both Mr. and Mrs. Benham were terrified by his narrow escape from an attack on his life as he was returning from the village store late one evening.

Not only were the Benhams ostracized by the area's loyal Southerners, but even the few individuals and families who attempted to befriend them were shunned. A dinner guest at the Benhams was later murdered, presumably for having had anything to do with the hated Yankees. A courageous Sunday's call from a village family brought down the wrath of the community against the visitors and likely provoked a melee and a shooting shortly thereafter.[61] As Mr. Benham pointed out, "It was as if we were so many criminals, of whose acquaintance one should be ashamed."[62]

The firing of the incompetent overseer, the inexperience of Northern white workers, and frustrations with balky mules soon cast serious doubts on the wisdom of the Benhams' venture. "The piece of ground looked as if it might have been the arena of a bullfight, or the rooting-place of a drove of hogs," they despaired. In addition "four plows out of sixteen were carried to the blacksmith shop for repairs."[63] The theft of hogs and garden produce took place with nightly regularity. Additional problems soon surfaced. The planting completed, Mr. Benham's payment to the laborers for their first month's work was followed by the immediate departure of all but two of the white workers who were never to be heard from again. Incessant rain and workers who refused to work in anything other than optimal weather conditions brought on a bumper crop of weeds that could never adequately be eradicated. Insects, buzzards, flies, millers, beetles, crickets, katydids, tree-toads, lizards, snakes, ants and mosquitoes all helped make life in the Southland a challenge. Then too there was the small-pox epidemic that took its toll on both workers and employers. Finally three crops of the army worms caused partners and friends to throw up their hands in despair. The Benhams chalked up their year's outlay and income as:

Promise	$108,000.00
Result	$6,564.27
Deficit	$101, 435.83

It was, indeed, as Mr. Benham termed it, "A Year of Wreck."

"You Northern Men Can't Live in This Country"

Loyal Southerners abhorred the carpetbaggers, the Northerners who rushed South following the war seeking economic and political advantages, and the scalawags, Southerners who sought opportunity by changing their allegiance and joining ranks with the growing popularity of the

Radical Republican regime.[64] It took but very little time for carpetbaggers to gain an odious reputation among Southerners, and certainly many
of those who came South to make a killing from a defeated, indigent populace deserved the rancor associated with their epithet.[65]

Particularly irksome to Southerners, naturally, was the air of superiority and self-righteousness so frequently exhibited by their former foe.
Help from Northerners was acceptable; advice and directions about how
to raise cotton, how to treat freedmen, how to reconstruct Southerners'
lives, traditions, and politics was not. For the most part Southerners
turned their backs on unsolicited Northern advice and firmly closed their
doors to Northern speculators and money-hungry carpetbaggers.

Planters and small farmers were delighted to see Northern money
invested in Southern enterprises; however, they were considerably less
pleased about competition from their recent enemies. Not a few Yankees
were threatened with death or the annihilation of their crops or mer-
chandise if they attempted to plant cotton or to run a business. A land
officer working for the Federal government advised a group of Northern
men looking for a cotton farm, "You are very rash; you northern men
can't live in this country. These people have no sympathy or friendship
for you; they will injure you in person and property. You are not only
risking your money, but your lives, and my advice is to get out of this
country just as fast as you can. The only way northern men can live here
is by coming in large columns. The people of all this country, from all I
can gather, have a deadly hatred of northern men."[66]

Southerners strenuously objected to Northerners attempting to grow
"rich on Southern money."[67] Even the governor of Mississippi, Adelbert
Ames, admitted in 1874 that in his experience the Northern man "is ever
an object of hatred and oppression to the old citizens."[68] A Wisconsin
man who was shot at and threatened with having his skull broken open
with an axe remarked that such abuse had a "tendency to weaken our faith
in the full reconciliation of the Southern people."[69]

As discouraged carpetbaggers abandoned the cotton fields and turned
their attention to seeking public office during the tumultuous postwar
years in the South, the antipathy of Southerners grew ever more virulent.
Southern newspapers were vitriolic in their condemnation of the "carpet-
bag fraternity." One editorial pointed out that hostility toward carpetbaggers "is due to the fact that they have come here not as friends but as
avowed public enemies. They have come not to perform the offices of
friendship, but to execute vengeance. They have come notoriously to
deprive the Southern whites of their rights of citizenship and to make them
aliens in the land of their birth; to deny them the privileges which are
dearer than all else to free-born Americans. Their mission is not simply

to confer suffrage on the negro, but to take it from the white citizen who has always enjoyed it, and to oppress him with political disabilities never dreamed of even by the authors of the harsh measures known as the military bills."[70]

The list of grievances continued. "They have crowded into our halls of legislation; spoken of us only in the language of insult and reproach; levied taxes to which they have contributed nothing; appropriated large salaries to themselves at the expense of a people overloaded with debt; and tortured their ingenuity to devise methods of displaying the hostility which they cherish towards the people upon whom these crying wrongs are executed."[71]

Marion Briscoe pictured a scene re-enacted in thousands of Southern towns. "The South was now going through the Reconstruction period. The little town of Boydton was filled with carpetbaggers. These men actually carried large suitcases made of carpet, and from these they received their name. Some of them were men of good appearance and bearing. Of course, they were politicians who were trying to make trouble for their own benefit. No one who lived in the South would speak to one of them, but they were thick-skinned and did not seem to care. Opposite the school there lived Ross Hamilton, a handsome mulatto, who had been elected to Congress since all this began. We would hang on the fence at the school to watch the carpetbaggers kiss the colored children, taking them in their arms, pitching them up into the air, and doing all they could to ingratiate themselves with the Negroes." Marion appended a note: "But they were very severe with Negroes when they stole and broke laws generally. My father (a lawyer) stood up for them and saved them from many dreadful punishments."[72]

Both carpetbaggers and scalawags received a cold shoulder (as did schoolmarms) from those who had no fear of reprisals as a result of their contempt. Betty Beaumont confessed that "white citizens hold aloof from this class of impostors; although, at the same time, they know there is danger in opposing them."[73] Good manners compelled Gertrude Thomas to at least call on the Northerners who had moved into her neighborhood. The visits, however, were described with a faint trace of disdain on the part of Gertrude. Although the Littles seemed to be wealthy and sociable, Gertrude was critical of their seemingly unkempt back piazza and its disarray of carpenter's tools and country-made soap drying in the sun. Another family, the Wilsons, she considered "very common. I did not attend the club meeting at their house and would not have called the other day but Mr. Thomas said 'it was best not to slight them.'" (By 1880, however, Gertrude Thomas had softened her views of Northerners somewhat, admitting that "at all times the cultivated educated Northern people are welcome.")

Upon her return from Europe following the surrender to the family home in Frankfort, Kentucky, Kate Thom wrote that they were "besieged with visitors. I am delighted to see the Confeds, but I must confess it is a great struggle for me to sit in the same room with the Yankees, and I don't think I can *possibly* be Christian enough to return their visits. A good many Southerners have moved here who are very nice people. I understand the Yankees are endeavoring to be very nice to our people, who are very *dilatory* in returning their civilities."[74]

In referring to the carpetbaggers, a Mississippi woman concurred with many of her countrymen in their determination to "hold aloof" from the abominable carpetbaggers and scalawags. The same woman, Betty Beaumont, denounced a young scalawag sheriff who was "much elevated by his new office; and bravely strives for money, forgetting that he ever pretended to be a true Southerner." The turncoat, despite the fact that he had served with the Confederate forces, had joined the Republicans and therefore "he can command a majority of votes in this County." His former friends, outraged by his arrogance and radical views, "have left him to enjoy his honorable office, with his white minority and colored majority."

Blanche Butler Ames (daughter of the famous Union General Benjamin F. Butler and wife of "Carpetbagger" Adelbert Ames, a former Union general, a U. S. senator from Mississippi and later governor of Mississippi) not only observed the antipathy of many Southern whites for the Carpetbaggers and Yankee school teachers who invaded the South, but also she herself experienced evidences of that alienation in her own personal life. Judging from some of her diary entries this lack of rapport might well have been the result of Blanche's own somewhat haughty attitude and cool responses to Southerners. On one of her infrequent visits to the Southland, Blanche Ames could find little good to say about the South particularly its climate, the food, the houses, the churches, the lack of refinement of the people, and the "whining" women. For the wife of a senator representing Mississippi, her caustic comments about women bemoaning the drastic changes in the South since the war were, to say the least, unbecoming.

In her diary, Blanche herself was guilty of whining about a breakfast companion: "I am disgusted with the woman's impertinence. Why does she whine to us? We do not know her, or wish to. She should understand that we care little or nothing about her sorrows and troubles." Blanche considered Mississippi "an unfortunate place," one which she could never regard "with favor, as a permanent place of residence."[75] (Little wonder Blanche found the South so inhospitable. Little wonder Blanche spent so little time in Mississippi, instead preferring the climate and comforts of her former home in Lowell, Massachusetts.)

In 1874 Blanche and her husband, by that time the governor of Mississippi, were the darlings of the Republicans and the blacks who elected him to office and anathema to white conservatives. Blanche wrote to her mother that she felt the lack of devoted friendly neighbors. "All are lynx-eyed, and one is always polite and kindly, but constantly on guard. *On a small scale*—it is something as you would feel and be situated as regards Washington and its people if you were living in the White House. The only difference being that with the exception of a few families, every white person in the city is inclined to be prejudiced against us."[76]

"Productions ... Could Be Made Very Profitable": Looking for New Business

It would indeed be a great injustice to label all Northerners who migrated southward at the war's end as predatory and unconscionable, for despite Southerners' great hatred of Yankees, the influx of Northerners after the war was frequently at the invitation of Southerners. (Real estate brokers, as noted, clearly did their part in encouraging Northerners.) Prompted by the South's desperate need for money, cities often made concerted efforts to lure Northern businessmen and engineers to come South—and, of course, bring their money and mechanical and business acumen with them.

The financial successes of Northern entrepreneurs such as Alexander Stewart in the dry goods business, Philip Armour in the meat packing business, and financiers such as Rockefeller, Carnegie and J. P. Morgan clued Southerners that there might be some economic lessons to be gleaned from their former enemies, that Northerners with money and Yankee know-how might be enticed to bring their gold and their talent southward and help boost an economy in ruins.

Cornelia Spencer, in particular, advocated taking some lessons in business from Northerners. In Northerners, Mrs. Spencer and others like her observed the activity and progress "of the people who got the better of us in the war." Denigration of the Yankees and an unwillingness to attempt to take lessons from Northern business and industrial giants, according to Mrs. Spencer, tended to thwart opportunities for women in the South. "On the one hand we have a dejected people, unhinged, demoralized, poverty-stricken; widows with children clinging to their skirts asking for bread. Young women begging to be told how they can get an education, how they can be doing something to help father and mother and raise the little ones."[77] On the other hand, she complained, the South had a superabundance of men in authority who sat with arms folded denouncing the Yankees and preventing any interchange of ideas and opportunities which might help the South to emulate the growth and prosperity being experienced in the North. Southerners, she pointed out, might gain some valuable information from their Northern brethren.

In some areas Northerners were ardently courted by ex–Confederates who foresightedly anticipated the advantages of attracting Northern capital and industry southward. On several occasions local officials in Petersburg, Virginia, for example, hosted large groups of Northern investors and writers in the hopes of attracting their support and their money. At one time some one hundred New York newspaper editors were brought to the city and given the royal treatment by the city's leaders. Soon other cities eagerly orchestrated similar campaigns.

The South's need for industrial development was paramount. With 20-20 hindsight, economists, agrarians, historians and even most Southerners agree that had the South abandoned its preoccupation with cotton and turned its attention to other avenues of production and to the development of factories and business interests, some of its postwar economic problems might have been averted. A far-sighted Mississippi woman explained at the time, "There are, no doubt, productions which could be made very profitable if the people would only turn their attention to other commercial interests as earnestly as they do to cotton...."[78]

Governor Johnson, of Georgia, in an optimistic speech pointed out that the Southerners had indeed started the war and although reduced to bankruptcy, former Confederates could reap advantages gained from the war. Capital instead of being tied up in slaves could be devoted to permanent land and household improvements, expansion of orchards, and the development of manufactures. "Attracted to this land emigrants from other parts of the world, and from the North, will come to settle among us...."[79]

Furthermore, it would indeed be an oversight to dismiss without mention the unsavory reputations garnered by countless administrators and administrations during the Radical Reconstruction. Even a brief examination of a period so rife with examples of bribery, fraudulent bond issues, misuse of funds, and outrageous waste and extravagance would necessitate volumes. Whether brought about by incompetence, inefficiency, inexperience or just plain greed, the graft and corruption pervading the South added up to huge losses for the already impoverished Southland.[80] Yet despite records of dishonesty and fraud on the part of Radical Republicans, scalawags, and carpetbaggers (and Conservative Democrats) during Reconstruction, historians point out that the Tweed Ring in New York City "supposedly stole more than all Southern politicians combined."[81]

7

Coping with a World
Out of Control

Southerners sought various means of coping with a world suddenly gone out of control. Edmund Ruffin, the Southern zealot famous for having fired one of the first shots of the war, committed suicide rather than live under Yankee domination. In a note penned shortly before putting a gun in his mouth and activating the trigger, Edmund Ruffin summarized convictions that no doubt reflected the opinions of countless other Southerners who, rather than commit suicide, chose less violent, less drastic solutions to their real or envisioned postwar problems. "I here declare my unmitigated hatred to Yankee rule—to all political, social & business connections with Yankees—& to the Yankee race. Would that I could impress these sentiments, in their full force, on every living southerner, & bequeath them to every one yet to be born! May such sentiments be held universally in the outraged & down-trodden South, though in silence & stillness, until the now far-distant day shall arrive for just retribution for Yankee usurpation, oppression, & atrocious outrages— & for deliverance & vengeance for the now ruined, subjugated, & enslaved Southern States! May the maledictions of every victim to their malignity, press with full weight on the perfidious Yankees people & their perjured rulers—& especially on those of the invading forces who perpetrated, & their leaders & high authorities who encouraged, directed, or permitted, the unprecedented & generally extended outrages of robbery, rapine & destruction, & house burning, all committed contrary to the laws of war on non-combatant residents, & still worse on aged men & helpless women!"[1]

Henry Hartford Cumming also resorted to Edmund Ruffin's suicide solution to the South's postwar problems. His deep depression exacerbated by fears that his wife and family would soon be reduced to abject poverty led him to commit suicide in the spring of 1866.[2]

189

"Visit of the Ku Klux." (*Harper's Weekly*, February 24, 1872.)

As a far less drastic means of coping with defeat, a good many Southerners counseled forgiveness and getting on with life as the only approach to a workable reconciliation with the North. Although she admitted that repressing their inordinate loathing of Yankees would require a supreme effort on the part of Southerners, Cornelia Spencer, as a Christian, advocated forgiveness as soon as possible. "If we are to be forgiven as we forgive, I think we had better do it as quick as we can. I am however, sensible of a great rising in my throat when I contemplate certain parties in the Yankee nation. I am, I do confess, at times in *no sort* of amity towards them. I have never been able to get up the least feeling of loyalty or interest in the star-spangled banner. On the contrary, I would like to spit on it this minute. Now of course this is not forgiveness. And yet I think myself a better Christian in this matter than a good many of my neighbors." In her letter to Ellen Summerell she reiterated her friend's query. "The question you propose is whether we are required to forgive & love them before they exhibit signs of repentance."[3]

At this point Mrs. Spencer's Christian background tended to frame her response, and in responding she made clear the distinction between forgetting and forgiving. "If we are to take our Master for an example the answer seems to be this. '*While we were yet sinners Christ died*_—. I really do believe we *ought* to choke down, trample out, scatter to the winds all our natural, & (casually speaking) *justifiable* resentments, & bitterness, & force ourselves to feel, look, speak kindly & forgivingly of these people. It will cost a mortal pang to do it, but it ought to be done, I believe, by Christians. And done *now*. If we wait till time has dulled our memories somewhat & worn off the keeness of the edge, we may begin to say I forgive—when it is only that we are forgetting."[4]

Even ministers sometimes had difficulty coping with the Christian doctrine of love and forgiveness. A South Carolina woman told of hearing the minister urging the members of his congregation to be faithful in following Christ until they reached the "'New Jerusalem, the golden city, not a desolate place like this [Columbia], but ever bright and fair, and I assure you, my friends, there will be no villainous Yankees there.'" Suddenly catching himself up short he added: "'Unless they have entirely new hearts.'"[5]

Forgiveness, of course, was utterly impossible for tens of thousands of Southerners who had given up a loved one to the cause or had suffered the wanton destruction of their homes and property by Yankee troops. A North Carolinian could find no place in his heart for forgiveness as he remembered Sherman's camp followers who in searching for buried treasure "entered the graveyard, dug up my dead children, opened their coffins, and left their bodies exposed to birds and beast, less vile than they. Tell me to forgive them? Never!" He insisted "If anybody … hates the wretches who followed Sherman's army more than I do, it is because his capacity for hating is greater than mine."[6]

"It Was a Sickening Sight": Battlefield Pilgrimages

Visiting the battlefield where a loved one breathed his last helped some women cope with their grief. Strange as it may seem, Civil War battlegrounds were compelling tourist areas. For some, the visits were grief-stricken pilgrimages, for others frantic searches for the final resting places of loved ones, for still others a recapturing of the heroism of their gallant men, or for the curious souvenir collector they constituted a treasure hunt. In March of 1866 Sarah Carter joined friends in what turned out to be a gruesome tour of Southern battlefields. At Seven Pines, Sarah cringed: "It seemed a quiet graveyard now that the roar of battle had long since died away. Our driver brought us three skulls, and there were numbers of ribs and ends of bones lying about on the carpet of fallen pine-needles. It was a sickening sight. We wandered around and saw how the men were buried in the places where they fell." At Fort Stedman many of the graves had been despoiled in an insensitive search for lead and iron. "Plenty of old canteens, mugs, tin plates, old shoes and knapsacks were scattered about, lovely purple lobelia and chickweed growing among them…. Oh, it was

"The Lost Found." (*Harper's Weekly*, February 4, 1866.)

dreadful!" En route home the visitors, traumatized by their experiences, "did not talk much, it was too sad." For women living close to the battlefields it was a shattering experience to see half buried bodies emerging from the mud and weeds following a heavy rain.[7]

Jennie Stephenson wrote of a ghastly clump of graves, the coloring of the former soldiers' clothes still preserved, in the meadow and in the garden near their home close to Petersburg. The children, she shuddered, used the skulls as playthings, making "a more repulsive sight than ever." According to Jennie: "The summer of 1866 was a time of searching through the county for the Union dead, to place in the cemetery. Five dollars was given for every collection of bones with a skull. So called spies, deserters, and anything resembling the form of a man was money. All were taken up and sold, and are now enshrined as heroes in their well kept cemeteries."[8]

For countless Southerners there were pilgrimages to particular graveyards to see a beloved's last resting place. Lizzie Hardin, her mother and sister, en route home to Kentucky after the war, paid their respects to the gravesite of a cousin, General Hardin Helm [Lincoln's Confederate brother-in-law] on the outskirts of Atlanta. Lizzie mourned: "We saw the graves of thousands of Confederate soldiers lying as close together as they ever stood on the field of battle. There they lay, unknown, forgotten, neglected, but *free*."[9]

Neither patriotism nor compassion but unabated curiosity prompted droves of tourists to seek out the homes of famous Southern generals. Mrs. Roger Pryor, whose husband had been an important general during the war, shunned the tourists who paraded by their home near Petersburg, Virginia, some even contriving to call, professing some vague common bond. "We were perfectly aware that they wished to see *us*, and not to gain, as they affected, information about the historic localities on the farm." Some of the uninvited callers were even emboldened enough to lecture them on the rights of their Negroes as well as Southerners' need to feel chastised for their rebellion.[10]

It was not the usual tourist's visit that fired the determination of a Northerner, Georgeanna Woolsey (famous for her services as a nurse at Gettysburg and on the hospital transports) to call on General Lee. Her errand was not to visit him in person but to deliver a very special package. During the war Georgeanna had become so incensed at the atrocities at the Federal prisons in Richmond that she collected editorials about the abuses from New York newspapers, and while visiting in Richmond shortly after the peace agreements deposited the bundle on General Lee's doorstep—after making sure that he was at home and the clippings would be given him.[11]

"Whatever Is, Is Right": Coping Through Religion

Millions of Southerners turned to their religion as a means of coping with the depression of defeat. As noted earlier the more religious Confederates resigned themselves to their losses as the manifestation of "God's will." Anne Thom echoed a familiar acceptance: "I trust things will be better than we think. God ruleth on earth, as well as in Heaven, & we must trust his wisdom & mercy to bring good out of all this seeming evil." However, not a few women were tormented over their husband's growing irreligion, their faith dashed by the war's appalling portrayal of man's inhumanity to man and by the depressing hopelessness of defeat. Edwin Fay confessed to his wife, Sarah: "Truly the Lord has forsaken his people—I fear the subjugation of the South will make an infidel of me. I cannot see how a just God can allow people who have battled so heroically for their rights to be overthrown. I can't I wont believe that my county is subjugated." A Virginia woman also agonized over the effect of the war on her husband. "This has been a sad, sad war. I see its evil effects everywhere—my own dear husband, I fear has lost faith in God—he doubts the necessity or efficacy of prayer! This is, I know, a time to try our souls. Our dearest hopes have been blighted, our homes & fortunes sacrificed, & some of our bravest & best lost to us— but still, God hath permitted it, & we must lay our hands upon our lips, & submit."[12]

Lizzie Hardin clung to her faith that "God is omnipotent; that in the a twinkling of an eye he could bring to nought all their devices!" (She was referring to Yankee oppression and humiliation.) However, the collapse of the Confederacy, she admitted, at times made it difficult to accept "whatever is, is right." Lizzie longed "for the unquestioning faith of a child." Instead, she wrote, "I feel like one who is groping in darkness and yet responsible for every step he takes."[13]

The death of a second step-son caused Margaret Junkin Preston to despair: "It is a sore blow to his precious father, to his sisters, and to us all. God grant it may be a sanctified affliction! We have surely need of chastisement, or it would not have been repeated so painfully, within so brief a period."[14]

Surely, Southerners were convinced, there would be some divine vengeance forthcoming for Northern injustices. Northern journalist John Dennett was asked "if, at the North, there was not among the intelligent classes, at any rate among the religious people, an expectation that God would visit upon that section some terrible retribution for the unjust war they had waged upon their brethren, the calamities they had inflicted on the South."[15]

It is scarcely surprising that an appeal to spiritualism and spiritualists held out great promise as a means of communing with loved ones lost on the field of battle. Rachel Craighead was awestruck by the experience when her mother sought out a spiritualist: "It is wonderful what he tells."[16] Gertrude Thomas on a trip to New York in 1870 visited a spiritualist with questions about her father and her babies who had died in infancy. However, Gertrude was somewhat put off by the spiritualist's vague reassurances and the less than direct communications. Somehow the medium seemed to be more concerned with his fees rather than with facts from the spirit world. Gertrude's attendance at two gatherings at the "church of the spiritualists" at Apollo Hall proved more rewarding. Impressed by the eloquent speaker she admitted, "I could not if I would and I do not know that I would if I could, note all the new startling doctrines he advanced."[17]

In New Orleans Madame La Blanch billed herself as "the only great Natural Clairvoyant and Spirit Visionist that has ever existed in the memory of man." Her powers did indeed seem impressive, particularly her "remedy to bring lovers together that never fails. It restores happiness between husband and wife." (All that and for "moderate terms!")[18]

Following the war countless women plunged into church activities and missionary work with a passion, some seeking to sublimate their troubles in charitable work for those even less fortunate, others seeking new avenues of volunteerism once their services as nurses and caregivers had lessened. While the men set about forming veterans' organizations and planning reunions, women devoted their efforts to founding veterans' hospitals, retirement homes for soldiers, and orphanages for children left parentless by the war.[19] That innate "mothering" that characterized women's activities in the aid societies and in their hospital work during the war soon found expression in efforts to establish and maintain Ladies' Hospitals and Relief Associations.

Back in New Orleans, for example, Frances Fearn discovered, as did thousands, considerable satisfaction in immersing herself in charitable works. With the passage of time Frances Fearn confessed that the old world existed only in memory, a new world of challenge and change had taken its place. There was indeed life after the defeat of the Confederacy and the loss of their fortune.[20]

"To Make Happy Their Short Holiday": *Coping Through Togetherness*

At first, in the wake of the surrender, partying and frivolity seemed almost sinful. In time, however, sadness and shock slowly gave way to relief that the bloodshed had finally ended. Soon the celebration of sheer survival burgeoned into an attempt to recapture the laughter and merriment that had so long been abandoned. Homecomings, reunions with friends and relatives for the first time in four years, the return of refugees to their old homes, all ushered in a heady exuberance that at least for the moment blurred the agony of defeat. One writer admitted that "one would have thought from the mirth and gayety that prevailed that our armies had been successful."[21]

Although there had been few real parties during the summer of 1865 in Washington, Georgia, Eliza Frances Andrews explained that "starvation parties" (gatherings where usually no refreshments other than water were served) constituted most of their entertainments. "We are too poor to have suppers often, but when we do get one we enjoy it famously."[22]

Everyone was "very blue," Ellen House reported, and queried, "How can a true Southerner be any thing else." Deeply disturbed by even the limited amount of socializing going on about her, Ellen remarked in her diary: "Yesterday there was a large picnic at Jenkins Mill, neither of us went [neither Ellen nor her sister]. I do not think this is any time for picnics &e. Tonight there is to be a dance at Mr. Buddins—a Union man. What the young men and girls can be thinking of to go there at such a time I cannot imagine."[23]

"Mine is a lonely home, My dear friend, the gay laughter and merry music which ever reigned supreme are all gone, & a lonely, sad heart wonders in the places once consecrated to mirth," wrote a young Southern belle. The loss of five brothers and her fiancé to the war had left her inconsolable. "The sacred emotions of the heart cannot be controlled, and we wander through life seeking in vain for the unattainable...."[24]

For a time Pauline DeCaradeuc (Heyward) was unable to bring herself to make merry and dance following the news of the collapse of the Confederacy. She took pains to explain that she did not "have the heart to dance, & go to pleasure parties—*What a mockery!*" When invited to a picnic at a neighbor's farm, Pauline declined. "The young men sent a buggy here for me, instead of hanging their disgraced heads over their paroles, or rallying on to Trans-Miss., they remained to dance & be merry over the death of their country, shame! shame!—of course, I sent their buggy back to them empty!" Three months later, however, Pauline accepted an invitation to the same neighbor's farm and "danced every dance."[25]

Once relief set in that the bloodshed was truly over Nannie Haskins, among others, described being caught up in a whirl of parties, dances, picnics—and tableaux—celebrating the return of the young heroes. After the "peace," young people tended to party with abandon, one Mississippi woman recalled. "We wanted to make happy their short holiday, before they took up life's burdens in earnest, and with willing hands and stout hearts worked for the support of aged fathers and mothers and young sisters."[26]

Kate Stone shared Pauline DeCaradeuc and Nannie Haskins' initial reluctance to party following the war. "There has been much visiting and various picnics and fish frys. I would not go at first. I felt like I did not want to see anybody or ever dance again. I felt fully forty years old, but Mamma made me go after a good cry. Once there I was compelled to exert myself, and soon I was enjoying it all. The burden of some of the years slipped from my shoulders, and I was young again." Kate added that she found "even poverty in company more bearable than when suffered alone." For Kate and her friends in the months after the war even a small party at a neighbor's home often occasioned as much excitement "as though it were the grand ball of a season."[27]

Martha Brent was relieved that "our loved ones were no longer standing up to be shot at. I made friends with a party of young folks and we were together, every night. What with music and dancing and rowing on the river in boats, I think there was never such a happy summer in my life. Though new clothes were an unknown quantity, we wore old ones and no one girl was better off than the rest!"[28]

The dearth of appropriate evening attire called forth ingenuity and resourcefulness on the part of most of the partiers. One young belle would probably have rivaled Scarlett O'Hara as she reported being "quite pleased with myself in a dress I had made out of an old pair of white window curtains."[29]

Marriages, now that beaux and fiancés had returned, took center stage. Girls' gossipy letters were filled with news of engagements and weddings. Hesitant during the war to refuse a proposal of marriage from a young hero about to return to the scene of battle, coquettes soon found it necessary to seriously accept or reject their young suitors' attentions. Kate Stone and her friend Mollie Moore "decided that the girls would all have to change their war customs, stop flirting, and only engage themselves when they really meant something. The days of lightly-won and lightly-held hearts should be over."[30]

Although they were not the exuberant, energetic socializing of dances and balls, the "getting up" of tableaux provided opportunities for "togetherness" for the young and even the not-so-young. The performances offered a creative outlet for participants as well as an interesting evening's diversion for audiences. The living representations of historical scenes, patriotic mottoes, literary characters, or popular sayings (successfully employed many years later by Flo Ziegfeld) were frequently integral parts of the soldiers' fairs and benefits conducted in both the South and the North to raise money for the troops during the war and for widows and orphans after the war. Floride Clemson described the fun of serving as "director, costumer, actor, & suggester" for her group's portrayals of "sleeping beauty, telling fortunes, Judith & Hollafernes, the witches in Macbeth, taking the veil, beheading Mary of Scotts, the fair Geraldine, in the magic mirror, the tea party at Chuzzlewits, the old maids' tea party, Mrs. Squires giving treakle, the real, & imaginary shepherdess, & the animating of Pigmalion's statute, a pantomime." The "suggester" added "I enjoyed it *hugely*."[31]

The medieval pageants, the popular antebellum tournaments, continued after "the late unpleasantness." "Knights" competed for swordsmanship and horseback riding honors while their "ladies" admired and applauded from the sidelines. In some areas the romanticism of earlier days continued unabated, yet in others the frivolity and pageantry had been eroded by the hard lessons of reality. In October of 1865 Floride Clemson told her diary: "There was a great tournament here. Some fourteen knights rode in various costumes, not at all knightly for the most. Two sent their lances to me to trim, & rode for me: Edwin Frost, & Ben Gaillard. My colors were red, white, & black. The Confederate colors, in mourning." The knights including "Great Mogul," an Indian, a "Highland Lad," "Billy Bow Legs," and the "Red Knight" apparently did their ladies proud, and in the evening Floride attended a fancy dress ball dressed as a Spanish lady. "I hear everyone say I was the best dressed lady in the room," she added modestly.[32]

At the August fair in 1870 Gertrude Thomas and her husband cheered on son Turner in his ride as "Henry of Navarre" in the Tournament of Knights. It was a high point of the summer when Turner dressed in black velvet and a white plumed hat was awarded first prize.[33]

For some very fortunate women there was the luxury of travel and vacationing at lakes and fashionable resorts. By 1867 small parties of those who had somehow managed to emerge unscathed financially journeyed to the Virginia springs for the mineral baths, the rest and relaxation—*and* the social life. Agnes Kirkland, a visitor from Maryland at White Sulphur Springs, detailed the daily rounds of "calling," teas, tableaux, and other entertainments. Of particular note during her stay was the friendship that developed between Agnes and General Lee and his wife, son and daughter, who were also guests at the Springs no doubt in the interests of Mrs. Lee's health and General Lee's own heart condition.[34]

As Northerners began to drift southward once again for the Virginia baths and the social scene, the mingling of former foes helped mitigate and even eradicate old enmities. It was during the Lees' visit to one of the most popular spas that General Lee was said to have gently admonished one of the visiting Southern belles for giving vent to her contempt for Yankees. When asked by the young lady if he had never felt resentment toward Yankees, he responded, "I believe I may say, looking into my own heart, and speaking as in the presence of God, that I never known one moment of bitterness or resentment."[35]

"A Terrible Nightmare": Crime and Violence as Outlets

In the chaos following the war, tens of thousands of Yankees, Negroes, Confederate veterans, jealous neighbors, and guerrilla factions turned to vicious acts of crime and violence as an outlet for their pent up vengeance and frustration. Few areas were immune from the rampant outbreak of crime at the war's end. A Mississippi woman pointed to "reports coming to town nearly every day, informing the authorities of lawless acts perpetrated on innocent, law-abiding citizens who are unable to protect themselves. Low pilfering and stealing are quite common, and there is but little safety for life or property."[36]

Not only civilians but even soldiers who survived the carnage on the battlefield were still vulnerable to the fiendish violence that characterized many areas of the postwar South. Ellen House was overjoyed with the return of her favorite brother, Johnnie, from twenty-two months of imprisonment on Johnson's Island. Her happiness was short lived, however, when he was murdered a few months later by a highwayman.[37]

Longing to accept an invitation to visit friends in Maryland, Floride Clemson was gravely disappointed not to be able to join the girls. "I only wish I could, as this country [Pendleton, South Carolina] is getting very unsafe. People are constantly called from their houses at night & shot, besides thefts of all kinds & degrees, are of daily occurrence. The country is in a terribly state, & will probably get worse, as the winter proceeds." Several months later with seemingly unintentional humor she wrote: "Matters are pretty quiet now except casual disturbances thefts & murders."[38]

"Bummers" and ruffians continued their vicious raids for weeks and months after the surrender. One woman related the diabolical details of a raid on her home within a month after peace had been declared.

SCENES IN MEMPHIS, TENNESSEE, DURING THE RIOT—SHOOTING DOWN NEGROES ON THE MORNING OF MAY 2, 1866.—[SKETCHED BY A. R. W.]

The Memphis race riots: "Shooting Down Negroes on the Morning of May 2, 1866." (*Harper's Weekly*, May 26, 1866.)

"Watches, jewelry, silver and every trinket of value [were] extracted. Locks burst, beds torn to pieces, and indeed every room thrown into the wildest confusion. What they could not take they destroyed, cutting in pieces such valuable things as boots, clothes and books, shattering glasses, china, combs and in short singling out the very articles they knew could only be replaced with difficulty." Upon entering the library they scattered every paper they could find "to the four winds." Apparently dissatisfied with the pandemonium generated by their first visit, several of the same group returned "once again to greet us." Any valuables or edibles missed before, she related, were quickly seized in their drunken revel which was celebrated with blasphemy and incredibly outrageous behavior. "What wonder Southern women were never reconstructed," the writer added.[39]

Unprotected women living in remote areas were particularly enticing prey for bedeviling thugs. Two dirty, unkempt women, a mother and daughter, came begging for help from John De Forest of the Freedmen's Bureau. The mother had long ago been widowed, and the daughter's husband and brother, in an attempt to avoid service with the Rebel army, had both been shot and killed by the Confederates. The women were in dire need of food and clothes; the daughter was shoeless, her feet swollen and raw from her two years without shoes. Snow, rain, and wind had filtered through the cracks of their cabin; the earthen floor had become a footbath of mud and water. Without the protection of men, the women were the targets of bullies and roughnecks who plagued them day and night.[40]

George Eggleston was outraged at the violence and denounced the marauders as the "offscourings of the two armies and of the suddenly freed Negro population—deserters from fighting regiments on both sides, and Negro desperadoes, who found common ground upon which to fraternize in their common depravity."[41] Robbery, house-breaking and entering, plundering and vandalism, as George Eggleston pointed out, were not the sole province of Northern or Western gangs of outlaws or of vengeful newly freed blacks. Confederate soldiers returning from the battlefields to their homes following their desertion or their discharge wantonly plundered both Confederate stores as well as private property.[42] Having been unpaid for months, veterans often looked at their thievery as "their due." Deserters stealthily bent on "doing all the harm they could" were often dreaded more than the Yankees.[43]

In isolated areas where residents were considerably outnumbered by their assailants, people were reluctant to seek retaliation by meeting violence with violence for fear of incurring even greater wrath from the terrorists. Edmund Ruffin detailed the work of marauding bands of white and black "bummers" in his Amelia County, Virginia, neighborhood.

"The depredations of the bands of armed robbers have been extended to this neighborhood, & are carried on boldly, & extensively, though confined to horses & mules as subjects for plunder." When the farms and residences of families scarcely three miles from his home were robbed, Ruffin was disappointed that the villains had met little or no resistance. However, he also observed that people were "afraid to resort to defence by arms, lest they should draw upon their families the worse misfortunes of having their dwellings burnt, if not some of the helpless inmates murdered."[44]

"As I look back to those days," Sara Handy recalled, "they appear as a terrible nightmare. We lay down at night in our clothes, not daring to go regularly to bed, for fear lest we might be roused at any hour by the blaze of our burning mills. I had a five-shooter, which I wore constantly, and thus felt that, to some degree, I held my fate in my own hands; but it is not an exhilarating consciousness to know that at any moment you may be called upon to save yourself from dishonor by taking your own life."[45]

"A Party of Men Went, at Night": The Ku Klux Klan

The greatest waves of violence, of course, came with the organization of the Ku Klux Klan. As a defense and/or retaliation against the dictatorial operations of the Radical Republicans, thousands of militant Southerners joined local groups of the Ku Klux Klan. By attempting to prevent freedmen from renting or owning land, from cohabiting with whites, from voting a Republican ticket, and from initiating a host of other acts of independence the Klan and other vigilante groups sought to "keep the Negro in his place" socially and economically. Blacks were whipped or beaten for moving from one plantation to another, for disrespect to their employers, for organizing black schools, for indolence. All too often the lynch law was summarily applied as a result of various legal or social transgressions on the part of blacks, while violence on the part of whites, including rape and murder, was simply glossed over as veritable white supremacy.

The Klan newspaper, the *Ku Klux Klan*, published weekly at Forrest, Mississippi, spelled out the Klan's vicious attitude toward blacks and the Klan's brazen defiance of the government, cursing anyone brave enough to condemn their activities. A Klan editor wrote in the December 14, 1871, issue of the *Ku Kluz Klan* "We are not afraid of anybody,

"Two Members of the Ku Klux Klan."
(*Harper's Weekly*, October, 27, 1866.)

or any government that holds a 'nigger' equal to a white man, and we don't care who knows it.... The negro is inferior to the white man, and the sooner the people know it the better."

Apparently Klan members were seemingly even more contemptuous of carpetbaggers than Negroes. Following a shoot-out in Starkville, Mississippi, in which several negroes succeeded in wounding two carpetbagger deputies, the *Ku Klux Klan* on December 14, 1871, carried an editorial from the *Vicksburg Herald* that concluded: "We are inclined to feel just a slight shade of regret that these irate Sambos did not succeed in their amiable purpose. We scarcely know a better use the negroes could be put to, than the killing of a score or so of carpet-bag officials of the State and National Government." In another article in the same edition, a Klanner surprisingly took to task a group of vigilantes who had hanged three Negroes for thievery and even begged their indulgence for the Negro. The paper insisted that the Negroes were completely under the control of the detested Radicals and the loyal leagues.

Investigations into the conditions in the South, which resulted in the voluminous testimony of the Federal government's Joint Select Committee to Investigate the Condition of Affairs in the Late Insurrectionary States, provide a heartbreaking litany of outrages and murders committed in the name of white supremacy.[46] Much of the violence was the work of the Ku Klux Klan; however, scores of other similar groups or "dens" were often organized under names such as the Knights of the Rising Sun the Invisible Empire, the Invisible Circle, the White Brotherhood, or the White Roses. (The ploy, of course, provided a hedge against having to admit to belonging to the Klan in case members were called to testify before a Federal investigating committee or in a court of law.) In addition to the larger organizations there was also a tremendous proliferation of "Clubs." Despite the fact that some groups were organized solely along political lines, others appeared to intersperse vigilante activities along with politics. (See the Susan Darden chapter in Part II for details of the various "Clubs.")

Although in June 1871 the committee circulated handbills begging people to come to the hearing places to testify, Klan members and informers were generally cowed by ultimatums reading "Death to all witnesses!" Oaths differed somewhat from Klan to Klan but in general members swore to support and defend the group, and come to the aid of a brother or members of his family who were in distress. Furthermore they promised never to "reveal the secrets of this order, or anything in regard to it that may come to my knowledge; and if I do may I meet a traitor's doom, which is Death, Death, Death."[47]

Despite the threat, some former Klansmen courageously testified as to the groups' lawlessness, while others resorted to outright lies and deceitful evasion during the committee's inquiries. Blacks in particular were threatened with dire results for testifying. Nevertheless, hosts of undaunted freedmen furnished shocking accounts of stabbings, beatings, whippings, rapes, murders, raids, burnings, castrations, thefts, threats of loss of work, loss of property, loss of crops, punishment of family members. Negroes were whipped and beaten for teaching in colored schools, for sending a child to school, for supposedly having "sassed white folks," for holding office, for voting the Republican ticket, for purchasing land, for being too "uppity," for even vaguely anticipating equality with whites. White men, too, were victims of Klan activities and were beaten for teaching Negro children, for boarding while teaching with black families, for proclaiming an equality of the races, for urging blacks to vote, for selling land to Negroes, for fraternization with blacks, for supporting Negroes in public office, for writing editorials for a Republican newspaper, for having meetings of Negroes in one's home, for urging blacks to violence if necessary to obtain their rights. Women, as well, testified to their whippings and beatings at the hands of the Klan.[48]

Freedmen were "Ku Kluxed" and were driven from their homes because they didn't work for someone or because they did work for someone. Masked men, professing to be agents of the devil, threatened blacks insisting that their victims would be carried off to a fiery inferno were they not to obey orders. Ku Kluxers confronted victims with questions about their voting and then beat or promised to kill them for having cast Republican ballots. In one election a man reported that, "A party of men went, at night, and took out two white men and three Negroes, one of them a colored woman, and whipped them most brutally. Two of them were managers of the box at the election, and the men told them that if they dared to hold an election at that box they would return and kill them."[49]

Not only freedmen but, as noted above, whites as well were victims of Klan brutality. Testimony before the Joint Committee revealed that a sixty-eight year old white man was whipped by a party of disguised men who "ordered him to come to town on sales day, and in the presence of the crowd publicly renounce his republican principles, and ask for pardon of the people for ever having identified himself with the republican party." The masked men promised they would kill him unless he repudiated his convictions.[50]

Certainly not all crime could be attributed to the Klan. In some areas resident whites made up their own vigilante committees. In those areas "getting lost" served as a euphemism for "murder." The Northern journalist John Dennett overheard a South Carolinian remark casually: "A heap of 'em [Negroes] out in my country get into the swamps and get lost. I don't know as it's true, but I've heard that there's men out there that haven't got anything else to do, and if you mention any nigger to 'em, and give 'em twelve dollars, the nigger's sure to be lost in a very few days."[51]

Eliza Frances Andrews was horrified by a friend's admission that in South Carolina "the men have a recipe for putting troublesome negroes out of the way that the Yankee can't get a key to. No two go out together, no one lets another know what he is going to do, and so, when mischievous negroes are found dead in the woods, nobody knows who killed them."[52] No doubt the South Carolina "recipe" accounted for hundreds of outright murders and the inability of authorities to arrest and punish the perpetrators.

James L. Orr, former Senator in the Confederacy, was critical of communities that professed ignorance of or fear of Klan or local vigilante activities. Testifying before the committee he concluded: "My supposition is that these parties engaged in midnight-marauding are pretty generally reckless young men, without a great deal of standing in the community, and if they happen to be detected, they can get on their horses and leave the country, and get out of the way. I think the better portion of the community are responsible for these acts, no further than that they do not use their influence, both morally and in actually enforcing the law. I think that is where the fault lies with them"[53]

Surely some of the atrocities were committed by "reckless young men," but apparently there were large numbers of otherwise responsible citizens who with a racist bent (the word racist, however, was not used in those days) or who in anti-Radical Republic defiance donned the white robes and beliefs of the Klan. Over the years it has been generally assumed that the Ku Klux Klan was composed essentially of the lower elements of society; however, revisionists point out that some judges, lawyers, bankers, and businessmen were also involved in Klan activities.[54]

Many years later former slaves in talks with WPA Writers' Project interviewers provided considerable detail about Ku Klux Klan activities. Ned Chaney of Lauderdale County, Mississippi, remembered Uncle Lem being "whupped" by the Klan "an' den dey cut his th'oat, an' some mo' niggers around there went de same way." (Information in the interview gives rise to the suspicion that the murders may have been the result of the freedmen owning and farming their own land, an activity deplored by Klan members. In many areas there were grave prohibitions about renting or selling land to blacks.) As for voting, Ned said his father had voted "onct because dat's what dey say do." (Perhaps he never voted again out of fear of the KKK.)

In some instances freedmen were inducted into Klan membership, Ned pointed out, and were used to ferret out information regarding the secret activities of blacks under suspicion by the Klan. (Some authorities believe that Negroes were not officially members of the Ku Klux Klan, but were "associates" and constituted "auxiliary" groups.) But, Ned continued: "nobody ever knowed de names of de Kloo Kluxes."[55] An article in the *Ku Klux Klan,* the KKK newspaper, of December 14, 1871, gave the following account of a Negro Ku Klux group. "We are reliably informed that on last Wednesday week, some eight or ten negroes went in the night to the residence of John Peeples', (col'd) and took Jack McLeod, (col'd,) out of the house into the woods and gave him four or five hundred stripes. They also went to the house of Richard Homer, (col'd,) after him, but he was not at home. This is the first and only case of Ku-Kluxing we have heard of in Montgomery."

In an article in the Klan newspaper preceding the above December 14, 1871, report of the Negro Klan's "visitation," the writer reiterated the Klan's ineradicable belief that "the negro is inferior to the White man." The writer continued, however, in a more enlightened vein: "We beg some indulgence from you for the negro. He has been gulled by mean men, and is more to be pitied than contemned."

Asked about the Klan by the WPA Project interviewers, Simon Hare of Lauderdale County, Mississippi, retorted "Show! Everybody knowed about Kloo Kluxes! One bunch of 'em came there one night, ridin' mules. Had things over dey eyes. You'd think hit was de devil. Git you off an' wuph you so you be sca'ed to show yo' face an' not go messin' wid white folks's business." Apparently Simon's father traveled with a lively group of freedmen and soon "we found out de diff'runce betwixt Radicals an' Democratics."[56]

"Many Brave Women Aided the Ku Klux Klan"

Few women discussed in detail the activities of the Klan in their areas; however, Betty Beaumont, of Woodville, Mississippi, admitted that the Klan "was probably organized for the sake of enforcing law and order during this period of anarchy, but, having been joined by many reckless characters, it in turn has grown into a perfect scourge." Mrs. Beaumont wrote of the Klan members' secrecy, their disguises, their blackened faces. "But it is seldom they are seen, as their work is done at night, by stealth. Their threats or warnings are sometimes given by marking the door of a residence, shop, or store with the outline of a coffin done in charcoal; and again a miniature coffin is made and placed in the domicile of the person whom they wish to injure or frighten, and a letter of explanation of what they may expect, if they do not conform to the required exactions of the company, is placed in the coffin. This is one of the least of the dastardly acts they commit." The Klan's lawlessness, Mrs. Beaumont observed, "is driving our best labor from our midst, both black and white, which will eventually impoverish the country, as labor is its wealth."[57]

Amidst all the violence there were women who tacitly or even overtly sanctioned at least some of the activities of the Klan. A DeSoto County, Mississippi, man provided specific details about the organization of his particular Klan, and admitted: "My wife, Mat, and Asa Doggett's wife were members, too. We had to take in a few women in order to have some one to make our uniforms and do any sewing for us."[58]

Mrs. William Hardin, a Nashville, Tennessee, widow, confessed that she was grateful for the protection provided by the Ku Klux Klan. "I cannot describe those terrible days, but of one thing I am sure, that many brave women aided the Ku Klux Klan to organize. They made their uniforms with their own hands. They kept their secrets and stood by them with unflinching devotion. In return the Ku Klux Klan were our only protection."[59]

Elizabeth Meriwether insisted that the Klan was "All that saved the South from utter destruction" and detailed, without apology, her husband's membership in the Klan as one of the lieutenants and counselors of General Nathan Bedford Forest, the Klan's Supreme Grand Wizard.

Forest was one of the friends who met with Minor Meriwether in the Meriwether home to formulate plans for the Memphis chapter of the Ku Klux Klan. Betty's curiosity about the "curious, long white garments—as if for a masked ball" that she had made for her husband and his repeated absences from home at night was answered as she watched him depart one evening with his "masked ball" garments. As her husband had instructed her Betty sat by a window and at midnight watched in astonishment as the "Ghostly Army," filed by their home. "It seemed to be an army of horses, but the horses' feet did not make the usual noise and clatter. Their hoofs were wrapped in cloth, their bodies were covered with flowing white cotton cloth, their riders wore white hoods and white gowns which trailed almost to the ground. Hardly a sound did either horses or riders make—truly, in the light of that midnight moon, it did seem like an army of ghosts." Aptly called "The Invisible Empire," the midnight marauders set about their devilish work of terrorizing and murdering hapless Negroes. To Betty Meriwether and thousands like her the Klan "accomplished a noble and a necessary work in the only way in which that work was then possible."[60]

When some of the Negroes refused to sign the work contracts mandated by the Freedmen's Bureau, Mrs. William Hardin foresaw serious problems looming ahead on her plantation. Informed that either they must sign and go to work or leave the plantation, many black workers refused to budge. As the situation worsened, suddenly out of the blue one night Mrs. Hardin's repose was shattered by one of the servants running into the room crying "Oh Mistess, de Ku Klux are here!" Calmly Mrs. Hardin opened the door and beckoned the men into the house. "Immediately the halls were full of men in their queer costumes. One who seemed to be the captain, asked me if the negroes were giving me any trouble. I told him they were all polite and respectful to me, but a few had declined to either sign the contract or leave the place. He simply said: 'They will give you no further trouble.' I begged them to be kind to the negroes."[61]

Kate Thom seemed to take a remarkably casual view of the violence that swept the Southland. In reporting from Frankfort, Kentucky, she wrote: "The negroes seem about the same. I understand their conduct has improved during the past week. A black boy was lynched here ten days ago, and the affair seems to have produced a salutary effect upon them all. He was seventeen years old, and attempted to violate a little girl of six, daughter of a Major in the Federal army. Five negroes have been hung for the same offence in the last two months."[62]

In contrast to the rampant persecution of blacks, a benevolent former owner from time to time braved retaliation from the Klan and provided shelter for an ex-slave at odds with the Klan. In 1870 a Mississippi woman recorded the visit of the Ku Klux Klan at a former slave's home. In sympathy for Albert, who had close ties to her family, she wrote: "Albert staid here Last night. He is in trouble." Three weeks later she wrote: "the kuklucks run Albert Black off from home Last Thursday for a false report."[63] Not all former owners, however, were courageous enough to befriend or shelter a black in trouble with the Klan. Too much togetherness and the owner herself could become a victim.

Women were not only witnesses to the violence of the era, but at times became the victims. Now and then they came through as heroines in the confrontations. Both during and after the war, Southern women had garnered a well-deserved reputation for being feisty, and upon numerous occasions they were credited with saving lives and property as a result of their spunkiness. A white Louisiana woman was responsible for fending off a delegation of hooded, black faced Ku Klux Klanners who appeared in the dark of night knocking at her door and ominously demanding a "private chat" with her brother Tom Hudnall. Apparently her brother had refused to join the democratic party and the Klanners had arrived to punished him for voting "the d——Negro ticket." As the appeals grew more insistent Mrs. Balfour at last summoned her brother to the door; however, at the sound of guns clicking for action, her brother dashed into the house returning with a double-barreled shotgun as his sister withdrew a knife from her blouse. Without further ado Mrs. Balfour faced the ringleader, knife in hand, and announced, "If you are to take my brother by force the sooner you come in the better for my brother and you too. I want you to come foremost, you bully ... as I am now ready to die by my brother's side." Somewhat startled by Mrs. Balfour's threat, the Klanners conferred and the ringleader finally backed down saying, "You may take it to yourself that you have saved your brother's life; we will now give him five days to leave this country." Needless to say Tom Hudnall made a speedy departure.[64]

In a confrontation not with Klanners but with Yankee "bummers" and town ruffians Margaret Beckwith proved herself equal to the occasion and forced the would-be molesters to back down and leave the premises. Members of the Beckwith family who were refugeeing in Lincolnton, North Carolina, were unaware of Lee's surrender; however, a band of vandals took advantage of their lack of knowledge to terrorize and plunder the frightened residents. At one point Margaret Beckwith courageously confronted a blue and gray clad wretch at the door who was threatening the family. Insisting that he knew the family had pistols in the home, he attempted to push his way past Margaret and into the house. Days earlier Margaret's father, who was not at home at the time, had given her a gun for protection which Margaret prudently carried in her pocket. "It was not loaded," she explained, "nor was I anxious to use it." However, as the would-be intruder grew ever more insolent and demanding, Margaret "pulled out the pistol & pointed it at him saying—'Yes, we have pistols—do you want them.' He began to back off, so I persisted— 'You had better take it'—but he dodged out of the range and disappeared." Word quickly spread that "all of us were armed—so we were not molested any more." Some time later an admiring little boy stopped Margaret on the street asking, "'Are you the lady who pointed the pistol at the Yankee?' So the story got out. I should have preserved that relic," Margaret reminisced, admitting, however, "The memory is surely enough."[65]

ᔥ

The blood curdling reports of murders, beating, whippings, and the general mistreatment of blacks and the unlikelihood of any of the perpetrators of those crimes ever being brought to trial finally resulted in the passage of the Enforcement Acts by Congress in 1870 and 1871 (the third act was called the Ku Klux Klan Act.) The chances of conviction of a white man for a crime against a black man were estimated to be about one in one hundred.[66] The acts, designed to curtail the activities of the Ku Klux Klan and other similar organizations and provide more stringent regulations for the apprehension and conviction of white terrorists, in time helped bring about the curtailment of Klan atrocities.

In later years some historians have maintained that the Ku Klux Klan may actually have lengthened Radical rule in the South. They suggest that the Klan's atrocities, as reported in the Northern newspapers, perhaps generated sympathy for blacks and the Radicals and at the same time served to reinforce in Northerners' minds the continued need for troops of occupation and the stringent subjugation of the former rebels.

"All I Want Is to Leave This Vile Place": Emigration

An infinite variety of reasons, depression over their lost cause, fear of Federal confiscation of their property, possible imprisonment for their Confederate wartime activities, the South's grave economic problems, personal finances, an inability to accept black-white equality, the threat of ultimate degradation under Radical Republican Reconstruction, etc., led thousands of Southerners to believe their only hope for the future resided with leaving the country.

A South Carolina woman wrote to her cousin of the despair that engulfed the men of the South in 1865. "I really felt sorry for all the gentlemen in Abbeyville. They are all so dejected with nothing to do and no heart to try to go to work. I never have seen Father as much depressed. It was sad to me to see him, for you know he is usually so cheerful. He says he thinks we ought to try to bear it as well as we can, wait patiently, and if we find we cannot live in the country, then will be time enough to talk about leaving. At present we cannot leave if we would. We have no money, no means of going etc. If we find we are obliged to go, we ought to form a colony, and as many relatives go together as possible."[67]

Disheartened following the war, Augusta Jane Evans (Wilson) joined the thousands of Southerners who eagerly hoped to find solace by leaving the country. "The only hope that now cheers me, is that of quitting forever this scourged, crushed, accursed country—once so irrepressibly dear to me,—now so odious and intolerable,—and finding a home in Mexico or Europe far from the repas[?] ... shadow of the 'Stars & Stripes.' Of the future of this *so-called Republic* I am hopeless,—the present does not invite contemplation,—and the past—our hallowed past is Too unutterly mournful to be dwelt upon."[68]

Rosa Postell, of Savannah, fervently hoped that with the end of the war and the release of her prisoner of war husband that they could "seek refuge ... far away from the horrors that await us here. Brazil or Australia, where many Southerners are now making their arrangements to migrate.... You can little dream of the painful future that must inevitably be our lot."[69]

Ann Beaufort Sims projected a bleak picture to her friend Hattie Palmer. "I am very anxious to leave the country. I see no prospect of anything in the future for southerners.... In all probability we will be taxed so heavily that we cannot stand it. The negro race are to be elevated. The white, particularly the higher class, will be called upon to bear the brunt of everything. Rather than endure this in my own native land, I prefer to leave." Plans of friends to emigrate to Brazil or Mexico tempted Ann who remarked that her father "would leave tomorrow if it were possible."[70] Eliza Frances Andrews pointed out that with all the talk about leaving the country "if all emigrate who say they are going to, we shall have a nation made up of women, negroes, and Yankees."[71]

Lizzie Hardin, a Kentuckian who had been sent south because of her Confederate biases, was particularly vehement in her denunciation of Yankees and in her interest in leaving the country. "It seems to me I am past feeling pleasure in anything. I hope I can never again love anything as I loved the cause that is lost. Oh! If only I could get out of the country. Not to claim any other for my own but only to find a place where

I may no longer see the suffering of the South. Some place where we might yet find rest for the 'sick heart and world-weary brain.'" A sort of "Manifest Destiny" theory as vindication for leaving the Southland appealed to Lizzie's mother: "That God, permitting us to be overrun, intends to send us out to new countries to carry the enlightenment of the Anglo-Norman race."[72] The diary of South Carolinian Pauline DeCaradeuc (Heyward) revealed her interest in leaving the country for Brazil. "All I want is to leave this vile place, to go to some other country. I hate everything here...." A month later on June 17, 1865, she continued: "We are all so anxious to go to Brazil, things are becoming more & more practicable too, thank God." Many of her friends instructed Pauline to add their names to the list of potential recruits for Brazil. Ardor cooled, however, when it was learned that their hero General Wade Hampton was not one of those emigrating to Brazil.[73]

Sarah Fay, was instructed in May 1865 by her husband, Edwin, who was serving with the Confederate Army in Opelousas, to be prepared to leave the country upon his return home at the end of the war. "Tis useless to disguise the fact that Gen'l Lee has sold the Confederacy. A wholesale proscription will follow and I will have to leave my country on your account. Were I a single man I would fight them forever but you are dearer to me than any country and I must make arrangements for your protection and support.... Confederate Money will not buy anything here now. I cannot even get shaved at the Barber Shop for it. It will require it to take us to Brazil where we will have to go for I never intend to take any Green Back. Save everything you can that can be converted into specie."[74]

"Oh my God," Edwin Fay begged, "why dost thou so afflict my beloved country. Is thy arm shortened so that it cannot save. I firmly believe that the Confederacy will gain its independence but it will be when *every man* is forced by Yankee tyranny to take up arms. I cannot wait for that time but must just as soon as I am released from the Army I must hasten out of the Country." Continuing, he reasoned: "If President Davis would come over here and take command and issue a heart stirring proclamation I think with the recruits he could get in a short time he could hold out for ten years and worry the Yankees into a recognition of the Confederacy."[75]

Her husband's growing depression became agonizing clear for Sarah Fay as he wrote: "My poor downtrodden Country! what can thy sons do who are true to thee. Exile alone awaits them. In a foreign land dearest we will have to seek an asylum. My heart bleeds. I know not what to do. I have no funds to pay our passage to Brazil. Three long years have I been separated from you but I fear it is only the Commencement of a separation. I can go to Brazil alone without money and I can make a home for you but then the long tedious separation. When shall our sorrows have an end...? Were it not for you dearest and our darlings I would imitate those noble spirits Mosby and Wade Hampton who have retreated into the vastnesses of the mountains and swear to lay down their arms only with their lives, but you are dearer to me than country and beneath another clime we will found a 'Nova Troja' where there may be peace and happiness yet to be found."[76]

Lack of money proved a great deterrent to thousands of would-be emigrants. "Never have I so longed to possess money and leave the country," Grace Elmore, of Columbia, South Carolina, confessed. "I could not leave it without grief, and ever through life would I long to see my native state. 'Tis inexpressibly mournful to feel the necessity of giving up one's country, to feel that even should that land become prosperous 'twould give no happiness to you, unless wholly free from the Yoke of the Yankee."[77]

Grace Elmore found it difficult to "make the state of subjugation ennobling; 'tis hard to resist the debasing influence of being a conquered people." In a return to her religious faith she added: "But we must strive against it. How I know not, but I feel within me God always leaves open a way by which one may rise to higher things, and tho' He has allowed us to be overcome, our hearts, our minds, our souls are still our own, and it rests with each of us to give up that to the hand of the destroyer, or to have our spirits strengthened by resisting the temptation to lower our standard of right, and by being purified thro' that." Taking heart Grace bravely wrote, "For the time our hands are tied, we can do nothing in open defense, but we women watch and pray and will meet our fate, horrible as it may be, with the same fortitude with which we have met everything, as it came."[78]

Brazil and Mexico proved popular locations for Southerners who were eager to escape the South's postwar trauma.[79] Brazil's warm climate, its government sympathetic to the Confederate cause, and the hope of the resumption of the Southern plantation way of life attracted thousands of Southerners. There some stalwart Confederates evolved into "Confederados" through their establishment of a permanent colony that exists to this day.[80] For some "adventurers," however, initial plans for a proposed resettlement in Brazil cooled rapidly thanks to an investigative trip to South America. Inability to speak the language and observations of general decay and idleness eventuated in a speedy return to native soil.[81]

The estimates of fifty failures for one successful venture discouraged many would-be Brazilian settlers. Lucy Durr's father found differences in climate, soil, products, and language to be daunting factors in resettlement in South America. Homesickness and the possibility of Brazil's emancipating her slaves, along with the preceding hurdles, sent Lucy's family and scores of other Southerners hastening back to the United States.[82]

Large numbers of disheartened ex–Confederates sought resettlement in Mexico as the answer to their escalating frustrations. Emperor Maximilian enthusiastically encouraged Southerners to migrate to Mexico, and in the fall of 1865 named Matthew Fontaine Maury, the former Confederate naval leader, to the office of Commissioner of Immigration and Colonization and appointed General John B. Magruder to head the Mexico City based Land Office of Colonization. Agents were then sent to Europe and the North to promote colonization. (Agents were to receive $100 a month and $300 a year for expenses.)[83]

The former governor of Louisiana, Henry Watkins Allen, as editor of the Maximilian sponsored *Mexican Times*, sent back glowing reports of the wondrous opportunities in Mexico. "It [Mexico] is the best country in the world for our people, and we expect large emigration."[84] Through the pages of the *Mexican Times* and in letters which were carried in Southern newspapers, Allen served as Maximilian's spokesman in advocating immigration: "We shall urge with all our influence, emigrants from the United States and Europe who wish rich, productive, and cheap lands, to come to this country without delay and accept the very liberal offers now made by the Imperial Government."[85] Allen promised that fortunes could easily be acquired by enterprising planters interested in raising cotton, sugar-cane, coffee, indigo cacao, tobacco, tropical fruit, corn, or wheat. To former Confederates he issued a special appeal: "To those who have drunk the cup of bitterness to the very dregs, we say, come to Mexico. Here you can get homes without money and without price.... The fortunes which you have lost can be regained here by a few years of industry and enterprise. Come then, and bring with you your families and your household goods. Let the maid and matron, the aged sire, the tender son, and the hired servants—all come."[86] Mexico, Allen wrote, provided a wealth of both financial as well as cultural opportunities; for example, "one could go to church in the morning, attend a bullfight in the afternoon, and hear an opera at night."[87]

Horace Greeley, editor of the *New York Tribune*, was taken to task by numerous Southerners for chiding the ex–Confederates for leaving the country and colonizing in Mexico and South America. Exile editor Allen countered Greeley's charges with: "You first abuse us for being rebels, and then denounce us for settling in Mexico." Allen pointed out that he had never carried an editorial denouncing the Federal government; therefore: "Mr. Greeley, why can't you let us alone?" Allen grew increasingly agitated as he admonished Greeley. "We know that you hate us, and that if you had the power, you would not only persecute us to death in this world, but consign us to that lake in the next, 'which burneth with fire and brimstone forever!'"[88]

To be sure, far more people threatened immigration than actually pulled up stakes and moved to Mexico. According to some estimates the Cordoba Valley area numbered scarcely more than 250 settlers, and the Cordoba colony itself involved some thirty American families. By the spring of 1866 settlers were becoming increasingly disenchanted with Mexico and were returning home resentful of what they believed had been false advertising. Even Maury himself had decided to leave Mexico, and in March 1866 returned to England to live out some three years of exile before returning to the United States in 1868.[89] Language problems, inadequate medical care, homesickness for family and friends, financial problems, and overcrowded conditions all took their toll on the colonists; however, it was essentially the political chaos in Mexico that lead to the dissolution of most of the Mexican settlements.

Although some Southerners took up lifelong residency in Europe or South America, most Southerners eventually returned home. Dissatisfaction with foreign governments and living conditions; an unsatisfactory economic climate; unhappiness with foreign school systems or the political situation; separation from family members; the enactment of universal amnesty; an improved outlook on economic conditions in the South sent many of these emigrants scurrying for the familiarity of their former homeland. At one time Canada had been a popular relocation area: it was close, one might join friends and neighbors, there was no language barrier. However, by 1870 most Southerners had moved elsewhere.[90]

Surprisingly, thousands of disgruntled Southerners headed North to large cities such as Chicago and New York seeking to pursue old careers or embark upon new ventures in a challenging, invigorating environment. Some historians estimate that by 1867, 20,000 Southerners were living in New York City.[91] The city, of course, was the center for much of the financial activity involving Southerners and loans. There Southerners' prewar indebtedness often had to be scaled down in order for Northerners to get any return on their money.

The inability of her husband (General Roger Pryor, CSA) to find work in Petersburg that would support her and their lively family of seven children led Mrs. Roger Pryor to pawn her watch and a greatly treasured cameo for $300, money that enabled her to first purchase quinine for her ailing husband's ravaging fever, buy a suit of clothes to replace his threadbare Confederate uniform, and then send him off to New York in search of remunerative work. In Petersburg, Mrs. Pryor kept the wolf at bay by giving piano lessons to the children in the neighborhood. After two grueling years of "fighting it out on this line," working first on the *Daily News* and then studying New York law and setting up a practice, the former general was able to send for Mrs. Pryor and their youngsters to join him in New York.[92]

Chicago, the railroad hub of the country, proved alluring to former rebels interested in working in connection with the burgeoning field of cross-country transportation, or in the development and production of the vast new array of manufactured products, or in the selling and promotion of those exciting new products. For many Southerners the North offered a new start, new work, new surroundings, new opportunities, good schools, and a happy release from the back-breaking work of the cotton fields.

Most Southerners who left the South, however, headed out for the untamed lands in the West, lured there by the opportunities for cheap land under the generous terms of the various Homestead Acts and the chance for relative independence. Over the years millions of settlers sought out homes and ranches in Texas. In the twenty years between 1860 and 1880 Texas rose from third from the last in population of the eleven Confederate states to number one in population in the South.[93]

Furthermore, the stampede of men seeking homesteading land in the West was augmented by a number of Southern widows and unmarried women who also applied for land. Some worked the land for themselves; others sought to augment a father's or a brother's holdings. In fact homesteading became such an attractive venture for young women that it was estimated that "in 1886 one-third of the land in the Dakotas was held by women." For some women their land claims served as a dowry; for others their holdings brought money for other investments or for college educations.[94]

In the eyes of many Southerners the departure of their fellow countrymen, especially to the North, was considered a despicable act, a deserting of the South for "filthy lucre's sake." Insisting that they had "sold their manhood," Mrs. Irby Morgan denounced them categorically and hoped "that they will never pollute the soil of our 'Sunny South' with their unhallowed feet" for having "sold their manhood."[95] Friends and neighbors were severely critical of the Roger Pryors for "forsaking" Virginia and taking up residence in New York. When it became known that many of his former associates decried him as a "Radical," Mrs. Pryor reported that her husband penned a lengthy discourse for the *Richmond Whig* in defense of his views on the need for good will between the two sections.[96]

"Sufficient Means to Subsist On": Black Relocation

Former slaves as well as elite whites also looked for a better life. Their freedom and the enormous upheaval of the labor situation in the South resulted in a tremendous exodus of freedmen from the southeastern states—some to Liberia under the auspices of the American Colonization Society, some to the cities, some to the North, some to the southwest, some westward, some to relocation in the South itself, the latter attracted by the free land available under the Homestead Act of June 1866.[97]

The Southern Homestead Act passed by Congress in 1866 held great promise for blacks and loyal whites. The act set aside over forty million acres of public lands in the states of Alabama, Arkansas, Florida, Louisiana and Mississippi for homesteads for freedmen and certain whites. Persons in the latter category who applied by January 1, 1867, were required to swear "that they have not borne arms against the United States Government."[98] The act was specifically set up to benefit landless Negroes and thus enable them to obtain land of their own and an independence that they so fervently desired. (The 1862 Homestead Act had excluded Confederates, and since the Dred Scott decision ruled against Negroes as citizens they too were specifically or by implication ineligible for homesteading land under the 1862 act. The new act made certain that there should be no distinction regarding color.) At first interested persons were allowed only eighty acres, but by mid 1868, they could apply for 160 acres. The stipulations required that the applicant must be the head of a family or 21 years of age, or "shall have performed service in the army or navy of the United States." The land must be for his own exclusive use for settlement and cultivation. The provision that the land could not be purchased outright was repealed in 1876.[99]

Although the act looked good on paper, it failed to provide the tremendous advantages for blacks that its authors had envisioned. For various reasons the Negroes were not always enabled to make the best use of the opportunity. First and foremost, as a result of their inability to read, many Negroes were probably unaware of the offer unless it was called to their attention by members of the Freedmen's Bureau. Furthermore, individuals seeking the homesteading land often discovered the nearest land office where they were to make their application was often miles away and wholly inaccessible. The allocated land was not always good, fertile land suited to the applicants' needs and interests. In fact Negroes testified that much of the homesteading land in the South was "worth nothing," and certainly not capable of producing cotton. Their accusations were corroborated by officials at the time and later historians have agreed that most of the quality land in those states had been "already claimed and settled before the war."[100] In some areas money-hungry and/or racist officials charged blacks exorbitant prices to enter a claim, or were indifferent to their appeals and summarily turned them away. Unfortunately countless numbers of blacks were duped by speculators who wrested their land away from them.[101]

Most Negro homesteaders encountered additional problems such as their need to earn a living as they prepared the land and planted their crops in anticipation of their first harvest. Their lack of basic farming equipment and the means to procure it brought down many a courageous homesteader. Even O. O. Howard himself (head of the Freedmen's Bureau) advised Negroes not to attempt to farm government land without "sufficient means to subsist on till they could get well under way."[102]

Resettlement in the West was not a viable option for most former bondsmen. Many of the above reasons in addition to rampant racism, want of transportation, inexperience and a lack of self-confidence discouraged most freedmen from seeking Homestead grants and taking on the frontier. Even fewer black women went west. In 1870 there were 436 blacks in Colorado, 789 in Nebraska, and only 172 in New Mexico.[103]

≈ 8 ∾

New Dimensions for Women

To be sure, life at best was no bed of roses for women—war or no war. Life itself was precarious, particularly childbirth. The life expectancy in 1860 was about forty-one years. For women who bore children the life expectancy was less than thirty-nine years as a result of the high death rate in childbirth. Nineteenth century infant mortality rates reached a shocking twenty to thirty percent. Thousands of mothers died before their youngest child reached maturity. Their children's health was a particularly grave concern for mothers, in view of the fact that in those days "children under the age of five accounted for half of all deaths."

Childbirth was a frightening time for women as death claimed one mother in every one hundred fifty-four live births—a death rate eighty-three times the 1992 maternal death rate.[1] Most women faced childbirth with at least some degree of trepidation. Lucy Neilson, of example, constantly feared for her life and wondered whether she would be alive to welcome the much anticipated visit of a niece.[2] Gertrude Thomas was surely not alone in frequently being tormented by "jealous thoughts" of a step-mother who might take her place were she to die in childbirth.[3]

"A Woman Alone in This Cold War"

The horrendous loss of men during the war, some 258,000 Confederates, meant not only that there would be tens of thousands of widows, but also that there would be tens of thousands of young, unmarried women who would of necessity give up any dreams of a husband, a house full of children, and "happily ever after."[4] Lucy Buck, of Front Royal, Virginia, never married, nor did any of her three sisters. On New Year's Day of 1873 Lucy confided to her diary that the hopes of bygone days had now turned into seasons "of trial and sorrow, as but a new season of uncertainty, care and toil." For Lucy her immersion in work provided solace, as it did for so many, from the disappointments and burdens of her postwar cares. "As to work—I've learned to regard that as a true though rough friend, winning one from too much thought of the non-returning Past, and helping me to dull the keen pain of the Present. 'Tis indeed 'The dull narcotic soothing pain.'" Convinced that God would not give her more to bear "than I have strength for," Lucy hoped that "He will continue to evolve some good for me out of all the evil that encompasses me."[5]

Younger women, with matrimonial prospects still in view, could jest about their unmarried state. Twenty-three year old Cordelia Scales, living near Holly Springs, Mississippi, joked about still remaining "an unmarried, staid & sober spinster." However, she reported that "two dreadful epidemics have been prevailing here to an alarming extent; small pox and matrimony." The latter, Cordelia wrote, "is fearfully increasing its number of victims & causing scores of my rash & unguided friends in the bloom of youth & beauty to rush madly & impetuously into that state of wedded bliss—'so called.' Poor creatures some of them, at least, deserved a better fate."[6] Cordelia had not long to bemoan her single status, for ten months later she was joined in matrimony with Ben Cottrell Gray on December 31, 1866.

Even as the war seemed to be winding down Maggie Lindsley pondered her future. "I wonder if Peace will find us prim and staid 'maiden ladies' locks and spectacles—This may be another thirty years war—who knows?"[7]

Kate Foster appeared less than optimistic about the life of a "spinster." By 1866 Kate was lamenting, "I am gradually verging on to an old maid—I must try to be a good one." Earlier she had reported: "My old friends are all leaving me behind in the lottery 'marriage.' I must hurry and find some one on whom to lavish my wealth of love & tenderness." Fannie Cooper also described the "marriage epidemic" taking place in her area, noting that "almost everyone is married." She added, "I am now *Miss Cooper* but don't enjoy the title much."

With the passage of time the single life seemed to become less and less appealing for Kate Foster as she wrote: "An old maid's life and one of struggle presents no allurements to a woman who feels that a woman's life is incomplete without Man's sustaining influence, each needing the other to create that soul music which is that result of a happy union. A woman alone, in this cold world, how sad it is—no eye in which to see the reflection of her own love."[8]

Much of Anna Maria Green's diary was punctuated with concerns about finding a suitable husband. As more and more of her friends married and left the area Anna Maria admitted: "The true secret of my present restless state of feeling is the dread of remaining single. Why is woman so created longing for the companionship of man and yet 'we should be woo'd and men not made to woo.'" She continued: "I almost feel that death were preferable to remaining alone in the world, and essentially so as a single woman. I do not feel that the life of a single woman is necessarily aimless or useless or wretched. But oh God! tis a struggle from which a sensitive, highly strung imaginative woman shrinks, feeling that she could face death—but not coldness and derision."[9]

Although there were scores of disappointed "spinsters" who remained with their families growing more bitter and mean-spirited with each year that passed, most unmarrieds made the best of their lot. The more enterprising women became realists and discovered a rich, rewarding life as teachers devoted to mothering other people's children or as caregivers of aged parents or orphaned nieces or nephews.

Elderly unmarried women often, unfortunately, tended to be shuffled around from one relative to another. In accordance with the dying wishes of her sister, Ann Hardeman took over much of the responsibility for raising her sister's six young children—although not in a home of her own. Conscientiously and lovingly "Aunt Ann" mothered her nieces and nephews in no fixed home, residing with her charges first in the home of one family member and then another. After the war, grief over the death of two nephews serving for the "Cause" plagued Ann's latter years of life. Ann lamented, "The old year with all its forebodings—our subjugation & all the consequences incident to a down trodden people has closed and though I still believe that God will sustain the right we are in sack cloth & ashes. Our hearts are bereaved of those who were far dearer to us than life."[10] For Ann her world centered on God and her church. Reading sermons and Bible passages and a disciplined two hours spent writing each day helped relieve the stress and anxiety over her uncertain living arrangements with various family members and worries over the futures of her two remaining nieces and nephews. Life was not easy for elderly, single women, and throughout Ann's diary ran feelings of almost unendurable loneliness, of deep concern over the lack of appreciation of her family, and of a depressing sense of being a bother to everyone. Ann counseled her niece Adelaide, "if you continue teaching you will be *beyond a doubt* an 'old Maid'!"—a situation Ann found to be wholly undesirable. Shortly before her death in 1868, Ann advised her niece to get married and avoid her own unenviable situation. "Here I am left without any resource—and feel that I am a dreg to everybody & do not know what to do with myself."[11]

"If She Keeps Up All the Corners"

In contrast to Ann Hardeman's dejection, Lou Thompson, single, living at home with her father and mother and younger brother in Kosciusko and Phoenix Mills in Attala County, Mississippi, found life both pleasurable and challenging. Surprisingly her diaries made little or no mention of the war, and life for Lou and her family in the postwar days appeared to continue much as usual, although in a manner somewhat routine. No doubt Lou's diaries depicted a life not noticeably different from countless of her contemporaries—a life focused on hard work, family, and friends. According to Lou's 1866–1872 diaries her days consisted of knitting, sewing, tatting, carding, spinning, weaving, quilting, gardening, cooking, canning, and ironing.

Sicknesses, weddings, family reunions, holiday festivities further added to her household responsibilities. A married sister and her husband staying with the Thompsons substantially increased the work but at the same time provided Lou with much needed help around the house. Diary entries repeatedly lamented "nothing but work from morning till night...."[12] Lou explained: "the chickens have to be looked after, the cows have to be milked, and its cook, cook, three times a day, then there is the garden to be worked, and mother says I would work in my flower yard if I done nothing else.... There is the washing and ironing too...." In other pages Lou described making a bonnet; planting fruit trees and raspberries; planting beans, collard seed, tomatoes, beets and peppers; gathering, canning and drying fruit; making tomato catsup; patching and twisting stocking thread; making soap; rendering lard; making sausage, souse, and chitterlings. These were no small tasks, she noted, and they keep "a housekeeper trotting from morning till night if she keeps up all the corners...."[13]

Lou regularly took time out from her house and garden chores to attend "preaching," prayer meetings, and church services. Faithfully recorded were the births, deaths, marriages, county fairs, and church activities of the communities (Phoenix Mills and Kosciusko). The local chapter of the Order of the Eastern Star captured Lou's attention and in about 1871 she joined and served as an officer in the group.

Countless pages of Lou's diary were replete with notations of company, company, and more company. Although she professed that she and her family loved company, just for fun one year Lou undertook to keep track of the number of meals the family served to guests outside of family and arrived at a total of 1,147 meals. Actually Lou's account of company meals was probably not too unusual, for company, visits from friends, relatives and neighbors were daily occurrences for most Southerners. Women throughout South recorded having "a great deal of company." One Tennessee woman complained that with the exception of one night her family had not had an evening alone for four months.

An added challenge for Lou came in response to the request of neighbors for her to teach school. At first Lou was a bit uneasy about teaching, but with increasing numbers and the growing enthusiasm of her scholars, Lou found the experience rewarding and pleasurable. Tuition was $1.50 and Lou reported that she studied as hard as her scholars. In addition the country fair offered opportunities for further outlets for Lou's talents and energies.

Some women even seemed to prefer the single life—at least ostensibly. Among the latter was Hannah Garlick Rawlings, who in her mid-twenties during the war years assumed the management of her family's property in Spotsylvania County and took over the teaching responsibilities of the children of the family. As the family's financial situation became ever more precarious with inflation and the devaluation of the currency, Hannah accepted work as a governess for a family in Orange County, Virginia.

The shortage of eligible bachelors seemed not to dismay Hannah Rawlings. In fact she laughingly responded to her sister's prodding: "Had I any *matrimonial intentions* I should certainly confide them to you, but I am accused of being too proud and cold-hearted to care for anyone. The fact is I never had a gentleman to tell me he loved me that I did not feel a wicked disposition to call him a *goose*. My friends look upon me, now, I believe, as a *hopeless case*. A little more than a year ago nearly every member of my family believed me to be engaged to a gentleman whom they regarded as too eligible a *parti* to be refused, but now they have given me up as incorrigible. A gentleman told me last summer 'he expected I would go into a convent yet, and if I did he hoped I would die the day I got there.' Wasn't that nice? Do you know where there's a convenient nunnery? But a truce to nonsense," she concluded.[14]

"They Are Now Members of Our Family"

In addition to the great numbers of "spinsters," the massive four year blood bath left tens of thousands of orphans and dependent widows at the mercy of relatives and friends. Extended families became commonplace as sisters took in their brother's orphaned children; fathers generously augmented their families with indigent in-laws; needy cousins, aunts and uncles were made welcome for months, or years, or forever.

Anna Maria Green's family, for example, was considerably enlarged by the addition of five of her Aunty Belle's orphaned children. "They are now members of our family, an intimate connection," she confided to her diary. Later, Anna Maria, upon observing the emaciated condition of yet another aunt, added, "I wish papa had wealth to provide comfortably for his sister besides taking care of Aunty Belle's orphan children."[15]

Now and then a marriage united a widow and a widower, thus creating an exuberant household of twenty-four children. One woman raised her own family of four as well as successively the children of her two widowed brothers, her household at times consisting of twenty people.[16] In addition to her own two daughters Mrs. Irby Morgan took in four granddaughters and four nieces. Apparently the melange worked well, for Mrs. Morgan reported that the girls had "a merry time of it." So great was the need for homes for orphans that newspapers carried plaintive appeals seeking people willing to adopt children bereft of parents or relatives to care for them.

The close family relationships so characteristic of the South were sometimes put to the test following the war. After a four year absence parents who had left children with grandparents or close relatives for safety during the war often suffered a difficult readjustment period. Pembroke Thom, a widower, left his two boys with their aunt while he was in Europe attempting to secure ships for the Confederate Navy. By May of 1866 when he finally was granted parole and could return to Maryland to claim his sons, their aunt was most reluctant to give the boys up. The boys, too, registered considerable hesitation about bonding with the strange, bearded man they were now to call father.[17]

Strained family relationships were certainly not unique following a four year husband/father separation. Young boys living with their mothers during the war years and serving as the "man in the house" found their role usurped with the return of their fathers. Josiah Gorgas, the Confederate Chief of Ordnance, experienced a somewhat troubled relationship with his son who had grown to adolescence during the four years.[18] Amanda McDowell's two brothers fought on opposite sides during the war, a division which, of course, resulted in some difficult family and community relationships upon their homecoming.

Not surprisingly, a wartime separation could result in marked degrees of incompatibly in a marriage. Bad habits such as smoking, drinking, and gambling acquired during a husband's service in the army, a possible uncouthness or an insensitivity to illness and death picked up from the savagery of the battlefield, the constant torture of an oozing stump or a festering wound, a spouse's restlessness for a more adventurous life than home and family—one or all could prove immensely unsettling to family life.

Countless women changed their role following the war from help-mate to breadwinner when of necessity they took over the family farm, the corner store, or taught school as a means of helping support their physically or mentally impaired husbands. A great many husbands chafed at their own inadequacies, and took out their frustrations in liquor, physical abuse, or just plain persistent ill-temper.[19]

In the 1860s and '70s the divorce rate was not the fifty-fifty probability it became in the later part of the twentieth century. As one observer commented, a mistake in marriage was a most disastrous situation especially for a wife who would gladly exchange an "Old Maid" title as "a delightful relief from worse evils."[20] Most marriages were lifetime propositions—"for better or for worse." The "for worse" could, of course, involve spousal abuse and irreconcilable differences. A Virginia woman told of a dreadful rumor making the rounds: "It is whispered Mrs. Levering has applied for a divorce. Mr. Levering, it is said, has become dissipated, & when in that state is unkind to his wife, & even threatens her life."[21] Madge Preston, living near Baltimore, confessed in her diary to being subjected to beatings and constant verbal abuse by her husband.[22]

Problems of alcoholism decimated lives and families in the postwar South. Men bowed down with failure and debt found comfort in alcohol. Rachel Craighead must have been agonizing over her husband's struggle with liquor when she confided to her diary, "Tom has not taken a chew of tobacco for a week nor a drink stronger than ale. I am so thankful—pray God for help [for] him." Reading between the lines of Gertrude Thomas's diary one suspects that Gertrude's husband may have had an alcohol problem. Virginia Clay, also, spent anxious days worrying over her husband Clement Clay's battle with alcohol.

"The Most Popular Women in Society Are Self-Supporting"

"Never did woman have a better opportunity to show this strength than at the close of the war, and right nobly did she meet the emergency and set herself to her work, encouraging and inspiring with hope Southern men, too many of whom had lost heart with their lost cause. It was the heart, the hope, the faith of Southern womanhood that set Southern men to working when the war was over, and in this work they led the way, filling the stronger sex with utter amazement at the readiness and power with which they began to perform duties to which they had never been used before." Thus read one assessment of the all-important postwar contributions of Southern women, a conclusion, certainly in many families, borne out in fact. (Note use of "stronger sex.")[23]

Countless editorials appeared in newspapers praising women and encouraging them in roles of strength and leadership in the unsettling times following the war. A *New Orleans Times* editorial quoted one accolade for women, saying they "think like heroes, and act like angels." The editorial, in language befitting the times, continued pointing out that "We must acknowledge, however, that the present crisis demands from our women more of a peculiar, and persistent heroism, than the battle field or crowded hospital, where their ministrations have so lately ended.... Now, if ever, her countrymen need her aid. They stand bewildered and perplexed on the threshold of the great change, where all old land marks are swept away, 'clinging to some eidolon of the past, stretching anxiously their vision to discern some of the possibilities of the future'.... More than ever now is she called upon to be the comforter, the assistant, of the father, husband, son and brother, who go from her roof to unaccustomed toil. Let her voice be to them a trumpet note of hope and encouragement! Let her reach forth her hands and say: 'Labor at your appointed work faithfully, as I shall at mine.... [I]Will strive earnestly and with one accord to strengthen your hands when they fail, to comfort your hearts when they are weary.... To the tender, loyal heart, and gentle hand, belong (we firmly believe) the strongest and clearest mark to be made upon this chaotic page of our eventful history.'"[24]

Women truly found their work cut out for them after the war in the support and inspiration of their war weary, disheartened husbands, fathers and brothers. As Wilbur Fisk Tillett reminded readers years later, "Was it not the brave-hearted wife that inspired the despairing husband when the war had ended to go to work and redeem his lost fortune, happy enough herself that she had a living husband to work with her, since so many of her sisters had to fight the battle with labor and poverty alone, while their husbands slept in the soldier's grave?" Tillett continued in affirming that it was the women with their words and hands who encouraged brothers and lovers to aspire to and to achieve a rewarding resumption of their prewar careers and work. "Many a trouble that utterly crushes strong man transforms weak woman into a tower of strength."[25]

Probably few Southern women found their immediate postwar work more demanding than Varina Howell Davis and Virginia Tunstall Clay. Their lives in the upper echelons of society suddenly came tumbling down with the fall of the Confederacy and the imprisonment of their husbands as two of the South's leading rebels. Virginia Tunstall Clay, wife of Clement Clay (a United States senator before the war, a member of the Confederate Senate for a two year term, and a special emissary to Canada

Virginia Tunstall Clay. (From Virginia Clay, *A Belle of the Fifties*.)

during the latter months of the war) and Varina Davis, wife of the president of the Confederacy, discovered totally new postwar roles awaiting them as they engaged in Herculean efforts to secure the release of their husbands from their incarceration at Fort Monroe. Both women were panic-stricken that their husbands might be sentenced to life imprisonment or worse yet be hanged as traitors.

Even though Virginia had long been a shrewd "maneuverer" throughout her husband's political career, her greatest challenge came in mounting an all out campaign to besiege President Johnson with letters on her husband's behalf from prominent politicians, editors, jurists, and longtime friends. Finally, according to Virginia's reminiscences, after angry confrontations in his Washington office, the chief executive realized he had met his match, dispensed with procrastination and signed papers for her husband's release. A strong woman? Yes indeed! Virginia Clay's determination must indeed have been awesome, for her husband was released some twelve months before Jefferson Davis.[26]

Varina Davis's problems, similar to those of Virginia Clay, were compounded by her responsibilities for her mother and her young children. Hoping for an escape from the notoriety surrounding her husband's incarceration, Varina sent her family to Montreal and devoted her every minute to securing a pass to visit her husband. Alarmed at his rapidly deteriorating health and horrified by the conditions of his imprisonment, Varina was struck by the need to seek public attention for her husband's situation, and immediately set about circulating details of his confinement to members of the press. It was a clever move on Varina's part, and the subsequent stories garnered interest as well as sympathy for Davis. As a result conditions at Fort Monroe were vastly improved, and an apartment was provided Varina and her husband. Even so, Varina doggedly continued her efforts to effect her husband's parole. Her persistence finally met with success and in May 1867 Davis was released. Although the Davises were plagued with financial problems for years to come, at least her husband was free from the confines of prison.[27]

$\wp$

When reassurance and resolution failed, women took over as the family's provider. Following the war Gertrude Thomas was devastated by her husband's deteriorating physical and financial condition. Lacking financial support (her husband having lost even her personal property through bad management) Gertrude undertook a teaching position and paid the taxes and the Thomases' workers from her salary. In an effort to help with the family's finances, socially prominent Mary Chesnut ignored her husband's derision and embarked on a thriving butter and eggs business working on shares with her maid. "The first half dollar [we earned was] for butter ... John C. and my husband laughed at my peddling—and borrowed money."[28]

Years later Southern women described in detail the immense changes in Southern womanhood that had come about as a result of the war. The antebellum concept of the "helpless woman," dependent and fragile, which had been so embedded in the Southern mentality, had been superseded by

LADY LOBBYISTS AT THE WHITE HOUSE.

"Lady Lobbyists at the White House." (*Harper's Weekly*, October 27, 1866.)

the acceptance and even admiration for a woman who could earn her own living instead of subsisting on the charity of her relatives. The women were eager to report that "Now ... a woman is respected and honored in the South for earning her own living."[29] Despite their pride in the emergence of "the independent woman," some women, however, appeared to qualify their statements with "when necessary" and clearly favored women taking up teaching rather than some "less genteel" profession.

One woman proudly announced that "in the two cities with which I am familiar the most popular women in society are self-supporting women...." However, she continued with typical Southern reservations as to women's sphere: "Still, I say, and I hope all my sisters in the South will say with me, far distant be the day when the women of this country will lay aside the modesty and delicacy that so well befit them and undertake to compete with men in business, or in public and political life."[30]

It was hoped that women's strides in acceptance in the field of public education would result in more challenging preparatory courses in schools throughout the country. "This increasing tendency among women to earn their own living by teaching has raised the standard of thoroughness in female education to some extent, though much is still to be desired, especially in the larger schools, where girls are too often sent to be 'graduated' rather than to be educated."[31] Women were quick to point out that indeed the sphere of women had definitely been widened; that women were taking their studies more seriously in preparation for the possibility that they might need to become self-supporting; and that they were aspiring to a broader culture and had become more resourceful and independent.[32] Scholars hoped that freeing the slaves had forced women to become self-sufficient in their own homes so that "culture and refinement may preside in the kitchen" as well as in the parlor.

A whole new world of challenging opportunities awaited women in their associations with the Grange, the huge organization founded in 1867 for the education and advancement of farmers. Grange activities opened new doors for tens of thousands of women who signed on as active members. One of the few organizations to open membership to women on an equal footing with men, the Grange provided social and educational outings for women who attended the classes, workshops, and conferences with their husbands or who elected independently to take advantage of the meetings and courses designed primarily for their enrichment. Women could find their voices in committees, or as officers, or as delegates to conventions. In Mississippi, for example, a statewide Grange was formed in 1872, its membership peaking in 1875. That same year the South as a whole accounted for some 210,000 Grange members.

"Refined" Women

For four long years Southern women had nursed the sick and wounded, organized auxiliaries to provide clothing and supplies for their loved ones on the battlefields, prepared tons of boxes of food to be sent to the frontlines, sewed mountains of uniforms for whole contingents of their fighting men, devoted endless hours to knitting, weaving and dyeing garments for their soldiers at war and for their families at home. Now at the war's end that profusion of inner resourcefulness and creativity sought expression and redirection.

During the war the lavish Northern Sanitary Commission fairs and the more modest local Southern fairs had succeeded in garnering huge proceeds for their parent organizations. In the postwar period women set about staging fairs, concerts, dinners, and other "benefits," the proceeds of which were devoted to helping to alleviate the plight of veterans and their families who were physically or economically devastated by the war. The tremendous output of time and energy devoted to the "entertainments" offered myriad creative outlets for the workers, helped provide challenge and diversion during difficult times, and developed a sense of camaraderie among the participants. In areas where women's rights and women's equality were odious concepts, where women's sphere was restricted to her home and church, the fairs and benefits were considered acceptable work for "refined" women. And it was usually the women who provided the inspiration and backbone for most enterprises. Furthermore, most bazaars netted sizable proceeds considering the straitened circumstances of the attendees. For example, bazaars held in New Orleans and Richmond each succeeded in bringing in $20,000, and fairs held in Augusta and Montgomery were successes with more than $10,000 in proceeds. Even small towns got caught up in the fair mania and took in as much as $1,000 in a two night event.[33]

The Southern Fair held in the spring of 1866 in Baltimore netted a handsome sum for the relief of needy veterans and their families. Real moneymakers were the diamond rings, gold bracelets and watches donated by the war's more fortunate survivors and raffled off at various sessions of the fair. Fancy goods and food items brought in tidy sums. Even President Johnson's wife sent "a superb bouquet" to the fair. Quite understandably the hit of the entire fair was the gift from one opulent donor of an attractive house and lot which brought in beaucoup dollars through the sale of raffle tickets. Manufactured goods, agricultural equipment, farm animals, demijohns of fifty-year-old wine were sold outright or ticketed for a lottery drawing. In addition to the proceeds from the fair itself, concerts, exhibitions, tableaux, lectures and other entertainments held in conjunction with the run of the fair helped swell the returns. The women managers of the fair earned high praise for their work. One newspaper declared: "The ladies—blessed angels! Are working with an energy, earnestness and industry never before surpassed. No sacrifice seems too great for them to make in this philanthropic cause. It is worthy of all praise and admiration."[34]

Naturally the fairs were not wholly devoid of problems such as the rascals who scattered red pepper and Scotch snuff on the floors of one building, deviltry that produced "a complete concert of sneezing and coughing from contralto down to basso profunda." As with most fairs pickpockets and thieves meandered through the crowds doing their mischief. Other miscreants bought goods with counterfeit bills and took good money in return. The *New Orleans Daily Picayune* suggested: "Such scoundrels ought to be doomed to live on earth forever, subject to gout, chronic rheumatism and toothache, unceasingly."[35]

In St. Louis the Southern Relief Fair concluded a most successful run with a Calico Ball which rocketed the sale of calico in the area to new heights. One store sold material for three hundred and fifty dresses in a twenty-four hour period. On some nights as many as three thousand patrons came to see the displays and entertainments. The gift of some two or three hundred high-crowned out-of-date men's hats were turned into ready cash with their sale at three dollars each. The gentlemen helped close the fair with a rush of humor by donning the hats and parading the aisles to the amusement of the attendees.[36]

In New Orleans the Ladies Benevolent Association devoted their efforts to staging splendid balls and tableaux for the benefit of widows and orphans, for limbs for disabled soldiers, and for protecting and marking the graves of the Confederate dead. Gentlemen were accepted as members upon the payment of fifty dollars.[37]

"Do Honor to Our Dead"

Southern women also discovered important new roles as they endeavored to commemorate the lives of their fallen heroes in Memorial Day ceremonies and the decoration of soldiers' graves. Women who had suffered so greatly in sacrificing their sons, fathers, brothers and fiancés to the war effort were appalled by appeals to them to forgive and forget. The defeat rendered futile their sacrifices and deprivations. Returning veterans could perhaps put the horrors of war behind them, but for the women those valiant men who had given their lives for their country must never be forgotten. Painful memories of their devastating losses prompted thousands of Southern women to channel those memories into a retreat to the past and the creation of memorial societies in an attempt to commemorate the sacrifices of their countrymen who gave their lives to a cause lost. The small Ladies Memorial Associations organized in various Southern communities soon blossomed into full-scale holidays complete with parades, speeches, and the laying of flowers at the gravesides of their war heroes. Although the women of Columbus, Georgia, claimed to have initiated the first real Memorial Day celebration, other Southern groups have challenged that claim.[38]

While numerous towns planned their memorials for April 26, the date of Johnston's surrender, others chose various dates in May for the decoration of Confederate graves and the accompanying processions, speeches, prayers, and hymn singing. Eulogies for the Confederate dead, reminders of their valor and sacrifices, and lengthy jeremiads over the Lost Cause traditionally constituted the framework of the day's speeches and commemorative services. Many Southerners soon found that establishing cemeteries and erecting monuments provided a valuable resource for preserving the past and at the same time serving as an outlet for bereavement.[39]

Floride Clemson described a memorial ceremony for the Confederate dead held in October of 1866 in Pendleton, South Carolina, and reenacted over the years in communities throughout the Southland. Some fifty women, Floride wrote, each "bore a banner for each of the martyrs draped with black with the name, date, & place of death on one side & an appropriate motto on the other." Following a visit to the Stone Church yard, where they placed wreaths on the graves, the women proceeded to the Baptist church and formed a procession. Leading the procession was a young woman carrying a banner for the returned soldiers, "with a flowery anchor in her hand, & dressed in white, with a long bridal veil. She was followed by a pack of children strewing flowers in the way of the returned soldiers…. We marched through the three grave yards; the Baptist, Methodist, & Episcopal, wreathing each soldiers grave as we came to it, with wreaths we wore over our shoulders." Speeches by Generals Wade Hampton and William Easley concluded the occasion. For various reasons Floride was critical of the ceremony, however, she admitted that she "had rather do honor to our dead with bad taste, than not at all."[40]

Pauline DeCaradeuc (Heyward) gave a more personal account of her family's observance of the decoration of the graves of the South's fallen sons. "Mother, Fa. [her father], Mannie & I fixed up our little cemetery, Oh, *so* sweetly, with all the exquisite spring flowers…." Later that day Pauline "went to the graves of some poor soldiers near & decked them too with our trifling tributes of flowers." Alice Palmer described the "not [to] be forgotten" memorial services in Charleston on June 16, 1866. "About one hundred soldiers are buried in private lots and a committee of ladies went up early to decorate the graves before 5 o'clock, but it rained in torrents and they were prevented. After the services over they went." Alice continued, "So many of our brave ones lie up there, sleeping their last sleep. It is too sad as you pass along to read on the stones of so many cut off in the bud of life."[41]

Ten years after Appomattox ten thousand Georgia residents turned out en masse in Augusta for the laying of the cornerstone for the erection of a monument to the Confederate dead. Highly visible attendees included large numbers of veterans identified by "scars, crutches, and empty sleeves."[42] As any southern traveler even today will verify, Augusta was merely one of the hundreds of cities throughout the South to erect one or more Confederate monuments in memory of their honored dead.

As might be expected the first public ceremonies to commemorate the Confederate dead with flowers and eulogies were not exactly popular with certain Federal military commanders in the South. At least one commander registered great displeasure over the "disloyal project" and did his best to prevent the observance. Betty Meriwether reported that in Memphis the commander agreed with certain Radicals that the ceremonies consisted of "putting treason on a pedestal" and sent out an order that "No loyal person will pay homage to rebels who had sought to overthrow the Nation. Peace has been declared, but the Government cannot permit rebels and traitors to eulogize rebellion and treason." The order was disregarded and the first "Decoration Day" in Memphis came off as planned despite the "fuming and grumbling" of the Yankee authorities.[43]

The founding of the United Daughters of the Confederacy, the Confederate Survivors Association, the Sons of the Confederacy, and the Children of the Confederacy helped further to perpetuate reverence for the Lost Cause and the men and women who sacrificed "the last full measure of devotion" for their convictions. As C. Vann Woodward, George C. Rable, and other historians have pointed out, Southerners continued to look back at the same time they looked ahead to new beginnings and a new South.[44]

"But When Will Women Have the Right to Vote?"

Perhaps because of their despondency over the outcome of the war, perhaps because of their need to take over the reins of farms and businesses as a result of a husband's physical or mental scars from the horrors of war, or perhaps because of their preoccupation in eking out a living for themselves and a houseful of young children after the loss of a husband to "the cause," or perhaps because of the Southern parameters of "women's sphere," or perhaps because of a hundred other reasons, Southern women were far behind their Northern sisters in taking up the crusade for women's rights. Southern women probably were not nearly so disappointed as some of their Northern counterparts that the Fifteenth Amendment restricted the suffrage to men and ignored women. (The efforts of the Radicals to reconstruct the South and provide equality for blacks and not for women irritated Elizabeth Cady Stanton. "Of course they [the Radicals] would rather see the experiment of equality tried in a southern plantation than at their own firesides, in their own beds."[45] In the late 1860s with the survival of her family a primary concern and in the climate of the prevailing philosophy, particularly in the South, that a women's interests should be limited to her home and her church, it is understandable that Southern women would have held few illusions about the possibility of being accorded the vote.

For Elizabeth Avery Meriwether, of Memphis, Tennessee, however, women's suffrage was always a vital issue. Although given comparatively little credit for being one of the first women in the South to publicly speak out for women's rights, over the years Elizabeth Avery Meriwether succeeded in carving out an admirable place for herself as an early feminist. As a young woman Betty was incensed by the discrimination against women. In 1867 while her husband and General Nathan Bedford Forest were busy organizing the Memphis chapter of the Ku Klux Klan in the Meriwether home, Betty was asked about her reactions to the plan. Betty agreed that intimidation might well deter uninformed black voters from bankrupting the South, however, she retorted, "But when will women have the right to vote?" In response to attempts to convince her that a woman's husband would take care of her interests, Betty wondered, "Who will take care of the interests of women who have no husbands?"[46]

It was Susan B. Anthony's arrest for voting in an election in the North that spurred on Betty to an unrelenting determination to vote in Memphis. Insisting that "taxation without representation is tyranny" Betty refused to pay taxes unless given an opportunity to make her wishes count through her vote. Perhaps because of her family connections or perhaps because the election officials considered her as simply a harmless "freak," Betty was issued a certificate to vote in Memphis "at any election during the year 1872." Whether her vote was tossed aside or actually counted made relatively little difference to Betty. "Counting my ballot is not important; what is important is to focus public attention on the monstrous injustice, as well as stupidity, of including educated women with felons and lunatics as persons denied the right of suffrage."[47]

As might be expected, a furor erupted over Betty's being allowed to cast a ballot. As Betty mused, "Some Southern papers thought the world was coming to an end, so horrified were they at the sight of a woman voting." One disparaging newspaper editorial read: "We enter our most earnest protest against the mothers, wives and daughters of Memphis being dragged into the corrupt cesspool of elections. We have been taught to look upon females as too pure to mingle in the strife and turmoil of the political arena and would feel greatly shocked to see some of our estimable female friends elbowed rudely at the polls in an effort to deposit their ballot. It will unsex woman to give her the ballot." On the other hand more enlightened editors commended her courage and saw her home and family as suffering not in the least from her interest in politics. "Has Queen Victoria neglected her nine children because of politics? Yet she opens Parliament, signs State papers and confers with her Ministers."[48]

For her first public speech Betty rented a theater in Memphis in 1876. A curious crowd appeared; a somewhat less than enthusiastic crowd left the theater following her talk. Undismayed, Betty continued her women's rights and temperance lectures. As Betty's speaking talents increased so did her notoriety and in 1881 she joined Elizabeth Cady Stanton and Susan B. Anthony in a speaking tour of New England.

In the South people generally accorded attention and respect to Betty's talks on temperance; however, conservatives were prone to blast her lectures on women's rights. One minister even attempted to prevent her giving her lecture. He accused Betty of passing herself off as a temperance lecturer in an attempt "to cover her infidel woman's rights doctrines." When the national democratic convention met in St. Louis in 1876 Betty attempted to rally the delegates to make women's suffrage a part of the Democratic platform, but her efforts met with derision. "The Resolutions Committee treated me as a joke, and the newspapers said nothing of my arguments; they talked only of my millinery and described the dress I wore."[49]

It took time but eventually other prominent South women took up the cause of women's suffrage. Although a latecomer, Gertrude Thomas, for example, at sixty-five years of age, joined the forces working for women's suffrage and was elected president of the Georgia Women's Suffrage Association in 1899. Virginia Clay-Clopton also became interested in women's rights and for four years, 1896–1900, presided over the Alabama Equal Suffrage Association.[50]

On the other hand, surprisingly, some of the most intelligent, well-educated women of the era were opposed to women's suffrage. Cornelia

Phillips Spencer of Chapel Hill, North Carolina, appeared to be of two minds concerning women and their role in the postwar world. Considered "the brightest woman in North Carolina" by many, and deemed by Governor Vance to be "the *smartest* man, too!" Mrs. Spencer advocated a better type of education for women, greater support for the common schools, and better trained teachers for the common schools. Although Mrs. Spencer devoted untold time and energy to the development of education in North Carolina and the progress of the University of North Carolina, she considered women subordinate to men. She saw many new fields opening their doors to women following the war, but maintained that "no amount of legislation can ever avail to enable woman to usurp man's place as head of this lower world, nor even to seat herself by his side as peer in those attributes and privileges which belong to him as sovereign."[51] While Northern women aggressively crusaded for voting rights, Mrs. Spencer spoke for thousands of Southern women who insisted that the suffrage and the acceptance of women as judges, senators, public orators, or presidents were "Forbidden Fruit" that would unsex a woman and "take her out of woman's plane."

Female suffrage, Mrs. Spencer prophesied, "will, I trust, be carried back to the depths of the sea and hopelessly drowned. I never could see any good to be derived from it, except in a very limited scene of action—in a church or school meeting. I cannot conceive what benefit would accrue to the country by doubling the popular vote—or what real tangible gain there would be to our sex from the exercise of this right. I can imagine an immense amount of evil,—public, social and domestic. I can imagine a thousand evils to woman herself—a sort of degradation in the eyes of men and angels. God forbid, for her own sake, that woman shall ever thus publicly step out of her own sphere into one for which she has no fitness morally, physically or intellectually, and where under all circumstances, she must cut at best, a very poor figure indeed." Mrs. Spencer's "Young Lady's Column," carried for many years in the *North Carolina Presbyterian*, no doubt served as an important influence on young women for years to come. (It should be noted that with time, Mrs. Spencer began to modify her views on woman's rights. Although apparently not fully convinced of the virtues of women's suffrage she at least admitted: "I confess to being so blinded and bigoted that only lately it has occurred to me that there might be some good in the other side of 'Woman's rights.' Only lately have I looked at it dispassionately and find to my inexpressible surprise and disgust that the female reformers out yonder in Wyoming, Chicago, New York, and where not, except down South, have really an argument or two on their side."[52])

With regard to women's rights Cornelia Spencer summarized her views, those shared by many conservatives, in her "Young Lady's Column" of April 22, 1874: "The laws of even Christian nations to this day ignore their rights and are unjust to them. However they have held their own and have got along pretty well on the whole. Now they are holding up their heads and asking for a little more…. What I say is this. Let the laws that bear unequally on them be modified, and let public opinion be so generously and liberally formed that they may safely and freely enlarge their sphere of action, increase their usefulness, strengthen their influence, improve their intellects and make themselves fit companions for and co-workers with good and true men, without impairing a single feminine grace, or losing sight for one moment of the great fact for woman, namely, that her true sphere in this world, whatever it be in the next, is a subordinate one. I did not say *inferior*, young ladies, I said *subordinate*. There can be but one head, and the man is the head."[53]

Despite her distaste for women's suffrage and her resolute position as to women's subservient role, Cornelia Spencer delighted in women being employed in occupations that women "can hold very gracefully," such as teaching, working in the Treasury Offices in Washington, in creative fields such as drawing, creating wallpaper designs or painting jewelry or china. She even urged women to aspire to become school-commissioners. Recognizing the "sterner necessities" requiring many women to make their own living in the world since the war and in her overall approval of women as teachers, Mrs. Spencer campaigned for schools "where women can be fitted for teachers—and they should be free schools," she argued.

Unless women were to become college teachers of higher mathematics or the classics, Mrs. Spencer considered such "abstract knowledge" a useless pursuit for most women. Instead she advocated a practical education that would make women "useful as well as ornamental, intelligent rather than accomplished, wise rather than learned." Higher education for women, practical or impractical, soon gained untold numbers of supporters who believed that "women could never fully develop their capabilities as long as they remained 'under guardianship' and were deprived of the education which the practice of self-government provided."[54]

The need for physical education for all women became a continuing crusade for Mrs. Spencer and scores of other physical health enthusiasts. Walking, not simply strolling, but routinely embarking on three or four mile hikes, Mrs. Spencer believed, would guard against weakened female stamina and would enable women to consider even more challenging endeavors.

In many respects Cornelia Spencer represented a growing group of shadowy ambivalent figures gradually emerging from the male dominated world of the past and slowly, cautiously embarking on tentative steps in the direction of a "brave new world" for women in the future. Her strong belief in equal justice for women, in spite of her negative attitude about extending the suffrage to women, led to Mrs. Spencer's advocacy of the need for equal pay for women. As public opinion was beginning to change, Mrs. Spencer saw woman as man's co-laborer and equal. "His helper and friend—never his rival, but certainly with a fully recognized and assured right to make her bread on as good terms as he—to be as much respected and as well paid as he, in all those departments of industry from which God and Nature have not excluded her." She seriously questioned "why a man should receive ten dollars for a piece of work, for which a woman, doing it equally well, can get but five...." In her column for Young Ladies, in words seemingly more twentieth century than nineteenth century, Mrs. Spencer apparently sanctioned women going into certain businesses but cautioned them to put forth great effort to please people and not to "screw their customers."[55]

In her hang-up with the past, Mrs. Spencer insisted that a cordial reception of women as orators speaking to audiences composed of both men and women was definitely not one of the lessons from the North to be emulated by Southerners. "Woman as an Orator! I have heard Lucy Stone and Mrs. Stanton and Lucretia Mott and others of that ilk. They are clever talkers—self possessed actresses, but when the world accepts their sharp incisive chatter, their shrill treble, their feeble feminine gesture in place of the thunder of Webster's argument, the clarion tones of Clay, the eagle glance of Prentice—why then I say, let the world slip. I for one shall be ashamed of it."[56]

Cornelia Spencer was certainly not alone in her distaste for women speakers. The *Natchez Courier* of May 25, 1870, for example, carried a succinct account of Mrs. Snodgrass's ill-fated lecture on women's rights in Henderson, Kentucky. "The audience laughed at her, and when the hat was passed around, contributed only twenty-five cents. The Snodgrass anathematized the town and left."

A writer for the *New Orleans Daily Picayune*, of June 8, 1866, spoke for untold numbers of Southerners—and Northerners as well—when he proclaimed: "The fair sex can gracefully preside in the parlor, but when leaving this, as a general thing, they are sadly out of place."

Not all women shared Mrs. Spencer's sentiments, as pointed out earlier, and some women began freely speaking their minds on political issues (although usually in small private groups) and attending political meetings. (See the picture of the Ladies Gallery during Johnson's Impeachment Trial in the Senate.) In 1871 when her husband was running for sheriff, Lucy Neilson of Columbus, Mississippi, joined her husband at his campaign gatherings. Although the only wife in attendance, her appearance was an innovation that sparked amazement and imitation. "They were very much amused at my coming out and vowed their wives should come next time. Said Mr. N. had taught them something worth remembering. We had a good laugh. I told them all I was running for deputy!"[57]

℘

As must be obvious women's transition out of the kitchen and into the workforce and into public life often met with considerable opposition. Southern men particularly were reluctant to accept women's emergence from "the cult of domesticity." Some men carried to the extreme their distaste for women who dared to venture outside the traditional "women's sphere." There were men who objected to women forming clubs even for educational or social stimulation. More than one man refused to read a book written by a woman. Ulysses S. Grant refused to allow his wife to work as a nurse with Annie Wittenmyer, the famous Civil War dietitian. The brothers of August Evans (Wilson), a well known writer of the time, talked her out of becoming a nurse. One minister "refused permission for a woman's prayer meeting on the grounds that if the women were left alone, 'who knows what they would pray for.'"

When Sarah Fay proposed taking a position teaching, her husband who was serving with the Confederate troops in Mississippi, was extremely discouraging. Edwin Fay explained to his wife that he much preferred Sarah's learning to spin and to weave to her reviewing Virgil. "But let me entreat you that during my absence you will become as domestic as you can possibly be...." With Sarah's response that she would spin when she quit teaching, her husband wrote: "I would like you to be like Penelope [the wife of Ulysses], a very domestic woman, that you might instruct your handmaids in all kinds of work." After countering her proposal with scores of questions calculated to put off the zealous schoolmistress, Sarah's husband agreed to go along with her decision, but added, "But is it necessary for my own beloved wife to descend to the unthankful occupation of teaching? And if you commence can you hold out? Will not your newborn energy fail?"[58]

Actually the traditional male dominance of Southerners continued to prevail and was reflected in the fact that only four southern states (Kentucky, Texas, Tennessee, and Arkansas) ratified the Nineteenth Amendment giving women the right to vote.[59]

Part II

FIVE WOMEN

℘ **9** ℭ

Susan Darden: Life in Postwar Mississippi

In page after page of her diary Susan Sillers Darden graphically depicts the uncertainties and frustrations of life near Fayette, Mississippi, following the war, descriptions which tend to mirror the anxieties of thousands of her fellow Southerners.[1] The daily catalog of events and problems interspersed with repeated references to illnesses and the deaths of family members and friends serves to document many of the postwar economic, political and racial problems confronting a defeated populace. Susan's perspective is that of a mature woman, who at forty-nine years of age at the end of the war had given birth to ten children, three of whom had died in infancy. Through her eyes the reader is provided with glimpses of the effects of the Civil War and Reconstruction on a well established Mississippi family. Scattered throughout Susan's diary are additional insights as to life in general for Southerners living in the tumultuous postwar world.

Although Susan's daily entries start off routinely with a brief notation of the weather, they then progress to the more consequential activities of the day. Often interjected among Susan's depiction of the Dardens' critical financial and labor troubles, however, are homey, domestic details of sewing, knitting, cooking, and baking: "sewing on my gingham basque," "lined my dress and sleeves," "knitting George's socks," "worked button holes for George's coat," "darned my gloves," "gathered some pecans," "cut up & stuffed 34 lbs. sausage meat," "put up some dried apples and pecans," "took up the butter." (It appeared the making and selling of butter had become a profitable business venture for Susan.)

In addition, almost daily reports of sicknesses and deaths punctuate Susan's diary: "Mollie Barker sick with pneumonia," "Lizzie sick with bilious fever," "Little Buckner very sick with flux," "Johnnie looks bad, had another spell of fever." Marriages in and around Fayette are duly recorded by Susan, often accompanied by terse, caustic comments regarding the couples involved. Of the Stampley wedding Susan dryly noted: "They are second cousins. The Stampley family believe in marrying cousins."[2]

The horrendous loss of life during the war rendered grief a constant companion for most Southerners. Susan Darden was no exception. Her diary was clouded with painful memories. Susan's eldest son, Buckner, and her brother Joseph were both casualties of the war. In 1862 Buckner died of wounds in the service of the Confederacy, and later brother Joseph was taken prisoner, contracted smallpox, and died just as the war was winding down. In an unrelenting lament Susan wept for Buckner. "Oh this cruel, cruel war—what ruin it has brought upon us. I hope my dear Buckner, my dear child, is happy where there is no trouble or trials for him to endure." In another entry she grieved: "It is 4 years today since our dear son came home, full of joy & life, to see Olivia [his sister] married. He is gone to that home from whence no traveler returns." Again and again she mourned: "Four years ago my dear son was suffering, far away in the Hospital, without a friend near. One year ago my dear brother, Joseph, was in the Hospital suffering with smallpox, from which he died 6 May 1865."

Additional entries in Susan's diary cite a shocking list of deaths within her personal circle of family and friends. Tortured by her melancholy reflections Susan despaired: "How happy we all were that day," [Olivia's wedding day] Susan remembered. "Oh, the sad change since then! Our dear child, Buckner, was with us, my dear sister was here, dear Sister Maria was here, Charley Scott was here. They are all gone to render their account to God; may it be a good one, may they be permitted to sit around the throne of God & sing praises to the most high. Dear Annie Briscoe is numbered with the dead, dear brother, Joseph, has been called away too. What a sad thought, when we think of so many that have died; and our unprofitable lives are still spared. Oh, may we improve it, while there is time afforded!"[3]

Economic Problems

Of special significance, of course, are Susan's entries portraying the economic chaos that engulfed the South at the war's end and considerably altered life for the Dardens. The Dardens' son-in-law, a physician, found it impossible to collect from many of his patients; the minister was hard put to derive a livable income from his parishioners; school teachers struggled to make ends meet.

With the Confederate economic system in shambles, debtors found it almost impossible to settle their indebtedness and creditors found it quite hopeless to collect on outstanding notes. Although the Dardens were probably monetarily better off than many of their neighbors, their financial situation was greatly strained by their inability to collect on monies they had loaned to friends and neighbors. "Mr. Darden went to Stephen Stampley's to collect $30.00 he owes us for peas bought last year, could not pay Mr. Darden anything."[4] (Susan always referred to her husband as "Mr. Darden," as was the custom of the times.) "Mrs. Dixson sent $1.00 for some meat, says she does not know how she is to live unless her uncle, Jack Burch, sends her the money that he owes her."[5] Mr. Darden had asked Ira Robertson about paying the money Ira owes him, "says he will pay it when he comes to Conference."[6] "Blount Stuart says he can't pay anything on his note this year."[7] Apparently one of the most difficult debts to collect on was Jesse Darden's claim against the Federal government. Jesse was forced to expend considerable time and energy in attempting to gain compensation for his $2,480 loss when the Yankees confiscated his horses mules, corn, wheat, etc.

Bankruptcies and foreclosures were commonplace. The demise of numerous businesses taking the meager savings of their backers with them served to compound the already perilous financial situation of countless Southerners. Many of the Dardens' friends lost huge sums of money when a seemingly reputable company apparently gave up the fight and declared bankruptcy. Susan reported in her diary: "Wes Whitney has just returned from Jackson, says there is great complaint of hard times, saw so many gentlemen that had money in Craig & Co's hands when they suspended business negotiations." She continued with a sobering list of their friends who suffered losses, including one woman's large investment of life insurance money.[8]

In January of 1868 Susan wrote of her soon-to-be son-in-law's distress over the possibility that he might lose his place: "has a mortgage of $3,000.00 on it; he paid $200.00, can't raise the balance. Col. Hamilton rented his place for $2500.00 & is not able to pay him anything. His merchant failed & he will lose all."[9] Still more family problems surfaced with the difficulties encountered by Susan's widowed sister-in-law who shortly after the death of her husband (Susan's husband's brother) "was very much troubled about her home being mortgaged; says she will never be able to pay the debt; thinks that her brother, Guilford Torrey, sold her interest in her father's place without her consent."[10]

One friend gave in to tears whenever he mentioned his family whom he feared would starve to death. Even son Buckner left a deeply mortgaged home when he went to war—a home that was about to be sold for the payment of back taxes. "Poor Buckner, everything he had was mortgaged.... How sad it makes me feel when I think of him & his home in Madison Parish—all a desolation now; so much hard work & many sleepless nights spent for naught—all for our enemies to ravage & destroy."[11]

Everyone, it seemed, wanted to borrow money, but unfortunately there was precious little to loan out. Everyone it seemed was hitting up Susan's husband for loans. "Wesley Whitney came this morn to borrow $600.00; has bought Jim Wiggington's Place (120 acres), just back of Fairgrounds near Fayette; Mr. Darden promised loan of the money; went to Fayette to see if Blount Stuart could pay him the $900.00 Blount owes Mr. Darden; Blount cannot pay the debt now, so Mr. Darden did not let Wesley Whitney have any money."[12]

Susan's diary entries were filled with notations such as "Henry Darden came up this eve, wanted to borrow money..." and "Alex Compton called this eve, wanted to borrow $100.00; Mr. Darden did not lend."[13] "Mr. Darden received letter from Jeff Whitney; attorney for Mrs. Issac Burch, her place mortgaged for supplies—Jeff wants to borrow $2200.00 from Mr. Darden, to lift the mortgage & give him deed of trust on the place."[14]

The list of would-be borrowers seemed infinite. "Pros Whitney wrote Mr. Darden that he wanted to borrow $100.00, & give a note for what he now owes & let Mr. Darden take a lien on 4 bales cotton to secure the payment; Mr. Darden has no money to loan."[15] "Dr. Guice wants to borrow $400.00 and give Deed of Trust on his house & lot, says Dick Truly is pushing him & he cannot collect his outstanding bills." It would appear Susan's husband had either sold provisions or loaned money to some of his freed blacks. "Hands owe Mr. Darden $1432.79, large amount for the way they work. Mr. Darden has money loaned to different ones to the amount of $6,513.42.[16]

Susan's husband appeared to be a shrewd, though compassionate businessman. In an attempt to save his son-in-law's property Susan's husband gave his note. On other occasions, however, Jesse was quick to snap up land at bargain prices that was being sold for back taxes. "Mr. Darden went to Fayette, bid in Cicero Stampley's land for $223.00; it was being sold for taxes." According to Susan, Cicero would have two years in which to redeem the land. (Those were stressful times. Fortunately or unfortunately wives were often kept in the dark about the dire financial status of their husbands and when Mr. Darden stopped at the Stampleys' home the next day, Cicero's wife did not know their land had been sold.) After repeated entreaties, Jesse finally obtained a Deed of Trust on Tom Darden's land "to secure payment of his note; which is $1100.00, with interest."[17] Apparently what little money Susan's husband had available he wisely invested in railroad bonds as the South began to rebuild and expand its railroad systems.

Anxiety over back taxes, current taxes, and future taxes plagued almost every Southern farmer—including the Dardens. Each year taxes alone seemed to eat up any profit that might be forthcoming. "We are taxed for every hog, sheep, beef we kill, for all the butter, eggs, & chicken we sell: & for everything we sell; it will take all we make to pay taxes," Susan complained.[18] In October of 1866 Susan was further disheartened when "Mr. Darden paid his Revenue Tax to Ely Jones today…$740.00. How hard to be robbed of our property & then have to pay this heavy TAX!"[19] As they watched a large portion of their income paid out in taxes, the Dardens, as did most Southerners, discovered it rough going in the postwar years.

Churches and their ministers were also experiencing difficult times as was evident in Susan's community. (See Jo Gillis Chapter.) During the catastrophic postwar years the support of one's family often became a titanic struggle, and contributions to one's church were relegated to a remote second place. Some ministers were forced to serve two congregations or to preach and teach in order to make ends meet. Churches were disbanded; ministers were suing for back pay. "Mr. Hall has written another letter to the session & members demanding $1000.00, as due him in equity for preaching…members had already given him $60.00, and agreed to give him $100.00 March 1871, when he went to get another situation."[20] Two years later Susan pointed out "The Masons are talking of closing the doors of the Presbyterian Church because the members have not defrayed half the expenses of the Masonic Hall." Several days later Susan's husband met with several Fayette men to attempt to raise the $300 needed to repair the church.[21]

Internal church politics added to the problems of the clergy and to the community. Congregations were prone to summarily ousting their ministers for behavior judged inappropriate by the members. Even their private lives were closely scrutinized. "Mr. Jones does not preach at Red Lick now, the members were so opposed to marrying Mrs. McGill."[22]

Swindlers, hoarders, rip-off artists were all out to make a fast buck. One judge charged everyone fifty cents to take the mandatory Oath of Allegiance. Some lawyers charged from $100 to $500 for drawing up applications for special pardons and sending them to Washington. (Johnson's

May 29, 1865, proclamation granted amnesty to most Southerners who would take the Oath of Allegiance; however, there were fourteen exceptions including the denial of amnesty to persons owning $20,000 or more of taxable property. Actually the latter groups were not totally excluded for they could petition President Johnson for a special pardon. Since the Dardens owned property worth over $20,000, they would have been required to seek a pardon via petition.) "Mr. Montgomery & Blount Stuart are going to send a petition to President Johnson to ask pardon. They will come under the Confiscation Act, they are worth $20,000.00. Mr. Darden will send a petition also." Four days later she added "Mr. Darden went to Fayette. Mr. Elliot of Port Gibson is charging $100.00 for sending the petitions on to Washington City to the President for those that are worth $20,000.00."[23]

Labor Problems

The sobering details of postwar life related in Susan's diary underscored the absolute desperation of farmers and businessmen in the years after the war. One man's mind was "very much disturbed on account of the state of affairs; he has not one but the cook; can't get hands, is in debt, has very little cotton; says he can't stand much more, will go distracted."[24]

Susan and her husband were typical of the thousands of Southerners experiencing critical labor problems. Within months after the surrender Susan noted: "The Provost Marshal in Fayette has issued orders for all planters to make written arrangements with their negroes about wages since June 1865; planters to give their names, ages & what class negroes they are."[25] In compliance with the mandate by the Freedmen's Bureau that all labor contracts with former slaves be witnessed, the Darden workers were summoned for an official document signing. "Jack Darden & Kie Glidewell came this eve to witness the negroes sign the agreement between them & Mr. Darden. He gives them $25.00; the women that suckle $15.00; those that do not suckle $18.00." Susan's husband later returned the signing favor. "Mr. Darden went to Jack's to witness the contract between him & the Freedmen he hired."[26]

Adherence to the terms of the contracts, as noted in Part I, frequently proved a bone of contention between employers and employees. Army officials and authorities representing the Freedmen's Bureau found themselves constantly flooded with complaints from irate workers and distraught employers each accusing the other of failure to abide by the agreements. Hiring and keeping laborers during those chaotic days posed immense problems. As the South began the vital reconstruction of its railroads, the possibility of more remunerative work in construction saw many workers abandoning the plantations at a moment's notice and heading for higher paying railroad jobs. A walk-out at harvesting time spelled disaster for plantation owners. "It will break up the planters if the hands leave the crops now & go off to work on the railroad," Susan anguished. The promise of better working conditions or rumors of greater ease in picking a cotton crop often lured workers off to a neighboring plantation thus leaving an owner stranded for help during crucial periods of the growing season.

The constant turnover of workers kept farmers at their wit's ends. "All of Capt Sam Montgomery's negroes left. Only 2 of Gabe Fowler's stayed. Jack went to Franklin (county) to hire hands; Henry went to Washington (Mississippi) to hire.... Sam Chamberlain has only been able to hire 4 negroes. Jack will have ten hands."[27] "Heard Jack Darden's hands leaving & going to Willie Stampley's to work."[28] Workers seemed to disappear with little provocation, or in fact with no provocation at all. "Jack came Sat. Wanted money to buy clothes. Mr. Darden did not give it to him—he said he would go & work & get the money. Mr. Darden told him not to come back if he left—he got his rations for this week & is gone. Mr. Darden ought not to have weighed his rations to him," Susan concluded.[29]

Shortly after Christmas in 1867, Susan's husband attended a meeting of residents of the county where they sought "to devise some rules about hiring the freedmen, passed resolutions & appointed committees." In response to the complaints about former bondsmen who refused to work at all the authorities advised the men to go to work and if they could not negotiate wages to at least "work for their bread and meat." The Freedmen were urged to "make the best contract they could, BUT GO TO WORK."[30]

Contract or no, many employers found their workers somewhat less than eager to resume or to undertake their designated responsibilities. The newly freed men violently resisted any assignments that might possibly return them to their former subservient condition. Freed slaves could now work if they wanted to, when they wanted to, for whatever compensation and under whatever conditions they could arrange. Susan was beside herself to know how to energize her servants. "My cows have not been milked since last Monday. What a trial to have a gang of free negroes on a place & can't get them to do anything."[31]

Directions to black "servants" that were formerly obeyed with alacrity now frequently went unheeded. In the postwar world, however, a moment's lapse and an impulsive lash with a whip could find a planter being hauled straight to the provost marshal's office for an accounting.

"Jack's Susan went to the Provost Marshal.... Jack had given her a few licks, which was the reason she went to the Marshal."[32] Accorded little satisfaction from the authorities, black Susan packed up her belongings and took off in a huff. Even Susan Darden in a moment of sheer exasperation almost forgot that she was no longer dealing with slaves. "The Freed women are doing so bad, cannot get them to go to the pen with Lucinda to milk. I wish I could get hold of them with a good cowhide."[33]

Unfortunately, despite their contracts, laborers often came out the losers when crop failures, as a result of weather conditions or an infestation of army worms left employers bereft of money or provisions to compensate their laborers. Disease as well as natural disasters and wolves took a toll on plantations. Susan told of one man who lost 20 freedmen with cholera and was reduced from six hundred acres to seventy-five acres. "How much trouble poor Jeff has had," Susan remarked.

Summer after summer there was either too much or too little rain. "We need rain so much, have little water in the cistern, had to haul water from Sol Stampley's creek Saturday to wash with."[34] Cutworms helped devastate crops that floods and droughts had left intact. A family member "was so distressed in his mind" as to see "nothing but ruin before him, only making 20 bales cotton & $3,000 in debt." Conscientious employers, such as Jesse Darden, spent many a sleepless night worrying about compensating his workers.

Some blacks were fortunate (or unfortunate) enough to come up with the wherewithal to purchase land (often poor land sold to unsuspecting blacks by conniving swindlers). When they found the land rocky and infertile many returned to their former owners. "Mr. Montgomery's hands are tired of their land they bought, have gone back & rented land from him."[35]

Retaining household help (white or black) brought on big headaches for most harried housewives. It was not surprising that women wanted— and *needed*—household help. Susan Darden detailed the menu for her "nice dinner" of January 6, 1866, for her family and a few friends: "stack cake & 2 Jelly cakes; apples, oranges, figs, coconut, raisins; almonds, pecans; candy & kisses; strawberries & whipt cream; transparent pudding; cucumber & mustard pickles; turkey, 2 baked chickens, 2 chicken pies, ham, baked ribs, backbones, sausages; Irish & sweet potatoes, rice, & onions." Such lavish menus apparently were not unusual. On another occasion Susan treated at least fourteen guests to "turkey, pig, beef, ham, oysters, & squab; my first mess peas, etc. For dessert had: cake, milk & peaches, grated coconut, transparent pudding, peach pie."[36] (One should realize that even a simple chicken dinner necessitated catching and killing the chicken, drawing and plucking the bird, carrying in the water to wash the chicken, bringing in the wood, building the fire, etc.)

Racial and Political Problems

Compounding the massive financial and labor problems of the times were the bitter racial and political enmities that bred mayhem and murder throughout the Southland. In certain respects Susan's diary chronicles many of the same economic problems encountered by tens of thousands of other white women in the postwar South. Susan's diary, however, warrants special attention. It is unique in the fact that few women diarists paint so personal a picture as does Susan of the malignant racial and political strife of her day. True, scores of diarists cite secondhand reports of atrocities committed in their communities. Susan's diary, however, reveals a family tragically caught up in the very eye of the storm.

Attitudes, one remembers, were polarized in much of Mississippi: conservative white Democrats against Radical Republican forces composed of scalawags, carpetbaggers and blacks. While the Radical Republicans were busily engaged in enticing blacks, via promises, speeches, barbecues, picnics—and violence, into Union Leagues or Loyal Leagues, Democrats were diligently organizing their own groups. Although the notorious Ku Klux Klan was the most infamous of the white groups, there were scores of other less well-known organizations such as the Knights of the Golden Circle, the Knights of the Black Cross, the Innocents, the Wide Awake Club, and a spate of Democratic "Clubs" or "White Leagues." (These groups often operated under innocuous aliases such as "mounted baseball clubs" or "musical clubs.")

Ostensibly the Loyal League groups and many of the Democratic clubs were political organizations, the former designed for the promotion and the support of the Republican party and the rights of freedmen; the latter organized to promote the interests of the Democratic party against Congressional reconstruction policies—and usually to effect the restoration of white supremacy.

Democratic politicians, of course, implored voters to join the "clubs." Articles such as the following editorial from the June 26, 1875, edition of *The Enterprise Courier* of Enterprise, Mississippi, maintained: "There is nothing so apt to insure success, as thorough organization; and to this end we advise our friends to organize clubs in every county district. There is no doubt but that the people need being stirred up, and awakened to the importance of the coming election, and while it is an easy task to elect Democrats, and honest competent officers in the county of Clarke, should we organize and make the effort to do so; it is equally certain that we will be defeated, if we do not recognize the necessity of entering into the campaign with our entire energies." The editorial went on to point out that "the opponents of good government," [referring to the Radical Republicans and the Loyal Leagues] have plans of operations that "on the slightest warning, can rally the faithful to the ballot-box. In this they have set an example which we would do well to imitate, for by so doing, we can place Clarke county under the control of men who will protect the interests of the people."

An article in the *Vicksburg Daily Herald* of January 21, 1875, called attention to the formation in Louisiana of "clubs," whose members were equipped with uniforms and arms. Club members insisted that the groups have been formed as means of "protection, a necessity occasioned by the existence of leagues among the blacks." In contrast the Republicans accused them "of being an armed body of volunteers, existing for the purpose of intimidating the blacks" and overthrowing the local government—an accusation that might well have been merited.

It is difficult to determine whether some of the "clubs" might possibly have devoted themselves exclusively to political issues or whether all clubs incorporated both political and racial goals. Since the two aspects were so intricately interwoven, one suspects a predominance of the latter group. Very possibly various clubs differed in their political and racial orientation.

Racial strife (actually the term "racism" did not gain currency until years later) was universal. For some individuals their black-white antipathies simply smoldered in verbal disparagement. For others, both Radical Republican converts and conservative Democrats, their pent up hostilities, with sufficient provocation, exploded in confrontations involving beatings, gunfire, murder and hangings. It would have been a most unusual person, black or white, who through intimidation, peer pressure or conviction did not find a home—or a shelter, in one of the organizations.

Somewhat surprisingly, it should be remembered, not all of the violence was spent on the opposition. Both groups at times took to task members of their own race who were "getting out of line." Men who beat their wives, women who were judged promiscuous, individuals who were straying from party lines, or who were growing too liberal in their racial attitudes could be threatened—or "paid a visit" by members of their own group.

Over the years tensions between the two parties and the two races continued to escalate. As would be expected, the Radical regime was as unpopular with the Dardens as with most of their conservative countrymen. Southerners who for generations had been steeped in the tradition of white supremacy viewed the Radical programs of black-white equality as an abomination. Subtle—and not so subtle—evidences of attitudes of racial superiority had long clouded the writing and thinking of vast numbers of Southerners. It was shocking, for example, for Susan to learn that in New Orleans "the negroes sat at the Hotel table with the whites & took 1st class seats in the Theatre; how awful to think of the poor Southern people."[37] When the blacks went into Fayette to register to vote in 1867, Susan was unable to repress her annoyance over having illiterate Negroes voting.[38] Susan seemed embarrassed for Dr. Hill, for black-white sexual relationships, and for the courts when she wrote: "Dr. Hill's case (living with colored woman & then deserting her) was to be tried...what a shame to have to try such cases in Court."[39]

Susan's contempt for the Radicals' success in securing the Negro vote for the Republicans was reflected in Susan's notation that: "The hands all went to vote today for Grant for President." In marked contrast, Jesse Darden's conservative planter vote was dutifully recorded in Susan's report. "Mr. Darden went to Fayette, voted for Greeley for President.[40] (Fortunately, evidences of racism were beginning to mellow in the next generation, and it was interesting to note that Susan's daughters braved the ridicule of some of their neighbors and friends and seemed to find a satisfying niche in teaching blacks to read and write for a salary of one dollar a month.)

The Radicals further incurred the wrath of the Dardens when Judge Shackleford was removed from office because he was unable to take the Iron Clad Oath of Allegiance. To take the Iron Clad Oath an individual needed to swear that he had never given aid in any way to the Confederacy. Naturally very few Southerners were eligible to sign that oath.

In turn the Radical Republicans did not take kindly to Southerners' criticism of their regime. Many Southerners found it the better part of wisdom to avoid vitriolic, public criticism of Radical Reconstruction. The Dardens were outraged when "Willie Marschalk was arrested & carried to Natchez, under negro guard, for having published an uncomplimentary article regarding 'Military Rule.'"

The Dardens' true Democratic colors came to the fore when in July of 1868 Susan's husband attended a mock burial of the Radical Constitution. "There was a procession with boxes with lights in them, the sides taken out & tissue paper with different mottos on them. Had a small coffin, within it the Constitution & some hair, had the coffin in the hearse. Buried it in the Public Square, between Robel's & Guilminot's, stomped on the grave & built a big fire on it." Susan concluded: "A big 'to do' generally. It looks like mockery to me."[41] (One assumes this was a celebration of the success of Mississippi whites in voting down the proposed new constitution. Enough black registrants, through intimidation or outright acts of terrorism, had supposedly been deterred from voting, thereby enabling the whites to control the vote. This action, of course, delayed Mississippi's readmission into the Union and participation in the presidential election.)

Clearly the racial confrontations that kept erupting throughout the South were common in the Fayette area as well. At the slightest provocation local residents stood ready to defend their own home territory or to put down violence in a neighboring area. News of racial unrest in nearby Vicksburg in 1874 incited Fayette area citizens into action. "The negroes are marching on Vicksburg," Susan wrote. "Were met by the citizens & 20 were killed & more wounded. Jesse (son) went to Fayette. Dr. Shannon telegraphed from Vicksburg the negroes burning houses in the surrounding countryside & threatening to kill the women & children. Put Darden got a Company of Men; were to start tonight to assist Vicksburg; so few came they disbanded & all went home ... too few to do any good at helping a place like Vicksburg."[42] (Trouble at that time was brewing in Vicksburg over taxation and fraud issues. Racial, political, and financial problems culminated on Sunday, December 6 and 7, when excited Negro and white forces confronted each other in the streets. In short order the overheated passions of the times exploded in rioting and violence that resulted in the death of two whites and more than twenty blacks — some accounts report thirty-five blacks died."[43]) In 1875 rumors that "The negroes threaten to burn Jackson, Miss, because the Democrats were elected," generated considerable apprehension for the Dardens and their neighbors.[44]

Elections, of course, always added fuel to an already growing conflagration and served as red flags to trigger-happy gun wielders. The following tragic accounts in Susan's diary reveal much about the racial strife of the period and the true nature and frequent vigilante activities of the "clubs."

Actually Susan does not openly report her husband's active participation in any of the violence of the area, and one would like to think that Susan and her husband were merely innocent observers of the outrages and murders being committed around them. Other members of the Darden family, however, were in the thick of confrontations in Mississippi and Louisiana that tore apart their lives.

Tempers were reaching the boiling point during the long hot days of summer in 1876 when Susan wrote that on July 31st "Mr. Darden and George [Susan's husband and son] went to Fayette, the Brandywine Club was there with their cannon. The darkies had said they were going to make the white men raise their hats to them & send a committee to wait on their wives. The different Clubs met in Fayette: Capt Harper, Mr. Vertner, Mr. John Martin, & Judge Shackleford spoke. The Radicals did not raise their pole, very few negroes there, everything passed off quietly."

Three months later on October 28th Susan described another potential confrontation. "Jesse & Mr. Darden went to Fayette to hear Lynch (colored) speak; they cheered him so he had to stop, ought to have let him speak; he left on the cars, freedmen followed him to the cars; the Clubs were ordered to follow on to see if Lynch got off the cars, he did not."

In November Susan's story, best told in her own words, continued innocuously enough with nephew Henry Darden's stopping at the Darden's home to borrow Susan's husband's gun "to go deer hunting in the morning." Suddenly there was an ominous turn of events, when four days later Susan wrote: "Mr. George Jones came here this morning at 3 A.M. for a gun; said Henry Darden & Walker Harper were ambushed & shot; they sent for Henry's wife, Ma & Pa."

The news must have come as a thunderbolt, and Susan's husband and son quickly set out to assess the situation. Upon their return home, the two men relayed the horrible news. "Drs. Richardson & McNair think Henry will die, shot in the groin, ball went up. He told Mr. Darden [Susan's husband] he was doing his duty & would act the same way again. Rev Mr. Lewis came out & talked with Henry." Earlier Susan had reported that her son Jesse's Club "was ordered out."

Susan's account of the shooting was somewhat garbled, possibly as a result of her distress. According to informants the shooting occurred when "The Club from Fayette were ordered to arrest Dave Bergaman, who had shot Charley Chess (both black); they were ordered to surround the house where the negroes were holding a prayer meeting, & they (Clubs) were fired upon, Henry was mortally wounded & Walker Harper shot badly on both sides (#2 small shot). He bled a good deal. Both are at Col Ed Field's; Capt Harper took Walker home this evening. The Club made the negro, at whose house the prayer meeting was held, tell the names of those that had come there with their guns; the negroes were in a cotton house when they fired & then ran away." Susan continued: "The Clubs from all round were there. They got 7 of the negroes; the others got away, some may have been shot *(wounded)*."

A day later Susan wrote "Mr. Gilbert came here at 1 P.M.; told us Henry was dying." Later "Mr. Gordon brought a new suit of clothes from Fayette; laid Henry out after Jesse got there; got his coffin in Rodney, Henry Key carried it out; buried him about sundown in Fayette cemetery…great many at his burying." Of particular note was Susan's relief over Henry's deathbed confession of faith. "Before he died they sent for Mr. Lewis; who prayed with Henry & received him into the church;

Henry professed to love his God, stated he was willing to die, penitent & exhorted all to make their peace with God and not postpone it as he had done. Was so anxious to see his 3 children & kiss them good-bye; Will Robertson went & brought Nettie in his lap; but Henry was dead when they got there; died at 4 A.M. this morning; talked to the last, TURNED ON HIS SIDE, & like he was going to sleep, died. Oh, what a dreadful thing to be shot down & leave wife & helpless children & heart broken parents."

A few days later Susan and her husband vainly tried to console Henry Darden's father. "Jack Darden came at 9 A. M. stayed to dinner; cried like his heart would break when he met us; it is hard for them to give upon their only child."

In the midst of her grief Susan was handed even more devastating news. "When Mr. Darden came after dark, he brought a dispatch from Curtis Smith that Mr. West (daughter Irene's husband) was shot on Saturday (November 4, 1876), by unknown persons, & died this morning. Oh, what dreadful news to us! Poor Irene has been so uneasy about him for sometime; poor little Laura was so distressed, cried so long wondering what her mama would do, Irene is in a delicate condition." (Pregnant)

Susan's husband and son took time for a hurried trip in to Fayette "to vote for President Tilden & Vice President Hendrcks, & Gen Chalmers," and the next day Susan's husband headed for Irene and her family. Five days later Susan's husband returned reporting that he found "Irene & Mrs. West & all friends in great distress." He then related the details of Irene's husband's death, the result of another racial confrontation. "Tommie West, with a number of his Club had started to a torch light procession in Bayou Sarah on Saturday night; they called at a negro's house (Tom Rice) to caution him about talking; Rice had been making some threats; while Tommie West was talking to the negro's wife 2 guns were fired, buckshot wounding Mr. West in the left groin about in the same place that Henry Darden's wound was located; there were also flesh wounds in Mr. West's arm. He drew his pistol, galloped his horse & ordered his men to surround the house. It was too late, the negro had got away."

"Mr. West thought he was fatally wounded at first; took him to Dr. Davis' that night; had Dr. Sterling, Dr. Derrick, Dr. Jones, & Dr. Davis with him. He begged for morphine when they got to Dr. Davis'; Cortey Smith & Jimmie Stewart were with him when he was shot; they took him home Sunday morn in a waggon; Cortey Smith went on ahead to tell Irene; & while telling her wept like a child. The Dr. assured Irene that the wound was not mortal; Mr. West did not say a word about dying was under influence of morphine all the time, suffered so much. Professor Andrews preached his funeral sermon at his burial Wednesday."

"Irene will have to come home to live," Susan surmised. "Darling Irene, what will become of her; Mr. West left nothing for her. Oh! how sad to think of his leaving his helpless family of wife and four children, dying without leaving a hope of the future; he was very popular, would have been elected Sheriff. The next highest Democrat was elected."[45]

Life and Times in Postwar Mississippi

Over the years it seems that the more things change, the more they remain the same. Many of the problems that have plagued families throughout history were also commonplace during the postwar years. During less stressful times, life for the Dardens and their friends took on more normal, although nonetheless challenging, aspects of family living. Not surprisingly the age old generation gap between parents and offspring surfaced in the Darden family. As a sophomore at Andrews Centenary College in Brandon, Mississippi, (tuition $35 for five months) son Jesse spent more time relaxing than studying. Extra monies for "wood, lights, books etc" had been sent; however, Jesse appeared disinterested in college. "I don't know what makes Jesse act so, for he promised his Pa he would apply himself if we would let him go to College; his Pa out of all patience with him."

Finding life at home far too restrictive, Susan's friend's grandson rebelled against his parents' constraints and "ran off from his Pa a short time ago (Freddie was using tobacco to excess, his parents opposed his habits & actions); they found Freddie in Natchez with the Butcher Fields; carried him home & Freddie left home the 2nd time, ran away; he was only 14 years old."[46]

Alcoholism and divorce (although the latter was uncommon) were problems threatening families in the 1860s and '70s as well as in the twentieth century. Susan reported that Ambrose Green's wife was "sueing for a divorce." According to Susan "he had 'gone on' in dissipation until his wife could not live with him; but had not drank any for three weeks & said he would not taste intoxicating drink again; he had put his property in wife and children's names."[47] Another acquaintance died "a drunkard to the last." Susan expressed immense sympathy for the latter man's widow left "without means to support a family."[48]

With a nine-year-old son at home the Dardens became "sandwiched" between care for a young child at home and concerns and financial responsibilities for a caretaker for Mr. Darden's elderly mother. "Ma fell last night, hurt herself so she can't walk today, has to lie in bed." More than a year later she wrote: "Mr. Darden went with me to see Ma, still has fever, very restless last night, had not sit up any today; we came home to dinner, went back tonight." A day later Jesse's mother died.[49]

Church activities, as with generations over the ages, constituted an intrinsic aspect of life for the Dardens as did Sabbath school for the younger Darden children and their friends. There was stiff competition for the prizes and honors awarded for perfect attendance and for memorizing Bible verses. Young George "got the penknife with 4 blades for committing the most verses in the Bible to memory. Will Liddell got the Bible; he could repeat 20 Chapters in the Bible. Carrie Whitney got a book in her class."[50] Susan's diaries contained repeated entries detailing church activities and the addition of new members. "Mr. David Harrison & wife joined the Church; it was unexpected to most persons. I pray they may be good citizens."[51]

Never was there room for boredom in Susan's busy life. Obviously the area around Fayette was not immune to the rampage of thefts and crime spawned in the aftermath of the war. Yet not all of the violence could be attributed to the aforementioned "clubs," or "Klanners" or "Radicals." In the absence of military rule, or even advantaged by military rule, many areas witnessed the rise of gangs of ruffians, some politically or racially oriented, other groups simply the residue of army "bummers." Irate citizens often took the law into their own hands. Susan's diary detailed the town's dispensing of "frontier justice" to one alleged criminal. Outraged over two shootings and the rape of a white woman, the local citizenry had experienced momentary satisfaction over the apprehending and jailing of the alleged culprit. However, without benefit of a trial or further preliminaries the men stormed the jail, hauled out the defenseless man and without further ado promptly hanged him. "They hung the negro that committed a rape upon her (Mrs. Kate Humphrey) Wednesday night. Broke the dungeon open; confined Merriman (Sheriff); and took the negro to Villine's butcher yard & hung him." A few days later Susan penned a further sad postscript to the tragedy. "Mrs. Kate Humphrey died yesterday, from the injuries received the night the negro raped her; leaves two little children."[52] (This hanging seems not to be the work of a "Club," but rather that of a quickly improvised group of self-appointed vigilantes.)

Tensions ran high during those years, and Susan's diary was punctuated with seemingly trivial, non-racial conflicts that were settled with gunfire. (A pistol seemed to be a necessary part of every man's attire.) In January of 1866, Susan wrote: "Ned Miller was murdered by a man he had gone in partnership with. They had a fist fight, Ned whipped him, the Man got his gun & shot Ned Miller. Mrs. Miller had a baby the day he was shot." (Domestic and family quarrels often resulted in gunshots.)

Fires, those set deliberately with malice and vengeance, and the accidental conflagrations touched off by lightening or carelessness could and did leave friends or neighbors bereaved and destitute. One man was left with eight small children when his home caught fire and evaporated into smoldering embers. Another man lost heavily when lightning struck his gin and thirty bales of cotton were consumed by fire. Flames from stoves, fireplaces, and lamps could result in tragedy, particularly for the elderly. "Miss Fannie Carpenter, of Natchez, was burned by her clothes catching on fire, she only lived 2 nights & a day following."[53] In another entry: "Fannie Hartwell had been sick, caught afire Saturday night & burned to death."[54]

Illnesses and deaths, as noted, were so commonplace that scarcely a page of Susan's diary was free from some dire notation of fatalities in the area. In Susan's heart-rending accounts of the death of an infant granddaughter in 1868 and in 1873 the death of her daughter Olivia (Tate), the reader is provided a window on two tragic accounts of death and dying in the late 1860s and 1870s.

During the spring of 1868, after weeks of anguish over the rapidly declining health of Olivia's newborn, Susan despaired: "Olivia's babe worse, head drawn back, & back drawn too; throws its head from side to side; been sick nearly 5 weeks." A few days later the Dardens' worst fears were realized. "Olivia's dear little babe died last night; 10:40 o'clock; babe screamed out all during the day, as if she were frightened, & 2 hours before she died had several hard convulsions; died easy when the breath went out of her. Mr. Darden, George, & I went. Mr. Jim Rowan went to Natchez for the coffin, plain, painted the color of mahogany, lined inside with a little pillow raised in the lining; cost $12.00.... The babe is buried where the other little babe & Dr. Tate's mother is buried; Dr. & Olivia were willing to give her up, she suffered so much."[55]

In 1866 Susan's daughter Olivia, the victim of some unidentified "female problem," had undergone an unsuccessful operation to relieve her condition. Seven years later in the spring of 1873 she had again returned to New Orleans for yet another risky operation. Within hours after the surgery the Dardens were horrified to learn that Olivia had died. "Oh! it was such a shock to me, so grieved, I hardly know what to do.... No one can imagine my feelings but those who have lost children in the same way."

Susan gave a chilling account of the death scene. Apparently the operation had been performed in a home, probably under grossly unsanitary conditions. Although the doctor had pronounced the operation a complete success, when he returned the next day and "found the bowl by her bedside, & said his heart sunk." Dr. Richardson was opposed to giving Olivia chloroform "but the dear child thought she could not stand the operation while she was conscious. Dr. Richardson says giving her chloroform was his only regret."

Benumbed and in a state of stupor Susan immediately left for New Orleans. Upon her arrival the distracted Susan was met by a Miss Austin (a nurse or an aide) who sought to comfort her by sharing with her the final moments of her daughter's life. Miss Austin "came into my room, threw her arms around my neck & wept hard & long. She then went with me to Mrs. Rochester's, where my darling child died. Mrs. Rochester [apparently the owner of the so-called hospital] was so very kind; told me all about my darling's death; said she had every attention possible."

Nineteenth century doctors and their aides, as in the case of Olivia, seemed coldly realistic in their responses to the piteous inquiries of their dying patients. It was a courageous Olivia who, according to Susan's diary "expressed her entire resignation to death when Mrs. Rochester told her death was near." Olivia, Susan was told, "had looked up at Mrs. Rochester soon before she died & said: 'Mrs. Rochester, am I dying now?' Mrs. Rochester told her, 'Yes. Honey; you have been dying for some time.' Then Olivia said 'Oh, Mrs. Rochester, what could I do without Him?'" A minister was called to the bedside: "prayed and talked with Olivia Friday; again Saturday Evening & was holding her hand when she breathed her last." Just before Olivia died "Mrs. Rochester had asked Olivia if she had any wish how she would be 'laid out'; Olivia had replied she would leave any choice with Mrs. Rochester, who laid her out in her wedding gown."

The next morning "the undertaker came with a metallic case, took the remains to his office, put the coffin in a zinc coffin with ice around it; there it remained till Tuesday evening when the corpse was carried & put on the 'Katie,'" a boat bound for home.

Whatever Dr. Richardson might have lacked in expertise in performing the surgery, he certainly made up for in insensitivity and avariciousness. Before Susan left to accompany her daughter's remains homeward, Dr. Richardson presented her with "his medical bill, $500.00; Mrs. Rochester's bill, $28.00; Mr. Johnson's bill for coffin, $85.00."

Two days later at Olivia's home the grief stricken Darden family had assembled. "Oh, none can tell the grief of my children when they met me. Mr. Will Johnson made some remarks, sung, & prayed. We had the coffin opened, but could not recognize the least feature; her face was all black, mouth open, eyes like they would fall out. It was terrible in the extreme to think we could not look upon our dear child again; buried her by her darling babes & husband."[56]

Three months later the appraisers met and concluded that Olivia's estate amounted to $795.00. This included: "9 oxen: $180.00; 6 cows & calves: $120.00; Webster: $125.00; Viola & colt: $100.00; 2 beds & bedding: $40.00; wardrobe: $25.00; 1 bookcase: $20.00; 1 center table: $10.00; bureau: $25.00; 1 lot chairs: $20.00; 1 desk: $10.00; 1 looking glass: $5.00; 1 clock: $5.00; 1 safe: $5.00; 1 carpet: $10.00; 1 cottage bed and bedding: $10.00; 1 marble washstand: $10.00."[57] Olivia's poor orphaned son would make his home with relatives.

&

To be sure not all of Susan's diary was gloom and doom. Throughout the course of her diary Susan enumerated the details of the constant stream of company, family and friends, who dropped in for tea, for dinner or for a week's visit. There were other bright spots—graduations, picnics, parties and dances for the young people, and for Susan and her husband concerts, evenings with the "Social Club" and days at the county fair. At the 1869 fair, Susan took a "red ribbon for butter." In 1871 she reported that at the fair "Mrs. Harper got prize vases for bouquets with greatest variety of flowers. Tom Baker was the successful Knight in the Riding Tournament."[58] The following year son George rode in the equestrian ring and Susan was awarded prizes for crowder peas and a medal for pecans.

Susan's husband, as was true of thousands of Southerners, became caught up in the activities of the Grange. Since the Grange was open to women as well as men, the reader might assume that Susan was encouraged to take part in their educational and social functions. The Dardens' commitment to education led to Mr. Darden's work in helping to establish a free white school in the district.

&

To almost everyone's surprise there was to be some compensation for losses by Yankee theft and appropriation during the war. It was indeed a happy day when "Mr. Fowler came this eve, going around finding out how much persons lost by Yankee confiscation.... Mr. Darden gave list of mules, horses, corn, wheat, etc; total valued at $2480.00; then went to Fayette to make oath to the list before a magistrate."[59]

&

As one pages through Susan's diary the reader develops a bonding with a warm-hearted, well disposed woman, passionately devoted to her family and friends. Life was not always kind to Susan—the death of a son and a brother in the war, the loss of two infant daughters and a baby son, the death of a grown daughter in 1873, the death of a son-in-law and a nephew as a result of political and racial strife, and a staggering list of deaths of grandchildren, in-laws, and friends. After the war the Dardens' antebellum well-being was severely threatened as economic and labor problems wracked their heretofore rather secure financial situation. It took a strong person to weather the vicissitudes of life in the postwar world. Susan Sillers Darden evidenced that stamina in full measure.

❧ **10** ☙

Virginia Smith Aiken:
"A New Order
of Things"

The 1872–73 diary of Virginia Carolina Smith Aiken, of Greenwood County, South Carolina, provides an excellent case study of a courageous Southern woman struggling to cope with the financial and psychological problems of her depressing postwar situation.

Prior to her marriage to widower David Wyatt Aiken, Virginia must have enjoyed a life of affluence and security as the daughter of one of the wealthiest men in South Carolina outside of Charleston. In the years following her father's death in 1855, his estate, as did so many, fell on hard times during the war. When in 1862 his executors sold his cotton mill stock for $207,350, the money was immediately invested in Confederate bonds. These and others of his holdings, of course, eroded to worthlessness during the collapse of the Confederacy.[1] The indebtedness of Virginia's husband (Mr. A. as she consistently referred to him in her diary) and the scarcity of money which made it impossible for him to collect on debts owed him was an all too familiar story enacted in home after home throughout the South. It was indeed a comedown for Virginia to have to scrimp and save and to deny herself and her family luxuries that she certainly must have been accustomed to during the antebellum years.[2] For Virginia and countless others like her[3] the austerity and uncertainties of life after the war completely upended her heretofore relatively sheltered life.

In her diary, Virginia found an outlet for her frustrations. In it she discovered a friend, a confidante, a listener to whom she could confess her innermost thoughts. There she could vent her irritation with a husband indifferent to her exhaustion brought on from her endless household duties and the daily care of some ten children. During the two year span of the diary, Virginia found her responsibilities augmented by a new addition to the family, or now and then diminished with a daughter or a son temporarily away from home and involved in teaching or farming. (Virginia's husband had two children from a previous marriage; together they had eleven children—thirteen in all.) Not surprisingly the centuries old complaints of women about family finances and overwork; about the trials of procuring and keeping domestic help; about their husbands' preoccupation with business and careers at the expense of family time and togetherness; about their disappointment in their children's lack of appreciation of the sacrifices made in their behalf, came through loud and clear in Virginia's lamentations.

The phenomenal success of Virginia's husband in the Confederate Army, where he enlisted as a private and soon rose to the rank of colonel, ill-prepared either of the Aikens for the rigors of the postwar world.[4] The war and the defeat had taken their toll on her husband, and Virginia at forty-four years of age found herself, as did so many Southern women, immersed in her husband's seemingly inextricable financial worries following the war.

Indebtedness was closing in on the Aikens. Unable to collect monies owed him, seemingly thwarted at every turn, Virginia's husband grew increasingly short-tempered, his irritability serving to set him at odds with the entire family. Diary entry after entry resounded with despondency over their situation. Mr. A., she wrote, "is so low spirited, & disheartened, by his failure to pay debts." With her husband's mounting frustrations Virginia despaired: "He seems miserable, & makes us all miserable, by the way he talks, says none of us try to help him, or try to take care of anything, & that we all seem bent upon destroying everything that belongs to him & that none of us do any work & oh! ever so much in that strain—Oh! what can I do to relieve him in any way—all I can do is to pray for him."[5] A few days later Virginia wrote: "Mr. A. wrote a great deal, he seems so restless & worried all the while. Oh! if he were only out of debt I would be happy."[6]

Mealtime was a particularly trying time for Virginia. Tired and hungry from his work in the barns and fields, Virginia's husband often unleashed his frustrations at the dinner table. Virginia's diary listened as she wept: "Somehow everything went wrong at the table." When the steak gave out that day, "Mr. A. got so vexed & was so impatient. All this made me feel so badly I couldn't eat any scarcely & and it was hard to choke back the tears." Her husband, she wrote, "never blames the cook, I am always at fault. He thinks I ought to know all about cooking when I do not." Although Virginia frequently wrote of baking cakes and other delicacies, she was disappointed that her husband seemed unaware and unappreciative of her "worrying work" in nursing a baby, caring for a houseful of children, doing the sewing, mending and planting of a garden.[7]

Virginia considered herself fortunate to have time to attend church once in three months. During the last of March in 1872, in an effort to give Virginia a slight breather and enable her to go to church, one of the older children volunteered to stay with "the little ones." The day was not an easy one even for young Mamie. "They worried her a little," Virginia reported to her diary. "Gus got red pepper in his mouth & squalled, of course, & in the midst of that, Joe fell out of the crib, she had left him asleep."

In February of 1872 Virginia was stunned by the enormity of the family's doctor's bills. "Oh the expense of this family is terrible, no wonder Mr. Aiken is so worried & harassed all the time to know how to make both ends meet."[8] Later Virginia was at a loss to raise the money for the family's dentist bills.

To be sure, the same endemic scarcities and irresponsibilities of hired labor experienced by their fellow countrymen also threatened the Aikens. "No labor, hard to get extra hands to plow, pick cotton or any thing else." Virginia noted.[9] For a brief time, however, the future brightened when Mr. A was able to hire two Englishmen to help with the field work, a step that "made Mr. A feel more like going to work." The sky soon darkened again, however, when about a month later one of the Englishmen left—"said he was not satisfied—didn't like the victuals."[10]

Virginia's affluent upbringing must have made her particularly resentful of her reduced condition. Economy became an all important consideration. For a time the family subsisted on two meals a days instead of three. New clothes and travel were out of the question as Virginia tried "to be more economical than ever this year."[11] Not surprisingly from time to time Virginia interjected a note of self-pity into her diary entries. Her daughters' trip into the village and the proud display of their purchases prompted Virginia's lament: "Tis tantalizing to see so many pretty things & not be able to get some. Oh! These peeps into the gay world unfits us for our duties, & makes us discontented with the quiet of our quiet home."[12] Unable to purchase a longed-for calico dress, Virginia resigned herself to her straitened situation "but as I have to stay at home it doesn't matter."[13]

Cares and Woes

At best the living definitely was not easy for most Southern women in the postwar world. Virginia's diary contained almost daily recordings

of colds, and fevers, and rheumatism, as well as more debilitating illnesses. "Children all ailing, eating too much trash," Virginia fretted.[14]
Punctuating Virginia's diary were frequent notations "My baby ailing
today" or "for the past three weeks my baby has been sick & so hard to
nurse." A visiting aunt observed Virginia's utter exhaustion and repeatedly cautioned: "Ginnie you ought to have a nurse. You are killing yourself trying to nurse in addition to your other work.!" This advice Virginia
dismissed sadly with the hard realities "that other work has to be done."[15]

Virginia herself was subject to frequent bouts of ill health. Childbirth, of course, was fraught with the very real possibilities of maternal
and infant death. Therefore the prospect of an addition to an already sizable family was not always an eagerly anticipated event. Having not yet
weaned her feverish, colicky baby, Virginia despaired in September of
1872: "I never felt as blue in my life & no wonder I have enough to make
me blue. I am in trouble again & that is sufficient to depress me. How
can I take care of any more children."[16] In March Virginia announced the
birth of new baby boy. The birth, however, was accompanied by complications. According to Virginia's diary as the doctor was an hour late in
arriving, no one was in the room with her to assist with the birth but her
husband. Fortunately Mr. Aiken had been successful in delivering their
new son.

As their family continued to increase the problems of educating so
many children became a growing concern. On the occasion of her six-
teenth wedding anniversary Virginia seemed particularly troubled. "What
a family I have in so few years—& now they are to be educated & this
troubles us both very much. We feel that we may have to leave our comfortable home & go to some village to school the children."[17]

Feeding such a large family was no small matter, especially during
those times of critical shortages following the war. Virginia often was
beside herself attempting to provide nourishing meals, or for that matter, meals at all, without eggs, butter, meat or milk. In addition to family meals, of course, there was always the additional work of
"company"—the invited guests as well as the unexpected "drop ins" who
stopped for tea or dinner—or for overnight—or for a fortnight. Unexpected guests required preparing extra food (often complicated by the
lack of any meat or sour milk), retrieving extra blankets from the garret,
making beds, and fixing up special rooms for the overnighters. "All this
tires me & hurts my feet terribly," Virginia explained, "for they are
swollen, but I get no sympathy, not even from my husband."[18]

Then too there was the Southern tradition of welcoming—or at least
accommodating—the total stranger who arrived in the dark of night
requesting food and a bed for a night's rest. Unfortunately such appeals

were not uncommon. One evening, for example, just as they were finishing dinner, "Two men with a drove of cattle wanted to stay all night so we took them in & had to cook supper for them & fix a room, so there was not much time for reading or relaxation." Another evening: "A man rode up & wanted to stay all night, so I had to take him." After supper "I had to fix a room. Oh! Such a bother, this is the third time this week we have had to entertain persons unexpectedly. We can not turn them off after night."[19]

Although Virginia was noticeably silent about most political affairs, no doubt being otherwise preoccupied, she expressed great sympathy for those involved in the postwar racial difficulties that rocked the state. Among the Aikens' visitors was a man attempting to hide out in order to escape arrest "on KKK difficulties." Virginia was most sympathetic: "I do feel so very sorry for him," Virginia confessed, "& all others thus situated. Oh! we poor Southern people have more than we can bear."[20]

On at least one other occasion the Aiken home served as a haven for a fleeing refugee. "Col Watts is with us tonight. He absents himself from home on account of the arrests the Yanks or radicals are making. A great many have left their homes. Tis distressing to think of the state of affairs in this State. We get no justice & no hearing, & all for political effect."[21]

Virginia repeatedly complained of being "broken down," and small wonder when meals often necessitated feeding from twelve to thirty people. At the holiday season, for example, Virginia was exhausted after overseeing a Christmas supper for over thirty people and a breakfast for thirty-three the following morning, the help having celebrated the holiday in a drunken stupor. "The tree looked very pretty & all got a good many presents & and they danced & played till 1 o'clock. Twas 2 o'clock when Mr. A and I went, & we both had to be up at daylight," to feed the thirty-three hungry breakfasters.

Following the Christmas celebration and when all of their guests had departed Virginia confided: "I am delighted it is all over. I think the children all enjoyed it, but I know I did not. I hope there will be no more entertainments here. It falls too hard on me & I am not able to go through with so much fatigue."[22] (Virginia was expecting a new baby in two months.)

Threshing and ginning seasons for most farmers involved a horrendous amount of work. For Virginia it meant preparing food for a dozen or more extra men who simply inhaled the food placed before them. Some mornings called for serving breakfast (and no doubt dinner also) to sixteen hands in addition to the members and overnight guests of her own family. The extra work "gave cook and myself ever so much trouble," Virginia admitted.[23]

There seemed no end to the countless stacks of clothing in need of sewing or mending. Frequent entries told of Virginia's dreary late night routine of mending "stockings & other things," while the rest of the family had retired early and were fast asleep. Virginia's garden, the source of a considerable amount of the Aikens' food supply, demanded much of Virginia's time and effort. Almost all of the family helped with the work. "We planted almost two barrels of Irish potatoes.... I cut up potatoes till my hands are sore."[24] A few days later she wrote: "Did a great deal in the garden before the rain—I sowed onion seed, lettuce, kale, sprouts, planted beans salsify, parsnips, carrots."[25]

Unfortunately, Mr. Aiken's ill humor occasioned by his preoccupation with his economic difficulties was evidenced in his persistent fault finding in the work of his young son. Fearful that his father would not approve of his work, son David put forth a supreme effort in the gardening and crop production. "David is completely broken down. He worried so to get the potatoes planted by 1 o'clock, but they did not finish till 3 o'clock; he was anxious to get some plowing done, which they couldn't finish, & he thinks his father will not like [it], because it was not finished, but I tell him father only expects him to do the best he can. He feels the responsibility so much & so do *I* in his absence," she added. "David had so much to do after we got back, feeding to look after etc., sheep not all up—& he so worried about them." Virginia hated to have their young son subjected to such exhausting overwork; nevertheless, she admitted, "he will have to learn for he'll have to make his living 'by the sweat of his brow.'"[26]

Securing responsible domestic help was a never ending problem and there seemed to be intermittent friction between Virginia and her servants. She repeatedly complained about her cook neglecting her work. "I can do nothing with her—yet if she were to leave, we could get no one else." Months later, Virginia was still annoyed with her kitchen help "poor cooking" (after all her directions), "clothes poorly done up." Employee theft was a common occurrence, but a loss that had to be tolerated in order to retain workers. "Tis so worrying to be surrounded by creatures you cannot trust," Virginia chafed.[27] Lacking servants, the Aiken daughters were assigned the distasteful tasks of "emptying the slops" and "bringing in the water." In desperation Virginia confessed, "I do feel so discouraged & like giving up."[28]

Occasionally the Aikens sat down to evaluate the "servant problem." "Mr. Aiken & I sat up late talking over the difficulty of getting on with or without servants. Mr. A. thinks we all ought to work more & perhaps if I ever get done having children, I may be able to work more, but in my present situation I am so miserably uncomfortable all the time I can do no more & the children all have much to do."[29]

On occasion Virginia was coerced into giving her help additional money in order to keep the peace. Contracts often proved worthless. One girl took leave when her father sent for her to come home to help pick cotton. Clara gathered up her child and her belongings and left in a huff after being accused of taking five cents. Although she later returned, she and another houseservant left at the end of January in 1873 despite their agreement to remain throughout the year.

The problems of what to do about newly freed blacks who had become a liability when their family and friends totally abandoned them to seek more lucrative work in distant areas compounded Virginia's troubles. With no younger people left to care for them in the slave quarters and their former owners financially unable to provide food, clothing or medical help to sustain them, some aged, infirm blacks had to be carted off to the poor house. Virginia's diary merely duplicates the accounts of other diarists who were forced to carry their aged former servants to asylums. "We sent Aunt Winny to the poor house ... there was no one to wait on her—she being the only colored person in the yard."[30] However, Aunt Winny was apparently not sent away sans raiment, for Virginia noted, "I have been sewing for Aunt Winny all day."

Postwar financial problems kept untold numbers of veterans, David Aiken included, on edge and at first preoccupied with simply eking out a living to support their families. Financial woes rendered countless husbands exhausted and indifferent to minor household concerns and annoying mother-child squabbles. Their support systems gone awry, women discovered they must more or less "go it alone." They themselves were forced to assume almost sole responsibility for the upbringing and disciplining of their children. Virginia's husband was often away from home for weeks at a time, and evenings at home were often spent working late into the night on proceedings of the State Agricultural Society, on Grange activities, or on columns for the *Rural Carolinian*. All too often the least little husbandly praise or appreciation, which would have done wonders for flagging egos, went unspoken. David Aiken's unsympathetic attitude, as Virginia broached the subjects of domestic help or problems with the children, was reflected in his brusque dismissal of the topic as he announced that it was time to go to sleep and "now don't let's talk on that subject if you please." The following day Virginia was in the depths of despair: "I lose all spirit & feel as if I would almost rather not live."[31] Often times Virginia lashed out in her diary at men's unreasonableness in "not seeing and appreciating all the work women do."

Virginia's self-esteem suffered further blows from what she saw as the rudeness and impudence of her children. Of course, mothers throughout the ages have complained of being unappreciated by their offspring.

Virginia Aiken was no exception. "I feel as if I am a mere cipher in my own house—run over by the children & servants." Their childish disrespect became yet another source of vexation for Virginia.

Fairs and the Grange

Household and family responsibilities clearly took center stage in Virginia's life; however, upon occasion local fairs and the activities of the Grange provided Virginia a welcome relief from the tedium of routine. As possibly part of his work for the Grange, or as a result of his great interest in agriculture, or perhaps with a possible political career in mind, or just for enlightenment or entertainment, Virginia's husband devoted days and weeks to the fairs. Although at first the fairs constituted a novelty for Virginia, she soon grew to resent his long absences from home and the expenses involved in her husband's participation. "I get discouraged, disheartened & disgusted...besides if Mr. Aiken only got paid for his services, I wouldn't mind it.... I just feel that he is taking bread out of the children's mouths to devote as much of his time (which is money) to an ungrateful public."[32] Proud that her husband and daughters took "premiums" at several exhibits at the fairs, Virginia was dismayed that her neighbors were jealous of their awards.

The fair season left Virginia with "too much responsibility when he is away. I am always glad when the season for the fairs are over for I have such a hard time. Mr. A goes away & takes the cook & all other help away & leaves the feeding & looking after stock to the children's care & then the wood & meat, meal & all other supplies give out & we just live from hand to mouth, not knowing one meal what we will eat the next."[33]

How Virginia could feel lonely at times with a houseful of young children is somewhat difficult to understand; however, the frequent absences of her husband on business trips and in his work with the newly formed Grange in South Carolina left Virginia feeling exasperated and resentful. "Oh! I so wish he could make a living for us by staying at home. I do have such a hard time when he is away for his back isn't turned till something goes wrong—the servants do as they please."[34]

The formation of a branch of the Order of the Patrons of Husbandry, the Grange, organized near the Aikens in April of 1872, provided an excellent outlet for David Aiken's agricultural interests and expertise, and in addition furnished Virginia with an opportunity for at least a few social gatherings away from the dreariness of household responsibilities. (The Grange, organized in Washington in 1867 for the purpose of pursuing advancements in agriculture and contributing to the education of farmers, captured the interest of hundreds of thousands of farmers and planters in both the North and the South. Within four years after its establishment in South Carolina in 1871 there were 350 local groups in the state. Virginia's husband was one of the leaders of the Grange movement and traveled extensively giving speeches and helping to organize new chapters throughout the state.

From its inception the Grange admitted women as equals with men, a unique feature which offered a much needed, socially approved camaraderie, as well as rewarding creative and social outlets for many overburdened farm women. Virginia's husband appears to have been one of the organizers of the Grange chapter at Bethlehem (La Purda Grange) and Virginia was enrolled as a charter member. At one of her first meetings in May, Virginia commented that it had been a "right pleasant meeting," but added, "The trouble with me is, I haven't time to spare to attend these meetings—tho' 1 think that is one good the order will do—give we poor hard working housekeepers a little recreation."[35]

Now and then Virginia became conscious of her enviable position in contrast to some of her less fortunate friends. One acquaintance had eight children and no help at all. Virginia's problems involving building her own fires, helping make the lard and sausage at hog killing time, canning endless jars of fruit and vegetables, boiling up jams and jelly, churning for three hours without success, allocating the allowances to the freedmen, arguing endlessly with neighbors over broken fences and straying livestock, tackling the mountains of sewing and mending, coping with the breakdown of their wagons and carriages, sustaining the crucial loss of a cow, all became minor complaints following the visit to a widowed friend with five little children—four of them sick in bed the day of her call. Virginia counted her blessings after her afternoon with her poor penniless friend struggling along alone, without a soul to help her.[36]

හ

Virginia Aiken may well have put up a good "front" for her family and friends; however, her diary tells a different story, that of a frenzied woman trying desperately to struggle through the vicissitudes of life in the post Civil War world. In reading Virginia Aiken's diary the reader becomes vicariously engrossed in the trials and anxieties weathered by the mother of a large family of young children, a woman whose personal domestic problems are complicated by the growing frustrations and consequent ill humor of her despondent husband. Actually, it would appear Virginia's complaints about her husband's preoccupation with his work were well-founded. During the postwar years her husband became increasing involved in politics and agricultural reform. From 1864 to 1866 he served as a representative in the South Carolina House. He was an energetic supporter of the Democratic party and consistently at odds with the Radical Republicans. In addition he was part owner and frequent essayist for the *Rural Carolinian.* Aiken organized a state Grange in South Carolina 1872, served on the national executive committee of the Grange in 1873, and headed the South Carolina Grange from 1875–1877. In 1876 he represented the Third District in Congress, where he continued to serve for many years. In Congress Aiken crusaded for tax reduction and elevating of the Department of Agriculture to Cabinet status. According to *American National Biography,* "he was widely acknowledged as the preeminent spokesman for the agrarian interests of the post–Civil War South."

The war had left the Aikens adrift in a welter of financial reverses, and at times Virginia appeared to be ready to give up on life itself. Although desperate for some even minuscule emotional support from her husband, the assistance of reliable help, the gaiety of a few hours of pleasure or release from her onerous household responsibilities, Virginia held fast to her daily routine. The reader can only hope that the social activities of the Grange, an improvement in their financial condition, the maturation of her children, and the rewards of her husband's successful political career would in time provide some well deserved happiness and relaxation. Indeed, Virginia was not alone in her cares and onerous responsibilities—her situation replicated that of thousands of Southern women in the postwar world.

୨ **11** ଓ

Anna Logan: From Affluence to Desperation

By the end of the war an idyllic life (on a twelve hundred acre plantation on the banks of the James River about forty miles from Richmond, Virginia), had eroded to a life of confusion and desperation for the James Logan family. Vivid impressions of the woeful plight of farmers and their families in the postwar world surface with persistent regularity throughout the pages of Anna Clayton Logan's memoir, "Recollections of My Life." Born in 1842 in Goochland County, Virginia, Anna was one of the Logans' eleven children. In antebellum times the family lived happily and comfortably at their plantation, "Dungeness," where two hundred slaves helped produce the bountiful cotton and sugar cane crops. Life was replete with parties, company, travel, and family activities. The war, of course, turned that world of comfort and luxury upside-down.

News of Lee's surrender, although slow in coming, was not unexpected. "We could hear the fighting going on, but had no news," Anna recalled. "We were so anxious about the boys [two of Anna's brothers were serving with the Confederate forces nearby] and our army. On April 9th General Robert E. Lee surrendered to General Grant. This sad news was brought to us by a straggler. We knew it was inevitable. Our soldiers, people and prisoners were starving and exhausted, dropping by the wayside as they marched. Where were our boys? We watched and prayed for them with anxious eyes."[1]

Fortunately Anna's two brothers survived the war. However, a $10,000 debt acquired years before the war (the money having enabled

"Ruined!" (*Harper's Weekly*, November 13, 1869.)

her father to purchase adjoining land), in addition to her father's inability to collect $30,000 owed him, plus insurmountable problems securing laborers brought the family to the brink of starvation themselves. "Our future was like Egyptian darkness. Our father and mother were helpless, with eleven children, only two educated, and no income. The servants had to be fed. They could not go. The liberal Federal government failed to keep the promise of 'forty-acres and a mule.' So they were a great care to us."[2]

"When we felt they were becoming a burden, we persuaded them to hire out," Anna remembered. "Our house servants were so well trained and well known, as our house had always been full, that they had no trouble finding new homes. Soon we were with no help. We had to bring in our wood and do our cleaning, and all the children helped. Everything was so hard on my parents. My father had no profession having been a planter. There was no business; everything was disorganized. I shuddered then with apprehension and shudder now at the recollection of the horrors."[3]

With the pervasive shortage of money in the South few Southerners could collect on old debts, and suddenly the Logans found themselves in imminent danger of losing their home. The Logans were in a bind—the $30,000 owed her father was impossible to collect and with no income there was little hope of paying off their indebtedness. In a last ditch effort to save their property (the owner of the mortgage had put out notices for the sale of their home), Anna hurried to Richmond to present their case to General Stoneman. As Anna ardently pled her case, the general listened attentively, and sympathetically granted an injunction. For at least a few more months the Logans could count on a roof over their heads!

"I wish I could blot out those horrible days," Anna wrote. "My parents found it hard to adjust themselves to the new regime. Bereft of every comfort, we had no money, no labor, no schools. Our friends were scattered. Our beautiful lands lay idle, and we were on the verge of starvation."[4] Anna's mother barely kept the family fed by sending Anna's younger brother to a jeweler in town each day with a silver spoon or fork, for which he received ninety cents.

Despite their poverty the Logans faithfully adhered to the Southern tradition of unstinting hospitality. Vast numbers of returning soldiers camped on the Logans' land en route home. At one time a regiment, or what was left of it, remained for three weeks. At one time the family's sympathies were extended to an elderly cousin who came in search of his son, wounded at the Battle of the Crater, and who remained with them for several months. His pitiful—and futile—search mirrored that of countless fathers frantic to find some word of a fallen boy. "He could not find his son at Petersburg, so came to us. Poor man, he asked every passing soldier if he could tell him of his son. After many weeks, the news came that his son had died of his wound. Even then, he stayed on, unable to communicate with his family in Lancaster. Finally, my father let him have the money, $40, with which he bought a horse and left for home. We were sorry to see him go."[5]

In the midst of their travail, however, there was a bright spot that would live forever as a cherished memory. Indeed, it was a very special afternoon when general Robert E. Lee returned the call of Anna's father and brothers and took lunch with the Logans. Anna's singing brought tears to the General's eyes and his "Thank you, my child" and the appreciative touch of his hand on her shoulder, for the moment, helped dispel the pall of gloom that had enveloped the Southland. "All of us were completely at sea as to our future, but we endeavored to forget in this never to be forgotten hour."[6]

The same loathing expressed by untold numbers of former Confederates over the rule of the provost marshals and the same bitterness over what Southerners considered the cruel incarceration of Jefferson Davis resounded in Anna's reminiscences. "The Provost Marshalls who were very common men made themselves most detestable. We felt an injustice of this treatment and the indignities put on our President. General Grant acted the gentleman in his terms of surrender to General Lee and soldiers, but I see little humanity in loading President Davis with irons, even if one viewed him as a traitor."[7]

As it turned out the Logans discovered that some Northerners were not all bad. Apprised of the dire straits of their suffering, friends and countless compassionate Northerners dispensed aid in the form of clothing and basic food supplies. "Only our northern friends offered a helping hand. One friend heard that our house had burned and came to find us, bringing food and clothes. Another New York friend sent us a sewing machine, the first I ever saw. It cost $300. Our southern friends seemed to resent our acceptance of these gifts, but had they been offered to them their viewpoint might have changed."[8]

In time things began looking up for the Logans when a cousin notified Anna of a teaching position in Salem, Virginia, and urged her to apply for it. Anna was overjoyed to be accepted, and particularly to have her sister Jeanie appointed as her assistant. In Salem Anna was successful with her school and "Dungeness" was soon sold to satisfy debts ("'at less than half its value'"). Shortly thereafter Anna's parents and most of the family moved to Salem.

Lacking money the Logans and thousands of other Southern families turned to bartering. When Anna's mother took in boarders to help defray expenses, one "guest" paid his bill in groceries and by selling a feather bed. Thanks to her teaching position, Anna was able to send two of her brothers to Roanoke College in exchange for taking two girls to study with her.

Fortunately, better days lay ahead for Anna when in 1869 she met a cousin (Robert H. Logan) whom she married two years later. However, proud Anna insisted that she extricate herself from debt before she would marry.

℘

In her memoirs Anna depicted a radically different change in lifestyles from her carefree antebellum days on their James River plantation home. As the war began Anna had completed her education at Miss Mead's school and was about to make her debut into Richmond society. Four years later the family scarcely knew where their next meal was coming from. Their home was being put up for sale to satisfy indebtedness, their servants had departed, their mother was reduced to taking in boarders, and Anna and her sister took teaching positions and gave music lessons to enable the family to survive. Unfortunately the Logan family's situation was certainly not unique in the annals of postwar Southern history.

ॐ **12** ॐ

Jo Gillis:
Preacher's Wife

ॐ) Ministers in particular experienced great difficulties in eking out a living for themselves and their families in the post-war world. With money either non-existent or in extremely short supply, countless Southerners, teetering on the brink of starvation, were hard put to support their immediate families, to say nothing of making even the most paltry contributions to their churches. Margaret Josephine Miles Gillis apparently self-sacrificed herself into her grave attempting to struggle along on the paltry income secured by her husband, the Reverend Neil Gillis, a Methodist Episcopal minister in the Alabama Conference.

The pages of Jo Gillis's diary tell the tale of a young mother straining under the incessant anxieties involved in the care of a sickly baby, coping with the depressed circumstances enveloping most ministers in the aftermath of the war; and endeavoring to discover a sliver of dignity for herself as the wife of what appeared to be an unappreciative, insensitive, often absentee husband. During her husband's periods of service as a circuit rider, Jo was left alone for long periods of time as her husband made the rounds of the churches in his district ministering to the needs of the parishioners. The work, although spiritually rewarding, was certainly not financially remunerative. Jo confessed in her diary that during some months she and her husband, who had served as chaplain with the Alabama Volunteers during the war, were dismayed to find that the congregations did not pay the Reverend Gillis enough to compensate them for more than their food.

ॐ

The end of the war signaled the beginning of bleak times for Jo Gillis. On January 22, 1865, Jo wrote: "As regards the war this seems the darkest time we have had. Pres. Davis against the views of almost every other man in the Confederacy relieved Joseph E. Johnston from the command of the Ten. Army, and put Hood in his place, and all has gone wrong ever since, 'till most the whole country nearly seems demoralized."

After a lapse of nine months, Jo, in October of 1865, took up her diary writing again. "Since I made my last entry oh! how changed everything has become. At the top of this page I said that was a dark hour for us but how much darker has it become. The Yankees have triumphed and we are now a downtrodden and oppressed people. The second day of April the Yankees took Selma and staid there a week burning portions of the city. I left Mr. Middleton's and came home to stay with the children [probably nieces and nephews] as Pa wanted to take his stock and get out of the way. April 10th six thousand Yanks marched up the wire road enroute for Montgomery, meeting with no resistance from our flying, demoralized cavalry."

The threat of a Union takeover and possible atrocities terrified an already apprehensive Jo—as well as most of the rest of the countryside. "Oh! I can never forget that week," she shuddered. "Mr. Gillis and Pa took the stock off, and Pollie, Leila, Bet and I were left here alone. The negroes were constantly running to us telling us tales of barbarity and cruelty, such as stripping the women to find their valuables, and whipping them, and other things more barbarous. Oh! what a miserable week. We were hourly expecting them here, but thank the good Lord they never came, although within a few minutes of us all the time. We could look out at any time of night and see all the flames of burning buildings."

"Then came the *awful* news that we were subjugated," Jo continued, "and our President in the hands of the enemy, and he is still a prisoner, his fate doubtful. Our property destroyed, negroes freed and no law or order. This is the present state of affairs."

Not being farmers the Gillises were exempt from the field-labor problems that engulfed most of the Southland However, the emancipation of slaves following the war rendered reliable domestic help increasingly hard to come by. Jo's girlhood experiences in a family financially well-off enough to have several servants ill-equipped her for the rigors of housekeeping—cooking, cleaning, washing, and ironing—or for the demanding responsibilities of attending their "delicate, fussy baby." Frustrated by inexperience Jo lamented: "Keeping house for myself is very difficult from keeping house for Pa. There I had servants that we were accustomed to and though *free* we could get *something* out of them."[1]

At rare intervals the Gillis family was fortunate enough to procure the services of temporary help. However, even those days left Jo exhausted and discouraged. Incensed by her "free negro" servants who left her kitchen in shambles each evening after preparing dinner, Jo wished "the Yanks *had* the free negroes strung around their necks and *all* in the bottom of the arctic ocean covered over with ice a hundred feet thick."[2]

Jo's annoyance with her "help" continued unabated. "The white people may work themselves to death to make some thing to eat and the trifling negroes laying round doing nothing, expecting big wages, and stealing all the white people can make to save their lives."[3]

With so little money coming in and so much being expended, Jo was further irritated by the constant complaints from the "hands" about wages. "Mr. G made a contract with a boy fifteen years old to give him six dollars a month, provisions, and one suit of clothes. (The best hands about here are only getting ten ($10) per month and rations.) This boy is very trifling, eats just what we have, and gets whatever he asks for, was this morning grumbling about his wages." Conceding defeat she despaired to her diary: "Oh! deliver me, deliver me from free negroes. I wish I could go where I would never see or hear of another."[4]

Earlier, despite her husband's wishes to the contrary, Jo had taught school in an attempt to help with the family's finances. This "independence" infuriated her husband who was extremely hurt by "her perversity." In a January 22, 1865, "catch up" entry in her diary Jo explained that she had opened a school in November of 1864 and taught for three months. "I have a very pleasant little school, and if I could always have a pleasant boarding house, had rather teach than do any thing else in the world, but Mr. G. says I shall never take another school." Despite Jo's confession of her great love of teaching, her husband was extremely reluctant to allow her to teach, and only begrudgingly consented to her once again conducting a school, apparently for a very short time, in 1867.

Since teaching school met with such violent opposition from her husband, Jo sought to secure a small return by selling some of her fancywork. However, even that venture met with failure—people simply did not have ready money to spend on anything other than necessities. "The people," she noted, "found my 'embroidery superior to any they ever saw' but they could not *buy* it."[5]

And yet the church women, Jo complained, had no qualms about making excessive, uncompensated demands on Jo's time and effort, simply because she was the "preacher's wife." "I must work *all* the time for other people for nothing," Jo observed. "They wanted me to do some work for them however, and I was their 'preacher's wife.' I could not refuse. My own work must be neglected...."[6]

Jo was consumed with self-doubts that manifest themselves in a morbid preoccupation over possible criticism from members of her husband's congregations. Poor Jo was terrified that people might be saying "'Ah!

Mrs. Gillis dont suit for a preacher's wife.' *God knows I know it*," she despaired, "but he also knows I do all I can." Jo admitted that the people had been "very kind to me in their way, but it does seem that people can *require* more of me than they do of any body else in the world."[7]

For at least four years, in the interests of economy, Jo denied herself any new clothes, for "it has taken all we could do to keep Mr. Gillis decently clad to appear before the public." The Rev. Gillis appeared to be inordinately focused on his own career and oblivious to the desperate condition of his wife's wardrobe. Embarrassed by her unsuitable clothing for church, she tried to hide her feelings from her husband. "He thinks I feel very comfortable and nice in my old sun bonnet at church. I do not desire finery and the surplus clothes I used to have, but I *do* want enough to keep me decent; even the plainest kind I would be satisfied. And if I could get paid for my work I could have this at least."[8]

In 1868 after yet another expensive, unsettling move, Jo wept into her diary: "This has been a year of suffering and toil. God alone knows what I *have* suffered. My darling baby has been sick the whole year—well only a few weeks at a time. He has been at the point of death several times. I have hardly known what it was to be well myself, still I have been obliged to toil and go through rain and heat, when I ought to have been in the bed. No one can know what I have suffered except a *woman* who has suffered the same, and through it all—Oh! God I wont write it."[9]

Their situation appeared almost hopeless as Jo glumly reflected: "Some times my spirit is weighed down with heaviness, and my lot in life seems *hard*, hard. God in heaven knows I *desire* to do my whole duty, but sometimes it does *not* seem right that I should be put upon by every body—not that I have been unkindly treated by any one but it seems the world is against me. Oh! most merciful Father help me to bear my trials."[10]

Committed to his calling as a minister, Jo's husband unstintingly devoted his time and energies to preaching despite the unrewarding financial returns. (The straitened conditions of ministers following the war was corroborated by Lucy Fletcher, a Richmond minister's wife, who saw their family finances dwindle drastically after the war. With the destruction of their church at the time of the occupation of Richmond, Lucy's husband decided to open a school in order to make ends meet. "Evidently ministers all over the South were suffering extreme economic hardships," she wrote.[11])

"I dont see how we are to live," Jo fretted. "Mr. Gillis thinks it his duty to preach and not for the world would I raise my voice against it. I *want* him to do good if he can, but the people seem no longer to care for preaching or preachers. They do not pay Mr. Gillis enough to pay his board. Misfortunes follow us. My poor husband worked himself nearly to death last year and came out deeply in debt."[12]

Unfortunately the new circuit in Conecuh County, Alabama, which Jo observed to be "poor" and "broken down," led to even more work and even less income for Jo and her husband. "Itinerating is harder and harder to stand. I would love to do good, but I cant for my life see how the ministers can remain in the Conference unless they just give their families over to starvation. I have been hungry *many* times this year because we had nothing but *fat* bacon and cornbread, and being sick [pregnant] my stomach turned from that."[13] Adding to the family's woes was "a tale going that the people ought not to pay any thing toward supporting Mr. Gillis, that his table is loaded with luxuries all the time."

Homebound and lonesome Jo admitted that the circuit was a difficult one, and she, as have women since time immemorial, accused her husband of having given his work "his whole time to the utter neglect of his home and family." Jo cried out for mercy: "God help this world, for it seems that destruction, ruin, and starvation stares us in the face."[14]

For Jo her diary was her confidante, an outlet for her trials and pent up emotions. During the long absences of her husband, Jo's diary was her best friend, her "listening ear." For Jo writing provided a momentary release from her stress-filled existence. However, it took relatively little time for her hardships as the wife of a Circuit Rider to take their toll. Plagued by hunger, overwork, her own delicate health, as well as that of her baby, Jo Gillis penned her last diary entry in September of 1868. Seven months pregnant and sleepless and exhausted from having spent the night nursing her desperately ill baby, Jo was heartsick when her husband casually announced that he would be "home very little from now till Conference." "*God have mercy on me,*" Jo anguished. "I know not *what* to do. I feel sometimes like reason will *certainly* be dethroned. This may be the last entry I shall ever make in my journal, and were I to express all my feelings they would be dark as mid-night."[15]

The frustrations of lack of money, lack of food, and perhaps most important of all lack of appreciation bore down heavily on Jo Gillis. On November 11, 1868, Jo gave birth to her second child. Ten days later Jo was dead—less than six years following her marriage and less than a month before her twenty-ninth birthday.

৪১

Perhaps it might be argued that the rigors of postwar life in Alabama were not entirely responsible for Jo's unhappiness. Some might call Jo the victim of an inferiority complex, a persecution complex, a martyr's complex, postwar depression, overwork, underappreciation, poor mental or physical health. But under whatever terminology Jo's miseries were no less agonizing for her. Her piteous outcries of distress can only tug at the heart.

ஐ 13 ଓ

Sally Perry: Plaintive Cries of Pain

The appalling list of war casualties obviously produced tens of thousands of lonely, long suffering, poverty stricken widows. Single-parent families so prevalent a century later were a ubiquitous feature of the postwar scene. Sally Randle Perry, whose husband, John, was killed at the Battle of Sharpsburg, reflected the despair, the anxieties, and the financial difficulties experienced by countless women widowed as a result of the war. Sally's plantation, "Ingleside," in Dallas County, Alabama, where she resided with her two children, had become for her "Bleak House." Her grief seemed overwhelming "and now I'm a widow. Ah! That mournful word. Little the world think[s] of the agony it contains!"[1]

The solitude of her late evening diary-keeping brought on rushes of sadness and apprehension. "I am lonely tonight," she told her journal. "My spirit is weary with Life's bitter struggles." To Sally the future appeared ominous. "And what hath the Future in store for me? Not a slight ray of light sheds its beam upon my pathway. How fickle a goddess is Fortune?"[2]

Grieving over the loss of her husband and further depressed by the surrender, Sally mourned the fearful toll of war dead, "a long ghostly band to haunt my memory." One would hope that Sally could summon a cheerier demeanor with her children; however, at night, alone with her thoughts, Sally was tormented by a barrage of melancholy reveries. Never long separated from thoughts of "the dear sleeper near the shores of the far-off Potomac," Sally was convinced that those who had given their

283

"I Can Not Sing the Old Songs." (*Harper's Weekly*, May 16, 1868.)

lives early in the war had been happy "believing they had left their country free. Those martyr dead had made doubly sacred the soil upon [which] their blood was spilled. The country that gave birth to such Patriots will surely rise again, Phoenix-like, purified from the ashes of the Past."[3]

Time and time again reality blurred as Sally relived the painful last good-bye with her husband at the Midway Pine—"the spot where I last parted with poor John as he left for the army. How well I remember that evening! How handsome he looked in his grey uniform & how I stood watching him as he dashed away. I listened sadly to the last sound of 'Nellie's' hoofs in the distance & when no longer heard I returned with my little ones to our now lonely home!"[4]

Sally found it difficult—if not impossible—to reconcile herself to the collapse of the Confederacy. "But the great Rebellion has been crushed. Our people feel the weight of the Conqueror's chain, and the iron has entered into the soul."[5] For Sally life under Yankee rule seemed insufferable.

The imprisonment and later trial of Jefferson Davis particularly angered Southerners. To them it was just one more Yankee oppression. With Sally it certainly proved to be a sore spot. "Our noble President languished years in the cold fortress of Monroe—and is even now in the capital (Richmond of our late Confederacy) on a trial for treason. *Treason*—it were as well to try every man, woman and child in the South—and exterminate the race at once. If he is guilty, we all are alike so. 'O Liberty, how many crimes are committed in thy name!'"[6]

Politics and governmental affairs during the Johnson and Radical reconstructions, of course, had taken a horrendous turn for the former rebels. The very idea of former slaves voting and being elected to office when their former owners were denied the privilege bred further bitterness and enmity among Southerners. The convention held in Montgomery in 1867 was especially disturbing to Sally. "What strange things do happen in this world of ours. Today in Ala—a slave state—a convention is being held in Montgomery—a motley crew (negroes & whites) elected by the negroes and renegades. What a mockery! What a humiliation for a proud people."[7] A year later Sally became further discouraged. "We have nothing bright to look upon either in the present or future. The political horizon is as black *as midnight*, as black as the hearts of those traitors who are bringing ruin upon us."[8]

From Sally's point of view the political scene looked bleak indeed. "The mongrel crew who lately assembled in convention in Montgomery have adjourned after having used every effort to fasten the vilest indignity upon our unhappy state. Verily much has been done to strengthen the *loyalty* of our people. We are indeed fallen in the South when *thieves* & adventurers from the *North*—traitors & renegades in the South—our former *slaves,* are allowed to disgrace the halls of our State House. O Justice! where is the sword! Liberty is dead. She breathed her last on Southern soil when Gen Lee surrendered his sword trusting to the honor of a Yankees blighted sword."[9]

Sally repeatedly echoed the South's denigration of carpetbaggers and Radicals. "After the war these Northern vultures still hover over the fair lands of the South to prey upon a helpless people. A political war of races has been begun.... O God where will it all end?"[10]

The pervasive loathing of Yankees that was felt by Sally and the older generation filtered own to even the youngest of children. The youngsters in Sally's home were sure that even Santa Claus had become a victim of Yankee predators. Young son John spread the word: "Did you know Santa Claus had been robbed? The Yankees stole all his money and cotton and darkies! I intend to ask the first Yankee about this that I meet in Selma!" "Poor child," Sally added, "He had been very much disturbed about this robbery. I fear he will have more cause still to be indignant, when he knows something of the wrongs of his country."[11]

Bringing up children alone in the turbulent postwar world was no easy task. Guilt-ridden, Sally berated herself for her lapses of patience with her children. Was she being too strict or too lenient? Was she inculcating the right values in her children? Were they developing the right moral standards? Deprived of a father were they becoming too effeminate? Was she overly protective? Were they receiving a proper education? Was she encouraging responsiblity, integrity, consideration in her youngsters?

These and hosts of other questions gnawed at Sally's conscience by day and murdered her sleep at night. "I have been out of humor all day—as irritable as if every nerve was on edge as it were. There are times and with temperament like mine when the slightest things will jar. I'm always saddened and remorseful after yielding to such feelings & still I yield again and again.... I cannot assimilate sufficiently to surrounding circumstances.... I wish I was different from myself—an adaption to circumstances is often conducive to our happiness.... Dreary & impatient & impulsive—no wonder that I'm so often miserable!"[12]

Parenting was understandably a monumental concern for Sally. "I feel so anxious about my children. I fear I do not possess that influence over them that I would wish. They obey as well as most children of their ages & I believe love their Mother. I fear that I have not enough patience with them—am too often irritable. Heaven knows I need so much of discipline myself, that I illy guide others. Suffering & sorrow is the pruning knife in the hands of God with which he lops off each excrescence of sin and shapes a human soul near his own."[13]

As the weeks passed Sally appeared to become more and more reclusive. Days passed with little to break the monotony of routine. Visiting and receiving callers held less and less interest for Sally. "This year I have communed less with the external world than I ever remember to have done before, and I suffer from the night."[14]

Memories of the happy days of earlier times continued to cloud Sally's every thought as she recalled: "But two short yrs ago her [Fortune's] favors were showered upon me. Now how changed. I am wicked to repine I know," she confessed. "Surely our God doeth all things well, but at times even His face seems hidden, and I grope my way in the darkness, oh! so desolate. And again my heart is filled with bitterness, and then I become almost reckless." All too often depression overwhelmed Sally. "At such hours were it not for the little ones entrusted to my care, Heaven alone knows what would become of me. In desperation Sally queried "Oh! how full this world is of sorrow and pain! Why do we cling to it?"[15]

As the days dragged on in numbing, vacuous succession, Sally's loneliness seemed to escalate rather than subside. "Wild, restless, impatient unhappy spirit, will you never cease your plaintive cries of pain, and vain longing for what is not? My eyes in vain seek to pierce the gloom which envelopes my life. There is no hope to cling to in the future—nothing for the weary foothold in the present and heartsick my soul still continues her search for peace!"[16]

On occasion Sally's grief and despondency gave test to her religious faith. Understandably, she sometimes was hard pressed to accept her husband's death, the demise of the Confederacy, and her troubled days as

Sally's faith (handwritten margin note)

manifestations of God's will. "Peace—blessed peace, shall I ever find it? Would that I could hear those words from on High—'Peace, my peace give I unto you,' then indeed would the wild waves of unrest be stayed."[17]

At other times her religious faith was Sally's sole comfort. "Well our God surely doeth all things well. His mercies are often in disguise." Sally sent constant appeals Heavenward in the hope that she would be able to "take up my cross daily & follow Him." In her increasingly frequent moments of helplessness she petitioned God: "O Thou, who art all Love & Mercy, look down in tender pity on earth's erring ones! Be Thou my strength, my guide & and my salvation; stand by me in the hour of trial & give me strength to resist the Evil One." The stress of daily life brought on "an intense longing for that land where the 'wicked cease from troubling and the weary are at rest.' O my Father, I pray that my steps may ever tend towards that happy land!"[18]

The opportunity for a house in Autaugaville, closer to her parents, proved tempting; however, the decision presented a serious dilemma. "Pa has returned from Autaugaville & says he has rented a house there. Ma is anxious that I should go there with my little ones another year, but I can not decide. I can not bear the thought of remaining on the plantation, filled as it will be, with strange negroes & still the thought of leaving home is inexpressibly sad. If the old srvts were here, I would feel secure—as it is, I know not what to do."[19]

During the war Sally had remained on the plantation "and no thought of fear ever disturbed me. The svts were never more kind, obedient and attentive to my slightest wish, than when all alone." Letters from Sally's husband were read to an eager audience of servants, all of whom wished to be remembered to him and hoped for his speedy return. Each had contributed some small token to be packed in the numerous boxes sent to their master on the battlefield. "When the news came that he had fallen, a wail arose from every little cabin. Often, before this—at night, I could hear old Uncle Harry (the old black preacher) praying at prayer meeting for 'Mars John' to come home once more."[20]

Such love (handwritten margin note)

Strong ties of loyalty had existed between Sally and her former servants. In fact Sally felt a deep debt of gratitude to one of the men who, as Wilson's Raiders were terrorizing the countryside, had brought a warning that enabled Sally to save "all the stock on the place." With all the able-bodied men in the army it was a frightening time for a woman to be alone on an isolated plantation It was also the time of a great display of fidelity on the part of Sally's corps of black men and women. "Old Uncle Harry hearing that the Yankees were coming, came tottering out on his old oaken stick," Sally recalled. "Came where I was standing & said—'Never mind Mistess—I'll stand right here & fight for you as long as I live.'"[21]

Whether Sally could ever become accustomed to the "new order of things" was questionable. In days gone by "we were accustomed to have around us the familiar faces, of svts who were born on the place—faces as familiar as those of our parents & and now each year is the signal for strange faces." Noting the "homing trend" of former servants, Sally was gravely disappointed when many of the old servants wished to return, yet had to be turned away. "I notice however that there is a universal tendency among the svts ever to return to their former homes & masters. Dick, who used to be a Foreman here, came a few days since & wished to bring all the old svts back, but he came too late, as the hands are already employed for the coming year."[22]

Gardening helped to occupy the lonely hours, but it too conjured up sad memories. "I must begin working my flower-beds next week. My strawberries too require extra labor just now. How I miss my old gardener 'Uncle Billy.' I miss his judicious care to make my garden again blossom as in days of yore. Ah! Those happy days of yore will never return again. What a pleasant home was mine, how happy I lived with my little ones among the svts, most of whom were born & many had grown gray on the old plantation." Sadly she added: "Ingleside is rapidly falling into a dilapidated condition. Alas! When can it ever be restored?"[23]

It was indeed a world turned topsy-turvy for Sally. With the departure of their servants Sally took over many of the household chores. "I'll commence house-keeping as if for the first time," Sally mused. "When I first married, I assumed control of a household of well-trained & experienced svts. I had nothing to do but to give orders & my wishes were executed. Now I must become acquainted with the practice as well as theory of a housewife's duties."[24]

For a woman heretofore totally unacquainted with the concept of "economy," the new age ushered in some revolutionary changes in Sally's life. In the absence of any nearby school Sally taught her children at home. The need to drastically reduce the family's expenses came as an unwelcome novelty to Sally. "Never have I known anything of want until now that *money* could furnish. My lessons of self-denial began *since* this war."[25]

The money crunch experienced by untold numbers of Southerners made vast inroads on Sally Perry's financial well-being. Unfortunately, business dealings held little interest for Sally. "Ah! that tiresome word business! Once the word had no meaning for me—now it is the synonym of all that is disagreeable," Sally complained.[26] In time disinterest and inexperience brought about serious consequences for the distracted Sally.

Inexperienced planters' wives, such as Sally, were prime candidates for disaster as they attempted to take over the role of plantation manager. When, where, what and how to plant, whether to rent, sell or struggle along against the forces of nature, crop failures, falling markets, "impressed" or dilapidated farm equipment, a worthless currency, and the influx of carpetbaggers were problems that challenged even the best of farmers.

In a world suddenly gone haywire Sally discovered that reliable advice about managing a plantation was hard to come by. Sally saw her hold on Ingleside slowly slipping away. "Life had so little of brightness for me that it seems a hollow mockery to make a happy face while my heart is full of tears. I have many things to trouble me now—the settlement of my business which has become much entangled in consequence of my bad management. I trusted too much on others when I should have depended alone on myself. Had I done this, how much better would it have been for me!"[27]

In relatively short order multitudinous problems culminated in immense losses for Sally and Ingleside. "Oh that I could now command one half the means that once were mine," Sally anguished.[28]

As the year (1867) drew to a close, a dispirited Sally struggled to get her life back together: "I am alone tonight—little ones are asleep. I sit & watch the dying of the year! O Time! What words can compute thy value & yet how lavishly we spend it, how recklessly throw it away. A few short hours & another year will have winged its flight to Eternity to appear as a virtue either for or against us!" In words reminiscent of Emerson in his poem "Days," as he chastised himself for failing to take advantage of the bountiful offerings each day presented, so Sally mourned the futility of her life. Pensively she continued: "Last thoughts rush upon me as the days of '67 rise successively before me. They pass me with averted faces as if more in sorrow than in anger—in sorrow that this mission to me has been all in vain."[29]

In the midst of her sorrows, the dawning of the new year was suddenly transformed into golden radiance as a bright sun broke through the clouds. "May this day be typical of this year which alas! is enveloped in clouds, but may yet show glimmers of sunlight at its close. I shall observe the omen whilst there is one ray of hope left."[30]

Some months later Sally, again consumed by grief, abandoned all hope. "Ingleside, dear Ingleside is tenanted by strangers—to be my home no more for many years."[31] Unable to shake her depression and as another new year approached Sally reflected on her inability "to have been able to have laid aside many little cares that troubled me last year by this time, but still new troubles spring up around my pathway. There are moments when I feel ready to sink in despair."[32]

At length Sally acknowledged that a move promised at least some release from her rapidly deteriorating situation. By spring Sally hoped to leave Alabama and find some quiet spot in Maryland where she could rear her children "to be what I would wish them to be."[33] Involved in a costly lawsuit, Sally expressed her bitterness at men so caught up with making money that they could make no allowances for those less fortunate. "'Tis strange that men, strong men—those who are able to go out & battle with the world, should still cling so strong to yellow gold, that they would still heap up their coffers with money robbed from the Orphan. What a fearful legacy they are entailing upon their children."[34]

In her last diary entry Sally appeared resigned to her sorrows. Even the weather seemed to personify her despondency. "This is a dreary day—typical of my life. The sun has hidden his face, and a mist of ... tears is softly falling."[35]

ϾϿ

And yet, in the midst of Sally's final paragraphs the reader is offered a glimmer of hope for a brighter tomorrow in the days to come. As Sally played with her children and joined in their merriment, at least for the moment, there appeared a ray of sunshine: "My spirit caught for a brief while the contagion of glee as I entered with a zest into their innocent sports."[36] The compassionate reader can only hope that somehow that momentary spark would augur a future replete with happier, more rewarding days for the desolate, bereaved Sally.

Epilogue

Some Southerners still look back in anger at the Civil War and Reconstruction. Some still feel a deep-seated bitterness, fostered by myth or fact, over the North's refusal to let Southerners leave the Union and carry out their own lives, over the maneuverings of the Radical Republicans, over what they consider to have been the North's unconscionable vengeance against the former rebels.

Heated conversations still rage over battles, strategies, racial problems, Yankees, Radical politics, carpetbaggers, and scalawags. The "ifs" of the Civil War and Reconstruction continue to challenge the imagination. What if England and France had sided with the Confederacy? What if the South's persistence had worn out the North? Would the postwar years have been different had Lincoln lived? How would the former slaves' situation have changed had the newly freed men been granted their "forty acres and a mule?" Could racism have been moderated by a more gradual emancipation replete with education and training for the newly freed men and women? What if the women's suffrage leaders had succeeded in obtaining voting rights for women as a part of the Fifteenth Amendment? What if the Radicals had not been so deeply committed to restructuring the South? What if Thaddeus Stevens and Charles Summer had chosen careers other than politics? What if the Radicals had not given up their crusade for the blacks? Could an 1865 "Marshall Plan" have helped pave the way to recovery? Could the Fourteenth and Fifteenth amendments been passed at that time had it not been for Radical Reconstruction? (Historians logically contend that the amendments could certainly not have been enacted without the Radicals. From the vituperation leveled against the Yankees and the African Americans in most of the excerpts here included, their points seem to be well-taken. Clearly the planters and the yeomen—many of the latter clung to their whiteness as their dearest personal possession—were adamant and often violent in their reluctance to accept the black man as their equals.) The "what ifs" aside, over the years, the South has had to live with its mistakes and its successes.

The Civil War had lasted for four years, Reconstruction for twelve years, three times as long as the war itself. Reconstruction ended with what some historians call the Bargain of 1877, whereby the Republican Rutherford B. Hayes was declared the winner of the hotly disputed election. (There were serious accusations of voting irregularities in Florida, South Carolina, and Louisiana.) The agreement was predicated on the understanding that Hayes would end federal intervention in the South. Reconstruction was officially over, but unfortunately many Americans continued to carry Reconstruction baggage with them for years to come.

Each of us finds it hard to love the person who bests us in a fight or in a verbal duel. We are not eager to humble our pride and keep company with the victor, and we surely hate to be reminded of the error of our ways, punished for our misdeeds and policed for fear of any further mischief on our part. It was a Herculean effort—often an impossible one— for Southerners to accept defeat devoid of bitterness and antagonism, to let bygones be bygones. For Southerners the road to recovery looked formidable.

Overall during those eventful twelve years of Reconstruction both Southern whites and Southern blacks chalked up important gains and losses. On the plus side the advances for the nation as a result of the war and Reconstruction are enormous. Slavery was abolished, the two sections were at least cosmetically reunited as one, the Fourteenth and Fifteenth amendments were enacted, education for both Negroes and whites was greatly expanded in the South, important Negro colleges were founded, the blacks began making their first steps toward independence and social equality.

In several areas the freedmen organized societies to purchase homes and lands that they could farm themselves and thereby become self-supporting. Margaret Ward attributed much of the freedwomen's independence to their organization of groups designed "to look after and provide for the wants of those who are out of a job." These societies known as the "Immaculate Doves," or the "Sistern," or the "Beloved Disciples," (often developed as outreaches of the black churches) provided emotional and financial support for their own members who were unemployed, down on their luck, or in want. Newly freed men organized and built their own churches and schoolhouses, and as a means of helping one another, blacks organized Mutual Aid Societies. In their thirst for knowledge and an education the freedmen themselves often pledged nails, work and money to construct the schools for their children. As noted earlier the reuniting of families and the pursuit of stable family lives became a top priority for former slaves following the war. Local demographic studies suggest that between 70 and 80 percent of postbellum black families were two-parent families.

For women the aftermath of war was particularly traumatic. For some the postwar years entailed lives of penury and adversity, while for others they opened whole new avenues of opportunity and self-fulfillment. The battlefield (or hospital) death of a husband, a father, or a brother left wounds that would fester as long as life itself. With the return of a husband, hobbled for life from the physical or mental scars of battle, many an already overworked wife found herself the sole support for her family. In addition to a frantic work schedule she became the chief provider of the tender loving care and the moral support departments for her despondent, dependent returnee. For distraught widows left with a houseful of young children to support, plus an abundance of financial naiveté and mounting debts, life became a living nightmare. Family responsibilities forced women into low paying clerical jobs, stressful teaching positions, injudicious business ventures, or even a permanent dependency on brothers for support. In the dreary months to follow countless women were relegated to unending days of loneliness, struggle, and stress.

Other more fortunate women were galvanized by the war and reconstruction into embarking on challenging, far more independent lifestyles than ever dreamed possible. Seeking a means of supporting their families or as an outlet for their energy and talents, a remarkable number of women moved out of the kitchen and into rewarding work as educators, writers, missionaries, club women, social workers, Grange members, businesswomen, fundraisers, government employees, and healthcare workers. Their sense of loss at the war's end evolved through the normal psychological progression of shock, disbelief, anger, resentment, guilt, and resignation. Finally, albeit partially, their grief was assuaged in memories, reminiscences and memorials. Southern women in particular embarked on a determined effort to ensure that the men who had given "the last full measure of devotion" to the Cause would long be remembered. The activities of philanthropic organizations devoted to the care of aged and infirm veterans and the war's innumerable war orphans, the ubiquitous Women's Memorial Societies, and the founding of the United Daughters of the Confederacy served commemorative, and, no doubt, therapeutic purposes. Although Southerners found the postwar years anything but serene or tranquil, there were times when women appeared to show their mettle in riding out the financial, political and racial chaos of the postwar world with greater assurance and endurance than did their male counterparts. As a result of resistance from male chauvinist husbands and brothers, and very possibly as a consequence of their preoccupation with

pressing family responsibilities, Southern women were incredibly delinquent in joining the advocates of female suffrage. Finally, at long last,
Southern activists abandoned a lost cause for a new cause—women's
rights.

And yet the failures of Reconstruction, the abandonment of the crusade for the rights and equality of freedmen as Northerners turned their
attention toward westward expansion and lucrative business ventures, the
development of the sharecropping system which relegated blacks to peas-
ant status, the Jim Crow laws, the "separate but equal" decision of the
Supreme Court, all left blacks an oppressed, segregated and forgotten
people until after World War II and the Civil Rights Acts of the 1960s.
Full rights of citizenship for African Americans that had supposedly been
enacted during Reconstruction were delayed for almost a hundred years.
In time Southerners began rethinking their dependence on cotton and
acknowledging their desperate need for industry. Decades later, however,
the South was still suffering from lack of industry, a sub-standard wage
scale, and the widespread poverty of both races.

Actually it was surprising that the South ever could get it all together
once again. Clearly Andrew Johnson and the Radicals were not entirely
successful in reconstructing the South. Instead, over the years the real
reconstruction of the South has evolved thanks to a combination of factors including the development of synthetics, the mobility provided by
the car and the airplane, the TVA, the Civil Rights Acts of the 1960s,
the focus on women's liberation, and the climate of low wages and mild
weather that attracted industry, vacationers, and retirees. It took time for
Southerners to emerge from defeat and to put hatred and ill will behind
them. In truth perhaps one of the South's most amazing accomplishments actually has been the gradual ebbing over the years of the seemingly ubiquitous anger and bitterness rife during those tumultuous years.

In later years despite the devastation at the war's end, despite the
South's catastrophic economic problems, its cataclysmic social, racial and
sectional animosities, and despite the rampant political dissension marking the Reconstruction era, the South almost miraculously did rise again—
not as a military threat to the country, not as a separate entity, but as a
vital, integral part of the United States of America, resplendent with its
Martin Luther Kings, its Rosa Parks, its Billy Graham, its William
Faulkners, Tennessee Williamses, Margaret Mitchells, Eudora Weltys,
and Maya Angelous, its Lyndon Johnsons and Jimmy Carters, Howard
Universities, and Coca Cola tycoons; its Satchmos, its Arthur Ashes, its
Bear Bryants, and its CNN.

Undeniably life after the Civil War and Reconstruction would never
again be the same—and that, indeed, is a blessing.

Chronology of the Reconstruction Era

January 16, 1865: Sherman's Field Order No. 15 set aside the South Carolina and Georgia Sea Islands for settlement of Negroes. Some 40,000 blacks were settled on the lands. Later President Johnson returned most of these lands to their original owners.

January 1865: Congress approved the Thirteenth Amendment, then sent to states for ratification. Ratified December 18, 1865.

1865–1867: termed "Presidential Reconstruction." President Johnson's May 29, 1865, proclamations involved the president's appointment of provisional governors in each of the Southern states and his order that state conventions to be held (whose delegates would be chosen by the "loyal" people of the state, to make constitutional changes and determine permanent voting and office-holding requirements. Johnson's plan required that the Thirteenth Amendment abolishing slavery be ratified, secession be declared illegal, and the Confederate debt be repudiated. During the summer of 1865 President Johnson's appointed provisional governors, arranged for conventions elected by voters who had taken the amnesty oath, and the conventions proceeded to revise the state constitutions. The ordinances of secession were repealed and the Thirteenth Amendment was ratified. On December 18, 1865, the Thirteenth Amendment was declared ratified and was added to the Constitution). When Congress convened in December of that year Johnson declared Reconstruction completed. Congress, however, took a dim view of Johnson's plan, rejected it, and in 1867 set up their own plan for Reconstruction. The Radicals, fearing Johnson's plan far too lenient, refused to admit members from the Confederate States. Instead they insisted on new state governments being set up with Rebels out and blacks given the franchise.

A second part of Johnson's May 29 proclamation was his issuance of a General Amnesty Proclamation whereby former Confederates "who would pledge to support the United States in the future and abide by any federal laws against slavery" would be granted "political rights and immunity from confiscation." There were certain exclusions, however, including important Confederate officials, high ranking army officers, and persons owning property worth $20,000 or more. The latter group could apply personally for presidential pardons, which began being awarded at some one hundred a day.

June 1865: Confederate prisoners of war, certain officers excepted, would be freed on the condition that they swear to the oath of allegiance. (See Joe Selby and George Washington Nelson, Jr. in Part I.) Actually this had been an on-and-off policy since the early days of the war.

October and November 1865: Southerners began enacting "Black Codes" in attempts to keep slaves in subjugation and restore white supremacy. The codes limited the social, economic, and political activity of Southern blacks. The confusion and turmoil engendered by the freeing of some four million former slaves, most of them bewildered by their newly acquired freedom and the uncertainties of their future homes, employment, and properties, posed a possible threat to the South as a whole and hastened the enactment of the "Black Codes" which severely restricted the freedmen's movements and their labor. Southerners envisioned resuming life in much of the antebellum tradition, but with freed black laborers.

December 1865: Appointment of the Joint Committee on Reconstruction to investigate conditions in the Southern states in order to determine whether any of their delegates should be admitted to Congress.

1866: The Ku Klux Klan founded in Pulaski, Tennessee.

1866: A Civil Rights Bill and a Bill to extend the Freedmen's Bureau were vetoed by President Johnson. Both bills, however, passed over Johnson's vetoes.

June 13, 1866: Congress approved the Fourteenth Amendment whereby all citizens would have equal protection of the laws. Repudiated by ten Southern states. Declared ratified July 28, 1868.

June 21, 1866: President Johnson signed the Southern Homestead Act providing over forty million acres of land for settlement by persons who would not be discriminated against on the basis of color.

1866: Riots in Memphis and New Orleans, during which many blacks died, served to weaken Johnson's stand.

July 16, 1866: Bill for extending the life of the Freedmen's Bureau, which was vetoed by President Johnson, was passed over his veto.

1866: Only Tennessee was willing to ratify the Fourteenth Amendment and thus became the only Southern state whose senators and representatives were seated in Congress. The other ten states refused to ratify the amendment and were denied readmission until deemed "entitled to such representation."

June 1866: Johnson ended confiscation.

July 1866: Tennessee was deemed "reconstructed" and restored to the Union.

March 2, 1867—1868: Passage of the Reconstruction Acts—over President Johnson's veto. The South (except Tennessee) was divided into five military districts, new governments were to be created in the South and blacks were enfranchised. These acts signaled the period known as Radical or Congressional Reconstruction. Southerners who had held any executive, legislative or judicial office and pledged to support the Constitution of the United States before the war and had thereafter been engaged in insurrection or "given aid or comfort to the enemies thereof" were barred from voting. (See Fourteenth Amendment.) These new governments would be provisional only and Rebel states would be re-admitted to the Union on the condition that they form new constitutions acceptable to Congress and they ratify the proposed Fourteenth Amendment. By 1868 six Southern states had complied and were readmitted to Congress. By 1870 Virginia, Georgia, Texas, and Mississippi had also completed the requirements.

September 7, 1867: President Johnson's second amnesty proclamation pardoned all but a few former rebels.

May 1868: The trial in the Senate for the removal of Johnson failed by one vote.

July 28, 1868: The Fourteenth Amendment giving Negroes citizenship was ratified.

February 1869: Congress approved the Fifteenth Amendment whereby no citizen would be deprived of the right to vote on the basis of race. It became part of Constitution in 1870.

December 1869: The first U. S. women's suffrage act passed in Wyoming.

1870 and 1871: Passage of the Enforcement Acts (the Third Enforcement Act, April 20, 1871, called the Ku Klux Klan Act) in attempts to curtail terrorist activity.

June 1872: Freedmen's Bureau Act was dissolved.

1873: A depression resulted in falling prices, thousands of bankruptcies, and the creation of untold numbers of debt-ridden, indigent Southerners. The conditions were particularly hard on blacks.

March 1, 1875: Civil Rights Act passed by Congress that outlawed racial discrimination in places of public accommodation and amusement. The act, however, did not mention public schools.

1876: The Centennial Exposition was held in Philadelphia. Women were given little attention until Elizabeth Cady Stanton and Susan B. Anthony appealed for "justice, we ask equality, we ask that all the civil and political rights that belong to citizens of the United States, be guaranteed to us and our daughters forever" in their Women's Declaration of Independence.

1877: In the Compromise of 1877 resulting from the disputed election between Samuel J. Tilden and Rutherford B. Hayes, Southern Democrats agreed to the inauguration of Hayes as president in exchange for the remaining Federal troops being withdrawn from the South. Thus "officially" ended Radical Reconstruction.

Notes

Introduction

1. Frank Jewel, in the Foreword to Eric Foner and Olivia Mahoney, *America's Reconstruction: People and Politics After the Civil War* (New York: Harper Collins Publishers, Inc., 1995).

2. Kathleen Christine Berkeley, "Elizabeth Avery Meriwether, 'An Advocate for Her Sex': Feminism and Conservatism in the Post-Civil War South," *Tennessee Historical Quarterly* 43 (Winter 1984): 397. Elizabeth Avery Meriwether, *Recollections of 92 Years 1824–1916* (Nashville, Tennessee: The Tennesee Historical Commission, 1958), v.

1— The Long War Ends

1. Cornelia Phillips Spencer, *The Last Ninety Days of the War in North Carolina* (New York: Watchman Publishing Company, 1866), 237–38.

2. "Diary of Elvira Bruce Seddon" Part II, *Goochland County Historical Society Magazine* 22 (1990): 8. Elvira was the eldest daughter of James Alexander Seddon, the Confederate Secretary of War.

3. Seddon, Diary, Part II, Vol. 22, 9.

4. Margaret Stanly Beckwith, Journal, Virginia Historical Society, Richmond. May 1, 1865.

5. G. Glenn Clift, ed., *The Private War of Lizzie Hardin: A Kentucky Confederate Girl's Diary of the Civil War in Kentucky, Virginia, Tennessee, Alabama, and Georgia* (Frankfort: Kentucky Historical Society, 1963), 235.

6. Louis P. Towles., ed. *A World Turned Upside Down: The Palmers of South Sante, 1818–1881* (Columbia: University of South Carolina Press, 1996), 471.

7. Towles, *A World Turned Upside Down*, 474.

8. Sarah Lois Wadley, Diary, 140 from the Sarah Lois Wadley Papers #1258, Southern Historical Collection, Wilson Library, University of North Carolina at Chapel Hill.

9. Clift, *The Private Life of Lizzie Hardin*, 231.

10. Towles, *A World Turned Upside Down*, 466.

11. Seddon, Diary, Part I, Vol. 21, 12.

12. Kate Mason Rowland, Memoirs of the War, Diary and Correspondence,

Eleanor S. Brockenbrough Library, The Museum of the Confederacy, Richmond, Virginia. Diary, April 2, 1865.

13. Nannie Haskins, Diary, Tennessee State Library and Archives, Nashville.

14. Kate S. Sperry, Diary, Winchester, Virginia, 1861–1866 (Accession 28532) Personal Papers Collection, Archives Research Services, The Library of Virginia, Richmond, Virginia.

15. Rives Lang Beaty, ed., "Recollections of Harriet Du Bose Lang," *South Carolina Historical Magazine* 59 (July 1958): 201.

16. Seddon, Diary, Part II, Vol. 22, 11.

17. Susan R. Jervey, and Charlotte St. Julien Ravenel, "Two Diaries from Middle St. John's Berkeley, South Carolina, February-May 1865," Journals kept by Miss Susan R. Jervey and Miss Charlotte St. Julien Ravenel, at Northampton and Pooshee Plantations, and Reminiscences of Mrs. (Waring) Henagan with Two Contemporary Reports From Federal Officials (Pinopolis, South Carolina: St. John's Hunting Club, 1921), April 20, 1865; Fannie E. Dickinson (Taylor), Diary, Virginia Historical Society, Richmond.

18. Sperry, Diary, 603.

19. Seddon, Diary, Part II, Vol. 23, 9.

20. James C. Bonner, ed., *The Journal of a Milledgeville Girl 1861–1867* (Athens: University of Georgia Press, 1964), 74.

21. Mary B.Goodwin, Diary 1860–1867 and Papers 1877–1890 (Accession 27846) Diary 1860–1867 Personal Papers Collection, Archives Research Services, The Library of Virginia, Richmond, Virginia. April 25, 1865.

22. Goodwin, Diary, May 7, 1865.

23. Beckwith, Jounral, May 1, 1865.

24. Daniel E. Sutherland, ed., *A Very Violent Rebel: The Civil War Diary of Ellen Renshaw House* (Knoxville: University of Tennessee Press, 1996), 161.

25. Clift, *The Private Life of Lizzie Hardin*, 232.

26. Confederate Letters Collection, Eleanor S. Brockenbrough Library, The Museum of the Confederacy, Richmond, Virginia.

27. Bell Irvin Wiley, ed., *"This Infernal War": The Confederate Letters of Sgt. Edwin H. Fay* (Austin: University of Texas Press, 1958), 446.

28. Wadley, Diary, 135.

29. Seddon, Diary, Part II, Vol. 22, 11.

30. *Our Women In the War. The Lives They Lived; The Deaths They Died* (Charleston, S.C.: The News and Courier Book Presses, 1885), 299.

31. Elizabeth Preston Allan, *The Life and Letters of Margaret Junkin Preston* (Boston: Houghton Mifflin and Company, 1903), 208.

32. Mary D. Robertson, *A Confederate Lady Comes of Age: The Journal of Pauline DeCaradeuc Heyward, 1863–1888* (Columbia: University of South Carolina Press, 1992), 74–75.

33. Towles, *A World Turned Upside Down*, 463.

34. Wadley, Diary, 140–141.

35. Andrew Buni, ed., "Reconstruction in Orange County, Virginia: A Letter from Hannah Garlick Rawlings to her sister Clarissa Lawrence Rawlings, August 9, 1865," *Virginia Magazine of History and Biography* 75 (January 1967): 459–465.

36. Jennie S. King, In Elizabeth (Porter) Pitts Collection, Tennessee State Library and Archives, Nashville. May 21, 1866.

37. Frances Butler Leigh, *Ten Years on a Georgia Plantation Since the War 1866–1877* (Savannah: Beehive Press, 1992), 4.

38. Sarah Matthews Handy, "In the Last Days of the Confederacy," *Atlantic Monthly* 87 (January 1901): 108.

39. Elliott Ashkenazi, ed., *The Civil War Diary of Clara Solomon: Growing Up in New Orleans, 1861–1862* (Baton Rouge: Louisiana State University Press, 1995), 374.

40. Beckwith, Journal, May 1, 1865.

41. Amanda Worthington, Diary, Worthington Family Papers, Mississippi Department of Archives and History, Jackson, 22.

42. Rowland, Diary, January 23, 1865.

43. Wadley, Diary, 140–141.

44. Wadley, Diary, 140.

45. Sperry, Diary, 607.

46. Clift, *The Private War of Lizzie Hardin*, 233.

47. Beckwith, Journal, May 5, 1865.

48. Charles M. McGee, Jr. and Ernest M. Lander, Jr., *A Rebel Came Home.* (Columbia: University of South Carolina Press, 1961), 83.

49. Wadley, Diary, 136.

50. Lucinda H. MacKethan, ed., *Recollections of a Southern Daughter: A Memoir by Cornelia Jones Pond of Liberty County* (Athens: University of Georgia Press, 1998), 88.

51. Sutherland, *A Very Violent Rebel*, 162.

52. Handy, "In the Last Days of the Confederacy," 110.

53. Catherine Thom Bartlett, ed., *"My Dear Brother," A Confederate Chronicle.* (Richmond, Virginia: The Dietz Press, 1952), 173.

54. Spencer, *Last Ninety Days*, 190.

55. Jervey and Ravenel, "Two Diaries from Middle St. John's Berkeley," April 22, 1865.

56. Amanda Virginia (Edmonds) Chappelear, Journals, Virginia Historical Society, Richmond, 357.

57. John Q. Anderson, ed., *Brokenburn: The Journal of Kate Stone 1861–1868* (Baton Rouge: Louisiana State University Press, 1995), 333, 341, 352. Selections reprinted by permission of Louisiana State University Press.

58. *Our Women in the War*, 218.

59. Virginia Walcott Beauchamp, ed., *A Private War: Letters and Diaries of Madge Preston 1862–1867* (New Brunswick: Rutgers University Press, 1987), 174–5

60. Robertson, *A Confederate Lady Comes of Age*, 74.

61. Towles, *A World Turned Upside Down*, 474.

62. William Kauffman Scarborough, ed., *The Diary of Edmund Ruffin*, Vol. 3 (Baton Rouge: Louisiana State University Press, 1989), 859, 905.

63. Quoted in Myrta Lockett Avary. *Dixie After the War* (Boston: Houghton Mifflin Company, 1937), 83.

64. Virginia L. French, Diary, Tennessee State Library and Archives, Nashville, 229.

65. Rachel Carter Craighead, Diaries 1855–1911, Tennessee State Library and Archives, Nashville. Also Microfilm. April 19, 1865.

66. Missouri Division, United Daughters of the Confederacy, *Reminiscences*

of the Women of Missouri During the Sixties (Jefferson City: The Hugh Stephens Printing Company, 1920), 294–98.

67. *Mobile Morning News*, May 11, 1865, quoted from the *Rochester Express*.

68. Clift, *The Private War of Lizzie Hardin*, 233.

69. George Cary Eggleston, *A Rebel's Recollections* (Bloomington: Indiana University Press, 1959), 184.

70. Sperry, Diary, April 25, 1865.

71. Bonner, *The Diary of a Milledgeville Girl*, 76.

72. Scarborough, *The Diary of Edmund Ruffin*, 854–55.

73. French, Diary, 227; Fletcher, Diary; Ellen Mordecai, Scrapbook and Miscellaneous Papers 1811–1885 (Accession 28685) S[usan] B. Treadway, Richmond, to Ellen M[ordecai], n.p. 19 April 1865, ALS, 3p., Personal Papers Collection, Archives Research Services, The Library of Virginia, Richmond, Virginia.

74. Eliza Frances Andrews. *The War-Time Journal of a Georgia Girl 1864–1865* (New York: D. Appleton and Company, 1908), 292.

75. Virginia Ingraham Burr, ed., *The Secret Eye. The Journal of Ella Gertrude Clanton Thomas, 1848–1899.* Copyright 1990 by Virginia Ingraham Burr and Gertrude T. Despeaux. Used by permission of the publisher, 285

76. Drew Gilpin Faust, "Altars of Sacrifice: Confederate Women and the Narratives of War," *Journal of American History* 76, No 4 (March 1990): 1200–1228.

77. Mrs. Roger A. Pryor, *Reminiscences of Peace and War* (New York: The Macmillan Company, 1904), 321. See Gabor S. Boritt, ed., *Why The Confederacy Lost* (New York: Oxford University Press, 1992) for further examination of the Confederate defeat.

78. Burr, *The Secret Eye*, 257, 260–61.

79. For further discussion see Willard E. Wight, "The Churches and the Confederate Cause," *Civil War History* 11 (March 1960): 361–373.

80. Mary H. Porter, *Eliza Chappell Porter: A Memoir* (Chicago: Fleming H. Revell Company, 1892), 163.

81. Allan, *The Life and Letters of Margaret Junkin Preston*, 143.

82. French, Diary, 227.

83. Dwight Franklin Henderson, ed., "The Private Journal of Georgiana Gholson Walker 1862–1865 With Selections from the Post-War Years 1865–1876," *Confederate Centennial Studies*, No. 25 (Tuscaloosa, Ala.: Confederate Publishing Company, Inc., 1963), 122.

84. Spencer, *Last Ninety Days*, 238 and 189 and Letters of Captain John Stewart Walker to his wife, held by Dr. Jack Jones, East Lansing, Michigan. Captain Walker left his wife a widow and his children orphans following his death at the Battle of Malvern Hill in July of 1862.

85. Grace Brown Elmore, Diary, South Caroliniana Library, University of South Carolina, Columbia, 91.

86. Kate D. Foster, Diary, In Kate D. Foster Papers, Rare Book, Manuscript, and Special Collections Library, Duke University, Durham, North Carolina, 20.

87. Seddon, Diary, Part II, Vol. 22, 11–12.

88. Seddon, Diary, Part II, Vol. 22, 11–13.

89. Sarah Rodgers Rousseau Espy, Diary (SPR 2), Alabama Department of Archives and History, Montgomery, June 2, 1866.

90. T. Conn Bryan, "A Georgia Woman's Civil War Diary: The Journal of

Minerva Leah Rowles McClatchey, 1864–65," *Collections of the Georgia Historical Society* 51, No. 2 (June 1967): 214.

91. Handy, "In the Last Days of the Confederacy," 108.

92. Seddon, Diary, Part II, Vol. 22, 13.

93. French, Diary, 231.

94. Mary Catherine Killebrew and Joseph Buckner, Collection, Tennessee State Library and Archives, Nashville, 61.

95. French, Diary, 231.

96. James P. Shenton, ed., *The Reconstruction: A Documentary History of the South After the War: 1865–1877* (New York: G. P. Putnam's Sons, 1963), 72.

97. Faust, "Altars of Sacrifice," 1201 and 1212. The numbers of family members engaged in active service in the Confederacy can become mindboggling. In researching his family history, genealogist Levin Culpepper of Meridian, Mississippi, discovered that his great, great, great grandfather (Joseph Culpepper 1765–1816) had twenty-one grandsons and three great grandsons who served in the war. And those were just the ones with the surname of Culpepper. There were others, the children of his three daughters that Levin has not yet counted. Thus more than twenty-four cousins were all engaged in fighting for the Confederacy.

98. Merton E. Coulter, *A History of the South VII The Confederate States of America 1861–1865* (Baton Rouge: Louisiana State University Press, 1950), 14.

99. James Wilford Garner, *Reconstruction in Mississippi* (Baton Rouge: Louisiana State University Press, 1968), 123.

100. Elmore, Diary, 104–5.

101. Espy, Diary, November 1863.

102. Seddon, Diary, Part II, Vol. 22, 14.

103. Tirza Willson Patterson, Papers, Tennessee State Library and Archives, Nashville, 4.

104. Beckwith, Journal, May 13, 1865.

105. Beckwith, Journal, *passim.*

106. Virginia Norfleet, Reminiscences, Privately Held, 4.

107. Norfleet, Reminiscences, 4.

108. Parthenia Antoinette Hague, *A Blockaded Family: Life in Southern Alabama During the Civil War* (Boston: Houghton Mifflin and Company, 1888), 174.

109. MacKethan, *Recollections of a Southern Daughter*, 83–85.

110. Craighead, Diary, April 30, 1865; May 16, 1865; April 8, 1865; December 31, 1865.

111. Towles, *A World Turned Upside Down*, 475.

112. Towles, *A World Turned Upside Down*, 475.

113. John Richard Dennett, *The South As It Is: 1865–1866* (New York: The Viking Press, 1965), 28.

114. *New Orleans Daily Picayune*, January 20, 1866.

115. Mary S. Whilden, *Recollections of the War: 1861–1865* (Columbia, South Carolina: The State Company, 1911).

116. Eggleston, *A Rebel's Recollections*, 180.

117. Handy, "In the Last Days of the Confederacy," 107.

118. E. Andrews, *The War-Time Journal of a Georgia Girl*, 196–97, 19.

119. Elmore, Diary, 98.

120. Hague, *A Blockaded Family*, 167.

121. Craighead, Diary, May 28, 1865.

122. Philip N. Racine, ed., *Piedmont Farmer: The Journals of David Golightly Harris, 1855–1870* (Knoxville: University of Tennessee Press, 1990), 366.

123. John Anderson, *Brokenburn*, 346; 350; Florence Anderson, Papers, Rare Book, Manuscript, and Special Collections Library, Duke University, Durham, North Carolina.

124. William M. Cash and Lucy Somerville Howorth, eds., *My Dear Nellie: The Civil War Letters of William L. Nugent to Eleanor Smith Nugent* (Jackson: University of Mississippi, 1977), 237.

125. Mobile Public Library, Local History and Genealogy, Civil War Collection, Mobile, Alabama.

126. Handy, "In the Last Days of the Confederacy," 110.

127. Emily Mason letter in Kate Mason Rowland Collection, Museum of the Confederacy, Richmond, Virginia.

128. E. Andrews, *The War-Time Journal of a Georgia Girl*, 193–94.

129. John Anderson, *Brokenburn*, 345–46.

130. Seddon, Diary, Part II, Vol. 22, 14.

131. Spencer, *Last Ninety Days*, 188–89.

132. Hague, *A Blockaded Family*, 165.

133. Matthew Jack Davis, "A Long Journey Home," *Civil War Times Illustrated* (May 1997): 16.

134. Eliza J. Kendrick (Lewis) Walker, "Other Days," *Alabama Historical Quarterly* 5 (Summer, 1943): 229.

135. Elmore, Diary, 95

136. Buni, "Reconstruction in Organge County, Virginia," 463.

137. Marion Knox Goode Briscoe, Memoir, Virginia Historical Society, Richmond.

138. Elizabeth W. Allston Pringle, *Chronicles of Chicora Wood* (New York: Charles Scribner's Sons, 1923), 249.

13 9. *Our Women in the War*, 214–218.

140. Mrs. Gordon Pryor Rice. Recollections. Virginia Historical Society, Richmond, Virginia. See also Notes on Virginia (Accession 24061) Personal Papers Collection, Archives Research Services, The Library of Virginia. Richmond, Virginia.

141. Elizabeth Avery Meriwether, *Recollections of 92 Years 1824–1916* (Nashville: The Tennessee Historical Commission, 1958), 164.

142. Bartlett, "*My Dear Brother*," 174.

143. *Our Women in the War*, 437

2—Gloomy Prospects Ahead

1. Jane F. Stephenson, "My Father and His Household, Before, During and After the War," In Blanton Family Papers, Virginia Historical Society, Richmond, 89. Of course, elite whites were not the only Southerners for whom life took a drastic turn after the surrender. See the account of the Union soldiers' sacking of the property of Willis Madden, considered the wealthiest black in

Culpeper County, Virginia. The destruction of his tavern and farm left him a ruined man, surrounded by debts, smothered in a deep depression from which he never fully recovered. (T.O. Madden, Jr. with Ann L. Miller, *We Were Always Free: The Maddens of Culpeper County, Virginia, a 200 Year Family History* [New York: W.W. Norton & Company, 1992], *passim*).

2. Mary Amarintha. Snowden, Correspondence, South Caroliniana Library, University of South Carolina, Columbia.

3. Elmore, Diary, 95.

4. Nannie Scott, *Nannie Scott of "Bel-Air" School* (Richmond: Dietz Press, 1971), 32. Edward Ball, *Slaves In The Family* (New York: Farrar, Straus and Giroux, 1998), 356.

5. Pringle, *Chronicles of Chicora Wood*, 11.

6. John William De Forest, *A Union Officer in the Reconstruction* (New Haven: Yale University Press, 1948), 66.

7. A child who had lost a father was considered an orphan. For more information concerning orphans see Catherine Clinton, *Civil War Stories* (Athens: University of Georgia Press, 1998), 43–80.

8. William Stanley Hoole, ed., "Reconstruction in West Alabama: The Memoirs of John L. Hunnicutt," *Confederate Centennial Studies* No. 11 (1959): 16.

9. Coulter, *A History of the South VII The Confederate States of America*, 2.

10. Walter Pritchard, "The Effects of the Civil War on the Louisiana Sugar Industry," *Journal of Southern History* 5 (August 1939): *passim*.

11. Eric Foner, *A Short History of Reconstruction 1863–1877* (New York: Harper & Row, Publishers, 1990), 78.

12. Quoted in J. Caryle Sitterson, "The McCollams: A Planter Family of the Old and New South," *Journal of Southern History* 6 (August, 1940): 363.

13. *New Orleans Daily Picayune*, December 31, 1865.

14. Leigh, *Ten Years on a Georgia Plantation*, 64–5.

15. Coulter, *A History of the South VII The Confederate States of America*, 14.

16. Garner, *Reconstruction in Mississippi*, 123 and Coulter, *A History of the South VII The Confederate States of America*, 14.

17. E. Andrews, *The War-Time Journal of a Georgia Girl*, 196–97, 138.

18. Samuel Carter III, *The Siege of Atlanta, 1864* (New York: Bonanza Books, 1973), 385.

19. *Official Records of the Union and Confederate Armies in the War of the Rebellion*, Series I, Vol. 43, Part I (Washington: Government Printing Office, 1921), 37; James I. Robertson, Jr., *Civil War Virginia: Battleground for a Nation* (Charlottesville: University Press of Virginia, 1991), 160–161; Edward H. Phillips, *The Shenandoah Valley in 1864: An Episode in the History of Warfare* (Charleston, South Carolina: The Citadel, The Military College of South Carolina, May 1965), 22.

20. Quoted in Phillips, *The Shenandoah Valley in 1864*, 17.

21. *Official Records of the Union and Confederate Armies in the War of the Rebellion*, Series I, Vol. 43, Part I, 29–30.

22. Margaretta Barton Colt, *Defend the Valley: A Shenandoah Family in the Civil War* (New York: Orion Books, 1994), 351.

23. Spencer, *Last Ninety Days*, 95.

24. Spencer, *Last Ninety Days*, 175.

25. Bryan, "A Georgia Woman's Civil War Diary," 213.

26. *Our Women in the War*, 367.
27. Aaron M. Boom, ed., "Testimony of Margaret Ketcham Ward on Civil War Times in Georgia," Parts I and II, *Georgia Historical Quarterly* 39 (September, December 1955): 391.
28. Boom, "Testimony of Margaret Ketcham Ward," 392.
2 9. Ned Chaney, Simon Hare, Sam Broach, Bessie Williams, Nettie Henry, WPA Federal Writers' Project, Meridian-Lauderdale County Public Library, Meridian, Mississippi.
30. Anne Middleton Holmes, *The New York Ladies' Southern Relief Association 1866–1867* (New York: The Mary Mildred Sullivan Chapter, United Daughters of the Confederacy, 1926), 65.
31. Sperry, Diary, 632.
32. Norfleet, Reminiscences, 14. Not a few of the personal items "appropriated" from Southerners found their way northward. A Georgia woman, while visiting in the North and attending a fashionable New York City church observed that her pew-mate was wearing a shawl, a ring and a bracelet that she was convinced had been stolen from her during the war by Yankee raiders. Following the service and in front of the rector, the objects were clearly identified by initials and pictures as belonging to the Southern lady. The possessions were promptly returned by the embarrassed New Yorker who was reluctant to divulge the sordid details of their acquisition. The article relating the incident in the *New Orleans Times* concluded with the caustic comment: "If Southern ladies want to know where their articles of missing jewelry and wardrobe furniture are, let them attend some fashionable 'up town' New York church, and if the men want to know what has become of their fine horses, shipped North by army officers and 'bummers,' let them spend an evening in Central Park." *New Orleans Times*, August 22, 1866, and John T. Trowbridge, *Picture of the Desolated South and the Work of Reconstruction 1865–1868* (Hartford Conn: L. Stebbins, 1868), 562.
Harriet Lang also had a remarkable story to relate. Following his release as a prisoner of war in the North, Harriet's father found it difficult to settle down to his prewar practice of law. In order to pay the taxes the family was compelled to sell much of their silver and jewelry. As the only solution to providing money for a trousseau and wedding reception for Harriet's eldest sister, Harriet's mother generously sent her silver, dented and blackened from having been hidden in the well during the war, to Baltimore to be sold. In a surprising turn of events the silver was returned some months later, cleaned and polished "as good as new," a gift of the company who had purchased it from the family! Beaty, "Recollections of Harriet Du Bose Kershaw Lang," 203.
33. Robert Selph Henry, *The Story of Reconstruction* (New York: Konecky and Konecky, 1991), 20; Avary, *Dixie After the War*, 160–61; Francis Butler Simkins and Robert Hilliard Woody, *South Carolina During Reconstruction* (Chapel Hill: University of North Carolina Press, 1932), 18.
34. Charles Martin, "A Reminiscence of the War Between the States by Charles T. Martin," Alabama Deptartment of Archives and History, Montgomery, Alabama.
35. Carol Bleser, ed., *The Hammonds of Redcliffe* (New York: Oxford University Press, 1981), 135.
36. Mary Custis Lee Letter to Emily Mason in Eleanor S. Brockenbrough Library, The Museum of the Confederacy, Richmond, Virginia.

37. Pryor, *My Day*, 272.
38. McKee Letters. Privately held by Charles D. Burks of Columbia, Missouri.
39. Hilary Abner Herbert, "Grandfather Talks About His Life Under Two Flags: Reminiscences, 1903" (SPR 4) Alabama Department of Archives and History, Montgomery.
40. Holmes, *The New York Ladies' Southern Relief Association*, 77–78.
41. Holmes, *The New York Ladies' Southern Relief Association*, 74–75.
42. *New Orleans Daily Picayune*, March 25, 1866.
43. Bartlett, "*My Dear Brother*," 176–77.
44. *Our Women in the War*, 440.
45. Mary Amarintha Snowden, Correspondence, Letter from Mrs. J. G. Lahater, January 24, 1866. (Precise date is unclear.) In South Caroliniania Library, University of South Carolina, Columbia.
46. *Our Women in the War*, 440.
47. Mary Edmondson, Diary of Mrs. Mary Edmondson of Phillips County Arkansas 1863–'64, United Daughters of the Confederacy, Richmond, Virginia.
48. Elmore, Diary, 103.
49. Spencer, *Last Ninety Days*, 71.
50. Buni, "Reconstruction in Organge County, Virginia," 461.
51. Buni, "Reconstruction in Organge County, Virginia," 461–62.
52. Buni, "Reconstruction in Organge County, Virginia," 462.
53. Southern Famine Relief Commission Report, New York Historical Society, New York City, January 26, 1867.
54. Southern Famine Relief Commission Report, January 31, 1867; February 1, 1867; February 2, 1867.
55. Southern Famine Relief Commission Report, February 2, 1867.
56. *Our Women in the War*, 121.
57. Southern diarists repeatedly despaired over the ruthless destruction of fields and farms by their own soldiers. A South Carolina woman lamented: "I am sorry to say that Wheeler's men have done us more damage than the Yankees. I did not mind it at first when I thought they had only taken things they needed, but I do blame them very much for their wanton destruction of property that they ought to protect. It is a shame and they ought to be exposed." Jervey and Ravenel, "Two Diaries from Middle St. John's Berkeley, South Carolina," 42.
58. Colt, *Defend the Valley*, 356.
59. Briscoe, Memoir, 186.
60. Virginia Meacham Gould, *Chained to the Rock of Adversity: To Be Free, Black & Female in the Old South* (Athens: University of Georgia Press, 1998), 89.
61. French, Diary, 241.
62. Robert Manson Myers, ed., *The Children of Pride: A True Story of Georgia and the Civil War* (New Haven, Yale University Press, 1972), 1303.
63. "*Maggie!*" *Maggie Lindsley's Journal: Nashville, Tennessee, 1864—Washington, D.C.,1865* (Southbury, Connecticut: Privately Printed, 1977).
64. Leigh, *Ten Years on a Georgia Plantation*, 10.
65. Allan, *The Life and Letters of Margaret Junkin Preston*, 210.
66. Bartlett, "*My Dear Brother*," 173.
67. Frances Fearn, *Diary of a Refugee* (New York: Frances Fearn, 1910), 118–119.

68. Fearn, *Diary of a Refugee*, 32–33.

69. Fearn, *Diary of a Refugee*, 44.

70. According to the *New Orleans Times*, General Howard, chief of the Freedman's Bureau, gave a speech in New York in which he divided the Southern people into four classes. "First—The men who engaged heartily in the war, but who have now given up slavery and are desirous of demonstrating their unqualified allegiance to the Government. Second—A large class, who at first pretended that they gave up the points at issue, but are making every effort to regain the power necessary to re-establish them. Third—The class that has always been defiant, and now seeks to keep up a state of disorder and commotion. Fourth—Those who have been and always would be Union people." Howard maintained: "The first class are quietly at work on their farms, exhibiting a wonderful degree of practical common sense. They are trying to conform to the lessons of the present. When they employ Negroes, they extend to them the privileges that belong to them as men." As he praised the first class, General Howard attributed the "mobs and disorders" taking place in the South to the next two classes. The editorial, of course, found serious fault with General Howard's speech, and the actions of Northerners calling them vindictive and vengeful. (*New Orleans Times*, November 2, 1866)

71. Spencer, *Last Ninety Days*, 71–72.

72. John Anderson, *Brokenburn*, 364.

73. John Anderson, *Brokenburn*, 364–65.

74. James M. McPherson, *Battle Cry of Freedom: The Civil War Era* (New York: Ballantine Books, 1988), 447.

75. Eggleston, *A Rebel's Recollections*, 101.

76. The speech was quite possibly delivered by the Reverend Moses D. Hoge, minister of Richmond's Second Presbyterian Church.

77. Seddon, Diary, Part I, Vol. 21, 11.

78. Espy, Diary.

79. Wadley, Diary, 139.

80. Clift, *The Private War of Lizzie Hardin*, 60.

81. Seddon, Diary, Part I, Vol. 21, 8.

82. Sarah G. Follansbee, Diary in Stringfellow-Follansbee Records (7N/A/9/e), Alabama Department of and Archives, Montgomery, 102.

83. Follansbee, Diary, April 27, 1865.

84. Beaty, "Recollections of Harriet Du Bose Kershaw Lang," 203.

85. John H. Kennaway, *On Sherman's Track; Or, The South After the War* (London: Seeley, Jackson and Halliday, 1867), 130.

86. C. Vann Woodward, ed., *Mary Chesnut's Civil War* (New Haven: Yale University Press, 1981), 733.

87. Wiley, "*This Infernal War*," 445.

88. Briscoe, Memoir, 186.

89. Margaret Newbold Thorpe, "Life in Virginia by a 'Yankee Teacher,' Margaret Newbold Thorpe," Edited by Richard L. Morton, *Virginia Magazine of History and Biography* 64, No. 2 (April 1956): 199 and 201.

90. Elizabeth Reynolds, Virginia Historical Society, Richmond.

91. John Anderson, *Brokenburn*, 368–69.

92. John Anderson, *Brokenburn*, 368–69.

93. John Anderson, *Brokenburn*, 377.

94. Espy, Diary, 72.

95. Thomas Nelson Page, "The Southern People During Reconstruction," *Atlantic Monthly* 88 (September 1901): 299.

96. Otto H. Olsen, ed., *Reconstruction and Redemption in the South* (Baton Rouge: Louisiana State University Press, 1980), 96 and Foner, *Short History*, 161.

97. *New Orleans Times*, August 21, 1866.

98. Suzanne D. Lebsock, "Radical Reconstruction and the Property Rights of Southern Women," *Journal of Southern History* 43, No. 2 (May 1977): 195–216.

99. Burr, *Secret Eye*, 310.

100. Burr, *Secret Eye*, 343.

101. Briscoe, Memoir, 176.

102. Betty Beaumont, *A Business Woman's Journal* (Philadelphia: T. B. Peterson & Brothers, 1888), 338.

103. Towles, *A World Turned Upside Down*, 678.

104. Alexander Melvorne Jackson. Papers (M16). McCain Library and Archives, The University of Southern Mississippi, Hattiesburg, Letters of September 18 and February 3, 1866.

105. Quoted in Michael Wayne, *The Reshaping of Plantation Society: The Natchez District, 1860–1880* (Baton Rouge: Louisiana State University Press, 1983), 80–81; 92–93; 173–74.

106. Willard L. Jones, "Cotton, the 'King' That Never Was," *Civil War Times* 2, No. 6 (October 1960): 16. Also see James L. Roark, *Masters Without Slaves: Southern Planters in the Civil War and Reconstruction* (New York: W. W.Norton & Company, 1977), 77.

107. Towles, *A World Turned Upside Down*, 501.

108. Anna Clayton Logan, in Virginia Historical Society, Richmond and in Goochland Historical Society, Goochland, Virginia. Excerpts published in "Recollections of My Life," Part II, *Goochland County Historical Society Magazine* 21 (1989): 24.

109. Rowland, Collection.

110. Kate Morrissette, "Social Life in the First Capital of the Confederacy" (SPR 443), Alabama Department of Archives and History, Montgomery, Alabama. For more information see the diaries of Sara Morgan Dawson and Sarah Follansbee that also provide colorful details of the destruction of Confederate cotton. Even many home owners whose houses were destroyed by the Federals or by their own handiwork rejoiced in the fact that despite their losses, their property would not further aggrandize the enemy. A Richmond resident told of friends who were "completely burnt out." Lucy Fletcher commented to her diary: "They make no complaint, no murmuring, indeed of all whom I have seen, some who have lost everything, I may say the same. All unite in saying, better burn and destroy everything than it should fall into the hands of our enemies." Lucy Muse Fletcher, Diary 1865, Rare Book, Manuscript, and Special Collections Library, Duke University, Durham, North Carolina. Historian James McPherson noted that "Southerners burned more of their own capital than the enemy had burned of Atlanta or Columbia." McPherson, *Battle Cry*, 846.

111. Jones, "Cotton, the 'King,'" 17.

112. Worthington Family Papers.

113 *Our Women in the War*, 321.

114. Adelicia Acklen, Papers, Tennessee State Library and Archives, Nashville

and Eleanor Graham, "Belmont 1. Nashville Home of Adelicia Acklen." *Tennessee Historical Quarterly* 30 (1971): 345–68.

115. Jones, "Cotton, the 'King,'" 17.

116. See *Official Records of the Union and Confederate Armies in the War of the Rebellion.* Series I, Vol. 44, 783.

117. George Winston Smith, "Cotton from Savannah in 1865," *Journal of Southern History* 21 (November 1955): 505.

118. *New Orleans Times,* June 6, 1865.

119. Coulter, *A History of the South,* 10.

120. *New Orleans Daily Picayune,* January 27, 1866.

121. Towles, *A World Turned Upside Down,* 486.

122. John T. Trowbridge, *The Desolate South 1865–1866: A Picture of the A History of the South, Battlefields and of the Devastated Confederacy,* Edited by Gordon Carroll (Boston: Little, Brown and Company, 1956), 306.

123. *New Orleans Daily Picayune,* January 27, 1866.

124. De Forest, *A Union Officer in the Reconstruction,* 44.

125 Quoted in Coulter, *A History of the South,* 8.

126. Celena Carnes, Correpsondence of Margaret McDowell (Venable) Hannah with Celena Carnes in Carrington Family Papers, Virginia Historical Society, Richmond. (Incidentally, In 1859 near the White House in Washington, Dan Sickles, a New York lawyer and Democratic congressman, shot and killed Philip Barton Key, whose father had composed the "Star Spangled Banner," when he discovered Key had had an affair with Sickles's wife. Later he served as a General with the Union forces despite his questionable reputation.)

3—A World Rife with Changes

1. *Report of the Joint Committee on Reconstruction, at the First Session Thirty-Ninth Congress.* Washington: Government Printing Office, 1866, Part III, 103.

2. Handy, "In the Last Days of the Confederacy," 9.

3. Ronnie W. Clayton, *Mother Wit: The Ex-Slave Narratives of the Louisiana Writers' Project* (New York: Peter Lang, 1990), 66.

4. Clayton, *Mother Wit,* 58.

5. Clayton, *Mother Wit,* 109–110.

6. Racine, Piedmont Farmer, 389 and Leon F. Litwack, *Been in the Storm So Long: The Aftermath of Slavery* (New York: Alfred A. Knopf, 1979), 179.

7. Durrell Family Collection. Excerpts from the *South Western Newspaper* 1864–66, New York Historical Society, 843.

8. Clayton, *Mother Wit,* 38.

9. Durrell Collection, 843. (Probably about July 22, 1865.)

10. Irby Morgan (Mrs.), *How It Was; Four Years Among the Rebels* (Nashville, Tennessee: Printed for the Author by Publishing House Methodist Episcopal Church, South, Barber & Smith Agents, 1892), 145.

11. Ned Chaney, Simon Hare, Sam Broach, Bessie Williams, Nettie Henry, WPA Federal Writers' Project, Meridian-Lauderdale County Public Library. Meridian, Mississippi.

12. Broach, WPA Federal Writers' Project.

13. Letitia Dabney Miller, Recollections. In Thomas Gregory Dabney Collection (M7), McCain Library and Archives, The University of Southern Mississippi, Hattiesburg.

14. John B. Cade. "Out of the Mouths of Ex-Slaves." *Journal of Negro History* 20 (July 1935): *passim.*

15. Handy, "In the Last Days of the Confederacy," 109.

16. Spencer, *Last Ninety Days*, 167.

17. Louis R. Wilson, ed. *Selected Papers of Cornelia Phillips Spencer.* Copyright 1953 by the University of North Carolina Press, renewed 1981 by Penelope Wilson and Elizabeth Wilson. Used by permission of the publisher, 112.

18. *Our Women in the War*, 368.

19. Burr, *Secret Eye*, 296.

20. *Our Women in the War*, 434.

21. *Report of the Joint Committee on Reconstruction*, Part II, 189.

22. Allan, *The Life and Letters of Margaret Junkin Preston*, 208.

23. Boom, "Testimony of Margaret Ketcham Ward on Civil War Times in Georgia," 395.

24. Eggleston, *A Rebel's Recollections*, 187.

25. Quoted in Anita Miller Stamper and Mary Edna Lohrenz, "Manuscript Sources for 'Mississippi Homespun: Nineteenth-Century Textiles and the Women Who Made Them,'" *Journal of Mississippi History* 53 (August 1991): 210

26. Quoted in Stamper and Lohrenz, "Manuscript Sources," 211.

27. Stamper and Lohrenz, "Manuscript Sources," 211.

28. Harvey Wish, ed., *Reconstruction in the South 1865–1877: First-Hand Accounts of the American Southland After the Civil War by Northerners & Southerners* (New York: Farrar, Straus and Giroux, 1965), 286.

29. Julie Saville, *The Work of Reconstruction: From Slave to Wage Laborer in South Carolina, 1860–1870* (New York: Cambridge University Press, 1994), 127.

30. Seddon, Diary, Part II, Vol. 22, 8.

31. Seddon, Diary, Part II, Vol. 22, 8.

32. Seddon, Diary, Part II, Vol. 22, 10–11.

33. Clift, *The Private War of Lizzie Hardin*, 224.

34. Foner, *Short History*, 37.

35. Charles L. Perdue, Jr., Thomas E. Barden, Robert K. Phillips, eds., *Weevils in the Wheat: Interviews with Virginia Ex-Slaves* (Bloomington: Indiana University Press, 1980), 268.

36. E. Andrews, *The War-Time Journal of a Georgia Girl*, 332–3.

37. John F. Wheless, Confederate Letter, Tennessee State Library and Archives, Nashville.

38. Whitelaw Reid, *After the War: A Southern Tour, May 1, 1865, to May 1, 1866* (New York: Moore, Wilstach & Baldwin, 1866), 52.

39. Quoted in Garner, *Reconstruction in Mississippi, 261.*

40. Jervey and Ravenel, "Two Diaries From Middle St. John's Berkeley, South Carolina," 36.

41. Quoted in Eugene D. Genovese, *Roll, Jordan, Roll: the World the Slaves Made* (New York: Pantheon Books, 1974), 606.

42. John Anderson, *Brokenburn*, 362.

43. Pringle, *Chronicles of Chicora Wood*, 160–268.

44. Beaumont, *A Business Woman's Journal, 354.*

45. Frank Durr in Jim Dawson, *Bits & Pieces: Studies in Lauderdale County Lore* Vol. 1 (Meridian Mississippi: Lauderdale County Department of Archives & History, Inc., 1995), Chapter Two.

46. John Anderson, *Brokenburn*, 366.

47. *Joint Committee on Reconstruction*, Part II, 196.

48. Clayton, *Mother Wit*, 215.

49. Perdue et al., *Weevils in the Wheat*, 196.

50. Clayton, *Mother Wit*, 109–110.

51. Towles, *A World Turned Upside Down*, 466.

52. Nettie Henry, Ned Chaney, Simon Hare, Sam Broach, Bessie Williams, Nettie Henry, WPA Federal Writers' Project, Meridian-Lauderdale County Public Library, Meridian, Mississippi.

53. N. Henry, WPA Federal Writers' Project, Meridian-Lauderdale County Public Library, Meridian, Mississippi.

54. Simon Hare, WPA Federal Writers' Project, Meridian-Lauderdale County Public Library, Meridian, Mississippi.

55. *Joint Committee on Reconstruction*, Part III, 101.

56. Cornelia Hancock, *South After Gettysburg: Letters of Cornelia Hancock 1863–1868*, Edited by Henrietta Stratton Jaquette (New York: Thomas Y. Crowell, 1937), 268.

57. Bonner, *The Diary of a Milledgeville Girl*, 126.

58. Allen W. Trelease, *White Terror: The Ku Klux Klan Conspiracy and Southern Reconstruction* (New York: Harper & Row, 1971), 132–35; xliv; Patrick W. Riddleberger, *1866: The Critical Year Revisited* (Carbondale: Southern Illinois University Press, 1979), 177–201.

59. Paul Escott, *Slavery Remembered: A Record of Twentieth Century Slave Narratives* (Chapel Hill: University of North Carolina Press, 1979), 157–58.

60. Burr, *Secret Eye*, 260–62.

61. Louisa McCord Smythe, Reminiscences, South Caroliniana Library, University of South Carolina, Columbia, 92.

62. N. Henry, WPA Federal Writers' Project; Trelease, *White Terror*, 290–93. See also Eric Foner and Olivia Mahoney, 121; Richard Nelson Current, *Those Terrible Carpetbaggers* (New York: Oxford University Press, 1988), 186–87; J. S. McNeilly, "The Enforcement Act of 1871 and the Ku Klux Klan in Mississippi" *Publications of Mississippi Historical Society* 9 (1908): 109–197.

63. Beaumont, *Business Woman's Journal*, 355.

64. *New Orleans Times*, July 6, 1866.

65. *Joint Committee on Reconstruction*, Part II, 243.

66. Burr, *Secret Eye*, 168.

67. Burr, *Secret Eye*, 168.

68. *Our Women in the War*, 217.

69. Escott, *Slavery Remembered, 133.*

70. Carol Bleser, *In Joy and in Sorrow: Women, Family, and Marriage in the Victorian South, 1830–1900* (New York: Oxford University Press, 1991), 106.

71. Roark, *Masters Without Slaves*, 184.

72. *Joint Committee on Reconstruction*, Part III, 31.

73. Wish, *Reconstruction in the South 1865–1877*, 293.

74. Perdue et al., *Weevils in the Wheat*, 72.

75. *New Orleans Daily Picayune*, January 5, 1866.

76. Elizabeth Hyde Botume, *First Days Amongst the Contrabands* (Boston: Lee and Shepard Publishers, 1893), 259–261; 230.

77. Cade, "Out of the Mouths of Ex-Slaves," 337.

78. Dennett, *The South As It Is*, 183.

79. Garner, *Reconstruction in Mississippi*, 262.

80. De Forest, *A Union Officer in the Reconstruction*, 29.

81. *Joint Committee on Reconstruction*, Part III, 19.

82. Hancock, *South After Gettysburg*, 280; 286.

83. William F. Mugleston, ed., "The Freedmen's Bureau and Reconstruction in Virginia: The Diary of Marcus Sterling Hopkins, a Union Officer," *Virginia Magazine of History and Biography* 86 (1978): 66.

84. De Forest, *A Union Officer in the Reconstruction*, 74.

85. Leigh, *Ten Years on a Georgia Plantation*, 23.

86. Rice, Recollections.

87. For interesting perspectives about the Freedmen's Bureau see Paul A. Cimbala and Randall M. Miller, eds., *The Freedmen's Bureau and Reconstruction* (New York: Fordham University Press, 1999) and George R. Bentley, *A History of the Freedmen's Bureau* (New York: Octagon Books, 1970).

88. Dennett, *The South As It Is*, 243–246.

89. Dennett, *The South As It Is*, 249.

90. Dennett, *The South As It Is*, 248–252.

91. Elmore, Diary, 100–105.

92. N. Henry, WPA Federal Writers' Project.

93. Clifford Stickney, Collection, Archives and Manuscripts Department, Chicago Historical Society.

94. James T. Currie, *Enclave: Vicksburg and Her Plantations 1863–1870* (Jackson: University Press of Mississippi, 1980), 147.

95. Botume, *First Days Amongst the Contrabands*, 195–199.

96. Mary Ames, *From a New England Woman's Diary in Dixie in 1865* (Springfield: The Plimpton Press, 1906), 96.

97. Trowbridge, *The Desolate South*, 288.

98. Thorpe, "Life in Virginia by a 'Yankee Teacher,'" 195.

99. Thorpe, "Life in Virginia by a 'Yankee Teacher,'" 195.

100. Botume, *First Days Amongst the Contrabands*, 231.

101. Sperry, Diary, 650.

102. Here and there in the midst of vast confusion and misery a ray of sunshine permeated the darkness. Case in point: A Beaufort woman and her family eagerly returned to the Sea Islands after the war only to find the home occupied by strangers. In the fall of 1866 the woman was appalled to suddenly discover their home was among those being offered for sale "for the taxes due." Some desperate moments occurred during the course of the sale in which her father narrowly succeeded in outbidding a Northern man and was given three days to attempt to raise the money. It would take a trip to Charleston, however, to seek to arrange a loan, and the delay threatened the loss of the property to a private sale. In a supreme act of kindness two Northern men came to their aid, secured the money "at their own risk" and saved the home for her family. "We shook hands with the Northerner that night, though up to that time we had said we would never give a handshake to any Yankee." *Our Women in the War*, 474.

103. Rowland, Collection.

104. *New Orleans Daily Picayune*, March 4, 1866.
105. *New Orleans Times*, July 19, 1866.
106. *New Orleans Times*, July 19, 1866.
107. *New Orleans Times*, July 19, 1866.
108. *New Orleans True Delta*, February 17, 1866.
109. For a concise description of the Bank and its demise see Bentley, *A History of the Freedmen's Bureau*, 145–148.
110. Kenneth M. Stampp, *The Era of Reconstruction 1865–1877* (New York: Vintage Books, 1967), 132–136 and the New Orleans *Daily Picayune*, February 13, 1866.
111. Joint Committee on Reconstruction, Part II, 236.
112. Joint Committee on Reconstruction, Part II, 235.
113. It is interesting to note that in Charleston and in some of the larger cities in the South there were a number of free public schools for Negroes even during the existence of slavery. After the war these schools were expanded. *Joint Committee on Reconstruction*, Part II, 251.

4—Help Wanted

1. *New Orleans Times*, July 19, 1866.
2. Lawrence N. Powell, *New Masters: Northern Planters During the Civil War and Reconstruction* (New Haven: Yale University Press, 1980), 109.
3. *New Orleans Daily Picayune*, May 13, 1866.
4. *New Orleans Daily Picayune*, December 28, 1865.
5. De Forest, *A Union Officer in the Reconstruction*, 158.
6. Roark, *Masters Without Slaves*, 271 and *New Orleans Daily Picayune*, January 3, 1866.
7. Gerald Schwartz, ed., *A Woman Doctor's Civil War: Esther Hill Hawks' Diary* (Columbia: University of South Carolina Press, 1984), 244.
8. Leigh, *Ten Years on a Georgia Plantation*, 103.
9. Leigh, *Ten Years on a Georgia Plantation*, 80.
10. Robert F. Futrell, "Efforts of Mississippians to Encourage Immigration, 1865–1880," *Journal of Mississippi History* 20 (April 1958): *passim*.
11. *New Orleans Picayune*, May 13, 1866.
12. Quoted in Foner, "A Short History," 64.
13. Killebrew, Collection, 62.
14. John Anderson, *Brokenburn*, 363.
15. Saville, *The Work of Reconstruction*, 23.
16. Although divorce had already separated Frances Butler's parents, the famous actress Fanny Kemble and Pierce Butler, the Civil War further deepened the rift. While Frances and her father held pro–South sympathies, her sister Sarah and their mother sided with the North.
17. Leigh, *Ten Years on a Georgia Plantation*, 39
18. Leigh, *Ten Years on a Georgia Plantation*, 37–46.
19. Leigh, *Ten Years on a Georgia Plantation*, 62.
20. De Forest, *A Union Officer in the Reconstruction*, 199.
21. Rebecca Smith, Alabama Department of Archives and History. (Probably an Alabama 1866 contract.)

22. Sally Elmore Taylor, Diary, South Caroliniana Library, University of South Carolina, Columbia, South Carolina.

23. Burr, *Secret Eye*, 358.

24. Burr, *Secret Eye*, 370; 368.

25. Bartlett, *"My Dear Brother,"* 185.

26. Southerners were proud of their progress in railroad building. According to a newspaper article, passengers could travel from New Orleans to New York in the record time of one hundred hours! Travel from New Orleans to Boston took one hundred and ten hours, travel to Chicago took sixty-four hours. *New Orleans Daily Picayune*, May 3, 1866. Rice, Recollections.

27. Elmore, Diary, 92.

28. S. Taylor, Diary.

29. Elmore, Diary 109.

30. Mary Jones was the widow of the Rev. Dr. Charles Colcock. Jones, a conscientious Georgia minister, called "Apostle to the Blacks," who during his lifetime had been devoutly committed to providing religious instruction for blacks.

31. Myers, *Children of Pride*, 1313.

32. Myers, *Children of Pride*, 1340–41. Cornelia Jones Pond in her Reminiscences recalled a typical instance of a disgruntled Negro who reported her father to the Freedmen's Bureau in Savannah. This time the Bureau officials also decided against the laborer, agreeing with Cornelia's family that he had not worked long enough in the fields to be awarded the same amount of compensation as the other workers. MacKethan, *Recollections of a Southern Daughter*, 90–1.

33. Myers, *Children of Pride*, 1369

34. Myers, *Children of Pride*, 1382; 1428.

35. Smythe, Reminiscences, 84–85.

36. Selby Family Collection in Manuscript Department, New York Historical Society New York, November 21, 1866.

37. Myers, *Children of Pride*, 1391.

38. Leigh, *Ten Years on Georgia Plantation*, 81.

39. Leigh, *Ten Years on Georgia Plantation*, 121 and Charles E. Wynes, "Fanny Kemble's South Revisited: The South As Seen Through the Eyes of Her Daughter, Frances," *Louisiana Studies* 11–12 (Fall 1972–3): 473–488.

40. Worthington, Diary, June 10, 1863.

41. Burr, *Secret Eye*, 370.

42. Bartlett, *"My Dear Brother,"* 189.

43. Amelia Akehurst Lines, *To Raise Myself a Little: The Diaries and Letters of Jennie, a Georgia Teacher, 1851–1866*, Edited by Thomas Dyer (Athens: University of Georgia Press, 1982), 197.

44. Michael O'Brien, *An Evening When Alone: Four Journals of Single Women in the South, 1827–67* (Charlottesville: The University Press of Virginia, 1993), 39.

45. John Rozier, ed., *The Granite Farm Letters: The Civil War Correspondence of Edgeworth & Sallie Bird* (Athens: University of Georgia Press, 1988), 289.

46. Towles, *A World Turned Upside Down*, 285

47. Tryphena Blanche Holder Fox, *A Northern Woman in the Plantation South: Letters of Tryphena Blanche Holder Fox 1856–1876*, Edited by Wilma King (Columbia: University of South Carolina Press, 1993), 158.

48. M. Robertson, *A Confederate Lady Comes of Age*, 113.

49. Betty Herndon Maury, *The Confederate Diary of Betty Herndon Maury 1861–63*, Edited by Alice Maury Parmelee (Washington: Privately Printed, 1938), 89.

50. Scott, *Nannie Scott of "Bel-Air" School*, 32.

51. Mary E. Harrison, Letter, South Caroliniana Library, University of South Carolina, Columbia.

52. Burr, *Secret Eye*, 265.

53. Samuel A. Agnew, Diaries, January 1, 1866-October 25, 1867, Lee County Library, Tupelo, Mississippi, January 5 and January 3, 1866.

54. Colt, *Defend the Valley*, 248.

55. Beckwith, Journal, Vol. I, 70.

56. Beckwith, Journal, Vol. II, 34.

57. Elmore, Diary, 93.

58. *Our Women in the War*, 116.

59. Bleser, *Hammonds of Redcliffe*, 144.

60. Espy, Diary, 106.

61. E. Andrews, *The War-Time Journal of a Georgia Girl*, 376–77.

62. K. Foster, Diary, November 15, 1863.

63. Woodward, *Mary Chesnut's Civil War*, 733.

64. Beckwith, Journal, Vol. 1, 71.

65. Wadley, Diary, September 16, 1865.

66. Colt, *Defend the Valley*, 233.

67. Espy, Diary, January 1866.

68. Towles, *A World Turned Upside Down*, 665.

69. Susan Sillers Darden, Diary, In Darden Family Papers, Mississippi Department of Archives and History, Jackson, 75.

70. Elmore, Diary, 92.

71. Myers, *Children of Pride*, 1405.

72. Myers, *Children of Pride*, 1308.

73. Fannie E. Dickinson (Taylor), Diary, Virginia Historical Society, Richmond.

74. Burr, *Secret Eye*, 366.

75. Burr, *Secret Eye*, 367. For trials involving domestic help see Burr, *passim*.

76. S. Taylor, Diary.

77. Blanche Butler Ames, *Chronicles from the Nineteenth Century: Family Letters of Blanche Butler and Adelbert Ames*. Vol. I (Privately Published, 1957), 644.

78. Wynes, "Fanny Kemble's South Revisited," 479.

79. Leigh, *Ten Years on a Georgia Plantation*, 72.

80. Boom, "Testimony of Margaret Ketcham Ward," 396–97; 200; 399.

81. *New Orleans Daily True Delta*, August 9, 1865.

82. *New Orleans Daily True Delta*, August 9, 1865. (Probably reprinted from *Raleigh Progress*.)

83. Norfleet, Reminiscences, 12.

5—The Rocky Road to Reconciliation

1. Rice, Recollections; Fletcher, Diary.

2. Father Abram Ryan, Papers, Tennessee State Library and Archives, Nashville, Letter, September 16, 1866.

3. Selby Family Collection, Letter, November 26, 1866.

4. Buni, "Reconstruction in Orange County, Virginia," 464.

5. *Joint Committee on Reconstruction*, Part III, 9.

6. *Joint Commttee on Reconstruction*, Part II, 267.

7. Stamper and Lohrenz, "Manuscript Sources," 217

8. Augusta Jane Evans Wilson, Papers (7N/Box 260), Alabama Department of Archives and History, Montgomery, Alabama.

9. Rosa Postell, "Sherman's Occupation of Savannah: Two letters," *Georgia Historical Quarterly* 50 (1966): 114.

10. Foster, Diary, July 18, 1865; M.B. Goodwin, Diary, July 2, 1865.

11. Eggleston, *A Rebel's Recollections*, 86.

12. Boom, "Testimony of Margaret Ketcham Ward," 396. In a Letter to Margaret Ward's son written in September of 1936, Margaret Mitchell wrote of his mother's lengthy testimony concerning the war and reconstruction before the United States Committee on Education and Labor: "I hope you will not think me foolishly enthusiastic when I write you that I think your mother's testimony is undoubtedly the most perfect and valuable and complete picture of a long gone day that I have come across in ten years of research into the period of the Sixties. If I had read that book, I am sure I would not have had to read hundreds of memoirs, letters and diaries to get the background of 'Gone With the Wind' in accurately." (George Ward Collection of Scrapbooks. Quoted in Boom, 271.)

13. Boom, "Testimony of Margaret Ketcham Ward," 401.

14. John Anderson, *Brokenburn*, 351.

15. George C. Benham, *A Year of Wreck: A True Story by a Victim* (New York: Harper & Brothers, 1880), 226.

16. Dennett, *The South As It Is*, 305.

17. John Anderson, *Brokenburn*, 357; 355.

18. Seddon, Diary, Part II, Vol. 22, 13.

19. Seddon, Diary, Part II, Vol. 22, 14.

20. Fox, *A Northern Woman in the Plantation South*, 165.

21. M. Robertson, *A Confederate Lady Comes of Age*, 76–77.

22. Florence Anderson, Papers. For a firsthand account of Jefferson Davis's trial see James Eliott Walmsley, "Some Unpublished Letters of Burton H. Harrison," in *Publications of the Mississippi Historical Society* 8 (1907): 81–85.

23. *Joint Committee on Reconstruction*, Part III, 10.

24. Gordon B. McKinney, "Women's Role in Civil War Western North Carolina," *North Carolina Historical Review* 69, No. 1 (1992): 52.

25. Schwartz, *A Woman Doctor's Civil War*, 243.

26. *Joint Committee on Reconstruction*, Part III, 14.

27. Hancock, *South After Gettysburg*, 217.

28. For a more detailed account of Catherine Minor's loyalty and postwar discrimination see Frank W. Klingberg, "The Case of the Minors: A Unionist Family Within the Confederacy," *Journal of Southern History* 13 (February-November 1947): 27–45; Frank W.Klingberg, "The Southern Claims Commission" in *University of California Publications in History* 50 (Berkeley: University of California Press, 1955), 222–226; and G.W Cable, ed., "War Diary of a Union Woman in the South," *Century Magazine* 38 (May-October 1889): 931–936.

29. Burr, *Secret Eye*, 336.

30. *New Orleans Daily True Delta*, August 25, 1865. (Probably reprinted from the *Mobile Advertiser*.)

31. *New Orleans Daily Picayune*, February 14, 1866.

32. M. Robertson, *A Confederate Lady Comes of Age*, 79.

33. M. Robertson, *A Confederate Lady Comes of Age*, 80.

34. *New Orleans Times*, May 15, 1865.

35. Fletcher, Diary and *Mobile News*, May 11, 1865.

36. Elmore, Diary, 87 and 91. Lucy Fletcher was shocked by Yankee behavior during the occupation of Richmond. Particularly offensive to a family friend was the "fastening of their horses in front of her door, while they visisted some disreputable houses in the neighborhood." Later, "a *long line* of horses awaiting their masters in the street" infuriated Lucy and the neighbors. "This is their boasted Yankee *morality*—a thing that was never done during the war or at any other time by our own officers, who without claiming any high degree of morality had yet sufficient *decency* and self-respect to show some consideration for the upright [?] respectable people in the neighborhood, & *such* profanity!" Fletcher, Diary.

37. French, Diary, 232.

38. French, Diary, 233–36.

39. Smythe, Reminiscences, 86.

40. Elmore, Diary, 96.

41. Towles, *A World Turned Upside Down*, 792.

42. Towles, *A World Turned Upside Down*, 492–93.

43. William P. Marchione, Jr., "Go South, Young Man! Reconstruction Letters of a Massachusetts Yankee," *South Carolina Historical Magazine*, 80 (January 1979): 34.

44. Eggleston, *A Rebel's Recollections*, 183; 181.

45. Handy, "*In The Last Days of the Confederacy*," 110.

46. Perdue et al., *Weevils in the Wheat*, 44.

47. Mary Burrows Fontaine, Letters, Eleanor S. Brockenbrough Library, The Museum of the Confederacy, Richmond, Virginia.

48. See "Ironclad Test Oaths of 1862 and January 24, 1865," in Harold Melvin Hyman, *Era of the Oath: Northern Loyalty Tests During the Civil War and Reconstruction* (Philadelphia: University of Pennsylvania Press, 1954), 158–59.

49. It should be noted that in most areas, taking the loyalty oath was strictly adhered to; however, in other areas and sometimes for minor positions the test oath was ignored or subjected to various interpretations. During the war in some areas of the occupied South, Union officials realized the farce involved in forcing most recalcitrant rebel civilians to swear their fidelity to the Federal government. In such sections primarily deserters and discharged Confederate soldiers were required to take the oath. Other officials relentlessly insisted on enforcement of the loyalty oath for "travelers, soldiers, or civilians." (Hyman, *Era of the Oath*, 35.) Widows frequently were required to take the loyalty oath under threat of having their property confiscated if they refused.

50. Mary Wilkinson, Papers, Historic New Orleans Collection, New Orleans, Louisiana.

51. Postell, "Sherman's Occupation of Savannah," 114.

52. Margaret Mackay Jones, ed., *Catherine Devereux Edmondston 1860–1866* (Mebane, North Carolina: Privately Published, n.d.), 108 and Beth G.Crabtree and James W. Patton, eds., "*Journal of a Secesh Lady": The Diary of Catherine Ann Devereux Edmondston 1860–1866* (Raleigh, North Carolina: Division of Archives and History, 1979), 716.

53. Emily V. Mason, "Memories of a Hospital Matron" in Charles G. Waugh and Martin H. Greenberg, *The Women's War in the South: Recollections and Reflections of the American Civil War* (Nashville, Tennessee: Cumberland House, 1999), 242. Taken from *Atlantic Monthly* 90 (September and October 1902): 305–318 and 475–485.

54. Fanny Kemble Wister, "Sarah Butler Wister's Civil War Diary," *Pennsylvania Magazine of History and Biography* 102 (July 1978): 304.

55. *Joint Committee on Reconstruction*, Part IV, 125.

56. Edmondson, Diary.

57. Bartlett, "*My Dear Brother*," 127.

58. Bartlett, "*My Dear Brother*," 127.

59. Bartlett, "*My Dear Brother*," 128–29.

60. Craighead, Diary, April 30, 1863. For a thoughtful analysis of the morality involved in subscribing to the Oath of Allegiance see *The Heavens Are Weeping: The Diaries of George Richard Browder 1852–1886*, Edited by Richard L. Troutman (Grand Rapids, Michigan: Zondervan Publishing House, 1987).

61. Selby Family Collection.

62. Richard Addison Wood and Joan Faye Wood, "For Better or for Worse," in Waugh and Greenberg, *The Women's War in the South*, 264.

63. Scott, *Nannie Scott of "Bel-Air" School*, 33.

64. Pringle, *Chronicles of Chicora Wood*, 260.

65. Botume, *First Days Amongst the Contrabands*, 31.

66. Quoted in Lillian Adele Kibler, *Benjamin F. Perry: South Carolina Unionist* (Durham, N.C.: Duke University Press, 1946), 407.

67. Reported in the *Chicago Tribune*, July 13, 1865. A far more detailed discussion of the Loyalty Oath, beginning with the Loyalty Oaths demanded of Federal civil servants in 1861, may be found in Harold Melvin Hyman's *Era of the Oath: Northern Loyalty Tests During the Civil War and Reconstruction*.

68. *New Orleans Times*, May 15, 1865; *New Orleans Daily Picayune*, May 11, 12, 1865.

69. Follansbee, Diary, April 30, 1865.

70. Allen Cabaniss, *The University of Mississippi: Its First Hundred Years* (Hattiesburg, Mississippi: University & College Press of Mississippi, 1971), 65.

71. Fletcher, Diary; April 9, 1865. Mrs. John Huske (Lucy London) Anderson, *North Carolina Women of the Confederacy* (Fayetteville, North Carolina: North Carolina Division, United Daughters of the Confederacy, 1926), 26.

72. *New Orleans Times*, May 15, 1865.

73. M.B. Goodwin, Diary, May 28. 1865.

74. M.B. Goodwin, Diary, June 4, 1865.

75. The number of teachers conducting schools for blacks even during the war was impressive. According to some statistics in the occupied South in January of 1865 about 750 people were teaching some 75,000 Negro children. One former slavewoman, for example, taught free Negro children for fifteen years in a makeshift schoolroom in her employer's yard. In order to circumvent the restrictions against teaching Negroes to read and write, the school was registered under the names of her employer's sons. Mary Weston, who conducted a school in her father's home, was twice arrested for doing so, and was ordered to hire a white woman "to sit in the room where she taught—then she was allowed to go on with her school." Schwartz, *A Woman Doctor's Civil War*, 199.

76. See Bentley, *A History of the Freedmen's Bureau*, 170.

77. Bentley, *A History of the Freedmen's Bureau*, *passim*.

78. *Joint Committee on Reconstruction*, Part III, 35.

79. Quoted in Trey Berry, "A History of Women's Higher Education in Mississippi, 1819–1882," *Journal of Mississippi History* 53, No. 4 (November 1991): 315.

80. L.D. Miller, Recollections.

81. Joseph C. Vance, "Freedmen's Schools in Albemarle County During Reconstruction," *Virginia Magazine of History and Biography* 61, No. 4 (October 1953): 432.

82. Allis Wolfe, "Women Who Dared: Northern Teachers of the Southern Freeemen, 1862–1872," Ph.D. diss., The City University of New York, 1982. Photocopy of Typescript. Ann Arbor, Michigan, University Microfilms International, 1982.

83. Quoted in Trey Berry "A History of Women's Higher Education in Mississippi," 314.

84. *Joint Committe on Reconstruction*, Part II, 267–68.

85. Hancock, *South After Gettysburg*, 234; 193; 223.

86. Schwartz, *A Woman Doctor's Civil War, 243*. Wayne E. Reilly, ed., *Sarah Jane Foster: Teacher of the Freedmen: A Diary and Letters* (Charlottesville: University Press of Virginia, 1990), *passim*.

87. Wolfe, "Women Who Dared," 107–108.

88. B. Ames, *Chronicles from the Nineteenth Century*, Vol. 1, 215.

89. Wolfe, "Women Who Dared," 105.

90. Reid, *After the War*, 46.

91. *Joint Committee on Reconstruction*, Part III, 34.

92. Quoted in Currie, *Enclave*, 193.

93. Botume, *First Days Amongst the Contrabands*, 258. The teachers of black children were not alone in coming under scrutiny; Southerners insisted on strict requirements for white female teachers of white children. The Committee on Teachers of the School Board of the City of New Orleans published a lengthy list of the teachers' duties and requirements in the August 17, 1866, issue of the *New Orleans Times*. Heading the list was the insistence that a teacher have an "unblemished moral character" and secondly "the necessary literary qualifications." Along with requirements of patience, kindness, firmness and impartiality came the recommendation that "The teacher of girls, especially, must be refined in manner and womanly in deportment. We want no masculine woman to teach our girls—no advocate of 'woman's rights.' We wish our daughters taught to be gentle, delicate and refined—not bold, forward, masculine." Furthermore, the committee stated that in their opinion "elderly ladies, or at any rate mothers are much better adapted to teaching and governing little children in the primary department than young girls are, and recommend that in all cases of equal qualifications in other respects the preference be given to such."

94. Albert T. Morgan, *Yazoo; Or, On the Picket Line of Freedom in the South* (Washington, D.C.: Published by Author, 1884), 112–13. Morgan soon garnered an unsavory reputation as a "Carpetbagger from Wisconsin," although at the same time there were hosts of devotees who accorded him a status approaching the divine. For more information on the Morgan story see *Yazoo; Its Legend and Legacies* by DeCell and Pritchard, 315–348.

95. Wolfe, "Women Who Dared," 105.

96. Bentley, *History of the Freedmen's Bureau*, 182.

97. E. F. Puckett, "Reconstruction in Monroe County," *Publications of the Mississippi Historical Society* 11 (1910): 117; 129. It was reported to have been Huggins' bloodstained shirt that was taken to Washington and used by Ben Butler in a speech before Congress detailing the Klan's villainy. This then apparently was the origin of the famous phrase "waving the bloody shirt." Trelease, *White Terror*, 294.

98. Puckett, "Reconstruction in Monroe County," 138–39; Hattie Magee, "Reconstruction in Lawrence and Jefferson Davis Counties," *Publications of the Mississippi Historical Society* 11 (1910): 196; M. G. Abney, "Reconstruction in Pontotoc County," *Publications of Mississippi Historical Society* 11 (1910): 258–59.

99. Bentley, *History of the Freedmen's Bureau*, 182, 179–80 and Wolfe, "Women Who Dared," 108.

100. Wolfe, *Women Who Dared*, 107–112.

101. *New Orleans Times*, June 16, 1869.

102. Perdue et al., *Weevils in the Wheat*, 29.

103. Wolfe, *Women Who Dared*, 157.

104. *Joint Committee on Reconstruction*, Part II, 197.

105. *Joint Committee on Reconstruction*, Part II, 199.

106. N. Henry, WPA Federal Writers' Project.

107. Hancock, *South After Gettysburg*, 282.

108. Thorpe, "Life in Virginia by a 'Yankee Teacher,'" 193.

109. Thorpe, "Life in Virginia by a 'Yankee Teacher,'" 193.

110. Perdue et al., *Weevils in the Wheat*, 285; 197.

111. See the Rollin sisters—Catherine de Medici, Charlotte Corday, and Louise Muhlbach whose Columbia, South Carolina, home was filled with "'beautiful carpets, elegant furniture, tasteful pictures, a one thousand dollar piano'" and where "salons" were held for some of the city's leading social and political leaders, including both blacks and whites. Simkins and Woody, *South Carolina During Reconstruction*, 368–69. The story of Frances Rollin is told in Catherine Clinton, *Civil War Stories* (Athens: University of Georgia Press, 1998), 99–111. Also see the autobiography of James Thomas, who at one time was was one of the wealthiest Negroes in the United States: Loren Schweninger, *From Tennessee Slave to St. Louis Entrepreneur: The Autobiography of James Thomas* (Columbia: University of Missouri Press, 1984), *passim*. See also the Johnsons of Natchez in Gould, *Chained to the Rock of Adversity: To Be Free, Black & Female in the Old South*, *passim*. It should be remembered that financially successful free black families often became slaveholders themselves. In Charleston in 1860 about four hundred slaves were owned by some one hundred free blacks. Some free blacks bought and employed relatives to save them from cruel treatment by their slaveowners. Clinton, *Civil War Stories*, 100. *Slave Testimony: Two Centuries of Letters, Speeches, Interviews, and Autobiographies*, edited by John W. Blassingame (Baton Rouge: Louisiana State University Press, 1977) contains many remarkable success stories of former slaves.

6—*The Radicals and Reconstruction*

1. *Chicago Tribume*, July 6, 1865.

2. *Chicago Tribune*, July 21, 1865.

3. *Joint Committee on Reconstruction*, Part III, 121.

4. *Joint Committee on Reconstruction*, Part II, 198.

5. *Joint Committee on Reconstruction*, Part II, 243.

6. *Joint Committee on Reconstruction*, Part II, 143; 141.

7. *Joint Committee on Reconstruction*, Part IV, 124; 37; 125.

8. For a detailed report of the aims and findings of the Joint Committee see various sections of the *Report of the Joint Committee on Reconstruction*.

9. Thaddeus Stevens, "Reconstruction," An address delivered at Lancaster, Pennsylvania on September 6, 1865, in *The American Mind: Selections from the Literature of the United States*, Edited by Harry R. Warfel et al. (New York: American Book Company, 1959), 579–584.

10. *New Orleans Daily Picayune*, January 24, 1866.

11. George C. Rable, *But There Was No Peace: The Role of Violence in the Politics of Reconstruction* (Athens: University of Georgia Press, 1984), 248.

12. Stampp, Kenneth M. and Leon F. Litwack, eds., *Reconstruction: An Anthology of Revisionist Writings* (Baton Rouge: Louisiana State University Press, 1969), 518; Stetson Kennedy, *After Appomattox: How the South Won the War* (Gainesville: University Press of Florida, 1995), 61.

13. Hodding Carter, *The Angry Scar: The Story of Reconstruction* (Garden City, New York: Doubleday & Company, 1959), 54. Stampp and Litwack, *Reconstruction: An Anthology*, 518.

14. Quoted in T. Harry Williams, "An Analysis of Some Reconstruction Attitudes," *Journal of Southern History* 12 (November 1946): 477.

15. Bonner, *The Diary of a Milledgeville Girl*, 127.

16. Darden, Diary, 76.

17. Clift, *The Private War of Lizzie Hardin*, 286.

18. Thorpe, "Life in Virginia by a 'Yankee Teacher,'" 202.

19. Frank Durr in Jim Dawson, *Bits & Pieces*, 19.

20. Botume, *First Days Amongst the Contrabands*, 263.

21. Meriwether, *Recollections of 92 Years 1824–1916*, v, and Berkeley, "Elizabeth Avery Meriwether, 'An Advocate for Her Sex,'" 397.

22. For an interesting discussion of the registration and voting procedures in South Carolina see Saville, *The Work of Reconstruction*, 143–198.

23. Beaumont, *Business Woman's Journal*, 300. For more information see Beaumont, *Business Woman's Journal*, 340–341.

24. Beaumont, *Business Woman's Journal*, 300.

25. Briscoe, Memoir, 173.

26. Rice, Recollections.

27. Harold M Hyman, ed., *New Frontiers of the American Reconstruction* (Urbana: University of Illinois Press, 1966), 73.

28. Avary, *Dixie After the War*, 346–47.

29. Charles L. Perdue, Jr., Thomas E. Barden, Robert K. Phillips, eds., *Weevils In The Wheat: Interviews with Virginia Ex-Slaves* (Bloomington: Indiana University Press, 1980), 23 and Charles Stearns, *The Black Man of the South, and the Rebels* (New York: Negro Universities Press, 1969), 207.

30. Beaumont, *Business Woman's Journal*, 340.

31. George J. Leftwich, "Reconstruction in Monroe County," *Publications of the Mississippi Historical Society* 9 (1906): 77.

32. Magee, "Reconstruction in Lawrence and Jefferson Davis Counties," 188.

33. Revisionist historians point to the fact that the surprising Democratic victories at the polls in Mississippi in 1875 appear to be the result of many white Republicans' dissatisfaction with certain Radical Republican principles and their consequent switch to the Democratic Party rather than the generally accepted theory that the Negroes were frightened away from the polls. David Donald, "The Scalawag in Mississippi Reconstruction," *Journal of Southern History* 10 (November 1944): 460.

34. Colt, *Defend the Valley*, 378.

35. Clift, *The Private War of Lizzie Hardin*, 282.

36. Richard T. Couture, ed., "Good Golly! Miss Mollie: The Massie Letters," Part III, *Goochland County Historical Society Magazine* 17 (1985): 12.

37. Richard W. Murphy, *The Nation Reunited: War's Aftermath* (Alexandria, Virginia: Time-Life Books, 1987), 67.

38. Worthington, Diary, October 6, 1865.

39. Burr, *Secret Eye*, 297–98.

40. Leigh, *Ten Years on a Georgia Plantation*, 132–33 and J. H. Jones, "Reconstruction in Wilkinson County," *Publications of the Mississippi Historical Society* 8 (1907): 161.

41. *Mobile News*, June 9, 1865 and *New Orleans Times*, June 12, 1865.

42. Alfred Lacey Hough, *Soldier in the West: The Civil War Letters of Alfred Lacey Hough*, Edited by Robert G. Athearn (Philadelphia: University of Pennsylvania Press, 1957), 192.

43. John Vance Lauderdale, *The Wounded River: The Civil War Letters of John Vance Lauderdale, M.D.*, edited by Peter Josyph (East Lansing: Michigan State University Press, 1993), 193–196.

44. Lauderdale, *The Wounded River*, 200.

45. Lauderdale, *The Wounded River*, 203.

46. Lauderdale, *The Wounded River*, 205.

47. Roark, *Masters Without Slaves*, 187.

48. Trowbridge, *The Desolate South*, 305.

49. *Mobile Daily News*, June 3, 1865. (Apparently extracted from the *New York Herald Tribune*.)

50. For a file of some 200 engaging letters inquiring about the weather, soil, and financial situation in the South, check out Henry Clements Collier, Collier Collection, Tennessee State Library and Archives, Nashville.

51. John Hammond Moore, *Columbia and Richland County: A South Carolina Community, 1740–1990* (Columbia: University of South Carolina Press, 1993), 224–25.

52. *The Weekly Clarion* [Jackson, Mississippi], April 24, 1869. (Reprinted from the *New York Times*.)

53. *Chicago Tribune*, August 7, 1865.

54. *New Orleans Times*, August 5, 1866.

55. Futrell, "Efforts of Mississippians to Encourage Immigration," 63.

56. Leigh, *Ten Years on a Georgia Plantation*, 81.

57. Qouted in David H.Overy, Jr., *Wisconsin Carpetaggers in Dixie* (Madison: The Department of History, University of Wisconsin, 1961), 53.

58. The inhospitality and trauma encountered by George Benham and his wife were similarly detailed in an astute part fact, part fiction account of another "crusader-adventurer" in Albion W.Tourgée's *A Fool's Errand by One of the Fools* (New

York: Fords, Howard, & Hulbert, 1880), a popular book of the 1880s. See Current's *Those Terrible Carpetbaggers* for a brief glimpse at the remarkable lives of Albion and Emma Tourgée and William Peirce Randel's *The Ku Klux Klan: A Century of Infamy* (Philadelphia: Chilton Books, 1965), for a discussion of Tourgée and *A Fool's Errand.* Also see Morgan's *Yazoo* for some of the author's experiences as a "Carpetbagger" in the South.

59. George C. Benham, *A Year of Wreck: A True Story by a Victim* (New York: Harper & Brothers, 1880), 91.

60. Benham, *A Year of Wreck*, 106.

61. Benham, *A Year of Wreck*, 228–29.

62. Benham, *A Year of Wreck*, 226.

63. Benham, *A Year of Wreck*, 101.

64. Although most people define carpetbaggers as Northerners seeking economic or political advantage in the South *after the war*, it would seem the term could as well be applied to any Northerners (sans carpetbags) seeking economic opportunity in the South either *during or after the war.*

65. Carpetbaggers, of course, took their name from the "suitcases" they toted which contained most of their worldly possessions. One man saw little justification in being denigrated as a "carpetbagger" merely because he "was born in the North, had fought for the country, and thought he had a right to live where he chose." (Tourgée, *A Fool's Errand*, 171.) It should be emphasized that despite their defamation by Southerners, the carpetbaggers were not necessarily the "dregs of Northern society." Many had been middle-class, educated businessmen, teachers, and even former Union veterans who had served in the South during the war. The word "scalawag" apparently came from Scalloway in the Shetland Islands and referred to "an undersized, worthless animal."

66. *Joint Committee on Reconstruction*, Part III, 19.

67. Dennett, *The South as It Is*, 273–74.

68. B. Ames, *Chronicles from the Nineteenth Century*, Vol. 1, *708.*

69. Quoted in Overy, *Wisconsin Carpetbaggers in Dixie*, 53.

70. The *Weekly Clarion*, February 1, 1869.

71. The *Weekly Clarion*, February 1, 1869.

72. Briscoe, *Memoir*, 171.

73. Beaumont, *Business Woman's Journal*, 340.

74. Bartlett, "*My Dear Brother*," 198.

75. B. Ames, *Chronicles from the Nineteenth Century*, Vol. 1, 217; 216.

76. B. Ames, *Chronicles from the Nineteenth Century*, Vol. 1, 667.

77. Wilson, *Selected Papers of Cornelia Phillips Spencer*, 195.

78. Beaumont, *Business Woman's Journal*, 302.

79. *Chicago Tribune*, July 26, 1865.

80. Stampp, *Era of Reconstruction*, 174–75.

81. Trelease, *White Terror*, xxix.

7—Coping with a World Out of Control

1. Scarborough, *The Diary of Edmund Ruffin*, 946.

2. Lee Ann Whites, *The Civil War as a Crisis in Gender: Augusta, Georgia, 1860–1890* (Athens: University of Georgia Press, 1995), 133.

3. Wilson, *Selected Papers of Cornelia Phillips Spencer*, 113.

4. Wilson, *Selected Papers of Cornelia Phillips Spencer*, 113.

5. *Our Women in the War*, 115.

6. *Our Women in the War*, 116.

7. Mildred Hill Bradford and Edna Earl Baldwin, eds., "Letters from the Folwell-Curtis Families 1845–1890," In History and Genealogy Division, Biloxi Public Library, Biloxi, Mississippi.

8. Stephenson, "My Father and His Household, Before, During and After the War."

9. Clift, *Private War of Lizzie Harden*, 261.

10. Mrs. Roger A. Pryor, *Reminiscences of Peace and War* (New York: The Macmillan Company, 1904), 391–92.

11. Anne L. Austin, *The Woolsey Sisters of New York: A Family's Involvement in the Civil War and a New Profession (1860–1900)* (Philadelphia American Philosophical Society, 1971), 109.

12. Bartlett, *"My Dear Brother,"* 173–74.

13. Clift, *Private War of Lizzie Hardin*, 281.

14. Allan, *The Life and Letters of Margaret Junkin Preston*, 156.

15. Dennett, *The South As It Is*, 21.

16. Craighead, Diary, September 1869.

17. Burr, *Secret Eye*, 339.

18. *New Orleans Daily Picayune*, December 28, 1865.

19. See Gaines M. Foster, *Ghosts of the Confederacy: Defeat, the Lost Cause, and the Emergence of the New South 1865 to 1913* (New York: Oxford University Press, 1987).

20. Fearn, *Diary of a Refugee, passim.*

21. William T. Alderson, ed., "The Civil War Diary of Captain James Litton Cooper, September 30, 1861 to January 1865," *Tennessee Historical Quarterly* 15 (June 1956): 173.

22. E. Andrews, *The War-Time Journal of a Georgia Girl*, 375.

23. Sutherland, *A Very Violent Rebel*, 163.

24. Merton E. Coulter, "Lost Generation: The Life and Death of James Barrow, C.S.A.," *Confederate Centennial Studies* No. 1 (1956): 102.

25. M. Robertson, *A Confederate Lady Comes of Age*, 83.

26. *Our Women in the War*, 325.

27. John Anderson, *Brokenburn*, 369; 357

28. Martha Buxton Porter Brent, Reminiscences (Accession 26501) Personal Papers Collection, Archives Research Services, The Library of Virginia, Richmond, Va.

29. Jervey and Ravenel, "Two Diaries from Middle St. John's Berkeley, South Carolina," 43. Gradually, and for the more affluent, private clubs began holding dances once again. Horse racing resumed its antebellum fascination for breeders, owners, jockeys, and spectators, and baseball enticed thousands of enthusiastic players and fans. In time concerts, operas, professional and amateur theatricals, circuses, and minstrel shows gradually emerged to offer a smorgasbord of entertainment for city-dwellers fortunate enough to be able to come up with the wherewithal for tickets. For the masses of rural residents there were opportunities for diversion and socializing at picnics, barbecues, agricultural fairs, church gatherings, and Grange activities. (Simkins and Woody, *South Carolina During Reconstruction*, 338–372.)

30. Anderson, *Brokenburn*, 354.
31. McGee and Lander, *A Rebel Came Home*, 97.
32. McGee and Lander, *A Rebel Came Home*, 93–94.
33. Burr, *Secret Eye*, 338. For more details of the tournaments see Avary, *Dixie After the War*, 171–75.
34. Colt, *Defend the Valley*, 382–83.
35. Nash K. Burger and John K Bettersworth, *South of Appomattox* (New York: Harcourt, Brace and Company, 1959), 43.
36. Beaumont, *Business Woman's Journal*, 301.
37. Sutherland, *A Very Violent Rebel, passim.*
38. McGee and Lander, *A Rebel Came Home*, 94–96.
39. *Our Women in the War*, 457–59.
40. De Forest, *A Union Officer in the Reconstruction*, 142–43.
41. Eggleston, *A Rebel's Recollections*, 181.
42. See earlier notation of Texas Regiment looting in E. Andrews, *The War-Time Journal of a Georgia Girl*, 193–94.
43. *Our Women in the War*, 290.
44. Scarborough, *The Diary of Edmund Ruffin*, 852.
45. Handy, "In the Last Days of the Confederacy," 107.
46. See purposes of Committee in Trelease, *White Terror*, 392.
47. Kennedy, *After Appomattox 195; 208.*
48. For example, see more detailed testimony in *Joint Committee on Reconstruction, passim;* Kennedy, *After Appomattox;* Trelease, *White Terror;* Walter L. Fleming, *Documentary History of Reconstruction: Political, Military, Social, Religious, Educational and Industrial 1865 to 1906*, Vol. 2 (New York: McGraw-Hill, 1966).
49. *Testimony Taken by the U.S. Congress: The Joint Select Committee to Inquire into the Condition of Affairs in the Late Insurrectionary States.* Vol.1 (Washington: Government Printing Office, 1872), 27.
50. *Testimony Taken by the U.S. Congress*, 27.
51. Dennett, *The South As It Is*, 261.
52. E. Andrews, *The War-Time Journal of a Georgia Girl*, 343.
53. *Testimony Taken by the U.S. Congress*, 7.
54. See Meriwether, *Recollections of 92 Years*, 202–9.
55. Ned Chaney, WPA Federal Writers' Project, Meridian-Lauderdale County Public Library, Meridian, Mississippi.
56. Simon Hare, WPA Federal Writers' Project, Meridian-Lauderdale County Public Library, Meridian, Mississippi.
57. Beaumont, *Business Woman's Journal*, 301–302.
58. Irby C. Nichols, "Reconstruction in DeSoto County," *Publications of Mississippi Historical Society* 11 (1910): 311.
59. Mrs. William F. Hardin, Letter written May 30, 1910, to the Florence Chapter of the United Daughters of the Confederacy printed in the *Florence Times*, Florence, Alabama.
60. Meriwether, *Recollections of 92 Years*, 202–9.
61. W.F. Hardin, Letter.
62. Bartlett, *"My Dear Brother,"* 198.
63. Stamper and Lohrenz, "Manuscript Sources," 191 and Narcisa Black, Diary, Mississippi Department of Archives and History, Jackson, September 13, 1870, and October 8, 1870.

64. Frank, F. Wetta, "'Bulldozing the Scalawags': Some Examples of the Persecution of Southern White Republicans in Louisiana During Reconstruction," *Louisiana History* 21, No. 1 (Winter, 1980): 49.

65. Beckwith, Journal, 33.

66. Rable, *But There Was No Peace*, 87.

67. M. Harrison, Letter.

68. A. Wilson, Letter to Mrs. J. H. Crisman, February 3, 1866.

69. Postell, "Sherman's Occupation of Savannah," 114.

70. Towles, *World Turned Upside Down*, 478.

71. E. Andrews, *The War-Time Journal of a Georgia Girl*, 184.

72. Clift, *The Private War of Lizzie Hardin*, 241; 250.

73. M. Robertson, *A Confederate Lady Comes of Age*, 76–79. Although General Hampton's home was one of the many destroyed during the war, he would not abandon the South. Instead he urged Southerners "to devote our whole energies to the restoration of law and order, the re-establishment of agriculture and commerce, the promotion of education and the rebuilding of our cities and dwellings which have been laid in ashes." Quoted in R. Henry, *The Story of Reconstruction*, 26–7.

74. Wiley, "*This Infernal War,*" 442.

75. Wiley, "*This Infernal War,*" 442.

76. Wiley, "*This Infernal War,*" 443–44.

77. Elmore, Diary, 93.

78. Elmore, Diary, 96; 103.

79. Enterprising speculators formed a host of Colonization Societies, such as the well-known Southern Colonization Society of Edgefield, South Carolina. The societies dispensed agents to various areas in the Western territories, in Latin America, and in Brazil to sound out the potential for former Confederates. Estimates run as high as 10,000 Southerners who left home for foreign lands. Cyrus B. Dawsey and James M. Dawsey, eds., *The Confederados: Old South Immigrants in Brazil* (Tuscaloosa: The University of Alabama Press, 1995), *passim*.

80. For an interesting study of "Brazilian fever," the South American migration and the melding of the two societies see Eugene C. Harter, *The Lost Colony of the Confederacy* (Jackson: University Press of Mississippi, 1985). Also see information on the Santa Barbara d'Oeste settlement near Americana in Brazil. Alan M. Tigay, "The Deepest South," *American Heritage* 49 (April 1998): 84–95.

81. Sitterson, "The McCollams," 361. Andrew McCollam registered great disappointment with his trip to Brazil in July of 1866 "with a people who do not speak my language or with whom I can not talk and in a country where everything is going to decay I must now confess to myself I have not the courage to settle."

82. Lucy Judkins Durr, "Brazilian Recollections" (Accession 319370 Personal Papers Collection, Archives Research Services, The Library of Virginia, Richmond, Virginia.

83. Maury chose for the first settlement a place nine miles southeast of Cordoba, which was to be called Carlota. Land was sold for $1 an acre "on five years' credit" and Maury expected that "By the time these lands are paid for they will be worth, even if no more settlers come to the Empire, $20, $30, or even $100 the acre, for they produce everything under the sun, and yield perpetual harvests."

Quoted in Carl Coke Rister, "Carlota, A Confederate Colony in Mexico," *Journal of Southern History* 11 (February 1945): 41, from Lewis Matthew Maury, letter November 27, 1865.

84. Durrell, Collection, 990. Letter dated January 17, 1866, printed December 3, 1865, in paper.

85. Quoted in Alfred J. Hanna, "A Confederate Newspaper in Mexico," *Journal of Southern History* 12 (February 1946): 70, from *Mexican Times*, September 3, 1866.

86. Quoted in Hanna from *Mexican Times*, September 16, 1865.

87. Hanna, "A Confederate Newspaper," 74. Before Allen's enthusiasm could wane, however, and little more than seven months after the first publication of the *Mexican Times*, Allen died following a brief illness, which perhaps had been complicated by his shattered right leg, a wound acquired during his service with the Confederate army.

88. Dawsey and Dawsey, *The Confederados*, 361.

89. Burger and Bettersworth, *South of Appomattox*, 64–73.

90. Daniel E. Sutherland, "Exiles, Emigrants, and Sojourners: The Post-Civil War Confederate Exodus in Perspective," *Civil War History* 31, No. 3 (September 1985): 251.

91. Richard W. Griffin, "Problems of the Southern Cotton Planters After the Civil War," *Georgia Historical Quarterly* 39 (1955):104. Also see Sutherland, "Exiles," 238 and 247; Sutherland, *The Confederate Carpetbaggers* (Baton Rouge: Louisiana State University Press, 1988), 42–45; Coulter, *A History of the South*, 187; Foster, *Ghosts*, 14–19.

92. Pryor, *Reminiscences*, 300–400. Roger was one of the lawyers secured by Benjamin Butler, Adelbert Ames's father-in-law, to help with Ames' impeachment-resignation problems at the beginning of his second term as governor of Mississippi. Roger Pryor later became a justice of the Supreme Court of New York and Mrs. Pryor achieved a handsome reputation for herself writing books and essays. For additional illustrations of Southerners heading North or West in search of opportunities see Mrs. Burton Harrison, *Recollections Grave and Gay* (New York: Scribner's Sons, 1911); LeConte Family Papers, Manuscripts Division, Bancroft Library, University of California, Berkeley; and Current, *Those Terrible Carpetbaggers*, 184–85.

93. Coulter, *A History of the South*, 186.

94. Sandra L Myres, *Westering Women and the Frontier Experience 1800–1915* (Albuquerque: University of New Mexico Press, 1982), 258. In *Westering Women* the author presents an interesting discussion of women homesteaders.

95. Irby Morgan (Mrs.), *How It Was*, 154.

96. Pryor, *My Day*, 325–329.

97. De Forest, *A Union Officer in the Reconstruction*, 130.

98. Michael L Lanza, *Agrarianism and Reconstruction Politics: The Southern Homestead Act* (Baton Rouge: Louisiana State University Press, 1990), 18.

99. Circular No. 9 War Department, Bureau of Refuges, Freedmen & Abandoned Lands reported in the *New Orleans Times*, July 9, 1866. In April of 1874 in Mississippi certain state lands of one hundred and sixty acres were to be made available to white or black heads of households for five cents an acre with the condition that they would live on the land and improve it for two years. Futrell, "Efforts of Mississippians to Encourage Immigration," 70.

100. Lanza, *Agrarianism and Reconstruction Politics*, 13.

101. Peter Kolchin, *First Freedom: The Responses of Alabama's Blacks to Emancipation and Reconstruction* (Westport, Connecticut: Greenwood Press, 1972), 134–5 and Michael Lanza, "One of the Most Appreciated Labors of the Bureau": The Freedmen's Bureau and the Southern Homestead Act," in Cimbala and Miller, *The Freedmen's Bureau and Reconstruction*, 67–92.

102. Quoted in Bentley, *History of the Freedmen's Bureau*, 145. For brief summaries of one such disastrous attempt to homestead in Florida see Bentley, 146 and Lanza in Cimbala and Miller, 81–82.

103. Myres, *Westering Women*, 85–86.

8—New Dimensions for Women

1. Shirley Blotnick Moskow, *Emma's World: An Intimate Look at Lives Touched by the Civil War Era* (Far Hills, New Jersey: New Horizon Press, 1990), 49, 162, 201; Myres, *Westering Women*, 156.

2. Stamper and Lohrenz, "Manuscript Sources for 'Mississippi Homespun,'" 212.

3. Although large families were the norm, not all women wanted more children and took steps to avoid additional pregnancies. Reliable condoms were being manufactured probably as early as 1844, about five years after the development of vulcanized rubber by Charles Goodyear. Moscow, *Emma's World*, 197. Although discrete donors often purged family letters or diary entries relating to birth control before sharing them with libraries or historical societies, enough evidence survives to indicate that women had some basic knowledge of contraception. In 1864 the vaginal diaphragm was added to douches, vaginal sponges, and the rhythm method of birth control. Advertisements in newspapers and magazines spelled out various contraceptive and abortive remedies and products. Myres, *Westering Women*, 154–155.

4. In 1870, for example, women outnumbered men by 36,000 in Georgia and by 25,000 in North Carolina. See Anne Firor Scott, *The Southern Lady: From Pedestal to Politics 1830–1930* (Chicago: The University of Chicago Press, 1970), 106.

5. Elizabeth R. Baer, ed., *Shadows on My Heart: The Civil War Diary of Lucy Rebecca Buck of Virginia* (Athens: University of Georgia Press, 1997), 321.

6. Cordelia Scales, "The Civil War Letters of Cordelia Scales," Edited by Percy L. Rainwater, *Journal of Mississippi History* 1, No. 1 (January 1939): 181.

7. *"Maggie!" Maggie Lindsley's Journal*, December 13, 1864.

8. K. Foster, Diary, *passim* and Fannie Cooper in Elizabeth (Porter) Pitts Collection, Tennessee State Library and Archives, Nashville.

9. Bonner, *The Diary of a Milledgeville Girl*, 116.

10. O'Brien, *An Evening When Alone*, 375

11. Quoted in O'Brien, *An Evening When Alone*, 46.

12. Lou E. Thompson, Diary/Attala County Records (M193), McCain Library and Archives, The University of Southern Mississippi. Hattiesburg, January 15, 1870.

13. Thompson, Diary, May 31, 1872.

14. Buni, "Reconstruction in Organge County, Virginia," 465.

15. Bonner, *The Diary of a Milledgeville Girl*, 72; 84.

16. Colt, *Defend the Valley*, 393.

17. Bartlett, *"My Dear Brother,"* 195–96.

18. Bleser, *In Joy and in Sorrow*, 233.

19. See cases in Burr, *Secret Eye*; Beauchamp, *A Private War*; Craighead, Diary; George C. Rable, *Civil Wars: Women and the Crisis of Southern Nationalism* (Urbana and Chicago: University of Illinois Press, 1989).

20. Stickney, Collection.

21. Bartlett, *"My Dear Brother,"* 174.

22. For a closer look at the life of a 19th century woman mistreated and belittled by an insensitive spouse see Beauchamp, *A Private War*, *passim.*

23. Wilbur Fisk Tillett, "Southern Womanhood As Affected By the War," *Century Illustrated Monthly Magazine* Vol.43, New Series Vol. 21 (November 1891—April 1892): 10.

24. *New Orleans Times*, August 5, 1866.

25. Tillett, "Southern Womanhood," 10.

26. Virginia Clay-Clopton, *A Belle of the Fifties: Memoirs of Mrs. Clay of Alabama* (New York: De Capo Press, 1969); Bell Irvin Wiley, *Confederate Women* (New York: Barnes & Noble, 1975); *Carol Bleser and Frederick Heath, "The Clays of Alabama: The Impact of the Civil War on a Southern Marriage,"* in Carol Bleser, *In Joy and in Sorrow.*

27. Varina Davis, *Jefferson Davis Ex-President of the Confederate States of America: A Memoir by His Wife* Vol. 2 (New York: Bedford Company, 1890); Wiley, *Confederate Women.* Also see Burke Davis, *The Long Surrender* (New York: Random House, 1985).

28. Burr, *Secret Eye, passim.* C. Vann Woodward and Elisabeth Muhlenfeld,eds., *The Private Mary Chesnut: The Unpublished Civil War Diaries* (New York: Oxford University Press, 1984), 237.

29. Tillett, "Southern Womanhood," 12.

30. Tillett, "Southern Womanhood," 11–12.

31. Tillett, "Southern Womanhood," 12.

32. Tillett, "Southern Womanhood," *passim.*

33. Foster, *Ghosts*, 39.

34. *New Orleans Daily Picayune*, April 17, 1866.

35. *New Orleans Daily Picayune*, April 11, 1866.

36. *New Orleans Times*, November 1, 1866.

37. *New Orleans Times*, May 13, 1871.

38. See Foster, *Ghosts*, 37–38.

39. Foster, *Ghosts*, 42–46.

40. McGee and Lander, *Rebel Came Home*, 114–15.

41. M. Robertson, *A Confederate Lady Comes of Age*, 102 and Towles, *A World Turned Upside Down*, 518. Also see Avary, *Dixie After the War*, 405–419.

42. For details of the speeches and the ceremony see Whites' book *The Civil War as a Crisis in Gender*, 160–198.

43. Meriwether, *Recollections of 92 Years*, 193–95.

44. C. Vann Woodward, *The Burden of Southern History* (New York: Vintage Books, 1960); Rable, *Civil Wars.*

45. Quoted in Wendy Hamand Venet, *Neither Ballots Nor Bullets: Women Abo-*

lutionists and the Civil War (Charlottesville: University Press of Virginia, 1991), 158.

46. Meriwether, *Recollections of 92 Years*, v.
47. Meriwether, *Recollections of 92 Years*, vi.
48. Meriwether, *Recollections of 92 Years*, 221.
49. Meriwether, *Recollections of 92 Years*, 224–225.
50. Bleser, *In Joy and in Sorrow*, 151.
51. Wilson, *Selected Papers of Cornelia Phillips Spencer*, 159.
52. Wilson, *Selected Papers of Cornelia Phillips Spencer*, 164 and 351.
53. Wilson, *Selected Papers of Cornelia Phillips Spencer*, 165–166. Sarah Jane Foster in an essay opposing women's suffrage wrote: "Let man, as befits their stronger frames, be the surgeons, doctors, lawyers, and statesmen of our land, but let the women seek to be such wives, mothers, and sisters as shall most purify and enoble these servants of the public." Reilly, *Sarah Jane Foster*, 20. In time some women who had earlier denounced women's speaking in public had revised their thinking and many even became speakers themselves. Gertrude Thomas eloquently spoke up for women at the convention of the Georgia Woman Suffrage Association in 1899, stating that women were not plucked from the head of man and therefore superior to men, nor were they taken from his foot and therefore were not inferior. Instead woman came from the side of man and that should be her position in life—standing at his side as his equal. Burr, *Secret Eye*, 453.
54. Wilson, *Selected Papers of Cornelia Phillips Spencer*, 262; Scott, *The Southern Lady: From Pedestal to Politics*, 166.
55. Wilson, *Selected Papers of Cornelia Phillips Spencer*, 276; 201.
56. Wilson, *Selected Papers of Cornelia Phillips Spencer*, 159.
57. Quoted in Stamper and Lohrenz, "Manuscript Sources for 'Mississippi Homespun,'" 209. Also see Neilson papers in Mississippi Department of Archives and History, Jackson, Mississippi.
58. Wiley, *"This Infernal War,"* 270, 214, 235.
59. For an interesting discussion of the ratification of the Nineteenth Amendment see Doris Weatherford, *A History of the American Suffragist Movement* (Santa Barbara, California: The Moschovitis Group, Inc., 1998).

9—Susan Darden

1. Susan's Diary is found among the Darden Papers at the Mississippi Department of Archives and History in Jackson, Mississippi. Fayette is located some twenty-three miles north of Natchez.
2. April 1872.
3. October 22, 1865.
4. February 22, 1868.
5. February 21, 1868.
6. October 30, 1870.
7. December 30, 1872.
8. January 21, 1872.
9. January 7, 1868.
10. August 19, 1872.

11. January 29, 1866.
12. December 30, 1870.
13. March 3, 1871.
14. May 1, 1873.
15. February 5, 1874.
16. February 1, 1872.
17. August 16, 1871; January 19, 1872.
18. February 8, 1866.
19. October 1, 1866.
20. July 16, 1871.
21. April 13–16, 1873.
22. November 1872.
23. August 28, 1865.
24. January 28, 1866.
25. August 1865.
26. January 1866.
27. January 8, 1866.
28. January 7, 1873.
29. April 1, 1872.
30. December 30, 1867.
31. January 1, 1871.
32. December 2, 1865.
33. December 10, 1865.
34. August 14, 1865.
35. January 1, 1873.
36. April 19, 1866.
37. May 22, 1867.
38. July 22, 1867.
39. November 22, 1870.
40. November 5, 1872.
41. July 11, 1868.
42. December 7, 1874.
43. Robert Selph Henry, *The Story of Reconstruction* (New York: Konecky & Konecky, 1991), 529–531. Also see Richard W. Murphy, *The Nation Reunited: War's Aftermath* (Alexandria, Virginia: Time-Life Books, 1987), 145–148.
44. November 10, 1875.
45. July through November 1875. (Personal note: What a surprise it was to find the story of Susan's son-in-law's death corroborated in an unexpected source. One day as my husband was engaged in genealogical research in the Mississippi archives, he called my attention to a distant relative of his, a victim of Reconstruction violence who turned out to be no other than Thomas Cage West (Susan's daughter's husband)! The account noted that Thomas West "was killed by a negro named Tom Rice, during the time he was running for the office of sheriff, was ambushed by said negro, supposedly a tool of the carpet-baggers, operating in the Star Hill community, on Nov. 6th, 1876.")
46. April 16, 1873.
47. May 22, 1873.
48. March 12, 1871
49. March 20, 1868 and May 30, 1869.

50. January 5, 1873
51. January 28, 1866
52. January 1873
53. January 15, 1866
54. January 6, 1873
55. March 13, 1868
56. April 5–11, 1873
57. July 8, 1873.
58. May 20, 1871
59. November 2, 1871.

10—Virginia Smith Aiken

1. Virginia Carolina Smith Aiken's diary is to be found among the David Wyatt Aiken papers in the South Caroliniana Library at the University of South Carolina in Columbia. The family background material comes from Margaret Watson, *Greenwood County Sketches* (Greenwood, S.C.: Attic Press, Inc., 1982), 9.
2. Watson, *Greenwood County Sketches, passim.*
3. For a similar story catch episodes in the life of Ella Gertrude Clanton Thomas in *The Secret Eye* by Virginia Ingraham Burr.
4. Virginia's brother Gus was killed during the war. In one of those stranger than fiction stories Gus was one of five Confederate colonels living on the same street in Abbeyville, South Carolina, who died in the war.
5. March 7, 1872.
6. March 10, 1872.
7. December 13, 1872
8. February 28, 1872.
9. November 13, 1872.
10. April 17, 1872.
11. April 1872.
12. April 1, 1872.
13. September 29, 1872.
14. June, 11, 1872.
15. April 27, 1872.
16. September 3, 1872.
17. January 31, 1873.
18. November 13, 1872.
19. December 19, 1872
20. April 23, 1872.
21. April 1, 1872.
22. December 26, 1872.
23. May 22, 1872.
24. March 30, 1872.
25. April 1, 1872.
26. March 30, 1872.
27. May 16, 1872.

28. June 11, 1872.
29. December 22, 1872.
30. January 31, 1873.
31. June 28–29, 1872.
32. November 12, 1872.
33. November 12, 1872
34. April 25, 1872.
35. May 31, 1872.
36. August 1872.

11—Anna Logan

1. Anna Clayton Logan, 26. Her "Recollections" are to found at the Goochland Historical Society, Goochland, Virginia. Excerpts have been published in "Recollections of My Life," *Goochland County Historical Society Magazine*, Parts I, II, Vols. 20, 21 (1988, 89).
2. "Logan, "Recollections," 27.
3. "Logan, "Recollections," 27.
4. "Logan, "Recollections," 28.
5. "Logan, "Recollections," 27.
6. "Logan, "Recollections," 29.
7. "Logan, "Recollections," 27.
8. "Logan, "Recollections," 27.

12—Jo Gillis

1. Margaret Josephine Miles Gillis, Diary 1860–1868 (SPR 5), in the Alabama Department of Archives and History, Montgomery, Alabama. 154
2. Gillis, Diary, 155.
3. Gillis, Diary. 155.
4. Gillis, Diary, 156.
5. Gillis, Diary, 160.
6. Gillis, Diary 160.
7. Gillis, Diary, 160.
8. Gillis, Diary, 161.
9. Gillis, Diary, 167
10. Gillis, Diary, 159.
11. Lucy Muse Fletcher, Diary 1865, Rare Book, Manuscript, and Special Collections Library. Duke University. Durham, North Carolina.
12. Gillis, Diary, 159.
13. Gillis, Diary, 167.
14. Gillis, Diary, 167; 162.
15. Gillis, Diary, 168.

13—Sally Perry

1. Sally Randle Perry, 8 (1867). Diary 1867–1868 (SPR 303) in the Alabama Department of Archives and History, Montgomery.
2. Perry, Diary, 11 (1867).
3. Perry, Diary, 9 (1867).
4. Perry, Diary, 23 (1867)
5. Perry, Diary, 9 (1867).
6. Perry, Diary, 9 (1867).
7. Perry, Diary, 9 (1867).
8. Perry, Diary, 49 (1868).
9. Perry, Diary, January 1, 1868.
10. Perry, Diary, January 2, 1868.
11. Perry, Diary, 31 (1867)
12. Perry, Diary, 22–23 (1867)
13. Perry, Diary. 33 (1867).
14. Perry Diary, 54 (1868).
15. Perry, Diary 11; 27 (1867).
16. Perry, Diary, 55 (1868).
17. Perry, Diary, 55 (1868).
18. Perry, Diary, 24, 47, 48, 53 (1867–68).
19. Perry, Diary, 14 (1867).
20. Perry, Diary, 14–15 (1867).
21. Perry, Diary, 15 (1867).
22. Perry, Diary, 26 (1867).
23. Perry, Diary, 26–27 (1867).
24. Perry, Diary, 35 (1867).
25. Perry, Diary, 31–32 (1867).
26. Perry, Diary, 35 (1867).
27. Perry, Diary, 31–32 (1867).
28. Perry, Diary, 24 (1867).
29. Perry, Diary, 38, December 31, 1867.
30. Perry, Diary, 39 January 1, 1868.
31. Perry, Diary, 60 December 7, 1868.
32. Perry, Diary, 61 (1868).
33. Perry, Diary, 60 (1868).
34. Perry, Diary, 61 (1868).
35. Perry, Diary, 60 (1868).
36. Perry, Diary, 60 (1868).

Bibliography

Abbott, Martin. *The Freedmen's Bureau in South Carolina*, 1865–1872. Chapel Hill: University of North Carolina Press, 1967.

_____. "A New Englander in the South, 1865: A Letter." *New England Quarterly* 33, No. 1 (March 1959): 388–393.

Abbott, Richard H. "The Republican Party Press in Reconstruction Georgia, 1867–1874." *Journal of Southern History* 61, No. 4 (November 1995): 725–760.

Abney, M. G. "Reconstruction in Pontotoc County. *Publications of Mississippi Historical Society* 11 (1910): 229–270.

Acklen, Adelicia. Papers. Tennessee State Library and Archives, Nashville.

Agnew, Samuel A. Diaries: January 1, 1866–October 25, 1867. Lee County Library, Tupelo, Mississippi.

Aiken, Charles S. *The Cotton Plantation South Since the Civil War*. Baltimore: The Johns Hopkins University Press, 1998.

Aiken, D. Wyatt. "The Grange: Its Origin, Progress and Educational Purposes." An address delivered at Washington, D. C., January 23, 1883.

"D. Wyatt Aiken," *American National Biography* Vol. 1. New York: Oxford University Press, 1999.

Aiken, Virginia Carolina Smith. Diary. In David Wyatt Aiken Papers. South Caroliniana Library, University of South Carolina, Columbia.

Alderson, William T., ed. "The Civil War Diary of Captain James Litton Cooper, September 30, 1861 to January 1865." *Tennessee Historical Quarterly* 15 (June 1956): 159–173.

Alford, J. W. *United States Bureau of Refugees, Freedmen and Abandoned Lands Report of Schools and Finances of Freedmen for January 1866–January 1867*. Washington, D. C.: Government Printing Office, 1866–1867.

Allan, Elizabeth Preston. *The Life and Letters of Margaret Junkin Preston*. Boston: Houghton, Mifflin and Company, 1903.

Allen, Ivan. *Atlanta from the Ashes*. Atlanta, Georgia: Ruralist Press, 1928.

Allison, W.B. In WPA Federal Writers' Project Meridian-Lauderdale County History, Meridian-Lauderdale County Public Library, Meridian, Mississippi.

Ames, Blanche Butler. *Chronicles from the Nineteenth Century: Family Letters of Blanche Butler and Adelbert Ames*. Volumes 1 and 2. n.p. Privately Published, 1957.

Ames, Mary. *From a New England Woman's Diary in Dixie in 1865*. Springfield: The Plimpton Press, 1906.

Anderson, Eric, and Alfred A. Moss, Jr., eds. *The Facts of Reconstruction: Essays in Honor of John Hope Franklin.* Baton Rouge: Louisiana State University Press, 1991.

Anderson, Florence. Papers. Rare Book, Manuscript, and Special Collections Library, Duke University, Durham, North Carolina.

Anderson, George M.S.J. "The Civil War Courtship of Richard Mortimer Williams and Rose Anderson of Rockville." *Maryland History Magazine* 80 (Summer 1985): 119–136.

Anderson, Jean Bradley. *Piedmont Plantation: The Bennehan-Cameron Family and Lands in North Carolina.* Durham, North Carolina: The Historic Preservation Society of Durham, North Carolina, 1985.

Anderson, John Q., ed. *Brokenburn: The Journal of Kate Stone 1861–1868.* Baton Rouge: Louisiana State University Press, 1995. Selections reprinted by permission of Louisiana State University Press.

Anderson, Mrs. John Huske (Lucy London). *North Carolina Women of the Confederacy.* Fayetteville, North Carolina: North Carolina Division, United Daughters of the Confederacy, 1926.

Andrews, Eliza Frances. *The War-Time Journal of a Georgia Girl 1864–1865.* New York: D. Appleton and Company, 1908.

Andrews, J. Cutler. *The South Reports the War.* Princeton, New Jersey: Princeton University Press, 1970.

Andrews, Matthew Page. *Women of the South in War Times.* Baltimore: The Norman, Remington Co., 1920.

Andrews, Sidney. "Three Months Among the Reconstructionists." *Atlantic Monthly* 27 (February 1866): 237–245.

Ash, Stephen V. "Civil War, Black Freedom, and Social Change in the Upper South: Middle Tennessee, 1860–1870." Ph.D. diss., University of Tennessee, Knoxville.

_____. *When the Yankees Came: Conflict and Chaos in the Occupied South, 1861–1865.* Chapel Hill: The University of North Carolina Press, 1995.

Ashkenazi, Elliott, ed. *The Civil War Diary of Clara Solomon: Growing Up in New Orleans, 1861–1862.* Baton Rouge: Louisiana State University Press, 1995.

Austin, Anne L. *The Woolsey Sisters of New York: A Family's Involvement in the Civil War and a New Profession (1860–1900).* Philadelphia: American Philosophical Society, 1971.

Avary, Myrta Lockett. *Dixie After the War.* Boston: Houghton Mifflin Company, 1937.

Baer, Elizabeth R., ed. *Shadows on My Heart: The Civil War Diary of Lucy Rebecca Buck of Virginia.* Athens: The University of Georgia Press, 1997.

Baker, La Fayette C. *The History of the United States Secret Service.* Philadelphia: L. C. Baker, 1867.

Ball, Edward. *Slaves in the Family.* New York: Farrar, Straus and Giroux, 1998.

Barrett, John Gilchrist. *The Civil War in North Carolina.* Chapel Hill: University of North Carolina Press, 1963.

Bartlett, Catherine Thom, ed. *"My Dear Brother": A Confederate Chronicle.* Richmond, Virginia: The Dietz Press, 1952.

Beaty, Rives Lang, ed. "Recollections of Harriet Du Bose Lang," *South Carolina Historical Magazine* 59 (1958): 159–170; 195–205.

Beauchamp, Virginia Walcott, ed. *A Private War: Letters and Diaries of Madge Preston 1862–1867.* New Brunswick: Rutgers University Press, 1987.

Beaumont, Betty. *A Business Woman's Journal.* Philadelphia: T.B. Peterson & Brothers, 1888.

_____. *Twelve Years of My Life: An Autobiography.* Philadelphia: T.B. Peterson & Brothers, 1887.

Beckwith, Margaret Stanly. Memoir. Virginia Historical Society, Richmond, Virginia.

Bell, William Dudley. "The Reconstruction Ku Klux Klan: A survey of the Writings on the Klan With a Profile and Analysis of the Alabama Klan Episode. 1866–1877." Ph. D diss., The Louisiana State University, 1973.

Belz, Herman. *Reconstructing the Union: Theory and Policy During the Civil War.* Ithaca, New York: Cornell University Press, 1969.

Benham, George C. *A Year of Wreck: A True Story by a Victim.* New York: Harper & Brothers, 1880.

Bennett, Lerone, Jr. *Black Power U.S.A.: The Human Side of Reconstruction 1867–1877.* Chicago: Johnson Publishing Co., 1967.

Bentley, George R. *A History of the Freedmen's Bureau.* New York: Octagon Books, 1970.

Berkeley, Kathleen Christine. "Elizabeth Avery Meriwether, 'An Advocate for Her Sex': Feminism and Conservatism in the Post-Civil War South." *Tennessee Historical Quarterly* 43 (Winter 1984): 390–407.

Berry, Trey. "A History of Women's Higher Education in Mississippi, 1819–1882." *Journal of Mississippi History* 53, No. 4 (November 1991): 303–319.

Bettersworth, John K. *Confederate Mississippi: The People and Policies of a Cotton State in Wartime.* Baton Rouge: Louisiana State University Press, 1943.

_____, ed. *Mississippi in the Confederacy: As They Saw It.* Baton Rouge: Louisiana State University, 1961.

Biloxi Public Library. Miscellaneous Newspaper Files, History and Genealogy Division. Biloxi, Mississippi.

Black, Narcisa. Diaries. Mississippi Department of Archives and History, Jackson, Mississippi.

Blassingame, John W. *Slave Testimony: Two Centuries of Letters, Speeches, Interviews, and Autobiographies.* Baton Rouge: Louisiana State University Press, 1977.

Bleser, Carol K. ed. *The Hammonds of Redcliffe.* New York: Oxford University Press, 1981.

_____. *In Joy and in Sorrow: Women, Family, and Marriage in the Victorian South, 1830–1900.* New York: Oxford University Press, 1991.

Bonner, James C., ed. *The Journal of a Milledgeville Girl 1861–1867.* Athens: University of Georgia Press, 1964.

Book of Rembrance 1861–1865. Anson County Library, Wadesboro, North Carolina.

Boom, Aaron M., ed. "Testimony of Margaret Ketcham Ward on Civil War Times in Georgia." Parts I and II. *Georgia Historical Quarterly* 39 (September, December 1955): 268–293, 375–401.

Boritt, Gabor S., ed. *Why the Confederacy Lost.* New York: Oxford University Press, 1992.

Botkin, B. A., ed. *A Civil War Treasury of Tales, Legends and Folklore.* New York: Promontory Press, 1981.

Botume, Elizabeth Hyde. *First Days Amongst the Contrabands.* Boston: Lee and Shepard Publishers, 1893.

Bradford, Mildred Hill, and Edna Earl Baldwin, eds. "Letters from the Folwell-Curtis Families 1845–1890." In History and Genealogy Division, Biloxi Public Library, Biloxi, Mississippi.

Brandon, Zillah. Diaries (SPR 262). Alabama Department of Archives and History, Montgomery, Alabama.

Breckinridge, Wm. C. P. "The Ex-Confederate, and What He Has Done in Peace." *Southern Historical Society Papers* 20 (January-December 1892): 225–238.

Brent, Martha Buxton Porter. Reminiscences (Accession 26501) Personal Papers Collection, Archives Research Services, The Library of Virginia, Richmond.

Briscoe, Marion Knox Goode. Memoir. Copy in Virginia Historical Society, Richmond.

Brown, D. Alexander. *The Galvanized Yankees.* Urbana: The University of Illinois Press, 1963.

Brownlee, Richard S. *Gray Ghosts of the Confederacy: Guerrilla Warfare in the West, 1861–1865.* Baton Rouge, Louisiana: Louisiana State University Press, 1958.

Bryan, T. Conn. "A Georgia Woman's Civil War Diary: The Journal of Minerva Leah Rowles McClatchey, 1864–65." *Collections of the Georgia Historical Society* 51, No. 2 (June 1967): 197–216.

Bryce, Mrs. Campbell. *The Personal Experiences of Mrs. Campbell Bryce During the Burning of Columbia, South Carolina by General W. T. Sherman's Army, February 17, 1865.* Philadelphia: Lippincott Press, 1899.

Buni, Andrew, ed. "Reconstruction in Organge County, Virginia: A Letter from Hannah Garlick Rawlings to Her Sister Clarissa Lawrence Rawlings, August 9, 1865." *Virginia Magazine of History and Biography* 75 (January 1967): 459–465.

Burger, Nash K. and John K. Bettersworth. *South of Appomattox.* New York: Harcourt, Brace and Company, 1959.

Burr, Virginia Ingraham, ed. *The Secret Eye: The Journal of Ella Gertrude Clanton Thomas, 1848–1889.* Copyright 1990 by Virginia Ingraham Burr and Gertrude T. Despeaux. Used by permission of the publisher.

Butchart, Ronald E. *Northern Schools, Southern Blacks, and Reconstruction: Freedmen's Education, 1862–1875.* Westport, Connecticut: Greenwood Press, 1980.

Cade, John B. "Out of the Mouths of Ex-Slaves." *Journal of Negro History* 20 (July 1935): 294–337.

Campbell, Edward D.C., Jr., and Kym S. Rice. *A Woman's War: Southern Women, Civil War and the Confederate Legacy.* Richmond: The Museum of the Confederacy and Charlottesville: The University Press of Virginia, 1996.

Capers, Gerald M., Jr. "Confederates and Yankees in Occupied New Orleans, 1862–1865." *Journal of Southern History* 30 (November 1964): 405–416.

Carnes, Celena. Correspondence of Margaret McDowell (Venable) Hannah with Celena Carnes. In Carrington Family Papers. Virginia Historical Society, Richmond.

Carter, Hodding. *The Angry Scar: The Story of Reconstruction.* Garden City, New York: Doubleday & Company, Inc., 1959.

Carter, Joseph C. *Magnolia Journey: A Union Veteran Revisits the Former Confederate States.* Tuscaloosa: The University of Alabama Press, 1974.

Carter, Samuel. *The Siege of Atlanta 1864.* New York: Bonanza Books, 1973.

Carter, Sarah S. "An Account of Visit to Richmond VA and Elsewhere Third Month 1866." Copy in Virginia Historical Society, Richmond, Virginia.

Cary, Harriette. "Diary of Miss Harriette Cary, Kept by Her from May 6, 1862, to July 24, 1862." *Tyler's Quarterly:* 105–173.

Cash, William M., and Lucy Somerville Howorth, eds. *My Dear Nellie: The Civil War Letters of William L. Nugent to Eleanor Smith Nugent.* Jackson: University of Mississippi, 1977.

Cassidy, Vincent H., and Amos E. Simpson. *Henry Watkins Allen of Louisiana.* Baton Rouge: Louisiana State University Press, 1964.

Chamberlain, Daniel H. "Reconstruction in South Carolina." *Atlantic Monthly* 87 (1901): 473–484.

Chaney, Ned; Simon Hare; Sam Broach; Bessie Williams; Nettie Henry. WPA Federal Writers' Project. Meridian-Lauderdale County Public Library, Meridian, Mississippi.

Chappelear, Amanda Virginia (Edmonds). Journals. Virginia Historical Society, Richmond.

Cimbala, Paul A., and Randall M. Miller, eds. *The Freedmen's Bureau and Reconstruction.* New York: Fordham University Press, 1999.

Civil War Letters. Historical File. Lee County Library, Tupelo, Mississippi.

Clark, Thomas D. "The Furnishing and Supply System in Southern Agriculture Since 1865." *Journal of Southern History* 12 (February 1946): 24–44.

Clark, Walter, ed. *Histories of the Several Regiments and Battalions from North Carolina in the Great War 1861-'65.* Vol. 1. Raleigh, N.C.: Published by the State, 1901.

Clay-Clopton, Virginia, *A Belle of the Fifties: Memoirs of Mrs. Clay of Alabama.* New York: Doubleday, Page & Company, 1905.

Clayton, Ronnie W. *Mother Wit: The Ex-Slave Narratives of the Louisiana Writers' Project.* New York: Peter Lang, 1990.

Clift, G. Glenn, ed. *The Private War of Lizzie Hardin: A Kentucky Confederate Girl's Diary of the Civil War in Kentucky, Virginia, Tennessee, Alabama, and Georgia.* Frankfort: The Kentucky Historical Society, 1963.

Clinton, Catherine. *Civil War Stories.* Athens: University of Georgia Press, 1998.

———. *Tara Revisited: Women, War, and the Plantation Legend.* New York: Abbeville Press, 1995.

———, and Nina Silber. *Divided Houses: Gender and the Civil War.* New York: Oxford University Press, 1992.

Cogan, Frances B. *All-American Girl: The Ideal of Real Womanhood in Mid-Nineteenth-Century America.* Athens: The University of Georgia Press, 1989.

Coleman, Kenneth, ed. *Athens, 1861–1865: As Seen Through Letters in the University of Georgia Libraries.* Athens: University of Georgia Libraries, Miscellanea Publications, No. 8, University of Georgia Press, 1969.

Collier, Henry Clements. Collier Collection. Tennessee State Library and Archives, Nashville.

Colt, Margaretta Barton. *Defend the Valley: A Shenandoah Family in the Civil War.* New York: Orion Books, 1994.

Commager, Henry Steele, ed. *The Blue and the Gray: The Story of the Civil War as Told by Participants.* Vols. I and II. New York: Crescent Books, 1950. (Reprint).

Cooper, Fannie. In Elizabeth (Porter) Pitts Collection. Tennessee State Library and Archives, Nashville.

Cottrell, Mary Jerdone (Denton). Diaries 1867 and 1869. Copy in Virginia Historical Society. Richmond.

Coulter, Merton E. *A History of the South VII the Confederate States of America 1861–1865.* Baton Rouge: Louisiana State University Press, 1950.

_____. "Lost Generation: The Life and Death of James Barrow, C.S.A." *Confederate Centennial Studies* No. 1 (1956):11–105.

_____, and Wendell Holmes Stephenson, eds. *A History of the South Volume VIII: The South During Reconstruction 1865–1877.* Baton Rouge: Louisiana State University Press, 1947.

Couture, Richard T., ed. "Good Golly! Miss Mollie: The Massie Letters: Part III." *Goochland County Historical Society Magazine* 17 (1985): 9–29.

Coxe, Elizabeth Allen. *Memories of a South Carolina Plantation During the War.* Privately printed, 1912.

Crabb, Alfred Leland. "The Twilight of the Nashville Gods." *Tennessee Historical Quarterly* 15 (1956): 305.

Crabtree, Beth G., and James W. Patton, eds. *"Journal of a Secesh Lady": The Diary of Catherine Ann Devereux Edmondston 1860–1866.* Raleigh, North Carolina: Division of Archives and History, 1979.

Craighead, Rachel Carter. Diaries 1855–1911. Tennessee State Library and Archives, Nashville. Microfilm.

Crow, Jeffrey J., Paul D. Escott, Charles L. Flynn, Jr. *Race, Class, and Politics in Southern History.* Baton Rouge: Louisiana State University Press, 1989.

Crowe, Charles, ed. *The Age of Civil War and Reconstruction, 1830–1900: A Book of Interpretative Essays.* Homewood, Illinois: The Dorsey Presss, 1966.

Cumming, Kate. Original handwritten sections from her book *Gleanings from Southland* in Kate Cumming Papers (LPR 164). Alabama Department of Archives and History, Montgomery, Alabama.

Current, Richard Nelson. *Those Terrible Carpetbaggers.* New York: Oxford University Press, 1988.

Currie, James T. *Enclave: Vicksburg and Her Plantations 1863–1870.* Jackson: University Press of Mississippi, 1980.

Darden, Susan Sillers. Diary. In Darden Family Papers. Mississippi Department of Archives and History, Jackson, Mississippi.

Davis, Angela Kirkham. "War Reminiscences: A Letter to My Nieces." Library, Historical Society of Fredrick County, Maryland.

Davis, Burke. *The Civil War: Strange and Fascinating Facts.* New York: Wings Books, 1982.

_____. *The Long Surrender.* New York: Random House, 1985.

_____. *Sherman's March.* New York: Vintage Books, 1980.

Davis, Matthew Jack. "A Long Journey Home." *Civil War Times Illustrated* (May 1997): 14–55.

Davis, Varina. *Jefferson Davis Ex-President of the Confederate States of America: A Memoir by His Wife.* Vol. 2. New York: Bedford Company, 1890.

Dawsey, Cyrus B., and James M. Dawsey, eds. *The Confederados: Old South Immigrants in Brazil.* Tuscaloosa: The University of Alabama Press, 1995.

Dawson, Jim. *Bits and Pieces: Studies in Lauderdale County Lore.* Vol. 1. Meridian: Lauderdale County Department of Archives and History, Inc., 1995.

Dawson, Sarah Morgan. *A Confederate Girl's Diary.* Edited by James I. Robertson, Jr. Bloomington: Indiana University Press, 1960.

DeCell, Harriet, and JoAnne Prichard. *Yazoo; Its Legends and Legacies.* Yazoo: Yazoo Delta Press, 1976.

de Fontaine, Mrs. F. G. "Old Confederate Days." *Confederate Veteran* 4, No. 9 (1896): 301–3.

De Forest, John William. *A Union Officer in the Reconstruction.* New Haven: Yale University Press, 1948.

Dennett, John Richard. *The South As It Is: 1865–1866.* New York: The Viking Press, 1965.

Dickinson, Fannie E. (Taylor). Diary. Virginia Historical Society, Richmond.

Donald, David. "The Scalawag in Mississippi Reconstruction." *Journal of Southern History* 10 (November 1944): 447–60.

Dorsey, Sarah A. *Recollections of Henry Watkins Allen, Brigadier General Confederate States Army, Ex-Governor of Louisiana.* New York: M. Doolady, 1866.

Douglass, Frederick. "Reconstruction." *Atlantic Monthly* 18 (December 1866): 761–765.

Du Bois, W. E. Burghardt. *Black Reconstruction in America: An Essay Toward a History of the Part Which Black Folk Played in the Attempt to Reconstruct Democracy in America, 1860–1880.* New York: Russell & Russell, 1963.

DuBose, John Witherspoon. *Alabama's Tragic Decade: Ten Years of Alabama 1865–1874.* Birmingham, Alabama: Webb Book Company, 1940.

Dulles, Foster Rhea. *The United States Since 1865.* Ann Arbor: The University of Michigan Press, 1969.

Dunning, William Archibald. *Reconstruction: Political and Economic 1865–1877.* New York: Harper & Brothers, 1937.

Durr, Lucy Judkins. "Brazilian Recollections" (Accession 319370) Personal Papers Collection, Archives Research Services, The Library of Virginia, Richmond, Virginia.

Durrell Family Collection. Excerpts from the *South Western Newspaper* 1864–66. New York Historical Society, New York.

Edmondson, Mary. Diary of Mrs. Mary Edmondson of Phillips County, Arkansas, 1863–64. United Daughters of the Confederacy, Richmond, Virginia.

Edwards, Laura F. *Gendered Strife and Confusion: The Political Culture of Reconstruction.* Urbana: University of Illinois Press, 1997.

Eggleston, George Cary. *A Rebel's Recollections.* Bloomington: Indiana University Press. 1959. Reprint. New York: Kraus Reprint Co., 1969.

Elmore, Grace Brown. Diary. South Caroliniana Library, University of South Carolina, Columbia.

Escott, Paul. *After Secession: Jefferson Davis and the Failrue of Confederate Nationalism.* Baton Rouge: Louisiana State University Press, 1978.

_____. *Slavery Remembered: A Rrecord of Twentieth Century Slave Narratives.* Chapel Hill: University of North Carolina Press, 1979.

_____, and Goldfield, David R., eds. *The South for New Southerners.* Chapel Hill: The University of North Carolina Press, 1991.

Espy, Sarah Rodgers Rousseau. Diary (SPR 2). Alabama Department of Archives and History, Montgomery, Alabama.

Evins, Janie Synatzske. "Arkansas Women: Their Contribution to Society, Politics, and Business, 1865–1900." *Arkansas Historical Quarterly* 44 (Summer 1985): 118–113.

Fairley, Laura Nan, and James T. Dawson. *Paths to the Past: An Overview History of Lauderdale County, Mississippi.* Meridian, Mississippi: Lauderdale County Department of Archives and History, 1988.

Farnham, Christie Anne, ed. *Women of the American South: A Multicultural Reader.* New York: New York University Press, 1997.

Faust, Drew Gilpin. "Altars of Sacrifice: Confederate Women and the Narratives of War." *Journal of American History* 76, No. 4 (March 1990): 1200–1228.

_____. *Mothers of Invention: Women of the Slaveholding South in the American Civil War.* Chapel Hill: The University of North Carolina Press, 1996.

_____. *Southern Stories: Slaveholders in Peace and War.* Columbia: University of Missouri Press, 1992.

Fearn, Frances. *Diary of a Refugee.* New York: Frances Fearn, 1910.

Fellman, Michael. *Inside War: The Guerrilla Conflict in Missouri During the American Civil War.* New York: Oxford University Press, 1989.

Felton, Rebeca Latimer. *Country Life in Georgia in the Days of My Youth.* Atlanta, Georgia: Index Printing Company, 1919.

Fitzgerald, Ruth Coder. *A Different Story: A Black History of Fredericksburg, Stafford and Spotsylvania, Virginia.* n.p. Unicorn, 1979.

Fleming, Walter L. *Documentary History of Reconstruction: Political, Military, Social, Religious, Educational and Industrial 1865 to 1906.* Volume 2. New York: McGraw-Hill Book Comany, 1966.

Fletcher, Lucy Muse. Diary 1865. Rare Book, Manuscript, and Special Collections Library, Duke University. Durham, North Carolina.

Follansbee, Sarah. Diary in Stringfellow-Follansbee Records (*7N/A/9/e*). Alabama Department of Archives and History, Montgomery, Alabama.

Foner, Eric. *Nothing But Freedom: Emancipation and its Legacy.* Baton Rouge: Louisiana State University Press, 1983.

_____. *A Short History of Reconstruction 1863–1877.* New York: Harper & Row, Publishers, 1990.

_____. *Slavery and Freedom in Nineteenth-Century America.* Oxford: Clarendon Press, 1994.

_____, and Olivia Mahoney. *America's Reconstruction: People and Politics After the Civil War.* New York: Harper Collins Publishers, Inc., 1995.

Fontaine, Mary Burrows. Letters. Eleanor S.Brockenbrough Library, The Museum of the Confederacy, Richmond, Virginia.

Foote, Shelby. *The Civil War: A Narrative: Fort Sumter to Perryville.* New York: Random House, 1958.

_____. *The Civil War: A Narrative: Red River to Appomattox.* New York: Random House, 1974.

Foster, Gaines M. *Ghosts of the Confederacy: Defeat, the Lost Cause, and the Emergence of the New South 1865 to 1913.* New York: Oxford University Press, 1987.

Foster, Kate D. Diary. In Kate D. Foster Papers. Rare Book, Manuscripts, and Special Collections Library, Duke University, Durham, North Carolina.

Fox, Tryphena Blanche Holder. *A Northern Woman in the Plantation South: Letters of Tryphena Blanche Holder Fox 1856–1876.* Edited by Wilma King. Columbia: University of South Carolina Press, 1993.

French, L. Virginia. Diary. Tennessee State Library and Archives, Nashville.

Fuke, Richard Paul. *Imperfect Equality: African Americans and the Confines of White Racial Attitudes in Post-Emancipation Maryland.* New York: Fordham University Press, 1999.

Futrell, Robert F. "Efforts of Mississippians to Encourage Immigration, 1865–1880." *Journal of Mississippi History* 20 (April 1958): 59–76.

Garcia, Celene Fremaux. *Celene: Remembering Louisiana 1850–1871.* Edited by Patrick J. Geary. Athens: University of Georgia Press, 1987.

Garner, James Wilford. *Reconstruction in Mississippi.* Baton Rouge: Louisiana State University Press, 1968.

Garrison, Webb. *A Treasury of Civil War Tales.* Nashville, Tennessee: Rutledge Hill Press, 1988.

Genovese, Eugene D. *Roll, Jordan, Roll: The World the Slaves Made.* New York: Pantheon Books, 1974.

Gillette, William. *Retreat from Reconstruction 1869–1879.* Baton Rouge: Louisiana State University Press, 1979.

Gillis, Margaret Josephine Miles. Diary 1839–1868 (SPR 5). Alabama Department of Archives and History, Montgomery, Alabama.

Girls of the Sixties. Collection in the South Caroliniana Library, University of South Carolina, Columbia.

Goodwin, Mary B. Diary 1860–1867 and Papers 1877–1890 (Accession 27846) Diary 1860–1867 Personal Papers Collection, Archives Research Services, The Library of Virginia, Richmond, Virginia.

Goodwin, Mary Frances (Archer). Papers. Virginia Historical Society, Richmond, Virginia.

Gould, Virginia Meacham. *Chained to the Rock of Adversity: To Be Free, Black and Female in the Old South.* Athens: University of Georgia Press, 1998.

Gragg, Rod. *The Illustrated Confederate Reader.* New York: Harper & Row, Publishers, 1989.

Graham, Eleanor. "Belmont 1. Nashville Home of Adelicia Acklen." *Tennessee Historical Quarterly* 30 (1971): 345–68.

Griffin, Richard W. "Problems of the Southern Cotton Planters After the Civil War." *Georgia Historical Quarterly* 39 (1955): 103–117.

Griggs, William Clark. *The Elusive Eden: Frank McMullan's Confederate Colony in Brazil.* Austin: University of Texas Press, 1987.

Grimball, John. "Diary of John Berkley Grimball. 1858–1865." *South Carolina Historical Magazine* 56 and 57 (1955, 1956): 8–30; 92–114; 157–177; 28–50; 88–102.

Grimball, Meta Morris. Journal. In Southern Historical Collection, Wilson Library, University of North Carolina, Chapel Hill.

Grimsley, Mark. "Burning Down the South." *Civil War Times Illustrated* 34, No. 4 (September/October 1995): 48–55.

_____. *The Hard Hand of War: Union Military Policy Toward Southern Civilians, 1861–1865.* New York: Cambridge University Press, 1995.

Hague, Parthenia Antoinette. *A Blockaded Family: Life in Southern Alabama During the Civil War.* Boston: Houghton, Mifflin and Company, 1888.

Hancock, Cornelia. *South After Gettysburg: Letters of Cornelia Hancock 1863–1868.* Edited by Henrietta Stratton Jaquette. New York: Thomas Y. Crowell, 1956.

Handy, Sara Matthews. "In the Last Days of the Confederacy." *Atlantic Monthly* 87 (January 1901): 104–10.

Hanna, Alfred J. "A Confederate Newspaper in Mexico." *Journal of Southern History* 12 (February 1946): 67–83.

Hardin, Mrs. William F. Letter written May 30, 1910 to the Florence Chapter of the United Daughters of the Confederacy printed in the *Florence Times.*

Harkison, Mary Eunice. Letter. South Caroliniana Library, University of South Carolina, Columbia.

Harris, William C. *The Day of the Carpetbagger: Republican Reconstruction in Mississippi.* Baton Rouge: Louisiana State University Press, 1979.

_____. *With Charity for All: Lincoln and the Restoration of the Union.* Lexington: The University Press of Kentucky, 1997.

Harrison, Mrs. Burton. *Recollections Grave and Gay.* New York: Scribner's Sons, 1911.

Harter, Eugene C. *The Lost Colony of the Confederacy.* Jackson: University Press of Mississippi, 1985.

Harwell, Richard B., ed. *The Confederate Reader.* New York: Longmans, Green and Co., 1957.

Haskins, Nannie. Papers. Tennessee State Library and Archives, Nashville.

Henderson, Dwight Franklin, ed. "The Private Journal of Georgiana Gholson Walker 1862–1865 With Selections from the Post-War Years 1865–1876." *Confederate Centennial Studies.* No 25. Tuscaloosa, Ala.: Confederate Publishing Company, Inc., 1963.

Hennig, Helen Kohn, ed. *Columbia: Capital City of South Carolina 1786–1936.* Columbia, S.C.: The State-Record Company, 1966.

Henry, Robert Selph. *The Story of Reconstruction.* Indianapolis: The Bobbs-Merrill Company, 1938. Reprint: New York: Konecky & Konecky, 1991.

Herbert, Hilary Abner. "The Conditions of the Reconstruction Problem." *Atlantic Monthly* 87 (February 1901): 145–157.

_____. "Grandfather Talks About His Life Under Two Flags: Reminiscences 1903" (SPR 4). Alabama Department of Archives and History, Montgomery, Alabama.

_____, et al. *Why the Solid South? Or, Reconstruction and Its Results.* Baltimore: R. H. Woodward & Company, 1890.

Hesseltine, Wiliam B., and David L.Smiley. *The South in American History.* Englewood Cliffs, N.J.: Prentice-Hall, Inc., 1960.

Hobson, Fannie Archer (Anderson). "An Account of the Evacuation of Richmond." Virginia Historical Society, Richmond, Virginia.

Hoehling, A.A., and Mary Hoehling. *The Day Richmond Died.* Lanham, Maryland: Madison Books, 1991.

_____, and _____. *The Last Days of the Confederacy.* New York: The Fairfax Press, 1981.

Holmes, Anne Middleton. *The New York Ladies' Southern Relief Association 1866–1867.* New York: The Mary Mildred Sullivan Chapter, United Daughters of the Confederacy, 1926.

Holmes, Emma. *The Diary of Miss Emma Holmes, 1861–1866.* Edited by John F. Marszalek. Baton Rouge: Louisiana State University Press, 1979.

Hoole, William Stanley, ed. "Reconstruction in West Alabama: The Memoirs of John L. Hunnicutt." *Confederate Centennial Studies* No. 11. Tuscaloosa, West Alabama: Confederate Publishing Company, 1959.

Horn, Stanley F., ed. *Tennessee's War 1861–1865 Described by Participants.* Nashville: Tennessee Civl War Centennial Commission, 1965.

Hough, Alfred Lacey. *Soldier in the West: The Civil War Letters of Alfred Lacey Hough.* Edited by Robert G. Athearn. Philadelphia: University of Pennsylvania Press, 1957.

Howe, M. A. DeWolfe, ed. *Home Letters of General Sherman.* New York: Charles Scribner's Sons, 1909.

Hubbard, Euclid. Diary. Privately held by Gary Hubbard, East Lansing, Michigan.

Huff, Archie, Jr. *Greenville: The History of the City and County in the South Carolina Piedmont.* Columbia: University of South Carolina Press, 1995.

Hunt, John Wilkins. "Story of the Hunt Family That First Came to Hardeman County Tennessee." Tennessee State Library and Archives, Nashville.

Hyman, Harold Melvin. *Era of the Oath: Northern Loyalty Tests During the Civil War and Reconstruction.* Philadelphia: University of Pennsylvania Press, 1954.

_____, ed. *New Frontiers of the American Reconstruction.* Urbana: University of Illinois Press, 1966.

_____, ed. *The Radical Republicans and Reconstruction 1861–1870.* Indianapolis: The Bobbs-Merrill Company, Inc., 1967.

Jackson, Alexander Melvorne. Papers (M16). McCain Library and Archives, The University of Southern Mississippi, Hattiesburg.

Jervey, Susan R. and Charlotte St. Julien Ravenel. "Two Diaries from Middle St. John's Berkeley, South Carolina, February–May 1865." Journals kept by Miss Susan R. Jervey and Miss Charlotte St. Julien Ravenel, at Northampton and Pooshee Plantations, and Reminiscences of Mrs. (Waring) Henagan with Two Contemporary Reports from Federal Officials. Pinopolis, South Carolina: St. John's Hunting Club, 1921.

Jones, Margaret Mackay, ed. *Catherine Devereux Edmondston 1860–1866.* Mebane, N.C.: Privately Published, n.d.

Jones, Willard L. "Cotton, the 'King' That Never Was." *Civil War Times 2*, No. 6 (October 1960): 16–17.

Judkins Family Papers (LPR 31). Alabama Department of Archives and History, Montgomery, Alabama.

Kennaway, John H. *On Sherman's Track; Or, the South After the War.* London: Seeley, Jackson, and Halliday, 1867.

Kennedy, Sarah Ann. Confederate Collection. Tennessee State Library and Archives, Nashville.

Kennedy, Stetson. *After Appomattox: How the South Won the War.* Gainesville: University Press of Florida, 1995.

Kennett, Lee. *Marching Through Georgia: The Story of Soldiers and Civilians During Sherman's Campaign.* New York: Harper Collins, 1995.

Kibler, Lillian Adele. *Benjamin F. Perry: South Carolina Unionist.* Durham, N.C.: Duke University Press, 1946.

Killebrew, Mary Catherine, and Joseph Buckner. Collection. Tennessee State Library and Archives, Nashville.

King, Jennie S. In Elizabeth (Porter) Pitts Collection. Tennessee State Library and Archives Nashville.

Kirchberger, Joe H. *The Civil War and Reconstruction: An Eyewitness History.* New York: Facts On File, Inc., 1991.

Klingberg, Frank Wysor. "The Case of the Minors: A Unionist Family Within the Confederacy." *Journal of Southern History* 13 (February-November 1947): 27–45.

_____. "The Southern Claims Commission" in *University of California Publications in History* Vol. 50. Berkeley: University of California Press, 1955.

Kolchin, Peter. *First Freedom: The Responses of Alabama's Blacks to Emancipation and Reconstruction.* Westport, Connecticut: Greenwood Press, 1972.

Kondert, Nancy T. "The Romance and Reality of Defeat: Southern Women in 1865." *Journal of Mississippi History* 35 (May 1973): 141–152.

Krug, Donna Rebecca Dondes. *The Folks Back Home: The Confederate Homefront During the Civil War*. Ph.D. diss., University of California at Irvine, 1990. Ann Arbor, Michigan: University Microfilms International.

Lacey, Nannie. "Reconstruction in Leake County." *Publications of Mississippi Historical Society* 11 (1910): 271–294.

Ladies Memorial Association of Appomattox Minute Book. Virginia Historical Society, Richmond, Virginia.

Lanza, Michael L. *Agrarianism and Reconstruction Politics: The Southern Homestead Act*. Baton Rouge: Louisiana State University Press, 1990.

Lauderdale, John Vance. *The Wounded River: The Civil War Letters of John Vance Lauderdale, M.D.* Edited by Peter Josyph. East Lansing: Michigan State University Press, 1993.

Lebsock, Suzanne D. "Radical Reconstruction and the Property Rights of Southern Women." *Journal of Southern History* 43, No. 2 (May 1977): 195–216.

_____. *"A Share of Honor": Virginia Women 1600–1945*. Richmond: The Virginia Women's Cultural History Project, 1984.

LeConte Family Papers. Manuscripts Division, Bancroft Library, University of California, Berkeley.

Lee, Mary Custis. Letters. Eleanor S. Brokenbrough Library, Museum of the Confederacy, Richmond.

Lee, Robert E. Jr. *My Father General Lee*. New York: Doubleday, 1960.

Lefler, Hugh Talmage, ed. *North Carolina History Told by Contemporaries*. Chapel Hill: The University of North Carolina Press, 1956.

Leftwich, George J. "Reconstruction in Monroe County." *Publications of Mississippi Historical Society* 9 (1906): 53–84.

Leigh, Frances Butler. *Ten Years on a Georgia Plantation Since the War 1866–1876*. Savannah: Beehive Press, 1992.

Letter to Andrew Johnson. Tennessee State Library and Archives, Nashville.

Letters from Confederate Women. The Museum of the Confederacy, Richmond, Virginia.

Lewis, Elsie M. "The Political Mind of the Negro, 1865–1900." *Journal of Southern History* 21 (May 1955): 189–202.

Lightfoot, Emmeline Allmand (Crump). Memoir. Virginia Historical Society, Richmond, Virginia.

Linden, Glenn M. *Voices from the Reconstruction Years, 1865–1877*. New York: Harcourt Brace College Publishers, 1999.

Lines, Amelia Akehurst. *To Raise Myself a Little: The Diaries and Letters of Jennie, a Georgia Teacher, 1851–1866*. Edited by Thomas Dyer. Athens: The University of Georgia Press, 1982.

Litwack, Leon F. *Been in the Storm So Long: The Aftermath of Slavery*. New York: Alfred A. Knopf, 1979.

Logan, Anna Clayton. in Goochland Historical Society, Goochland, Virginia. Excerpts published in "Recollections of My Life." *Goochland County Historical Society Magazine* 20, 21 (1988, 1989): 43–59 and 15–30.

Lohrenz, Mary Edna and Anita Miller Stamper. *Mississippi Homespun: Nineteenth-Century Textiles and the Women Who Made Them*. Jackson: Mississippi Department of Archives and History, 1989.

MacKethan, Lucinda H., ed. *Recollections of a Southern Daughter: A Memoir by Cornelia Jones Pond of Liberty County*. Athens: The University of Georgia Press, 1998.

Maclean, Clara Dargan. "Return of a Refugee." *Southern Historical Society Papers* 13 (January to December 1885): 502–515.

Madden, T. O., Jr., with Ann L. Miller. *We Were Always Free: The Maddens of Culpeper County, Virginia, a 200 Year Family History.* New York: W.W. Norton & Company, 1992.

Magee, Hattie. "Reconstruction in Lawrence and Jefferson Davis Counties." *Publications of the Mississippi Historical Society* 11 (1910): 163–204.

"Maggie!" Maggie Lindsley's Journal: Nashville, Tennessee, 1864–Washington, D. C., 1865. Connecticut: Privately printed, 1977.

Mann, Lizzie Jackson. Recollections of the Civil War 1861–65. Virginia Historical Society, Richmond, Virginia.

Marchione, William P., Jr. "Go South, Young Man! Reconstruction Letters of a Massachusetts Yankee." *South Carolina Historical Magazine* 80 (January 1979): 18–35.

Marquette, C.L. ed. "Letters of a Yankee Sugar Planter." *Journal of Southern History* 6, No. 4 (November 1940): 521–548.

Martin, Charles. "A Reminiscence of the War Between the States by Charles T. Martin." Alabama Deptartment of Archives and History, Montgomery, Alabama.

Martin, Josephine, W., ed. *Dear Sister: Letters Written on Hilton Head Island 1867.* Beaufort, South Carolina: Beaufort Book Company, 1977.

Mason, Emily. Papers. Eleanor Brokenborough Library, Museum of the Confederacy, Richmond.

Mason, Emily V. "Memories of a Hospital Matron." *Atlantic Monthly* 90 (September and October 1902): 305–318 and 475–485. Also in Waugh, Charles G. and Martin H. Greenberg. *The Women's War in the South: Recollections and Reflections of the Americacn Civil War.* Nashville, Tennessee: Cumberland House, 1999.

Massey, Mary Elizabeth. *Bonnet Brigades.* New York: Alfred A. Knopf, 1966.

_____. "The Making of a Feminist." *Journal of Southern History* 39, No. 1 (February 1973): 3–22.

Maury, Betty Herndon. *The Confederate Diary of Betty Herndon Maury 1861–63.* Edited by Alice Maury Parmelee. Washington: Privately printed, 1938.

Maury, Matthew Fontaine. "The American Colony in Mexico." *De Bow's* Series 2 (January–June 1866): 622–630.

May, Robert E. "Southern Elite Women, Sectional Extremism, and the Male Sphere: The Case of John A. Quitman's Wife and Female Descendants, 1847–1931." *Journal of Mississippi History* 50, No.4 (November 1988): 251–285.

McBryde, Lucy Newton. Collection. South Caroliniana Library, University of South Carolina, Columbia.

McDonald, Cornelia. *A Diary with Reminiscences of the War and Refugee Life in the Shenandoah Valley 1860–1865.* Nashville: Cullom & Ghertner, 1935.

McDowell, Amanda (1861–1865), and Lela McDowell Blankenship (1943). *Fiddles in the Cumberlands.* New York: Richard R. Smith, 1943.

McFeely, William S. *Yankee Stepfather: General O.O. Howard and the Freedmen.* New York: W.W. Norton, 1968.

McGee, Charles M., Jr., and Ernest M. Lander, Jr. *A Rebel Came Home.* Columbia: University of South Carolina Press, 1961.

McKee Letters. Privately held by Charles D. Burks of Columbia, Missouri.

McKinney, Gordon B. "Women's Role in Civil War Western North Carolina." *North Carolina Historical Review* 69, No. 1 (1992): 37–56.

McNeilly, J. S. "The Enforcement Act of 1871 and the Ku Klux Klan in Mississippi." *Publications of the Mississippi Historical Society* 9 (1908): 109–197.

McPherson, James M. *Battle Cry of Freedom: The Civil War Era.* New York: Ballantine Books, 1988.

Meriwether, Elizabeth Avery. *Recollections of 92 Years 1824–1916.* Nashville, Tennessee: The Tennesee Historical Commission, 1958.

Miers, Earl Schenck. *The General Who Marched to Hell: William Tecumseh Sherman and His March to Fame and Infamy.* New York: Alfred A. Knopf, 1951.

Miller, Letitia Dabney. Recollections. In Thomas Gregory Dabney Collection (M7). McCain Library and Archives, The University of Southern Mississippi, Hattiesburg.

Miller, Robert Delmert. "Of Freedom and Freedmen: Racial Attitudes of White Elite in North Carolina During Reconstruction 1865–1877." Ph.D. diss., University of North Carolina, Chapel Hill.

Moore, John Hammond. *Columbia and Richland County: A South Carolina Community, 1740–1990.* Columbia: University of South Carolina Press. 1993.

Mordecai, Ellen. Scrapbook and Miscellaneous Papers 1811–1885 (Accession 28685) S[usan] B. Treadway, Richmond, to Ellen M[ordecai], n.p. 19 April 1865, ALS, 3p., Personal Papers Collection, Archives Research Services, the Library of Virginia, Richmond, Virginia.

Moreno, Paul. "Racial Classifications and Reconstruction Legislation." *Journal of Southern History* 61, No. 2 (May 1995): 271–304.

Morgan, Albert T. *Yazoo; Or, on the Picket Line of Freedom in the South.* Washington, D.C.: Published by Author, 1884.

Morgan, Irby (Mrs.) *How It Was; Four Years Among the Rebels.* Nashville, Tennessee: Printed for the author by Publishing House Methodist Episcopal Church, South, Barber & Smith Agents, 1892.

Morrison, Mary E. (Rambant). Memoir. Copy in Virginia Historical Society, Richmond, Virginia.

Morrissette, Kate. "Social Life in the First Capital of the Confederacy" (SPR 443). Alabama Department of Archives and History, Montgomery, Alabama.

Morton, Patricia, ed. *Discovering the Women in Slavery: Emancipating Perspectives on the American Past.* Athens: University of Georgia Press, 1996.

Morton, Richard L. "'Contrabands' and Quakers in the Virginia Peninsula, 1862–1869." *Virginia Magazine of History and Biography* 61 (October 1953): 419–429.

Moskow, Shirley Blotnick. *Emma's World: An Intimate Look at Lives Touched by the Civil War Era.* Far Hills, New Jersey: New Horizon Press, 1990.

Mugleston, William F., ed. "The Freedmen's Bureau and Reconstructin in Virginia: The Diary of Marcus Sterling Hopkins, A Union Officer." *Virginia Magazine of History and Biography* 86 (1978): 45–102.

Murphy, Richard W. *The Nation Reunited: War's Aftermath.* Alexandria, Virginia: Time-Life Books, 1987.

Myers, Robert Manson, ed. *The Children of Pride: A True Story of Georgia and the Civil War.* New Haven, Connecticut: Yale University Press, 1972.

Myres, Sandra L. *Westering Women and the Frontier Experience 1800–1915.* Albuquerque, New Mexico: University of New Mexico Press, 1982.

Neagles, James C. *Confederate Research Sources: A Guide to Archive Collections.* Salt Lake City, Utah: Ancestry Publishing, 1986.

Neilson, Lucy Irion. Papers. Mississippi Department of Archives and History, Jackson, Mississippi.

Newberry, J. S. *The U.S. Sanitary Commission in the Valley of the Mississippi During the War of the Rebellion 1861–1866.* Cleveland: Fairbanks, Benedict & Co., 1871.

Nichols, Irby C. "Reconstruction in DeSoto County." *Publications of the Mississippi Historical Society* 11 (1910) 295–316.

Noland, Julia Tigner, and Blanche Connelly Saucier. *Confederate Greenbacks: Mississippi Plantation Life in the '70s and '80s.* San Antonio, Texas: The Naylor Company, 1940.

Norfleet, Virginia. Reminiscences. Privately held by Frances Smith, East Lansing, Michigan.

Nunn. W. C. *Escape from Reconstruction.* Westport, Connecticut: Greenwood Press, 1956. (Reprint)

"Oaths, Amnesties and Rebellion." *Debow's Review:* After the War Series 1 (January–June 1866): 283–303.

O'Brien, Michael. *An Evening When Alone: Four Journals of Single Women in the South, 1827–67.* Charlottesville: The University Press of Virginia, 1993.

Official Records of the Union and Confederate Navies in the War of the Rebellion. Series II, Volume 1. Washington: Government Printing Office, 1921.

Olsen, Otto H., ed. *Reconstruction and Redemption in the South.* Baton Rouge: Louisiana State University Press, 1980.

"Original Memorial Day" Editorial Cartoon by Frank Spangler in Photograph Vertical Files-Subject-Memorial Day, Alabama Department of Archives and History, Montgomery, Alabama.

Our Women and the War: The Lives They Lived, the Deaths They Died. Charleston, S.C.: The News and Courier Book Presses, 1885.

Overy, David H., Jr. *Wisconsin Carpetbaggers in Dixie.* Madison, Wisconsin: The Department of History, University of Wisconsin, 1961.

Padgett, James A., ed. "Reconstruction Letters from North Carolina: Part II Letters to John Sherman." *North Carolina Historical Review* 18, No. 3 (July 1941): 278–300.

Page, Dave. "A Fight for Missouri." *Civil War Times Illustrated* 34, No. 3 (July/August 1995): 34–38.

Page, Thomas Nelson. "The Southern People During Reconstruction." *Atlantic Monthly* 88 (September 1901): 289–304.

Parsons, Jeanette Hepburn, Papers (7N/Box 178). Alabama Department Archives and History, Montgomery, Alabama.

Patrick, Rembert. *Fall of Richmond.* Baton Rouge: Louisiana State University, 1960.

_____. *The Reconstruction of the Nation.* New York: Oxford University Press, 1967.

Patrick, Robert. *Reluctant Rebel: The Secret Diary of Robert Patrick 1861–1865.* Edited by F. Jay Taylor. Baton Rouge: Louisiana State University Press, 1959.

Patterson, Tirza Willson. Papers. Tennessee State Library and Archives, Nashville.

Pearson, Alden B., Jr. "A Middle-Class, Border-State Family During the Civil War." *Civil War History* 22, No. 4 (December 1976): 318–336.

Pearson, Elizabeth Ware. *Letters from Port Royal 1862–1868*. New York: Arno Press, 1969.

Pease, William H. "Three Years Among the Freedmen: William C. Gannett and the Port Royal Experiment." *Journal of Negro History* 42 (April 1957): 98–117.

Pennypacker, Margaret Muse. Reminiscences 1860–1864. Personal Papers Collection, Archives Research Collection, The Library of Virginia, Richmond, Virginia.

Perdue, Charles L., Jr, Thomas E. Barden, Robert K. Phillips, eds. *Weevils in the Wheat: Interviews with Virginia Ex-Slaves*. Bloomington: Indiana University Press, 1980.

Perman, Michael. *Reunion Without Compromise: The South and Reconstruction: 1865–1868*. New York: Cambridge University Press, 1973.

Perry, Sally Randle. Diary 1867–1868 (SPR 303). In Alabama Department of Archives and History, Montgomery, Alabama.

"Petition of Ladies of Petersburg, Va., for Release of President Davis, Oct. 1865." *Southern Historical Society Papers* 24 (January–December 1896): 240–242.

Phillips, Edward H. *The Shenandoah Valley in 1864: An Episode in the History of Warfare*. Charleston, South Carolina: The Citadel, the Military College of South Carolina, May 1965.

Phillips, Sarah Ella. "Reminiscences of War and Episode of Wilson's Raid Near Selma, Alabama April 1865" (SPR 7). Alabama Department of Archives and History, Montgomery, Alabama.

Phipps, Shelia. "IU32 North Cameron Street: 'Secesh Lives Here.'" *Winchester-Frederick County Historical Society Journal* 8 (1993): 51–68.

Pike, James S. *The Prostrate State: South Carolina Under Negro Government*. New York: D. Appleton, 1874.

Porcher, F.A. "The Last Chapter of the History of Reconstruction in South Carolina." *Southern Historical Society Papers* 13 (January–December 1885): 47–87.

Porter, Mary H. *Eliza Chappell Porter: A Memoir*. Chicago: Fleming H. Revell, 1892.

"Portrait of an Old Confederate." *Louisa County Historical Magazine* 23, No. 1 (Spring 1997): 25–32.

Postell, Rosa. "Sherman's Occupation of Savannah: Two Letters." *Georgia Historical Quarterly* 50 (1966): 109–115.

Powell, Lawrence N. *New Masters: Northern Planters During the Civil War and Reconstruction*. New Haven, Connecticut: Yale University Press, 1980.

Powers, Bernard E., Jr. *Black Charlestonians: A Social History, 1822–1885*. Fayetteville, Arkansas: The University of Arkansas Press, 1994.

Pringle, Elizabeth W. Allston. *Chronicles of Chicora Wood*. New York: Charles Scribner's Sons, 1923.

Pritchard, Walter. "The Effects of the Civil War on the Louisiana Sugar Industry." *Journal of Southern History* 5 (August 1939): 315–332.

Pryor, Mrs. Roger A. *My Day: Reminiscences of a Long Life*. New York: Macmillan, 1909.

_____. *Reminiscences of Peace and War*. New York: The Macmillan Company, 1904.

Puckett, E. F. "Reconstruction in Monroe County." *Publications of the Mississippi Historical Society* 11 (1910): 103–162.

Quarles, Benjamin. *The Negro in the Making of America*. New York: Simon & Schuster, 1987.

Rable, George C. *But There Was No Peace: The Role of Violence in the Politics of Reconstruction*. Athens: The University of Georgia Press, 1984.

_____. *Civil Wars: Women and the Crisis of Southern Nationalism*. Urbana and Chicago: University of Illinois Press, 1989.

Racine, Philip N., ed. *Piedmont Farmer: The Journals of David Golightly Harris, 1855–1870*. Knoxville: The University of Tennessee Press, 1990.

Randall, J. G. *The Civil War and Reconstruction*. Boston: D. C. Heath, 1937.

Randel, William Peirce. *The Ku Klux Klan: A Century of Infamy*. Philadelphia: Chilton, 1965.

Reid, Whitelaw. *After the War: A Southern Tour. May 1, 1865, to May 1, 1866*. New York: Moore, Wilstach & Baldwin, 1866.

Reidy, Joseph P. *From Slavery to Agrarian Capitalism in the Cotton Plantation South*. Chapel Hill: University of North Carolina Press, 1992.

Reilly, Wayne E., ed. *Sarah Jane Foster: Teacher of the Freedmen: A Diary and Letters*. Charlottesville: University Press of Virginia, 1990.

Rennolds, Elizabeth Gordon. Memoir. Virginia Historical Society, Richmond, Virginia.

Report to the Contributors to the Pennsylvania Relief Association for East Tennessee, by a Commision Sent by the Executive Committee to Visit That Region and Forward Supplies to the Loyal and Suffering Inhabitants. Philadelphia: Printed for the Association, 1864.

Report of the Joint Committee on Reconstruction, at the First Session Thirty-Ninth Congress. Washington: Government Printing Office, 1866.

Reynolds, John S. *Reconstruction in South Carolina*. Columbia, South Carolina: The State Company, 1905.

Reynolds, Elizabeth. Virginia Historical Society, Richmond.

Rice, Mrs. Gordon Pryor. Recollections. Virginia Historical Society, Richmond, Virginia. See also Notes on Virginia (Accession 24061) Personal Papers Collection, Archives Research Services, The Library of Virginia. Richmond, Virginia.

Richards, Caroline Cowles. *The Diary of Caroline Cowles Richards 1852–1872*. Canandaigua, N. Y:. Caroline Cowles Richards, 1908.

Richardson, Joe M. "'We Are Truly Doing Missionary Work': Letters from American Missionary Association Teachers in Florida 1864–1874." *Florida Historical Quarterly* 54, No. 2 (October 1975): 178–195.

Riddleberger, Patrick W. *1866: The Critical Year Revisited*. Carbondale: Southern Illinois University Press, 1979.

Ripley, C. Peter. *Slaves and Freedmen in Civil War Louisiana*. Baton Rouge: Louisiana State University Press, 1976.

Roark, James L. *Masters Without Slaves: Southern Planters in the Civil War and Reconstruction*. New York: W.W. Norton & Company, 1977.

Robertson, James I., Jr. *Civil War Virginia: Battleground for a Nation*. Charlottesville: University Press of Virginia, 1991.

Robertson, Mary D. *A Confederate Lady Comes of Age: The Journal of Pauline DeCaradeuc Heyward, 1863–1888*. Columbia, South Carolina: University of South Carolina Press, 1992.

Rose, Peter I., ed. *Americans from Africa: Slavery and its Aftermath*. New York: Atherton, 1970.

Rose, Willie Lee. *Rehearsal for Reconstruction: The Port Royal Experiment*. Indianapolis: Bobbs-Merrill, 1964.

354 Bibliography

_____. *Slavery and Freedom*. Edited by William W. Freehling. New York: Oxford University Press, 1982.
Rowland, Kate Mason. Memoirs of the War: Diary and Correspondence. Eleanor S. Brockenbrough Library, The Museum of the Confederacy, Richmond, Virginia.
Rozier, John, ed. *The Granite Farm Letters: The Civil War Correspondence of Edgeworth and Sallie Bird*. Athens: The University of Georgia Press, 1988.
Rush, Lucinda Lenore. "The Civil War Diary of Kate Mason Rowland." A. M. diss.,Virginia Polytechnic Institute and State University, October 1972.
Rutherford, Mildred Lewis. Miss Rutherford's Scrap Book: "Woman's War Work, 1861–1865": Valuable Information About the South. Vol. 8 Georgia Historical Society, Savannah.
Ryan, Father Abram. Papers. Tennessee State Library and Archives, Nashville.
Ryan, Mary P. *Women in Public: Between Banners and Ballots, 1825–1880*. Baltimore: The Johns Hopkins University Press, 1990.
Sansing, David Gaffney. "The Role of the Scalawag in Mississippi Reconstruction." Ph.D. diss., University of Southern Mississippi, Hattiesburg, Mississippi.
_____, ed. *What Was Freedom's Price?* Jackson: University Press of Mississippi, 1978.
Saville, Julie. *The Work of Reconstruction: From Slave to Wage Laborer in South Carolina, 1860–1870*. New York: Cambridge University Press, 1994.
Scales, Cordelia. "The Civil War Letters of Cordelia Scales." Edited by Percy L. Rainwater. *Journal of Mississippi History* 1, No. 1 (January 1939): 169–181.
Scarborough, William Kauffman, ed. *The Diary of Edmund Ruffin*. Volume III. Baton Rouge: Louisiana State University Press, 1989.
Scheiner, Seth M., ed. *Reconstruction: A Tragic Era?* New York: Holt, Rinehart and Winston, 1968.
Schwartz, Gerald, ed. *A Woman Doctor's Civil War: Esther Hill Hawks' Diary*. Columbia: University of South Carolina Press, 1984.
Schweninger, Loren. *From Tennesse Slave to St. Louis Entrepreneur: The Autobiography of James Thomas*. Columbia: University of Missouri Press, 1984.
Scott, Anne Firor. *The Southern Lady: From Pedestal to Politics 1830–1930*. Chicago: The University of Chicago Press, 1970.
Scott, Mary White. Diary. Library, Headquarters of the United Daughters of the Confederacy, Richmond, Virginia.
Scott, Nannie. *Nannie Scott of "Bel-Air" School*. n.p. Dietz Press, 1971.
Seddon, Elvira Bruce. "The Diary of Elvira Bruce Seddon." *Goochland County Historical Society Magazine* 21, 22 (1989, 1990): 6–14 and 7–15.
Sefton, James E. *The United States Army & Reconstruction 1865–1877*. Baton Rouge: Louisiana State University Press, 1967.
Selby Family Collection. In Manuscript Department, New York Historical Society, New York.
Shackelford, Maria Louisa (Mrs. Edmund Fontaine). "To My Grandchildren." In Meade Family Papers. Virginia Historical Society, Richmond.
Shenton, James P., ed. *The Reconstruction: A Documentary History of the South After the War: 1865–1877*. New York: G.P. Putnam, 1963.
Sherman, William T. Letter. Special Collections. Chicago Public Library.
Silber, Nina. *The Romance of Reunion: Northerners and the South, 1865–1900*. Chapel Hill: University of North Carolina Press, 1993.

Silver, James W. "Confederate Morale and Church Propaganda." *Confederate Centennial Studies* No. 3 (1957): 7–114.

_____. *Mississippi in the Confederacy as Seen in Retrospect.* Baton Rouge: Louisiana State University Press, 1961.

Simkins, Francis B. "New Viewpoints of Southern Reconstruction." *Journal of Southern History* 5 (February 1939): 49–61.

_____, and James Welch Patton. *The Women of the Confederacy.* Richmond: Garrett and Massie, 1936.

_____, and Robert Hilliard Woody. *South Carolina During Reconstruction.* Chapel Hill: The University of North Carolina Press, 1932.

Sitterson, J. Caryle. "The McCollams: A Planter Family of the Old and New South." *Journal of Southern History* 6 (August 1940): 347–382.

Six Women's Slave Narratives. New York: Oxford University Press, 1988.

Smedes, Susan Dabney. *Memorials of a Southern Planter.* Edited by Fletcher M. Green. New York: Alfred A. Knopf, 1965.

Smith, George Winston. "Cotton from Savannah in 1865." *Journal of Southern History* 21 (November 1955): 495–512.

Smith, Rebecca. Labor Contract (SPR 73). Alabama Department of Archives and History, Montgomery, Alabama.

Smythe, Louisa McCord. Reminiscences. South Caroliniana Library, University of South Carolina, Columbia.

Snowden, Mary Amarintha. Correspondence. South Caroliniana Library, University of South Carolina, Columbia.

Southern Famine Relief Commission Report. New York Historical Society.

Spencer, Cornelia Phillips. *The Last Ninety Days of the War in North Carolina.* New York: Watchman, 1866.

Spencer, Judith Ann. "Their Faltering Footsteps: Hardships Suffered By the Confederate Civilians on the Homefront in the American Civil War." M.S. diss. North Texas State University, 1977. (Microfilm: University Microfilms, Ann Arbor, Michigan.)

Sperry, Kate S. Diary, Winchester, Virginia, 1861–1866 (Acession 28532) Personal Papers Collection, Archives Research Services, The Library of Virginia, Richmond, Virginia.

Stamper, Anita Miller, and Mary Edna Lohrenz. "Manuscript Sources for 'Mississippi Homespun: Nineteenth-Century Textiles and the Women Who Made Them.'" *Journal of Mississippi History* 53 (August 1991): 185–217.

Stampp, Kenneth M. *The Era of Reconstruction 1865–1877.* New York: Vintage Books, 1967.

_____, and Leon F. Litwack, eds. *Reconstruction: An Anthology of Revisionist Writings.* Baton Rouge: Louisiana State University Press, 1969.

Stearns, Charles. *The Black Man of the South, and the Rebels.* New York: Negro Universities Press, 1969.

Stephenson, Jane F. "My Father and His Household, Before, During and After the War." In Blanton Family Papers. Virginia Historical Society, Richmond, Virginia.

Stephenson, William. *Sallie Southall Cotten: A Woman's Life in North Carolina.* Greenville, North Carolina: Pamlico, 1987.

Sterkx, H.E. *Partners in Rebellion: Alabama Women in the Civil War.* Rutherford: Fairleigh Dickinson University Press, 1970.

Sterling, Dorothy, ed. *We Are Your Sisters: Black Women in the Nineteenth Century.* New York: W.W. Norton, 1984.

Stevens, James M. Stevens Collection. Biloxi Public Library. Biloxi, Mississippi.

Stevens, Thaddeus. "Reconstruction," An address delivered at Lancaster, Pennsylvania on September 7, 1865. In *The American Mind: Selections From the Literature of the United States.* Edited by Harry R. Warfel, et al., New York: American Book Company, 1959. 579–584.

Stone, Alfred H. "A Mississippian's View of Civil Rights, States Rights, and Reconstruction." *Journal of Mississippi History* 10 (January–October 1948): 181–239.

Sublett, Emmie. Letter. Eleanor S. Brockenbrough Library, The Museum of the Confederacy, Richmond, Virginia.

Sullivan, Charles. *The Mississippi Gulf Coast: Portrait of a People.* Northridge, California: Windsor Publications, 1985.

Sulzby, James F., Jr. *Johnson's Island: A Paper on the Confederate Prison at Johnson's Island, Ohio.* Birmingham, Alabama: Dr. Ralph W. Beeson, 1988.

Sutherland, Daniel E. *The Confederate Carpetbaggers.* Baton Rouge: Louisiana State University Press, 1988.

_____. "Exiles, Emigrants, and Sojourners: The Post-Civil War Confederate Exodus in Perspective." *Civil War History* 31, No. 3 (September 1985): 237–256.

_____. "A Special Kind of Problem: The Response of Household Slaves and Their Masters to Freedom." *Southern Studies* 20, No. 2 (Summer 1981): 151–166.

_____, ed. *A Very Violent Rebel: The Civil War Diary of Ellen Renshaw House.* Knoxville: The University of Tennessee Press, 1996.

Swint, Henry L., ed. *Dear Ones at Home: Letters from Contraband Camps.* Nashville: Vanderbilt University Press, 1966.

Tatum, Georgia Lee. *Disloyalty in the Confederacy.* Chapel Hill: The University of North Carolina Press, 1934.

Taylor, J. E. *With Sheridan Up the Shenandoah Valley in 1864: Leaves from a Special Artist's Sketch Book and Diary.* Cleveland, Ohio: The Western Reserve Historical Society, 1989.

Taylor, Joe Gray. *Louisiana Reconstructed 1863–1877.* Baton Rouge: Louisiana State University Press, 1974.

Taylor, Mrs. Thomas; Mrs. Smythe, Mrs. August Kohn, Miss Poppenheim, Miss Martha B. Washington, eds. *South Carolina Women in the Confederacy.* Columbia, S.C.: The State Company, 1903.

Taylor, Sally Elmore. Diary. South Caroliniana Library, University of South Carolina, Columbia, South Carolina.

Testimony Taken by the U.S. Congress: The Joint Select Committee to Inquire Into the Condition of Affairs in the Late Insurrectionary States. Volume I. Washington: Government Printing Office, 1872.

Thom Family Papers. Virginia Historical Society, Richmond, Virginia.

Thomas, Emory M. *The Confederacy as a Revolutionary Experience.* Englewood Cliffs, New Jersey: Prentice-Hall, 1971.

Thompson, Lou E. Diary/Attala County Records (M193). McCain Library and Archives, The University of Southern Mississippi. Hattiesburg.

Thorpe, Margaret Newbold. "Life in Virginia by a 'Yankee Teacher,' Margaret Newbold Thorpe." Edited by Richard L. Morton. *Virginia Magazine of History and Biography* 64, No. 2 (April 1956): 180–207.

Tigay, Alan M. "The Deepest South." *American Heritage* 49 (April 1998): 84–95.

Tillett, Wilbur Fisk. "Southern Womanhood as Affected by the War." *Century Illustrated Monthly Magazine* 43 New Series 21 (November 1891–April 1892): 9–16.

"To the Friends of the Southern Cause." South Caroliniana Library, University of South Carolina, Columbia.

Tourgée, Albion W. *A Fool's Errand by One of the Fools*. New York: Fords, Howard, & Hulbert, 1880.

Towles, Louis P., ed. *A World Turned Upside Down: The Palmers of South Sante, 1818–1881*. Columbia: University of South Carolina Press, 1996.

Trapnell, Frederica H., ed. Virginia Tucker-Henry B. Brooke Correspondence 1831–1869. Central Rappahannock Regional Library, Fredericksburg, Virginia.

Trefousse, Hans L. *Reconstruction: America's First Effort at Racial Democracy*. New York: Van Nostrand Reinhold, 1971.

———. *Thaddeus Stevens: Nineteenth-Century Egalitarian*. Chapel Hill: The University of North Carolina Press, 1997.

Trelease, Allen W. *White Terror: The Ku Klux Klan Conspiracy and Southern Reconstruction*. New York: Harper & Row, 1971.

Trowbridge, John T. *The Desolate South 1865–1866: A Picture of the Battlefields and of the Devastated Confederacy*. Edited by Gordon Carroll. Boston: Little, Brown and Company, 1956.

———. *Picture of the Desolated South and the Work of Reconstruction 1865–1868*. Hartford Conn: L. Stebbins, 1868.

Trudeau, Noah Andre. *Out of the Storm: The End of the Civil War, April–June 1865*. Boston: Little, Brown and Company, 1994.

Twitchell, Harvey. *Carpetbagger from Vermont: The Autobiography of Marshall Harvey Twitchell*. Edited by Ted Tunnell. Baton Rouge: Louisiana State University Press, 1989.

United Daughters of the Confederacy. Missouri Division. *Reminiscences of the Women of Missouri During the Sixties*. Jefferson City: The Hugh Stephens Printing Co., 1920.

Vance, Joseph C. "Freedmen's Schools in Albemarle County During Reconstruction." *Virginnia Magazine of History and Biography* 61, No. 4 (October 1953): 430–438.

VanPelt, Harriet. Papers. Privately held by Ruth Ann Runquist, East Lansing, Michigan.

Venet, Wendy Hamand. *Neither Ballots Nor Bullets: Women Abolitionists and the Civil War*. Charlottesville: University Press of Virginia, 1991.

Wadley, Sarah Lois in the Sarah Lois Wadley Papers #1285, Southern Historical Collection, Wilson Libary, University of North Carolina at Chapel Hill.

Walker, Eliza J. Kendrick (Lewis). "Other Days." *Alabama Historical Quarterly* 5 (Spring 1943): 71–97 and (Summer 1943): 209–233.

Walker, John Stewart. Letters to his Wife. Held by Dr. Jack Jones, East Lansing, Michigan.

Walker, Peter F. *Vicksburg: A People at War, 1860–1865*. Chapel Hill: University of North Carolina Press, 1960.

Walmsley, James Eliott. "Some Unpublished Letters of Burton N. Harrison." *Publications of the Mississippi Historical Society* 8 (1907): 81–85.

War of the Rebellion: A Compilation of the Official Records of the Union and Confederate Armies. Washington: Government Printing Office, 1893.

Warren, Robert Penn. *Jefferson Davis Gets His Citizenship Back*. Lexington, Kentucky: The University of Kentucky Press, 1980.
Watkins, Ruth. "Reconstruction in Newton County." *Publications of the Mississippi Historical Society* 11 (1910): 205–228.
Watson, Margaret. *Greenwood County Sketches: Old Roads and Early Families*. Greenwood, South Carolina: Attic Press, 1982.
Waugh, Charles G., and Martin H. Greenberg. *The Women's War in the South: Recollections and Reflections of the American Civil War*. Nashville, Tennessee: Cumberland House, 1999.
Wayne, Michael. *The Reshaping of Plantation Society: The Natchez District, 1860–1880*. Baton Rouge: Louisiana State University Press, 1983.
Weatherford, Doris. *A History of the American Suffragist Movement*. Santa Barbara, California: The Moschovitis Group, Inc., 1998.
Weeks, Charles Miller. Papers. Archives and Manuscripts Department, Chicago Historical Society.
Weiner, Marli F., ed. *Heritage of Woe: The Civil War Diary of Grace Brown Elmore 1861–1868*. Athens: University of Georgia Press, 1997.
_____. *Mistresses and Slaves: Plantation Women in South Carolina, 1830–80*. Urbana: University of Illinois, 1998.
Weland, Gerald. *O.O. Howard, Union General*. Jefferson, North Carolina: McFarland & Company, Inc., 1995.
Wellman, Manly Wade. *The County of Warren, North Carolina, 1586–1917*. Chapel Hill: The University of North Carolina Press, 1959.
Wells, W. Calvin. "Reconstruction and Its Destruction in Hinds County." *Proceedings of Mississippi Historical Society*. 9 (1906): 85–108.
Wetta, Frank F. "'Bulldozing the Scalawags': Some Examples of the Persecution of Southern White Republicans in Louisiana During Reconstruction." *Louisiana History* 21, No. 1 (Winter, 1980): 43–58.
Wharton, Vernon Lane. *The Negro in Mississippi 1865–1890*. Chapel Hill: The University of North Carolina Press, 1947.
Wheeler, Richard. *Voices of the Civil War*. New York: Thomas Y. Crowell Company, 1976.
_____. *Witness to Appomattox*. New York: Harper & Row, 1989.
Wheless, John F. Confederate Letter. Tennessee State Library and Archives, Nashville.
Whilden, Mary S. *Recollections of the War: 1861–1865*. Columbia, South Carolina: The State Company, 1911.
Whites, Lee Ann. *The Civil War as a Crisis in Gender: Augusta, Georgia, 1860–1890*. Athens: The University of Georgia Press, 1995.
Whyte, James H. *The Uncivil War: Washington During the Reconstruction 1865–1878*. New York: Twayne Publishers, 1958.
Wiener, Jonathan M. "Female Planters and Planters' Wives in Civil War and Reconstruction: Alabama, 1850–1870." *Alabama Review* 30, No. 2 (April 1977): 135–149.
Wight, Willard E. "The Churches and the Confederate Cause." *Civil War History* 11 (March 1960): 361–373.
Wiley, Bell Irvin. *Confederate Women*. New York: Barnes & Noble, 1975.
_____. *Southern Negroes 1861–1865*. New York: Rinehart & Company, Inc., 1938.
_____, ed. *"This Infernal War": The Confederate Letters of Sgt. Edwin H. Fay*. Austin: University of Texas Press, 1958.

Wilkinson, Mary. Papers. Historic New Orleans Collection, New Orleans, Louisiana.

Williams, T. Harry. "An Analysis of Some Reconstruction Attitudes." *Journal of Southern History* 12 (November 1946): 469–486.

Wilson, Augusta Evans. Papers (7N/Box 260). Alabama Department of Archives and History, Montgomery, Alabama.

Wilson, Louis R., ed. *Selected Papers of Cornelia Phillips Spencer.* Copyright 1953 by the University of North Carolina Press, renewed 1981 by Penelope Wilson and Elizabeth Wilson. Used by permission of the publisher.

Wilson, Woodrow. "The Reconstruction of the Southern States." *Atlantic Monthly* 87 (January 1901): 1–15.

Winters, John D. *The Civil War in Louisiana.* Baton Rouge: Louisiana State University Press, 1963.

Wish, Harvey, ed. *Reconstruction in the South 1865–1877: First-Hand Accounts of the American Southland After the Civil War by Northerners & Southerners.* New York: Farrar, Straus and Giroux, 1965.

Wister, Fanny Kemble, ed. "Sarah Butler Wister's Civil War Diary." *Pennsylvania Magazine of History and Biography* 102 (July 1978): 271–327.

Wolfe, Allis. "Women Who Dared: Northern Teachers of the Southern Freemen, 1862–1872." Ph.D. diss., The City University of New York, 1982. Photocopy of Typescript. Ann Arbor, Michigan. University Microfilms International, 1982.

Woloch, Nancy. *Women and the American Experience.* New York: Alfred A. Knopf, 1984.

Wood, Richard Addison, and Joan Fare Wood, eds. "For Better or for Worse," in Charles G. Waugh and Martin H. Greenberg, *The Women's War in the South, Recollections and Reflections of the American Civil War.* Nashville, Tennessee: Cumberland House, 1999.

Woodward, C. Vann. *The Burden of Southern History.* New York: Vintage Books, 1960.

_____, ed. *Mary Chesnut's Civil War.* New Haven: Yale University Press, 1981.

_____, and Elisabeth Muhlenfeld. *The Private Mary Chesnut: The Unpublished Civil War Diaries.* New York: Oxford University Press, 1984.

Worthington, Amanda. Diary. In Worthington Family Papers. Mississippi Department of Archives and History, Jackson, Mississippi.

Wright, Gavin. *Old South, New South: Revolutions in the Southern Economy Since the Civil War.* New York: Basic Books, 1986.

Wynes, Charles E. "Fanny Kemble's South Revisited: The South As Seen Through the Eyes of Her Daughter, Frances." *Louisiana Studies* 11–12 (Fall 1972-3): 473–488.

Young, Mary. *"All My Trials, Lord": Selections from Women's Slave Narratives.* New York: Franklin Watts: A Division of Grolier Publishing, 1995.

Newspapers

Chicago Daily Times
Chicago Daily Tribune

Daily South Carolinian
Daily True Delta (New Orleans)
Detroit Advertiser and Tribune
Harper's Weekly
Mobile Daily News
New Orleans Daily Picayune
New Orleans Times
Richmond Dispatch
Weekly Clarion (Jackson, Mississippi)
Wilmington Journal

Index